About P

Pearson is the world's learning company, with presence across 70 countries worldwide. Our unique insights and world-class expertise comes from a long history of working closely with renowned teachers, authors and thought leaders, as a result of which, we have emerged as the preferred choice for millions of teachers and learners across the world.

We believe learning opens up opportunities, creates fulfilling careers and hence better lives. We hence collaborate with the best of minds to deliver you class-leading products, spread across the Higher Education and K12 spectrum.

Superior learning experience and improved outcomes are at the heart of everything we do. This product is the result of one such effort.

Your feedback plays a critical role in the evolution of our products and you can contact us – reachus@pearson.com. We look forward to it.

Praise for *Deep Learning Illustrated*

"Over the next few decades, artificial intelligence is poised to dramatically change almost every aspect of our lives, in large part due to today's breakthroughs in deep learning. The authors' clear visual style provides a comprehensive look at what's currently possible with artificial neural networks as well as a glimpse of the magic that's to come."
—*Tim Urban, writer and illustrator of Wait But Why*

"This book is an approachable, practical, and broad introduction to deep learning, and the most beautifully illustrated machine learning book on the market."
—*Dr. Michael Osborne, Dyson Associate Professor in Machine Learning, University of Oxford*

"This book should be the first stop for deep learning beginners, as it contains lots of concrete, easy-to-follow examples with corresponding tutorial videos and code notebooks. Strongly recommended."
—*Dr. Chong Li, cofounder, Nakamoto & Turing Labs; adjunct professor, Columbia University*

"It's hard to imagine developing new products today without thinking about enriching them with capabilities using machine learning. Deep learning in particular has many practical applications, and this book's intelligible clear and visual approach is helpful to anyone who would like to understand what deep learning is and how it could impact your business and life for years to come."
—*Helen Altshuler, engineering leader, Google*

"This book leverages beautiful illustrations and amusing analogies to make the theory behind deep learning uniquely accessible. Its straightforward example code and best-practice tips empower readers to immediately apply the transformative technique to their particular niche of interest."
—*Dr. Rasmus Rothe, founder, Merantix*

"This is an invaluable resource for anyone looking to understand what deep learning is and why it powers almost every automated application today, from chatbots and voice recognition tools to self-driving cars. The illustrations and biological explanations help bring to life a complex topic and make it easier to grasp fundamental concepts."
—*Joshua March, CEO and cofounder, Conversocial; author of Message Me*

"Deep learning is regularly redefining the state of the art across machine vision, natural language, and sequential decision-making tasks. If you too would like to pass data through deep neural networks in order to build high-performance models, then this book—with its innovative, highly visual approach—is the ideal place to begin."
—*Dr. Alex Flint, roboticist and entrepreneur*

Deep Learning Illustrated

A Visual, Interactive Guide to Artificial Intelligence

Jon Krohn
with Grant Beyleveld
and Aglaé Bassens

 Pearson

Authorized adaptation from the United States edition, entitled *Deep Learning Illustrated: A Visual, Interactive Guide to Artificial Intelligence*, 1st Edition, ISBN 978-0-13-511669-2 by Krohn, Jon; Beyleveld, Grant; Bassens, Aglae, published by Pearson Education, Inc, Copyright © 2020.

Indian Subcontinent Adaptation
Copyright © 2020 Pearson India Education Services Pvt. Ltd

ISBN 978-93-539-4546-6

First Impression

This edition is manufactured in India and is authorized for sale only in India, Bangladesh, Bhutan, Pakistan, Nepal, Sri Lanka and the Maldives. Circulation of this edition outside of these territories is UNAUTHORIZED.

Published by Pearson India Education Services Pvt. Ltd, CIN: U72200TN2005PTC057128.

Head Office: 15th Floor, Tower-B, World Trade Tower, Plot No. 1, Block-C, Sector 16, Noida 201 301, Uttar Pradesh, India.
Registered Office: The HIVE, 3rd Floor, Metro zone, No 44, Pillaiyar Koil Street, Jawaharlal Nehru Road, Anna Nagar, Chennai 600 040, Tamil Nadu, India.
Phone: 044-66540100
Website: in.pearson.com; Email: companysecretary.india@pearson.com

Printed in India at Sai Printo Pack Pvt Ltd, New Delhi.

◆

For Gigi
—Jon

◆

Contents

Figures

Tables

Examples

Foreword

Machine learning is considered by many to be the future of statistics and computer engineering as it reshapes customer service, design, banking, medicine, manufacturing, and hosts of other disciplines and industries. It is hard to overstate its impact on the world so far and the changes it will bring about in the coming years and decades. Of the multitude of machine learning methods applied by professionals, such as penalized regression, random forests, and boosted trees, perhaps the most excitement-inducing is deep learning.

Deep learning has revolutionized computer vision and natural language processing, and researchers are still finding new areas to transform with the power of neural networks. Its most profound impact is often seen in efforts to replicate the human experience, such as the aforementioned vision and language processing, and also audio synthesis and translations. The math and concepts underlying deep learning can seem daunting, unnecessarily deterring people from getting started.

The authors of *Deep Learning Illustrated* challenge the traditionally perceived barriers and impart their knowledge with ease and levity, resulting in a book that is enjoyable to read. Much like the other books in this series—*R for Everyone, Pandas for Everyone, Programming Skills for Data Science,* and *Machine Learning with Python for Everyone*—this book is welcoming and accessible to a broad audience from myriad backgrounds. Mathematical notation is kept to a minimum and, when needed, the equations are presented alongside understandable prose. The majority of insights are augmented with visuals, illustrations, and Keras code, which is also available as easy-to-follow Jupyter notebooks.

Jon Krohn has spent many years teaching deep learning, including a particularly memorable presentation at the New York Open Statistical Programming Meetup—the same community from which he launched his Deep Learning Study Group. His mastery of the subject shines through in his writing, giving readers ample education while at the same time inviting them to be excited about the material. He is joined by Grant Beyleveld and Aglaé Bassens who add their expertise in applying deep learning algorithms and skillful drawings.

Deep Learning Illustrated combines theory, math where needed, code, and visualizations for a comprehensive treatment of deep learning. It covers the full breadth of the subject, including densely connected networks, convolutional neural nets, recurrent neural nets, generative adversarial networks, and reinforcement learning, and their applications. This makes the book the ideal choice for someone who wants to learn about neural networks with practical guidance for implementing them. Anyone can, and should, benefit from, as well as enjoy, their time spent reading along with Jon, Grant, and Aglaé.

—*Jared Lander*
Series Editor

Preface

Commonly called *brain cells*, billions of interconnected *neurons* make up your nervous system, and they enable you to sense, to think, and to take action. By meticulously staining and examining thin slices of brain tissue, the Spanish physician Santiago Cajal (Figure P.1), was the first[1] to identify neurons (Figure P.2), and in the early half of the twentieth century, researchers began to shed light on how these biological cells work. By the 1950s, scientists inspired by our developing understanding of the brain were experimenting with computer-based *artificial* neurons, linking these together to form *artificial neural networks* that loosely mimic the operation of their natural namesake.

Armed with this brief history of neurons, we can define the term *deep learning* deceptively straightforwardly: Deep learning involves a network in which artificial neurons— typically thousands, millions, or many more of them—are stacked at least several layers deep. The artificial neurons in the first layer pass information to the second, the second to the third, and so on, until the final layer outputs some values. That said, as we literally illustrate throughout this book, this simple definition does not satisfactorily capture deep learning's remarkable breadth of functionality nor its extraordinary nuance.

As we detail in Chapter 1, with the advent of sufficiently inexpensive computing power, sufficiently large datasets, and a handful of landmark theoretical advances, the first wave of the deep learning tsunami to hit the proverbial shore was a standout performance in a leading machine vision competition in 2012. Academics and technologists took note, and in the action-packed years since, deep learning has facilitated countless now-everyday

Figure P.1   Santiago Cajal (1852–1934)

---

1. Cajal, S.-R. (1894). *Les Nouvelles Idées sur la Structure du Système Nerveux chez l'Homme et chez les Vertébrés*. Paris: C. Reinwald & Companie.

Figure P.2   A hand-drawn diagram from Cajal's (1894) publication showing the growth of a neuron (a–e) and contrasting neurons from frog (A), lizard (B), rat (C), and human (D) samples

applications. From Tesla's Autopilot to the voice recognition of Amazon's Alexa, from real-time translation between languages to its integration in hundreds of Google products, deep learning has improved the accuracy of a great number of computational tasks from 95 percent to 99 percent or better—the tricky few percent that can make an automated service feel as though it works by magic. Although the concrete, interactive code examples throughout this book will dispel this apparent wizardry, deep learning has indeed imbued machines with superhuman capability on complex tasks as diverse as face recognition, text summarization, and elaborate board games.[2] Given these prominent advances, it is unsurprising that "deep learning" has become synonymous with "artificial intelligence" in the popular press, the workplace, and the home.

These are exciting times, because, as you'll discover over the course of this book, perhaps only once in a lifetime does a single concept disrupt so widely in such a short period of time. We are delighted that you too have developed an interest in deep learning and we can't wait to share our enthusiasm for this unprecedentedly transformative technique with you.

How to Read This Book

This book is split into four parts. Part I, "Introducing Deep Learning," is well suited to any interested reader. This part serves as a high-level overview that establishes what deep learning is, how it evolved to be ubiquitous, and how it is related to concepts like AI, machine learning, and reinforcement learning. Replete with vivid bespoke illustrations, straightforward analogies, and character-focused narratives, Part I should be illuminating for anyone, including individuals with no software programming experience.

---

2. See bit.ly/aiindex18 for a review of machine performance relative to humans.

In contrast, Parts II through IV are intended for software developers, data scientists, researchers, analysts, and others who would like to learn how to apply deep learning techniques in their field. In these parts of the book, essential underlying theory is covered in a manner that minimizes mathematical formulas, relying instead on intuitive visuals and hands-on examples in Python. Alongside this theory, working code run-throughs available in accompanying Jupyter notebooks[3] facilitate a pragmatic understanding of the principal families of deep learning approaches and applications: natural language processing (Chapter 8), machine vision (Chapter 9), game playing (Chapter 10), and image generation (Chapter 11). For clarity, wherever we refer to code, we will provide it in `fixed-width font, like this`.

If you find yourself yearning for more detailed explanations of the mathematical and statistical foundations of deep learning than we offer in this book, our two favorite options for further study are:

1. Michael Nielsen's e-book *Neural Networks and Deep Learning*,[4] which is short, makes use of fun interactive applets to demonstrate concepts, and uses mathematical notation similar to ours
2. Ian Goodfellow (introduced in Chapter 3), Yoshua Bengio (Figure 1.10), and Aaron Courville's book *Deep Learning*,[5] which comprehensively covers the math that underlies neural network techniques

Scattered throughout this book, you will find amiable trilobites that would like to provide you with tidbits of unessential reading that they think you may find interesting or helpful. The *reading trilobite* (as in Figure P.3) is a bookworm who enjoys expanding your knowledge. The *trilobite calling for your attention*, meanwhile (as in Figure P.4), has noticed a passage of text that may be problematic, and so would like to clarify the situation. In addition to trilobites habituated within sidebars, we made liberal use of footnotes. These

Figure P.3   The reading trilobite enjoys expanding your knowledge.

---

3. `github.com/the-deep-learners/deep-learning-illustrated`
4. Nielsen, M. (2015). *Neural Networks and Deep Learning*. Determination Press. Available for free at: `neuralnetworksanddeeplearning.com`
5. Goodfellow, I., et al. (2016). *Deep Learning*. MIT Press. Available for free at: `deeplearningbook.org`

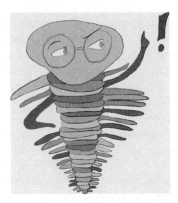

Figure P.4   This trilobite calls attention to tricky passages of text. Look out for it!

are likewise not essential reading but provide quick explanations of new terms and abbreviations, as well as citations of seminal papers and other references for you to follow up with if you're so inclined.

For much of this book's content, corresponding video tutorials are also available. Although the book provided us with an opportunity to flesh out theoretical concepts more thoroughly, the videos enable you to become familiar with our Jupyter notebooks from a different perspective, in which the importance of each line of code is described verbally as it is typed out.[6]

---

6. Many of the Jupyter notebooks covered in this book are derived directly from the videos, which were all recorded prior to writing. In some places, we decided to update the code for the book, so while the video version and the book version of a given code notebook align quite closely, they may not always be strictly identical.

Acknowledgments

We're grateful to the team at untapt, particularly Andrew Vlahutin, Sam Kenny, and Vince Petaccio II, who supported us while we wrote this book, with extra-special mention to the neural-network-loving Ed Donner, who ceaselessly encourages us to pursue our passions in the field of deep learning.

Additionally, we're grateful to the dozens of members of the Deep Learning Study Group[7] who regularly attend our stimulating and vibrant sessions at untapt's New York offices. Because the book is derived from our Study Group discussions, it is difficult to imagine how the book would otherwise have been conceived.

Thanks to our technical reviewers for invaluable feedback that noticeably improved the book's content: Alex Lipatov, Andrew Vlahutin, Claudia Perlich, Dmitri Nesterenko, Jason Baik, Laura Graesser, Michael Griffiths, Paul Dix, and Wah Loon Keng. Thanks to the book's editors and managers—Chris Zahn, Betsy Hardinger, Anna Popick, and Julie Nahil—whose meticulousness and thoughtfulness ensured the book's quality, clarity, and presentation. Thanks to Jared Lander, who leads the New York Open Statistical Programming community that both seeded our Deep Learning Study Group and facilitated meeting Pearson's Debra Williams Cauley. Special thanks are due to Debra herself, who has backed our colorful publication ideas from the day we met her and who has been instrumental in ensuring their success. Thanks as well to the scientists and machine learning experts who mentored us academically, and who continue to inspire us, particularly Jonathan Flint, Felix Agakov, and Will Valdar.

Finally, countless thanks are due to our families and our friends, who not only put up with us working through our time with them on vacations and weekends, but also selflessly motivate us as we do.

---

7. deeplearningstudygroup.org

About the Authors

Jon Krohn is Chief Data Scientist at the machine learning company untapt. He presents an acclaimed series of tutorials published by Addison-Wesley, including *Deep Learning with TensorFlow LiveLessons* and *Deep Learning for Natural Language Processing LiveLessons*. Jon teaches his deep learning curriculum in-classroom at the New York City Data Science Academy and guest lectures at Columbia University. He holds a doctorate in neuroscience from the University of Oxford and, since 2010, has been publishing on machine learning in leading peer-reviewed journals, including *Advances in Neural Information Processing Systems*.

Grant Beyleveld is a data scientist at untapt, where he works on natural language processing using deep learning. He holds a doctorate in biomedical science from the Icahn School of Medicine at New York City's Mount Sinai hospital, having studied the relationship between viruses and their hosts. He is a founding member of deeplearningstudygroup.org.

Aglaé Bassens is a Belgian artist based in Paris. She studied Fine Arts at The Ruskin School of Drawing and Fine Art, Oxford University, and University College London's Slade School of Fine Arts. Along with her work as an illustrator, her practice includes still life painting and murals.

Introducing Deep Learning

1

Biological and Machine Vision

Throughout this chapter and much of this book, the visual system of biological organisms is used as an analogy to bring deep learning to, um . . . life. In addition to conveying a high-level understanding of what deep learning is, this analogy provides insight into how deep learning approaches are so powerful and so broadly applicable.

Biological Vision

Five hundred fifty million years ago, in the prehistoric Cambrian period, the number of species on the planet began to surge (Figure 1.1). From the fossil record, there is evidence[1] that this explosion was driven by the development of light detectors in the trilobite, a small marine animal related to modern crabs (Figure 1.2). A visual system, even a primitive one, bestows a delightful bounty of fresh capabilities. One can, for example, spot food, foes, and friendly-looking mates at some distance. Other senses, such as smell, enable animals to detect these as well, but not with the accuracy and light-speed pace of vision. Once the trilobite could see, the hypothesis goes, this set off an arms race that produced the Cambrian explosion: The trilobite's prey, as well as its predators, had to evolve to survive.

In the half-billion years since trilobites developed vision, the complexity of the sense has increased considerably. Indeed, in modern mammals, a large proportion of the *cerebral cortex*—the outer gray matter of the brain—is involved in visual perception.[2] At Johns

---

1. Parker, A. (2004). *In the Blink of an Eye: How Vision Sparked the Big Bang of Evolution*. New York: Basic Books.
2. A couple of tangential facts about the cerebral cortex: First, it is one of the more recent evolutionary developments of the brain, contributing to the complexity of mammal behavior relative to the behavior of older classes of animals like reptiles and amphibians. Second, while the brain is informally referred to as *gray matter* because the cerebral cortex is the brain's external surface and this cortical tissue is gray in color, the bulk of the brain is in fact *white* matter. By and large, the white matter is responsible for carrying information over longer distances than the gray matter, so its neurons have a white-colored, fatty coating that hurries the pace of signal conduction. A coarse analogy could be to consider neurons in the white matter to act as "highways." These high-speed motorways have scant on-ramps or exits, but can transport a signal from one part of the brain to another lickety-split. In contrast, the "local roads" of gray matter facilitate myriad opportunities for interconnection between neurons at the expense of speed. A gross generalization, therefore, is to consider the cerebral cortex—the gray matter—as the part of the brain where the most complex computations happen, affording the animals with the largest proportion of it—such as mammals, particularly the great apes like *Homo sapiens*—their complex behaviors.

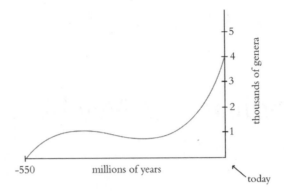

Figure 1.1   The number of species on our planet began to increase rapidly 550 million years ago, during the prehistoric Cambrian period. "Genera" are categories of related species.

Figure 1.2   A bespectacled trilobite

Hopkins University in the late 1950s, the physiologists David Hubel and Torsten Wiesel (Figure 1.3) began carrying out their pioneering research on how visual information is processed in the mammalian cerebral cortex,[3] work that contributed to their later being awarded a Nobel Prize.[4] As depicted in Figure 1.4, Hubel and Wiesel conducted their research by showing images to anesthetized cats while simultaneously recording the activity of individual neurons from the *primary visual cortex*, the first part of the cerebral cortex to receive visual input from the eyes.

Projecting slides onto a screen, Hubel and Wiesel began by presenting simple shapes like the dot shown in Figure 1.4 to the cats. Their initial results were disheartening: Their efforts were met with no response from the neurons of the primary visual cortex. They grappled with the frustration of how these cells, which anatomically appear to be the gateway for visual information to the rest of the cerebral cortex, would not respond to

---

3. Hubel, D. H., & Wiesel, T. N. (1959). Receptive fields of single neurones in the cat's striate cortex. *The Journal of Physiology, 148,* 574–91.
4. The 1981 Nobel Prize in Physiology or Medicine, shared with American neurobiologist Roger Sperry.

Figure 1.3   The Nobel Prize-winning neurophysiologists Torsten Wiesel (left) and David Hubel

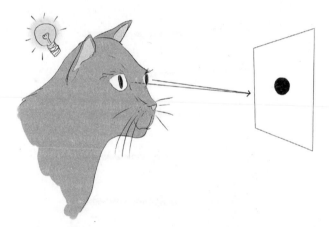

Figure 1.4   Hubel and Wiesel used a light projector to present slides to anesthetized cats while they recorded the activity of neurons in the cats' primary visual cortex. In the experiments, electrical recording equipment was implanted within the cat's skull. Instead of illustrating this, we suspected it would be a fair bit more palatable to use a lightbulb to represent neuron activation. Depicted in this figure is a primary visual cortex neuron being serendipitously activated by the straight edge of a slide.

visual stimuli. Distraught, Hubel and Wiesel tried in vain to stimulate the neurons by jumping and waving their arms in front of the cat. Nothing. And then, as with many of the great discoveries, from X-rays to penicillin to the microwave oven, Hubel and Wiesel made a serendipitous observation: As they removed one of their slides from the projector, its straight edge elicited the distinctive crackle of their recording equipment to alert them that a primary visual cortex neuron was firing. Overjoyed, they celebrated up and down the Johns Hopkins laboratory corridors.

The serendipitously crackling neuron was not an anomaly. Through further experimentation, Hubel and Wiesel discovered that the neurons that receive visual input from the eye are in general most responsive to simple, straight edges. Fittingly then, they named these cells *simple* neurons.

As shown in Figure 1.5, Hubel and Wiesel determined that a given simple neuron responds optimally to an edge at a particular, specific orientation. A large group of simple neurons, with each specialized to detect a particular edge orientation, together is able to represent all 360 degrees of orientation. These edge-orientation detecting simple cells then pass along information to a large number of so-called *complex* neurons. A given complex neuron receives visual information that has already been processed by several simple cells, so it is well positioned to recombine multiple line orientations into a more complex shape like a corner or a curve.

Figure 1.6 illustrates how, via many hierarchically organized layers of neurons feeding information into increasingly higher-order neurons, gradually more complex visual stimuli can be represented by the brain. The eyes are focused on an image of a mouse's

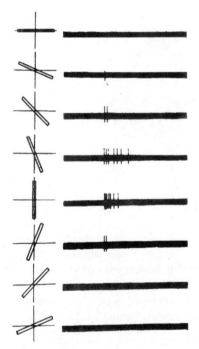

Figure 1.5   A simple cell in the primary visual cortex of a cat fires at different rates, depending on the orientation of a line shown to the cat. The orientation of the line is provided in the left-hand column, while the right-hand column shows the firing (electrical activity) in the cell over time (one second). A vertical line (in the fifth row from the top) causes the most electrical activity for this particular simple cell. Lines slightly off vertical (in the intermediate rows) cause less activity for the cell, while lines approaching horizontal (in the topmost and bottommost rows) cause little to no activity.

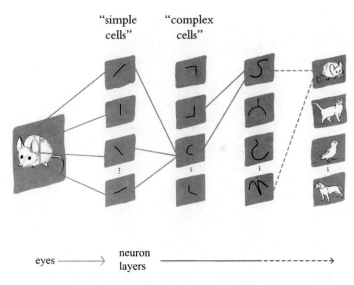

"simple cells"   "complex cells"

eyes ⟶   neuron layers ⟶

Figure 1.6 A caricature of how consecutive layers of biological neurons represent visual information in the brain of, for example, a cat or a human

head. Photons of light stimulate neurons located in the retina of each eye, and this raw visual information is transmitted from the eyes to the primary visual cortex of the brain. The first layer of primary visual cortex neurons to receive this input—Hubel and Wiesel's *simple cells*—are specialized to detect edges (straight lines) at specific orientations. There would be many thousands of such neurons; for simplicity, we're only showing four in Figure 1.6. These simple neurons relay information about the presence or absence of lines at particular orientations to a subsequent layer of *complex cells*, which assimilate and recombine the information, enabling the representation of more complex visual stimuli such as the curvature of the mouse's head. As information is passed through several subsequent layers, representations of visual stimuli can incrementally become more complex and more abstract. As depicted by the far-right layer of neurons, following many layers of such hierarchical processing (we use the arrow with dashed lines to imply that many more layers of processing are not being shown), the brain is ultimately able to represent visual concepts as abstract as a mouse, a cat, a bird, or a dog.

Today, through countless subsequent recordings from the cortical neurons of brain-surgery patients as well as noninvasive techniques like magnetic resonance imaging (MRI),[5] neuroscientists have pieced together a fairly high-resolution map of regions that are specialized to process particular visual stimuli, such as color, motion, and faces (see Figure 1.7).

---

5. Especially *functional* MRI, which provides insight into which regions of the cerebral cortex are notably active or inactive when the brain is engaged in a particular activity.

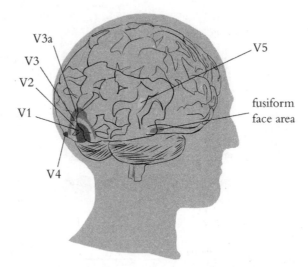

Figure 1.7   Regions of the visual cortex. The V1 region receives input from the eyes and contains the simple cells that detect edge orientations. Through the recombination of information via myriad subsequent layers of neurons (including within the V2, V3, and V3a regions), increasingly abstract visual stimuli are represented. In the human brain (shown here), there are regions containing neurons with concentrations of specializations in, for example, the detection of color (V4), motion (V5), and people's faces (fusiform face area).

Machine Vision

We haven't been discussing the biological visual system solely because it's interesting (though hopefully you did find the preceding section thoroughly interesting). We have covered the biological visual system primarily because it serves as the inspiration for the modern deep learning approaches to machine vision, as will become clear in this section.

Figure 1.8 provides a concise historical timeline of vision in biological organisms as well as machines. The top timeline, in blue, highlights the development of vision in trilobites as well as Hubel and Wiesel's 1959 publication on the hierarchical nature of the primary visual cortex, as covered in the preceding section. The machine vision timeline is split into two parallel streams to call attention to two alternative approaches. The middle timeline, in pink, represents the deep learning track that is the focus of our book. The bottom timeline, in purple, meanwhile represents the traditional machine learning (ML) path to vision, which—through contrast—will clarify why deep learning is distinctively powerful and revolutionary.

The Neocognitron

Inspired by Hubel and Wiesel's discovery of the simple and complex cells that form the primary visual cortex hierarchy, in the late 1970s the Japanese electrical engineer

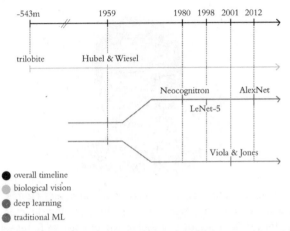

Figure 1.8   Abridged timeline of biological and machine vision, highlighting the key historical moments in the deep learning and traditional machine learning approaches to vision that are covered in this section (see page 327 for the color image)

Kunihiko Fukushima proposed an analogous architecture for machine vision, which he named the *neocognitron*.[6] There are two particular items to note:

1. Fukushima referred to Hubel and Wiesel's work explicitly in his writing. Indeed, his paper refers to three of their landmark articles on the organization of the primary visual cortex, including borrowing their "simple" and "complex" cell language to describe the first and second layers, respectively, of his neocognitron.
2. By arranging artificial neurons[7] in this hierarchical manner, these neurons—like their biological inspiration in Figure 1.6—generally represent line orientations in the cells of the layers closest to the raw visual image, while successively deeper layers represent successively complex, successively abstract objects. To clarify this potent property of the neocognitron and its deep learning descendants, we go through an interactive example at the end of this chapter that demonstrates it.[8]

LeNet-5

While the neocognitron was capable of, for example, identifying handwritten characters,[9] the accuracy and efficiency of Yann LeCun (Figure 1.9) and Yoshua Bengio's (Figure 1.10) *LeNet-5* model[10] made it a significant development. LeNet-5's hierarchical

---

6. Fukushima, K. (1980). Neocognitron: A self-organizing neural network model for a mechanism of pattern recognition unaffected by shift in position. *Biological Cynbernetics, 36,* 193–202.

7. We define precisely what *artificial neurons* are in Chapter 7. For the moment, it's more than sufficient to think of each artificial neuron as a speedy little algorithm.

8. Specifically, Figure 1.19 demonstrates this hierarchy with its successively abstract representations.

9. Fukushima, K., & Wake, N. (1991). Handwritten alphanumeric character recognition by the neocognitron. *IEEE Transactions on Neural Networks, 2,* 355–65.

10. LeCun, Y., et al. (1998). Gradient-based learning applied to document recognition. *Proceedings of the IEEE, 2,* 355–65.

Figure 1.9   Paris-born Yann LeCun is one of the preeminent figures in artificial neural network and deep learning research. LeCun is the founding director of the New York University Center for Data Science as well as the director of AI research at the social network Facebook.

Figure 1.10   Yoshua Bengio is another of the leading characters in artificial neural networks and deep learning. Born in France, he is a computer science professor at the University of Montreal and codirects the renowned Machines and Brains program at the Canadian Institute for Advanced Research.

architecture (Figure 1.11) built on Fukushima's lead and the biological inspiration uncovered by Hubel and Wiesel.[11] In addition, LeCun and his colleagues benefited from superior data for training their model,[12] faster processing power, and, critically, the backpropagation algorithm.

Backpropagation, often abbreviated to *backprop*, facilitates efficient learning throughout the layers of artificial neurons within a deep learning model.[13] Together with the researchers' data and processing power, backprop rendered LeNet-5 sufficiently reliable

---

11. LeNet-5 was the first *convolutional neural network*, a deep learning variant that dominates modern machine vision and that we detail in Chapter 10.

12. Their classic dataset, the handwritten MNIST digits, is used extensively in Part II, "Essential Theory Illustrated."

13. We examine the backpropagation algorithm in Chapter 7.

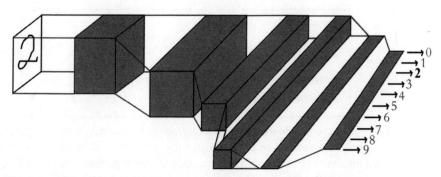

Figure 1.11   LeNet-5 retains the hierarchical architecture uncovered in the primary visual cortex by Hubel and Wiesel and leveraged by Fukushima in his neocognitron. As in those other systems, the leftmost layer represents simple edges, while successive layers represent increasingly complex features. By processing information in this way, a handwritten "2" should, for example, be correctly recognized as the number two (highlighted by the output shown on the right).

to become an early commercial application of deep learning: It was used by the United States Postal Service to automate the reading of ZIP codes[14] written on mail envelopes. In Chapter 9, on machine vision, you will experience LeNet-5 firsthand by designing it yourself and training it to recognize handwritten digits.

In LeNet-5, Yann LeCun and his colleagues had an algorithm that could correctly predict the handwritten digits that had been drawn without needing to include any expertise about handwritten digits in their code. As such, LeNet-5 provides an opportunity to introduce a fundamental difference between deep learning and the traditional machine learning ideology. As conveyed by Figure 1.12, the traditional machine learning approach is characterized by practitioners investing the bulk of their efforts into engineering features. This *feature engineering* is the application of clever, and often elaborate, algorithms to raw data in order to preprocess the data into input variables that can be readily modeled by traditional statistical techniques. These techniques—such as regression, random forest, and support vector machine—are seldom effective on unprocessed data, and so the engineering of input data has historically been a prime focus of machine learning professionals.

In general, a minority of the traditional ML practitioner's time is spent optimizing ML models or selecting the most effective one from those available. The deep learning approach to modeling data turns these priorities upside down. *The deep learning practitioner*

---

14. The USPS term for postal code.

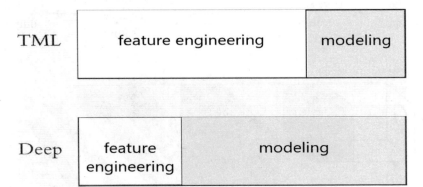

Figure 1.12 Feature engineering—the transformation of raw data into thoughtfully transformed input variables—often predominates the application of traditional machine learning algorithms. In contrast, the application of deep learning often involves little to no feature engineering, with the majority of time spent instead on the design and tuning of model architectures.

typically spends little to none of her time engineering features, instead spending it modeling data with various artificial neural network architectures that process the raw inputs into useful features automatically. This distinction between deep learning and traditional machine learning is a core theme of this book. The next section provides a classic example of feature engineering to elucidate the distinction.

The Traditional Machine Learning Approach

Following LeNet-5, research into artificial neural networks, including deep learning, fell out of favor. The consensus became that the approach's automated feature generation was not pragmatic—that even though it worked well for handwritten character recognition, the feature-free ideology was perceived to have limited breadth of applicability.[15] Traditional machine learning, including its feature engineering, appeared to hold more promise, and funding shifted away from deep learning research.[16]

To make clear what feature engineering is, Figure 1.13 provides a celebrated example from Paul Viola and Michael Jones in the early 2000s.[17] Viola and Jones employed rectangular filters such as the vertical or horizontal black-and-white bars shown in the figure. Features generated by passing these filters over an image can be fed into machine learning algorithms to reliably detect the presence of a face. This work is notable because the

---

15. At the time, there were stumbling blocks associated with optimizing deep learning models that have since been resolved, including poor weight initializations (covered in Chapter 7), covariate shift (also in Chapter 7), and the predominance of the relatively inefficient sigmoid activation function (Chapter 6).

16. Public funding for artificial neural network research ebbed globally, with the notable exception of continued support from the Canadian federal government, enabling the Universities of Montreal, Toronto, and Alberta to become powerhouses in the field.

17. Viola, P., & Jones, M. (2001). Robust real-time face detection. *International Journal of Computer Vision, 57,* 137–54.

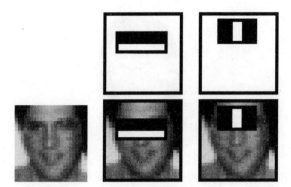

Figure 1.13   Engineered features leveraged by Viola and Jones (2001) to detect faces reliably. Their efficient algorithm found its way into Fujifilm cameras, facilitating real-time auto-focus.

algorithm was efficient enough to be the first real-time face detector outside the realm of biology.[18]

Devising clever face-detecting filters to process raw pixels into features for input into a machine learning model was accomplished via years of research and collaboration on the characteristics of faces. And, of course, it is limited to detecting faces in general, as opposed to being able to recognize a particular face as, say, Angela Merkel's or Oprah Winfrey's. To develop features for detecting Oprah in particular, or for detecting some non-face class of objects like houses, cars, or Yorkshire Terriers, would require the development of expertise in that category, something that could again take years of academic-community collaboration to execute both efficiently and accurately. Hmm, if only we could circumnavigate all that time and effort somehow!

ImageNet and the ILSVRC

As mentioned earlier, one of the advantages LeNet-5 had over the neocognitron was a larger, high-quality set of training data. The next breakthrough in neural networks was also facilitated by a high-quality public dataset, this time much larger. *ImageNet*, a labeled index of photographs devised by Fei-Fei Li (Figure 1.14), armed machine vision researchers with an immense catalog of training data.[19,20] For reference, the handwritten digit data used to train LeNet-5 contained tens of thousands of images. ImageNet, in contrast, contains tens of *millions*.

The 14 million images in the ImageNet dataset are spread across 22,000 categories. These categories are as diverse as container ships, leopards, starfish, and elderberries. Since 2010, Li has run an open challenge called ILSVRC (the ImageNet Large Scale Visual Recognition Challenge) on a subset of the ImageNet data that has become the premier

---

18. A few years later, the algorithm found its way into digital Fujifilm cameras, facilitating autofocus on faces for the first time—a now everyday attribute of digital cameras and smartphones alike.
19. image-net.org
20. Deng, J., et al. (2009). ImageNet: A large-scale hierarchical image database. *Proceedings of the Conference on Computer Vision and Pattern Recognition*.

Figure 1.14   The hulking ImageNet dataset was the brainchild of Chinese-American computer science professor Fei-Fei Li and her colleagues at Princeton in 2009. Now a faculty member at Stanford University, Li is also the chief scientist of A.I./ML for Google's cloud platform.

ground for assessing the world's state-of-the-art machine vision algorithms. The ILSVRC subset consists of 1.4 million images across 1,000 categories. In addition to providing a broad range of categories, many of the selected categories are breeds of dogs, thereby evaluating the algorithms' ability not only to distinguish widely varying images but also to specialize in distinguishing subtly varying ones.[21]

AlexNet

As graphed in Figure 1.15, in the first two years of the ILSVRC all algorithms entered into the competition hailed from the feature-engineering-driven traditional machine learning ideology. In the third year, all entrants *except one* were traditional ML algorithms. If that one deep learning model in 2012 had not been developed or if its creators had not competed in ILSVRC, then the year-over-year image classification accuracy would have been negligible. Instead, Alex Krizhevsky and Ilya Sutskever—working out of the University of Toronto lab led by Geoffrey Hinton (Figure 1.16)—crushed the existing benchmarks with their submission, today referred to as AlexNet (Figure 1.17).[22,23] This was a watershed moment. In an instant, deep learning architectures emerged from the fringes of machine learning to its fore. Academics and commercial practitioners scrambled to grasp the fundamentals of artificial neural networks as well as to create software libraries—many of them open-source—to experiment with deep learning models on their own data and use cases, be they machine vision or otherwise. As Figure 1.15 illustrates, in

21. On your own time, try to distinguish photos of Yorkshire Terriers from Australian Silky Terriers. It's tough, but Westminster Dog Show judges, as well as contemporary machine vision models, can do it. Tangentially, these dog-heavy data are the reason deep learning models trained with ImageNet have a disposition toward "dreaming" about dogs (see, e.g., `deepdreamgenerator.com`).
22. Krizhevsky, A., Sutskever, I., & Hinton, G. (2012). ImageNet classification with deep convolutional neural networks. *Advances in Neural Information Processing Systems, 25*.
23. The images along the bottom of Figure 1.17 were obtained from Yosinski, J., et al. (2015). Understanding neural networks through deep visualization. *arXiv: 1506.06579*.

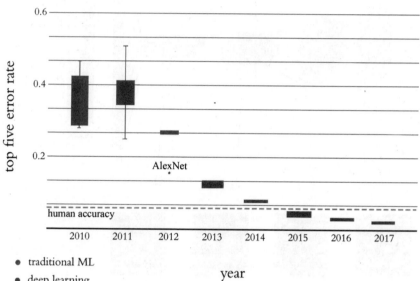

ILSVRC Results

Figure 1.15   Performance of the top entrants to the ILSVRC by year. AlexNet was the victor by a head-and-shoulders (40 percent!) margin in the 2012 iteration. All of the best algorithms since then have been deep learning models. In 2015, machines surpassed human accuracy.

Figure 1.16   The eminent British-Canadian artificial neural network pioneer Geoffrey Hinton, habitually referred to as "the godfather of deep learning" in the popular press. Hinton is an emeritus professor at the University of Toronto and an engineering fellow at Google, responsible for managing the search giant's Brain Team, a research arm, in Toronto. In 2019, Hinton, Yann LeCun (Figure 1.9), and Yoshua Bengio (Figure 1.10) were jointly recognized with the Turing Award—the highest honor in computer science—for their work on deep learning.

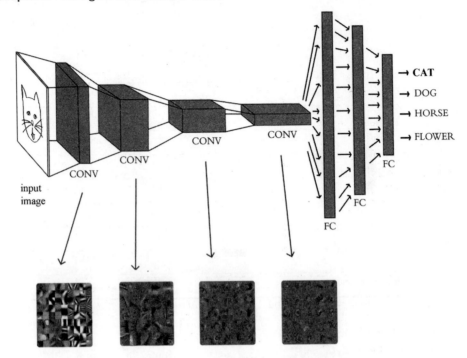

Figure 1.17   AlexNet's hierarchical architecture is reminiscent of LeNet-5, with the first (left-hand) layer representing simple visual features like edges, and deeper layers representing increasingly complex features and abstract concepts. Shown at the bottom are examples of images to which the neurons in that layer maximally respond, recalling the layers of the biological visual system in Figure 1.6 and demonstrating the hierarchical increase in visual feature complexity. In the example shown here, an image of a cat input into LeNet-5 is correctly identified as such (as implied by the bold "CAT" output). "CONV" indicates the use of something called a convolutional layer, and "FC" is a fully connected layer; we formally introduce these layer types in Chapters 6 and 9, respectively.

the years since 2012 all of the top-performing models in the ILSVRC have been based on deep learning.

Although the hierarchical architecture of AlexNet is reminiscent of LeNet-5, there are three principal factors that enabled AlexNet to be the state-of-the-art machine vision algorithm in 2012. First is the training data. Not only did Krizhevsky and his colleagues have access to the massive ImageNet index, they also artificially expanded the data available to them by applying transformations to the training images (you, too, will do this in Chapter 9). Second is processing power. Not only had computing power per unit of cost increased dramatically from 1998 to 2012, but Krizhevsky, Hinton, and Sutskever also programmed two GPUs[24] to train their large datasets with previously unseen efficiency. Third is architectural advances. AlexNet is deeper (has more layers) than LeNet-5, and

---

24. Graphical processing units: These are designed primarily for rendering video games but are well suited to performing the matrix multiplication that abounds in deep learning across hundreds of parallel computing threads.

it takes advantage of both a new type of artificial n euron[25] and a nifty t rick[26] that helps generalize deep learning models beyond the data they're trained on. As with LeNet-5, you will build AlexNet yourself in Chapter 9 and use it to classify images.

Our ILSVRC case study underlines why deep learning models like AlexNet are so widely useful and disruptive across industries and computational applications: They dramatically reduce the subject-matter expertise required for building highly accurate predictive models. This trend away from expertise-driven feature engineering and toward surprisingly powerful automatic-feature-generating deep learning models has been prevalently borne out across not only vision applications, but also, for example, the playing of complex games (the topic of Chapter 4 and natural language processing (Chapter 2.[27] One no longer needs to be a specialist in the visual attributes of faces to create a face-recognition algorithm. One no longer requires a thorough understanding of a game's strategies to write a program that can master it. One no longer needs to be an authority on the structure and semantics of each of several languages to develop a language-translation tool. For a rapidly growing list of use cases, one's ability to apply deep learning techniques outweighs the value of domain-specific proficiency. While such proficiency formerly may have necessitated a doctoral degree or perhaps years of postdoctoral research within a given domain, a functional level of deep learning capability can be developed with relative ease—as by working through this book!

TensorFlow Playground

For a fun, interactive way to crystallize the hierarchical, feature-learning nature of deep learning, make your way to the TensorFlow Playground at `bit.ly/TFplayground`. When you use this custom link, your network should automatically look similar to the one shown in Figure 1.18. In Part II we return to define all of the terms on the screen; for the present exercise, they can be safely ignored. It suffices at this time to know that this is a deep learning model. The model architecture consists of six layers of artificial neurons: an input layer on the left (below the "FEATURES" heading, four "HIDDEN LAYERS" (which bear the responsibility of learning, and an "OUTPUT" layer (the grid on the far right ranging from -6 to $+6$ on both axes).The network's goal is to learn how to distinguish orange dots (negative cases from blue dots (positive cases based solely on their location on the grid. As such, in the input layer, we are only feeding in two pieces of information about each dot: its horizontal position (X_1 and its vertical position (X_2. The dots that will be used as training data are shown by default on the grid. By clicking the *Show test data* toggle, you can also see the location of dots that will be used to assess the performance of the network as it learns. Critically, these test data are not available to the network while it's learning, so they help us ensure that the network generalizes well to new, unseen data.

---

25. The rectified linear unit (ReLU), which is introduced in Chapter 6.
26. Dropout, introduced in Chapter 7.
27. An especially entertaining recounting of the disruption to the field of machine translation is provided by Gideon Lewis-Kraus in his article "The Great A.I. Awakening," published in the *New York Times Magazine* on December 14, 2016.

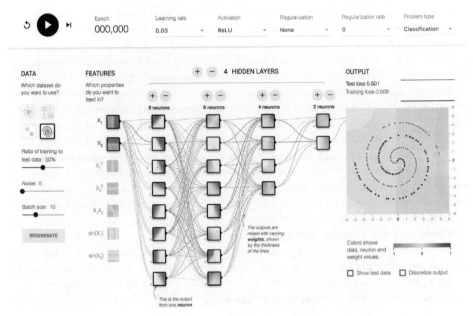

Figure 1.18   This deep neural network is ready to learn how to distinguish a spiral of orange dots (negative cases) from blue dots (positive cases) based on their position on the X_1 and X_2 axes of the grid on the right (see page 327 for the color image).

Click the prominent *Play* arrow in the top-left corner. Enable the network to train until the "Training loss" and "Test loss" in the top-right corner have both approached zero—say, less than 0.05. How long this takes will depend on the hardware you're using but hopefully will not be more than a few minutes.

As captured in Figure 1.19, you should now see the network's artificial neurons representing the input data, with increasing complexity and abstraction the deeper (further to the right) they are positioned—as in the neocognitron, LeNet-5 (Figure 1.11), and AlexNet (Figure 1.17). Every time the network is run, the neuron-level details of how the network solves the spiral classification problem are unique, but the general approach remains the same (to see this for yourself, you can refresh the page and retrain the network). The artificial neurons in the leftmost hidden layer are specialized in distinguishing edges (straight lines), each at a particular orientation. Neurons from the first hidden layer pass information to neurons in the second hidden layer, each of which recombines the edges into slightly more complex features like curves. The neurons in each successive layer recombine information from the neurons of the preceding layer, gradually increasing the complexity and abstraction of the features the neurons can represent. By the final (rightmost) layer, the neurons are adept at representing the intricacies of the spiral shape, enabling the network to accurately predict whether a dot is orange (a negative case) or blue (a positive case) based on its position (its X_1 and X_2 coordinates) in the grid. Hover over a neuron to project it onto the far-right "OUTPUT" grid and examine its individual specialization in detail.

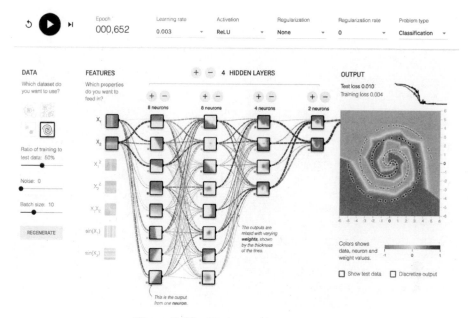

Figure 1.19   The network after training

Quick, Draw!

To interactively experience a deep learning network carrying out a machine vision task in real time, navigate to `quickdraw.withgoogle.com` to play the Quick, Draw! game. Click *Let's Draw!* to begin playing the game. You will be prompted to draw an object, and a deep learning algorithm will guess what you sketch. By the end of Chapter 9, we will have covered all of the theory and practical code examples needed to devise a machine vision algorithm akin to this one. To boot, the drawings you create will be added to the dataset that you'll leverage in Chapter 11 when you create a deep learning model that can convincingly mimic human-drawn doodles. Hold on to your seat! We're embarking on a fantastic ride.

Summary

In this chapter, we traced the history of deep learning from its biological inspiration through to the AlexNet triumph in 2012 that brought the technique to the fore. All the while, we reiterated that the hierarchical architecture of deep learning models enables them to encode increasingly complex representations. To concretize this concept, we concluded with an interactive demonstration of hierarchical representations in action by training an artificial neural network in the TensorFlow Playground. In Chapter 2, we will expand on the ideas introduced in this chapter by moving from vision applications to language applications.

Human and Machine Language

In Chapter 1, we introduced the high-level theory of deep learning via analogy to the biological visual system. All the while, we highlighted that one of the technique's core strengths lies in its ability to learn features automatically from data. In this chapter, we build atop our deep learning foundations by examining how deep learning is incorporated into human language applications, with a particular emphasis on how it can automatically learn features that represent the meaning of words.

The Austro-British philosopher Ludwig Wittgenstein famously argued, in his posthumous and seminal work *Philosophical Investigations*, "The meaning of a word is its use in the language."[1] He further wrote, "One cannot guess how a word functions. One has to look at its use, and learn from that." Wittgenstein was suggesting that words on their own have no real meaning; rather, it is by their use within the larger context of that language that we're able to ascertain their meaning. As you'll see through this chapter, natural language processing with deep learning relies heavily on this premise. Indeed, the word2vec technique we introduce for converting words into numeric model inputs explicitly derives its semantic representation of a word by analyzing it within its contexts across a large body of language.

Armed with this notion, we begin by breaking down deep learning for natural language processing (NLP) as a discipline, and then we go on to discuss modern deep learning techniques for representing words and language. By the end of the chapter, you should have a good grasp on what is possible with deep learning and NLP, the groundwork for writing such code in Chapter 8.

Deep Learning for Natural Language Processing

The two core concepts in this chapter are *deep learning* and *natural language processing*. Initially, we cover the relevant aspects of these concepts separately, and then we weave them together as the chapter progresses.

---

1. Wittgenstein, L. (1953). *Philosophical Investigations*. (Anscombe, G., Trans.). Oxford, UK: Basil Blackwell.

Deep Learning Networks Learn Representations Automatically

As established way back in this book's Preface, deep learning can be defined as the layering of simple algorithms called *artificial neurons* into networks several layers deep. Via the Venn diagram in Figure 2.1, we show how deep learning resides within the machine learning family of *representation learning* approaches. The representation learning family, which contemporary deep learning dominates, includes any techniques that learn features from data automatically. Indeed, we can use the terms "feature" and "representation" interchangeably.

Figure 1.12 lays the foundation for understanding the advantage of representation learning relative to traditional machine learning approaches. Traditional ML typically works well because of clever, human-designed code that transforms raw data—whether it be images, audio of speech, or text from documents—into input features for machine learning algorithms (e.g., regression, random forest, or support vector machines) that are adept at weighting features but not particularly good at learning features from raw data directly. This manual creation of features is often a highly specialized task. For working with language data, for example, it might require graduate-level training in linguistics.

A primary benefit of deep learning is that it eases this requirement for subject-matter expertise. Instead of manually curating input features from raw data, one can feed the data directly into a deep learning model. Over the course of many examples provided to the deep learning model, the artificial neurons of the first layer of the network learn

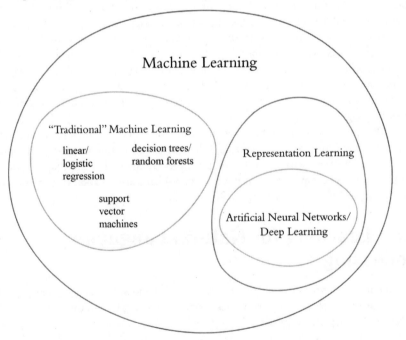

Figure 2.1   Venn diagram that distinguishes the traditional family from the representation learning family of machine learning techniques

how to represent simple abstractions of these data, while each successive layer learns to represent increasingly complex nonlinear abstractions on the layer that precedes it. As you'll discover in this chapter, this isn't solely a matter of convenience; learning features automatically has additional advantages. Features engineered by humans tend to not be comprehensive, tend to be excessively specific, and can involve lengthy, ongoing loops of feature ideation, design, and validation that could stretch for years. Representation learning models, meanwhile, generate features quickly (typically over hours or days of model training), adapt straightforwardly to changes in the data (e.g., new words, meanings, or ways of using language), and adapt automatically to shifts in the problem being solved.

Natural Language Processing

Natural language processing is a field of research that sits at the intersection of computer science, linguistics, and artificial intelligence (Figure 2.2). NLP involves taking the naturally spoken or naturally written language of humans—such as this sentence you're reading right now—and processing it with machines to automatically complete some task or to make a task easier for a human to do. Examples of language use that do not fall under the umbrella of *natural* language could include code written in a software language or short strings of characters within a spreadsheet.

Examples of NLP in industry include:

- *Classifying documents*: using the language within a document (e.g., an email, a Tweet, or a review of a film) to classify it into a particular category (e.g., high urgency, positive sentiment, or predicted direction of the price of a company's stock).

- *Machine translation*: assisting language-translation firms with machine-generated suggestions from a source language (e.g., English) to a target language (e.g., German or Mandarin); increasingly, fully automatic—though not always perfect—translations between languages.

- *Search engines*: autocompleting users' searches and predicting what information or website they're seeking.

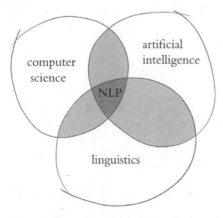

Figure 2.2   NLP sits at the intersection of the fields of computer science, linguistics, and artificial intelligence.

- *Speech recognition*: interpreting voice commands to provide information or take action, as with virtual assistants like Amazon's Alexa, Apple's Siri, or Microsoft's Cortana.

- *Chatbots*: carrying out a natural conversation for an extended period of time; though this is seldom done convincingly today, they are nevertheless helpful for relatively linear conversations on narrow topics such as the routine components of a firm's customer-service phone calls.

Some of the easiest NLP applications to build are spell checkers, synonym suggesters, and keyword-search querying tools. These simple tasks can be fairly straightforwardly solved with deterministic, rules-based code using, say, reference dictionaries or the-sauruses. Deep learning models are unnecessarily sophisticated for these applications, and so they aren't discussed further in this book.

Intermediate-complexity NLP tasks include assigning a school-grade reading level to a document, predicting the most likely next words while making a query in a search engine, classifying documents (see earlier list), and extracting information like prices or named entities[2] from documents or websites. These intermediate NLP applications are well suited to solving with deep learning models. In Chapter 8, for example, you'll leverage a variety of deep learning architectures to predict the sentiment of film reviews.

The most sophisticated NLP implementations are required for machine translation (see earlier list), automated question-answering, and chatbots. These are tricky because they need to handle application-critical nuance (as an example, humor is particularly transient), a response to a question can depend on the intermediate responses to previous questions, and meaning can be conveyed over the course of a lengthy passage of text consisting of many sentences. Complex NLP tasks like these are beyond the scope of this book; however, the content we cover will serve as a superb foundation for their development.

A Brief History of Deep Learning for NLP

The timeline in Figure 2.3 calls out recent milestones in the application of deep learn-ing to NLP. This timeline begins in 2011, when the University of Toronto computer scientist George Dahl and his colleagues at Microsoft Research revealed the first major

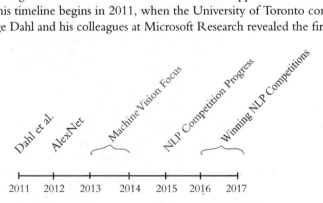

Figure 2.3   Milestones involving the application of deep learning to natural language processing

---

2. *Named entities* include places, well-known individuals, company names, and products.

breakthrough involving a deep learning algorithm applied to a large dataset.[3] This break-through happened to involve natural language data. Dahl and his team trained a deep neural network to recognize a substantial vocabulary of words from audio recordings of human speech. A year later, and as detailed already in Chapter 1, the next landmark deep learning feat also came out of Toronto: AlexNet blowing the traditional machine learning competition out of the water in the ImageNet Large Scale Visual Recognition Challenge (Figure 1.15). For a time, this staggering machine vision performance heralded a focus on applying deep learning to machine vision applications.

By 2015, the deep learning progress being made in machine vision began to spill over into NLP competitions such as those that assess the accuracy of machine translations from one language into another. These deep learning models approached the precision of traditional machine learning approaches; however, they required less research and development time while conveniently offering lower computational complexity. Indeed, this reduction in computational complexity provided Microsoft the opportunity to squeeze real-time machine translation software onto mobile phone processors—remarkable progress for a task that previously had required an Internet connection and computationally expensive calculations on a remote server. In 2016 and 2017, deep learning models entered into NLP competitions not only were more efficient than traditional machine learning models, but they also began outperforming them on accuracy. The remainder of this chapter starts to illuminate how.

Computational Representations of Language

In order for deep learning models to process language, we have to supply that language to the model in a way that it can digest. For all computer systems, this means a quantitative representation of language, such as a two-dimensional matrix of numerical values. Two popular methods for converting text into numbers are one-hot encoding and word vectors.[4] We discuss both methods in turn in this section.

One-Hot Representations of Words

The traditional approach to encoding natural language numerically for processing it with a machine is *one-hot encoding* (Figure 2.4). In this approach, the words of natural language in a sentence (e.g., "the," "bat," "sat," "on," "the," and "cat") are represented by the columns of a matrix. Each row in the matrix, meanwhile, represents a unique word. If there are 100 unique words across the corpus[5] of documents you're feeding into your

---

3. Dahl, G., et al. (2011). Large vocabulary continuous speech recognition with context-dependent DBN-HMMs. *Proceedings of the International Conference on Acoustics, Speech, and Signal Processing.*

4. If this were a book dedicated to NLP, then we would have been wise to also describe natural language methods based on word frequency, e.g., TF-IDF (term frequency-inverse document frequency) and PMI (pointwise mutual information).

5. A *corpus* (from the Latin "body") is the collection of all of the documents (the "body" of language) you use as your input data for a given natural language application. In Chapter 8, you'll make use of a corpus that consists of 18 classic books. Later in that chapter, you'll separately make use of a corpus of 25,000 film reviews. An example of a much larger corpus would be all of the English-language articles on Wikipedia. The largest corpuses are crawls of all the publicly available data on the Internet, such as at commoncrawl.org.

The bat sat on the cat.

words
the	1	0	0	0	1	0
bat	0	1	0	0	0	0
on	0	0	0	1	0	0

n_{unique_words}

Figure 2.4   One-hot encodings of words, such as this example, predominate the traditional machine learning approach to natural language processing.

natural language algorithm, then your matrix of one-hot-encoded words will have 100 rows. If there are 1,000 unique words across your corpus, then there will be 1,000 rows in your one-hot matrix, and so on.

Cells within one-hot matrices consist of binary values, that is, they are a 0 or a 1. Each column contains at most a single 1, but is otherwise made up of 0s, meaning that one-hot matrices are *sparse*.[6] Values of one indicate the presence of a particular word (row) at a particular position (column) within the corpus. In Figure 2.4, our entire corpus has only six words, five of which are unique. Given this, a one-hot representation of the words in our corpus has six columns and five rows. The first unique word—the—occurs in the first and fifth positions, as indicated by the cells containing 1s in the first row of the matrix. The second unique word in our wee corpus is bat, which occurs only in the second position, so it is represented by a value of 1 in the second row of the second column. One-hot word representations like this are fairly straightforward, and they are an acceptable format for feeding into a deep learning model (or, indeed, other machine learning models). As you will see momentarily, however, the simplicity and sparsity of one-hot representations are limiting when incorporated into a natural language application.

Word Vectors

Vector representations of words are the information-dense alternative to one-hot encodings of words. Whereas one-hot representations capture information about word location only, *word vectors* (also known as *word embeddings* or *vector-space embeddings*) capture information about word meaning as well as location.[7] This additional information renders

---

6. Nonzero values are rare (i.e., they are *sparse*) within a sparse matrix. In contrast, *dense* matrices are rich in information: They typically contain few—perhaps even no—zero values.

7. Strictly speaking, a one-hot representation is technically a "word vector" itself, because each column in a one-hot word matrix consists of a vector representing a word at a given location. In the deep learning community, however, use of the term "word vector" is commonly reserved for the dense representations covered in this section—that is, those derived by word2vec, GloVe, and related techniques.

word vectors favorable for a variety of reasons that are catalogued over the course of this chapter. The key advantage, however, is that—analogous to the visual features learned automatically by deep learning machine vision models in Chapter 1—word vectors enable deep learning NLP models to automatically learn linguistic features.

When we're creating word vectors, the overarching concept is that we'd like to assign each word within a corpus to a particular, meaningful location within a multidimensional space called the *vector space*. Initially, each word is assigned to a random location within the vector space. By considering the words that tend to be used around a given word within the natural language of your corpus, however, the locations of the words within the vector space can gradually be shifted into locations that represent the meaning of the words.[8]

Figure 2.5 uses a toy-sized example to demonstrate in more detail the mechanics behind the way word vectors are constructed. Commencing at the first word in our corpus and moving to the right one word at a time until we reach the final word in our corpus, we consider each word to be the *target word*. At the particular moment captured in Figure 2.5, the target word that happens to be under consideration is word. The next target word would be by, followed by the, then company, and so on. For each target word in turn, we consider it relative to the words around it—its *context words*. In our toy example, we're using a context-word window size of three words. This means that while word is the target word, the three words to the left (a, know, and shall) combined with the three words to the right (by, company, and the) together constitute a total of six context words.[9] When we move along to the subsequent target word (by), the windows of context words also shift one position to the right, dropping shall and by as context words while adding word and it.

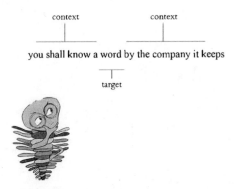

context   context
___ ___   ___ ___
      | |

you shall know a word by the company it keeps

⊤
|
target

Figure 2.5   A toy-sized example for demonstrating the high-level process behind techniques like word2vec and GloVe that convert natural language into word vectors

---

8. As mentioned at the beginning of this chapter, this understanding of the meaning of a word from the words around it was proposed by Ludwig Wittgenstein. Later, in 1957, the idea was captured succinctly by the British linguist J.R. Firth with his phrase, "You shall know a word by the company it keeps." Firth, J. (1957). *Studies in linguistic analysis*. Oxford: Blackwell.

9. It is mathematically simpler and more efficient to not concern ourselves with the specific ordering of context words, particularly because word order tends to confer negligible extra information to the inference of word vectors. Ergo, we provide the context words in parentheses alphabetically, an effectively random order.

Two of the most popular techniques for converting natural language into word vectors are *word2vec*[10] and *GloVe*.[11] With either technique, our objective while considering any given target word is to accurately predict the target word given its context words.[12] Improving at these predictions, target word after target word over a large corpus, we gradually assign words that tend to appear in similar contexts to similar locations in vector space.

Figure 2.6 provides a cartoon of vector space. The space can have any number of dimensions, so we can call it an *n*-dimensional vector space. In practice, depending on the richness of the corpus we have to work with and the complexity of our NLP application, we might create a word-vector space with dozens, hundreds, or—in extreme cases—thousands of dimensions. As overviewed in the previous paragraph, any given word from our corpus (e.g., king) is assigned a location within the vector space. In, say, a 100-dimensional space, the location of the word king is specified by a vector that we can call v_{king} that must consist of 100 numbers in order to specify the location of the word king across all of the available dimensions.

Human brains aren't adept at spatial reasoning in more than three dimensions, so our cartoon in Figure 2.6 has only three dimensions. In this three-dimensional space, any given word from our corpus needs three numeric coordinates to define its location within

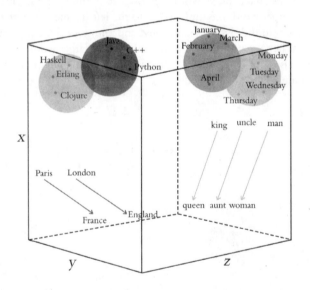

n – dimensional space

Figure 2.6   Diagram of word meaning as represented by a three-dimensional vector space (see page 328 for the color image).

10. Mikolov, T., et al. (2013). Efficient estimation of word representations in vector space. *arXiv:1301.3781.*
11. Pennington, J., et al. (2014). GloVe: Global vectors for word representations. *Proceedings of the Conference on Empirical Methods in Natural Language Processing.*
12. Or, alternatively, we could predict context words given a target word. More on that in Chapter 8.

the vector space: x, y, and z. In this cartoon example, then, the meaning of the word king is represented by a vector v_{king} that consists of three numbers. If v_{king} is located at the coordinates $x = -0.9$, $y = 1.9$, and $z = 2.2$ in the vector space, we can use the annotation [-0.9, 1.9, 2.2] to describe this location succinctly. This succinct annotation will come in handy shortly when we perform arithmetic operations on word vectors.

The closer two words are within vector space,[13] the closer their meaning, as determined by the similarity of the context words appearing near them in natural language. Synonyms and common misspellings of a given word—because they share an identical meaning—would be expected to have nearly identical context words and therefore nearly identical locations in vector space. Words that are used in similar contexts, such as those that denote time, tend to occur near each other in vector space. In Figure 2.6, Monday, Tuesday, and Wednesday could be represented by the orange-colored dots located within the orange days-of-the-week cluster in the cube's top-right corner. Meanwhile, months of the year might occur in their own purple cluster, which is adjacent to, but distinct from, the days of the week; they both relate to the date, but they're separate subclusters within a broader *dates* region. As a second example, we would expect to find programming languages clustering together in some location within the word-vector space that is distant from the time-denoting words—say, in the top-left corner. Again here, object-oriented programming languages like Java, C++, and Python would be expected to form one subcluster, while nearby we would expect to find functional programming languages like Haskell, Clojure, and Erlang forming a separate subcluster. As you'll see in Chapter 8 when you embed words in vector space yourself, less concretely defined terms that nevertheless convey a specific meaning (e.g., the verbs created, developed, and built) are also allocated positions within word-vector space that enable them to be useful in NLP tasks.

Word-Vector Arithmetic

Remarkably, because particular movements across vector space turn out to be an efficient way for relevant word information to be stored in the vector space, these movements come to represent relative particular meanings between words. This is a bewildering property.[14] Returning to our cube in Figure 2.6, the brown arrows represent the relationship between countries and their capitals. That is, if we calculate the direction and distance between the coordinates of the words Paris and France and then trace this direction and distance from London, we should find ourselves in the neighborhood of the coordinate representing the word England. As a second example, we can calculate the direction and distance between the coordinates for man and woman. This movement through vector space represents gender and is symbolized by the green arrows in Figure 2.6. If we trace the green direction and distance from any given male-specific term (e.g., king, uncle), we should find our way to a coordinate near the term's female-specific counterpart (queen, aunt).

---

13. Measured by Euclidean distance, which is the plain old straight-line distance between two points.
14. One of your esteemed authors, Jon, prefers terms like "mind-bending" and "trippy" to describe this property of word vectors, but he consulted a thesaurus to narrow in on a more professional-sounding adjective.

$$V_{king} - V_{man} + V_{woman} = V_{queen}$$
$$V_{bezos} - V_{amazon} + V_{tesla} = V_{musk}$$
$$V_{windows} - V_{microsoft} + V_{google} = V_{android}$$

Figure 2.7 Examples of word-vector arithmetic

A by-product of being able to trace vectors of meaning (e.g., gender, capital-country relationship) from one word in vector space to another is that we can perform *word-vector arithmetic*. The canonical example of this is as follows: If we begin at v_{king}, the vector representing king (continuing with our example from the preceding section, this location is described by [-0.9, 1.9, 2.2]), subtract the vector representing man from it (let's say v_{man} = [-1.1, 2.4, 3.0]), and add the vector representing woman (let's say v_{woman} = [-3.2, 2.5, 2.6]), we should find a location near the vector representing queen. To make this arithmetic explicit by working through it dimension by dimension, we would estimate the location of v_{queen} by calculating

$$x_{queen} = x_{king} - x_{man} + x_{woman} = -0.9 + 1.1 - 3.2 = -3.0$$
$$y_{queen} = y_{king} - y_{man} + y_{woman} = 1.9 - 2.4 + 2.5 = 2.0 \qquad (2.1)$$
$$z_{queen} = z_{king} - z_{man} + z_{woman} = 2.2 - 3.0 + 2.6 = 1.8$$

All three dimensions together, then, we expect v_{queen} to be near [-3.0, 2.0, 1.8].

Figure 2.7 provides further, entertaining examples of arithmetic through a word-vector space that was trained on a large natural language corpus crawled from the web. As you'll later observe in practice in Chapter 8, the preservation of these quantitative relationships of meaning between words across vector space is a robust starting point for deep learning models within NLP applications.

word2viz

To develop your intuitive appreciation of word vectors, navigate to bit.ly/word2viz. The default screen for the word2viz tool for exploring word vectors interactively is shown in Figure 2.8. Leaving the top-right dropdown box set to "Gender analogies," try adding in *pairs* of new words under the "Modify words" heading. If you add pairs of corresponding gender-specific words like princess and prince, duchess and duke, and businesswoman and businessman, you should find that they fall into instructive locations.

The developer of the word2viz tool, Julia Bazińska, compressed a 50-dimensional word-vector space down to two dimensions in order to visualize the vectors on an xy-coordinate system.[15] For the default configuration, Bazińska scaled the x-axis from the words she to he as a reference point for gender, while the y-axis was set to vary

---

15. We detail how to reduce the dimensionality of a vector space for visualization purposes in Chapter 8.

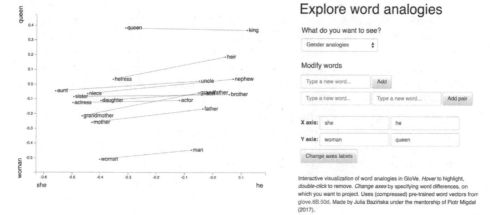

Figure 2.8   The default screen for word2viz, a tool for exploring word vectors interactively

from a commonfolk base toward a royal peak by orienting it to the words **woman** and **queen**. The displayed words, placed into vector space via training on a natural language dataset consisting of 6 billion instances of 400,000 unique words,[16] fall relative to the two axes based on their meaning. The more regal (**queen**-like) the words, the higher on the plot they should be shown, and the female (**she**-like) terms fall to the left of their male (**he**-like) counterparts.

When you've indulged yourself sufficiently with word2viz's "Gender analogies" view, you can experiment with other perspectives of the word-vector space. Selecting "Adjectives analogies" from the "What do you want to see?" dropdown box, you could, for example, add the words **small** and **smallest**. Subsequently, you could change the *x*-axis labels to **nice** and **nicer**, and then again to **small** and **big**. Switching to the "Numbers say-write analogies" view via the dropdown box, you could play around with changing the *x*-axis to **3** and **7**.

You may build your own word2viz plot from scratch by moving to the "Empty" view. The (word vector) world is your oyster, but you could perhaps examine the country-capital relationships we mentioned earlier when familiarizing you with Figure 2.6. To do this, set the *x*-axis to range from **west** to **east** and the *y*-axis to **city** and **country**. Word pairs that fall neatly into this plot include **london—england**, **paris—france**, **berlin—germany** and **beijing—china**.

While on the one hand word2viz is an enjoyable way to develop a general understanding of word vectors, on the other hand it can also be a serious tool for gaining insight into specific strengths or weaknesses of a given word-vector space. As an example, use

---

16. Technically, 400,000 *tokens*—a distinction that we examine later.

the "What do you want to see?" dropdown box to load the "Verb tenses" view, and then add the words lead and led. Doing this, it becomes apparent that the coordinates that words were assigned to in this vector space mirror existing gender stereotypes that were present in the natural language data the vector space was trained on. Switching to the "Jobs" view, this gender bias becomes even more stark. It is probably safe to say that any large natural language dataset is going to have some biases, whether intentional or not. The development of techniques for reducing biases in word vectors is an active area of research.[17] Mindful that these biases may be present in your data, however, the safest bet is to test your downstream NLP application in a range of situations that reflect a diverse userbase, checking that the results are appropriate.

Localist Versus Distributed Representations

With an intuitive understanding of word vectors under our figurative belts, we can contrast them with one-hot representations (Figure 2.4), which have been an established presence in the NLP world for longer. A summary distinction is that we can say word vectors store the meaning of words in a *distributed* representation across n-dimensional space. That is, with word vectors, word meaning is distributed gradually—*smeared*—as we move from location to location through vector space. One-hot representations, meanwhile, are *localist*. They store information on a given word discretely, within a single row of a typically extremely sparse matrix.

To more thoroughly characterize the distinction between the localist, one-hot approach and the distributed, vector-based approach to word representation, Table 2.1 compares them across a range of attributes. First, one-hot representations lack nuance; they are simple binary flags. Vector-based representations, on the other hand, are extremely nuanced: Within them, information about words is smeared throughout a continuous, quantitative space. In this high-dimensional space, there are essentially infinite possibilities for capturing the relationships between words.

Second, the use of one-hot representations in practice often requires labor-intensive, manually curated taxonomies. These taxonomies include dictionaries and other specialized reference language databases.[18] Such external references are unnecessary for vector-based representations, which are fully automatic with natural language data alone.

Third, one-hot representations don't handle new words well. A newly introduced word requires a new row in the matrix and then reanalysis relative to the existing rows of the corpus, followed by code changes—perhaps via reference to external information sources. With vector-based representations, new words can be incorporated by training the vector space on natural language that includes examples of the new words in their

---

17. For example, Bolukbasi, T., et al. (2016). Man is to computer programmer as woman is to homemaker? Debiasing word embeddings. *arXiv:1607.06520*; Caliskan, A., et al. (2017). Semantics derived automatically from language corpora contain human-like biases. *Science 356*: 183–6; Zhang, B., et al. (2018). Mitigating unwanted biases with adversarial learning. *arXiv:1801.07593*.

18. For example, WordNet (wordnet.princeton.edu), which describes synonyms as well as *hypernyms* ("is-a" relationships, so furniture, for example, is a hypernym of chair).

Table 2.1   Contrasting attributes of localist, one-hot representations of words with distributed, vector-based representations

One-Hot	Vector-Based
Not subtle	Very nuanced
Manual taxonomies	Automatic
Handles new words poorly	Seamlessly incorporates new words
Subjective	Driven by natural language data
Word similarity not represented	Word similarity = proximity in space

natural context. A new word gets its own new n-dimensional vector. Initially, there may be few training data points involving the new word, so its vector might not be very accurately positioned within n-dimensional space, but the positioning of all existing words remains intact and the model will not fail to function. Over time, as the instances of the new word in natural language increases, the accuracy of its vector-space coordinates will improve.[19]

Fourth, and following from the previous two points, the use of one-hot representations often involves subjective interpretations of the meaning of language. This is because they often require coded rules or reference databases that are designed by (relatively small groups of) developers. The meaning of language in vector-based representations, meanwhile, is data driven.[20]

Fifth, one-hot representations natively ignore word similarity: Similar words, such as couch and sofa, are represented no differently than unrelated words, such as couch and cat. In contrast, vector-based representations innately handle word similarity: As mentioned earlier with respect to Figure 2.6, the more similar two words are, the closer they are in vector space.

Elements of Natural Human Language

Thus far, we have considered only one element of natural human language: the *word*. Words, however, are made up of constituent language elements. In turn, words themselves are the constituents of more abstract, more complex language elements. We begin with the language elements that make up words and build up from there, following the schematic in Figure 2.9. With each element, we discuss how it is typically encoded from the traditional machine learning perspective as well as from the deep learning perspective. As we move through these elements, notice that the distributed deep learning

---

19. An associated problem not addressed here occurs when an in-production NLP algorithm encounters a word that was not included within its corpus of training data. This *out of vocabulary* problem impacts both one-hot representations and word vectors. There are approaches—such as Facebook's *fastText* library—that try to get around the issue by considering subword information, but these approaches are beyond the scope of this book.

20. Noting that they may nevertheless include biases found in natural language data. See the sidebar beginning on page 31.

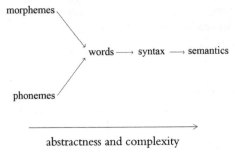

Figure 2.9   Relationships between the elements of natural human language. The leftmost elements are building blocks for further-right elements. As we move to the right, the more abstract the elements become, and therefore the more complex they are to model within an NLP application.

representations are fluid and flexible vectors whereas the traditional ML representations are local and rigid (Table 2.2).

Phonology is concerned with the way that language sounds when it is *spoken*. Every language has a specific set of *phonemes* (sounds) that make up its words. The traditional ML approach is to encode segments of auditory input as specific phonemes from the language's range of available phonemes. With deep learning, we train a model to predict phonemes from features automatically learned from auditory input and then represent those phonemes in a vector space. In this book, we work with natural language in text format only, but the techniques we cover can be applied directly to speech data if you're keen to do so on your own time.

Morphology is concerned with the forms of words. Like phonemes, every language has a specific set of *morphemes*, which are the smallest units of language that contain some meaning. For example, the three morphemes out, go, and ing combine to form the word outgoing. The traditional ML approach is to identify morphemes in text from a list of all the morphemes in a given language. With deep learning, we train a model to predict the occurrence of particular morphemes. Hierarchically deeper layers of artificial neurons can then combine multiple vectors (e.g., the three representing out, go, and ing) into a single vector representing a word.

Table 2.2   **Traditional machine learning and deep learning representations, by natural language element**

Representation	Traditional ML	Deep Learning	Audio-Only
Phonology	All phonemes	Vectors	True
Morphology	All morphemes	Vectors	False
Words	One-hot encoding	Vectors	False
Syntax	Phrase rules	Vectors	False
Semantics	Lambda calculus	Vectors	False

Phonemes (when considering audio) and morphemes (when considering text) combine to form *words*. Whenever we work with natural language data in this book, we work at the word level. We do this for four reasons. First, it's straightforward to define what a word is, and everyone is familiar with what they are. Second, it's easy to break up natural language into words via a process called *tokenization*[21] that we work through in Chapter 8. Third, words are the most-studied level of natural language, particularly with respect to deep learning, so we can readily apply cutting-edge techniques to them. Fourth, and perhaps most critically, for the NLP models we'll be building, word vectors simply work well: They prove to be functional, efficient, and accurate. In the preceding section, we detail the shortcomings of localist, one-hot representations that predominate traditional ML relative to the word vectors used in deep learning models.

Words are combined to generate *syntax*. Syntax and morphology together constitute the entirety of a language's grammar. Syntax is the arrangement of words into phrases and phrases into sentences in order to convey meaning in a way that is consistent across the users of a given language. In the traditional ML approach, phrases are bucketed into discrete, formal linguistic categories.[22] With deep learning, we employ vectors (surprise, surprise!). Every word and every phrase in a section of text can be represented by a vector in n-dimensional space, with layers of artificial neurons combining words into phrases.

Semantics is the most abstract of the elements of natural language in Figure 2.9 and Table 2.2; it is concerned with the *meaning* of sentences. This meaning is inferred from all the underlying language elements like words and phrases, as well as the overarching context that a piece of text appears in. Inferring meaning is complex because, for example, whether a passage is supposed to be taken literally or as a humorous and sarcastic remark can depend on subtle contextual differences and shifting cultural norms. Traditional ML, because it doesn't represent the fuzziness of language (e.g., the similarity of related words or phrases), is limited in capturing semantic meaning. With deep learning, vectors come to the rescue once again. Vectors can represent not only every word and every phrase in a passage of text but also every logical expression. As with the language elements already covered, layers of artificial neurons can recombine vectors of constituent elements—in this case, to calculate semantic vectors via the nonlinear combination of phrase vectors.

Google Duplex

One of the more attention-grabbing examples of deep-learning-based NLP in recent years is that of the Google Duplex technology, which was unveiled at the company's I/O developers conference in May 2018. The search giant's CEO, Sundar Pichai, held spectators in rapture as he demonstrated Google Assistant making a phone call to a Chinese-food restaurant to book a reservation. The audible gasps from the audience were in response to the natural flow of Duplex's conversation. It had mastered the cadence of a human conversation, replete with the *uh*'s and *hhhm*'s that we sprinkle into conversations

---

21. Essentially, tokenization is the use of characters like commas, periods, and whitespace to assume where one word ends and the next begins.
22. These categories have names like "noun-phrase" and "verb-phrase."

while we're thinking. Furthermore, the phone call was of average audio quality and the human on the line had a strong accent; Duplex never faltered, and it managed to make the booking.

Bearing in mind that this is a demonstration—and not even a live one—what nevertheless impressed us was the breadth of deep learning applications that had to come together to facilitate this technology. Consider the flow of information back and forth between the two agents on the call (Duplex and the restaurateur): Duplex needs a sophisticated speech recognition algorithm that can process audio in real time and handle an extensive range of accents and call qualities on the other end of the line, and also overcome the background noise.[23]

Once the human's speech has been faithfully transcribed, an NLP model needs to process the sentence and decide what it means. The intention is that the person on the line doesn't know they're speaking to a computer and so doesn't need to modulate their speech accordingly, but in turn, this means that humans respond with complex, multipart sentences that can be tricky for a computer to tease apart:

> "We don't have anything tomorrow, but we have the next day and Thursday, anytime before eight. Wait no . . . Thursday at seven is out. But we can do it after eight?"

This sentence is poorly structured—you'd never write an email like this—but in natural conversation, these sorts of on-the-fly corrections and replacements happen regularly, and Duplex needs to be able to follow along.

With the audio transcribed and the meaning of the sentence processed, Duplex's NLP model conjures up a response. This response must ask for more information if the human was unclear or if the answers were unsatisfactory; otherwise, it should confirm the booking. The NLP model will generate a response in text form, so a text-to-speech (TTS) engine is required to synthesize the sound.

Duplex uses a combination of *de novo* waveform synthesis using Tacotron[24] and WaveNet,[25] as well as a more classical "concatenative" text-to-speech engine.[26] This is where the system crosses the so-called uncanny valley:[27] The voice heard by the

---

23. This is known as the "cocktail-party problem"—or less jovially, "multitalker speech separation." It's a problem that humans solve innately, isolating single voices from a cacophony quite well without explicit instruction on how to do so. Machines typically struggle with this, although a variety of groups have proposed solutions. For example, see Simpson, A., et al. (2015). Deep karaoke: Extracting vocals from musical mixtures using a convolutional deep neural network. *arXiv:1504.04658*; Yu, D., et al. (2016). Permutation invariant training of deep models for speaker-independent multi-talker speech separation. *arXiv:1607.00325*.

24. `bit.ly/tacotron`

25. `bit.ly/waveNet`

26. Concatenative TTS engines use vast databases of prerecorded words and snippets, which can be strung together to form sentences. This approach is common and fairly easy, but it yields stilted, unnatural speech and cannot adapt the speed and intonation; you can't modulate a word to make it sound as if a question is being asked, for example.

27. The uncanny valley is a perilous space wherein humans find humanlike simulations weird and creepy because they're too similar to real humans but are clearly *not* real humans. Product designers endeavor to avoid the uncanny valley. They've learned that users respond well to simulations that are either very robotic or not robotic at all.

restaurateur is not a human voice at all. WaveNet is able to generate completely synthetic waveforms, one sample at a time, using a deep neural network trained on real waveforms from human speakers. Beneath this, Tacotron maps sequences of *words* to corresponding sequences of *audio features*, which capture subtleties of human speech such as pitch, speed, intonation, and even pronunciation. These features are then fed into WaveNet, which synthesizes the actual waveform that the restaurateur hears. This whole system is able to produce a natural-sounding voice with the correct cadence, emotion, and emphasis. During more-or-less rote moments in the conversation, the simple concatenative TTS engine (composed of recordings of its *own* "voice"), which is less computationally demanding to execute, is used. The entire model dynamically switches between the various models as needed.

To misquote Jerry Maguire, you had all of this at "hello." The speech recognition system, NLP models, and TTS engine all work in concert from the instant the call is answered. Things only stand to get more complex for Duplex from then on. Governing all of this interaction is a deep neural network that is specialized in handling information that occurs in a sequence.[28] This governor tracks the conversation and feeds the various inputs and outputs into the appropriate models.

It should be clear from this overview that Google Duplex is a sophisticated system of deep learning models that work in harmony to produce a seamless interaction on the phone. For now, Duplex is nevertheless limited to a few specific domains: scheduling appointments and reservations. The system cannot carry out general conversations. So even though Duplex represents a significant step forward for artificial intelligence, there is still much work to be done.

Summary

In this chapter, you learned about applications of deep learning to the processing of natural language. To that end, we described further the capacity for deep learning models to automatically extract the most pertinent features from data, removing the need for labor-intensive one-hot representations of language. Instead, NLP applications involving deep learning make use of vector-space embeddings, which capture the meaning of words in a nuanced manner that improves both model performance and accuracy.

In Chapter 8, you'll construct an NLP application by making use of artificial neural networks that handle the input of natural language data all the way through to the output of an inference about those data. In such "end-to-end" deep learning models, the initial layers create word vectors that flow seamlessly into deeper, specialized layers of artificial neurons, including layers that incorporate "memory." These model architectures highlight both the strength and the ease of use of deep learning with word vectors.

---

28. Called a *recurrent neural network*. These feature in Chapter 8.

3

Machine Art

In this chapter, we introduce some of the concepts that enable deep learning models to seemingly *create* art, an idea that may be paradoxical to some. The University of California, Berkeley, philosopher Alva Noë, for one, opined, "Art can help us frame a better picture of our human nature."[1] If this is true, how can machines create art? Or put differently, are the creations that emerge from these machines, in fact, art? Another interpretation—and one we like best—is that these creations are indeed art and that programmers are artists wielding deep learning models as brushes. We're not the only ones who view these works as bona fide artistry: generative adversarial network (GAN)-produced paintings have been snapped up to the tune of $400,000 a pop.[2]

Over the course of this chapter, we cover the high-level concepts behind GANs, and you will see examples of the novel visual works they can produce. We will draw a link between the latent spaces associated with GANs and the word-vector spaces of Chapter 2. And we will cover a deep learning model that can be used as an automated tool for dramatically improving the quality of photos. But before we do any of that, let's grab a drink . . .

A Boozy All-Nighter

Below Google's offices in Montreal sits a bar called *Les 3 Brasseurs*, a moniker that translates from French to "The 3 Brewers." It was at this watering hole in 2014, while a PhD student in Yoshua Bengio's renowned lab (Figure 1.10), that Ian Goodfellow conceived of an algorithm for fabricating realistic-looking images,[3] a technique that Yann LeCun (Figure 1.9) has hailed as the "most important" recent breakthrough in deep learning.[4]

Goodfellow's friends described to him a *generative model* they were working on, that is, a computational model that aims to produce something novel, be it a quote in the style of Shakespeare, a musical melody, or a work of abstract art. In their particular case, the

---

1. Noë, A. (2015, October 5). What art unveils. The *New York Times*.
2. Cohn, G. (2018, October 25). AI art at Christie's sells for $432,500. The *New York Times*.
3. Giles, M. (2018, February 21). The GANfather: The man who's given machines the gift of imagination. *MIT Technology Review*.
4. LeCun, Y. (2016, July 28). *Quora.* bit.ly/DLbreakthru

friends were attempting to design a model that could generate photorealistic images such as portraits of human faces. For this to work well via the traditional machine learning approach (Figure 1.12), the engineers designing the model would need to not only catalog and approximate the critical individual features of faces like eyes, noses, and mouths, but also accurately estimate how these features should be arranged relative to each other. Thus far, their results had been underwhelming. The generated faces tended to be excessively blurry, or they tended to be missing essential elements like the nose or the ears.

Perhaps with his creativity heightened by a pint of beer or two,[5] Goodfellow proposed a revolutionary idea: a deep learning model in which two artificial neural networks (ANNs) act against each other competitively as adversaries. As illustrated in Figure 3.1, one of these deep ANNs would be programmed to produce forgeries while the other would be programmed to act as a detective and distinguish the fakes from real images (which would be provided separately). These adversarial deep learning networks would play off one another: As the *generator* became better at producing fakes, the *discriminator* would need to become better at identifying them, and so the generator would need to produce even more compelling counterfeits, and so on. This virtuous cycle would eventually lead to convincing novel images in the style of the real training images, be they of faces or otherwise. Best of all, Goodfellow's approach would circumnavigate the need to program features into the generative model manually. As we expounded with respect to

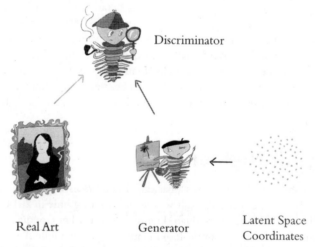

Discriminator

Real Art   Generator   Latent Space
                                         Coordinates

Figure 3.1   High-level schematic of a generative adversarial network (GAN). Real images, as well as forgeries produced by the generator, are provided to the discriminator, which is tasked with identifying which are the genuine articles. The orange cloud represents latent space (Figure 3.4) "guidance" that is provided to the forger. This guidance can either be random (as is generally the case during network training; see Chapter 11) or selective (during post-training exploration, as in Figure 3.3).

---

5. Jarosz, A., et al. (2012). Uncorking the muse: Alcohol intoxication facilitates creative problem solving. *Consciousness and Cognition, 21*, 487–93.

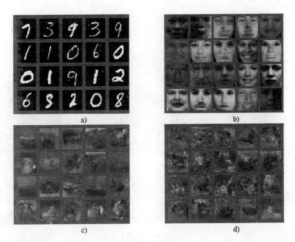

Figure 3.2   Results presented in Goodfellow and colleagues' 2014 GAN paper

machine vision (Chapter 1) and natural language processing (Chapter 2), deep learning would sort out the model's features automatically.

Goodfellow's friends were doubtful his imaginative approach would work. So, when he arrived home and found his girlfriend asleep, he worked late to architect his dual-ANN design. It worked the first time, and the astounding deep learning family of generative adversarial networks was born!

That same year, Goodfellow and his colleagues revealed GANs to the world at the prestigious Neural Information Processing Systems (NIPS) conference.[6] Some of their results are shown in Figure 3.2. Their GAN produced these novel images by being trained on (a) handwritten digits;[7] (b) photos of human faces;[8] and (c) and (d) photos from across ten diverse classes (e.g., planes, cars, dogs).[9] The results in (c) are markedly less crisp than in (d), because the GAN that produced the latter featured neuron layers specialized for machine vision called *convolutional* layers,[10] whereas the GAN that produced the former used a more general layer type only.[11]

Arithmetic on Fake Human Faces

Following on from Goodfellow's lead, a research team led by the American machine learning engineer Alec Radford determined architectural constraints for GANs that guide considerably more realistic image creation. Some examples of portraits of fake humans

6. Goodfellow, I., et al. (2014). Generative adversarial networks. *arXiv:1406.2661.*
7. From LeCun's classic MNIST dataset, which we use ourselves in Part II.
8. From the Hinton (Figure 1.16) research group's Toronto Face database.
9. The CIFAR-10 dataset, which is named after the Canadian Institute for Advanced Research that supported its creation.
10. We detail these in Chapter 9.
11. *Dense* layers, which are introduced in Chapter 4 and detailed in Chapter 6.

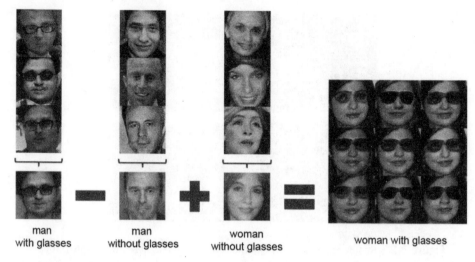

Figure 3.3　An example of latent-space arithmetic from Radford et al. (2016)

that were produced by their *deep convolutional* GANs[12] are provided in Figure 3.3. In their paper, Radford and his teammates cleverly demonstrated interpolation through, and arithmetic with, the *latent space* associated with GANs. Let's start off by explaining what latent space is before moving on to latent-space interpolation and arithmetic.

The latent-space cartoon in Figure 3.4 may be reminiscent of the word-vector space cartoon in Figure 2.6. As it happens, there are three major similarities between latent spaces and vector spaces. First, while the cartoon is only three-dimensional for simplicity and comprehensibility, latent spaces are n-dimensional spaces, usually in the order of hundreds of dimensions. The latent space of the GAN you'll later architect yourself in Chapter 11, for example, will have $n = 100$ dimensions. Second, the closer two points are in the latent space, the more similar the images that those points represent. And third, movement through the latent space in any particular direction can correspond to a gradual change in a concept being represented, such as age or gender for the case of photorealistic faces.

By picking two points far away from each other along some n-dimensional axis representing age, interpolating between them, and sampling points from the interpolated line, we could find what appears to be the same (fabricated) man gradually appearing to be older and older.[13] In our latent-space cartoon (Figure 3.4), we represent such an "age" axis in purple. To observe interpolation through an authentic GAN latent space, we recommend scanning through Radford and colleagues' paper for, as an example, smooth rotations of the "photo angle" of synthetic bedrooms. At the time of writing, the state

---

12. Radford, A., et al. (2016). Unsupervised representation learning with deep convolutional generative adversarial networks. *arXiv:1511.06434v2*.

13. A technical aside: As is the case with vector spaces, this "age" axis (or any other direction within latent space that represents some meaningful attribute) may be orthogonal to all of the n dimensions that constitute the axes of the n-dimensional space. We discuss this further in Chapter 8.

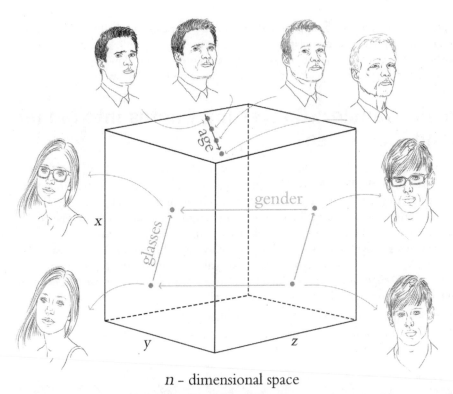

n – dimensional space

Figure 3.4   A cartoon of the latent space associated with generative adversarial networks (GANs). Moving along the purple arrow, the latent space corresponds to images of a similar-looking individual aging. The green arrow represents gender, and the orange one represents the inclusion of glasses on the face. (see page 328 for the color image).

of the art in GANs can be viewed at bit.ly/InterpCeleb. This video, produced by re-searchers at the graphics-card manufacturer Nvidia, provides a breathtaking interpolation through high-quality portrait "photographs" of ersatz celebrities.[14,15]

Moving a step further with what you've learned, you could now perform arithmetic with images sampled from a GAN's latent space. When sampling a point within the latent space, that point can be represented by the coordinates of its location—the resulting vector is analogous to the word vectors described in Chapter 2. As with word vectors, you can perform arithmetic with these vectors and move through the latent space in a semantic way. Figure 3.3 showcases an instance of latent-space arithmetic from Radford and his coworkers. Starting with a point in their GAN's latent space that represents a man with glasses, subtracting a point that represents a man *without* glasses, and adding a point

14. Karras, T., et al. (2018). Progressive growing of GANs for improved quality, stability, and variation. *Proceedings of the International Conference on Learning Representations.*
15. To try your hand at distinguishing between real and GAN-generated faces, visit whichfaceisreal.com.

representing a *woman* without glasses, the resulting point exists in the latent space near to images that represent women *with* glasses. Our cartoon in Figure 3.4 illustrates how the relationships between meaning in latent space are stored (again, akin to the way they are in word-vector space), thereby facilitating arithmetic on points in latent space.

Style Transfer: Converting Photos into Monet (and Vice Versa)

One of the more magical applications of GANs is *style transfer.* Zhu, Park, and their coworkers from the Berkeley Artificial Intelligence Research (BAIR) Lab introduced a new flavor of GAN[16] that enables stunning examples of this, as shown in Figure 3.5. Alexei Efros, one of the paper's coauthors, took photos while on holiday in France and the researchers employed their CycleGAN to transfer these photos into the style of the Impressionist painter Claude Monet, the nineteenth-century Dutch artist Vincent Van Gogh, and the Japanese Ukiyo-e genre, among others. If you navigate to `bit.ly/cycleGAN`, you'll be delighted to discover instances of the inverse (Monet paintings converted into photorealistic images), as well as:

- Summer scenes converted into wintry ones, and vice versa
- Baskets of apples converted into baskets of oranges, and vice versa

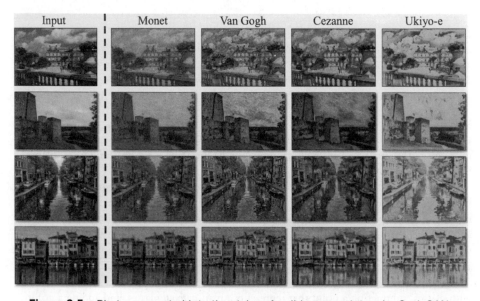

Figure 3.5   Photos converted into the styles of well-known painters by CycleGANs

---

16. Called "CycleGANs" because they retain image consistency over multiple cycles of network training. Zhu, J.-Y., et al. (2017). Unpaired image-to-image translation using cycle-consistent adversarial networks. *arXiv:1703.10593.*

- Flat, low-quality photos converted into what appear to be ones captured by high-end (single-lens reflex) cameras
- A video of a horse running in a field converted into a zebra
- A video of a drive taken during the day converted into a nighttime one

Make Your Own Sketches Photorealistic

Another GAN application out of Alexei Efros's BAIR lab, and one that you can amuse yourself with straightaway, is *pix2pix*.[17] If you make your way to bit.ly/pix2pixDemo, you can interactively translate images from one type to another. Using the edges2cats tool, for example, we sketched the three-eyed cat in the left-hand panel of Figure 3.6 to generate the photorealistic(-ish) mutant kitty in the right-hand panel. As it takes your fancy, you are also welcome to convert your own creative visions of felines, shoes, handbags, and building façades into photorealistic analogs within your browser. The authors of the pix2pix paper call their approach a *conditional* GAN (cGAN for short) because the generative adversarial network produces an output that is conditional on the particular input provided to it.

Creating Photorealistic Images from Text

To round out this chapter, we'd like you to take a *gan*der at the truly photorealistic high-resolution images in Figure 3.7. These images were generated by StackGAN,[18] an

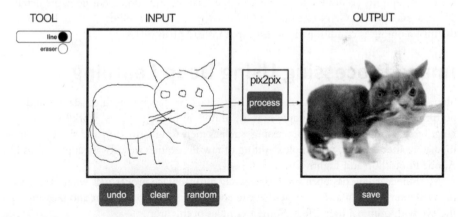

Figure 3.6 A mutant three-eyed cat (right-hand panel) synthesized via the pix2pix web application. The sketch in the left-hand panel that the GAN output was conditioned on was clearly not doodled by this book's illustrator, Aglaé, but one of its other authors (who shall remain nameless).

17. Isola, P., et al. (2017). Image-to-image translation with conditional adversarial networks. *arXiv:1611.07004*.
18. Zhang, H., et al. (2017). StackGAN: Text to photo-realistic image synthesis with stacked generative adversarial networks. *arXiv:1612.03242v2*.

Figure 3.7   Photorealistic high-resolution images output by StackGAN, which involves two GANs stacked upon each other

approach that *stacks* two GANs on top of each other. The first GAN in the architecture is configured to produce a rough, low-resolution image with the general shape and colors of the relevant objects in place. This is then supplied to the second GAN as its input, where the forged "photo" is refined by fixing up imperfections and adding considerable detail. The StackGAN is a cGAN like the pix2pix network in the preceding section; however, the image output is conditioned on *text* input instead of an image.

Image Processing Using Deep Learning

Since the advent of digital camera technology, image processing (both on-device and postprocessing) has become a staple in most (if not all) photographers' workflows. This ranges from simple on-device processing, such as increasing saturation and sharpness immediately after capture, to complex editing of raw image files in software applications like Adobe Photoshop and Lightroom.

Machine learning has been used extensively in on-device processing, where the camera manufacturer would like the image that the consumer sees to be vibrant and pleasing to the eye with minimal user effort. Some examples of this are:

- Early face-recognition algorithms in point-and-shoot cameras, which optimize the exposure and focus for faces or even selectively fire the shutter when they recognize that the subject is smiling (as in Figure 1.13)

- Scene-detection algorithms that adjust the exposure settings to capture the whiteness of snow or activate the flash for nighttime photos

In the postprocessing arena a variety of automatic tools exists, although generally photographers who are taking the time to postprocess images are investing considerable time and domain-specific knowledge into color and exposure correction, denoising, sharpening, tone mapping, and touching up (to name just a few of the corrections that may be applied).

Historically, these corrections have been difficult to execute programmatically, because, for example, denoising might need to be applied selectively to different images and even different parts of the same image. This is exactly the kind of intelligent application that deep learning is poised to excel at.

In a 2018 paper from Chen Chen and his collaborators at Intel Labs,[19] deep learning was applied to the enhancement of images that were taken in near total darkness, with astonishing results (Figure 3.8). In a phrase, their deep learning model involves convolutional layers organized into the innovative *U-Net*[20] architecture (which we break down for you in Chapter 9). The authors generated a custom dataset for training this model: the See-in-the-Dark dataset consists of 5,094 raw images of very dark scenes using a short-exposure image[21] with a corresponding long-exposure image (using a tripod for stability) of the same scene. The exposure times on the long-exposure images were 100 to 300 times those of the short-exposure training images, with actual exposure times in the range of 10 to 30 seconds. As demonstrated in Figure 3.8, the deep-learning-based image-processing pipeline of U-Net (right panel) far outperforms the results of the traditional pipeline (center panel). There are, however, limitations as yet:

- The model is not fast enough to perform this correction in real time (and certainly not on-device); however, runtime optimization could help here.

- A dedicated network must be trained for different camera-models and sensors, whereas a more generalized and camera-model-agnostic approach would be favorable.

- While the results far exceed the capabilities of traditional pipelines, there are still some artifacts present in the enhanced photos that could stand to be improved.

- The dataset is limited to selected static scenes and needs to be expanded to other subjects (most notably, humans).

Figure 3.8   A sample image (left) processed using a traditional pipeline (center) and the deep learning pipeline by Chen et al. (right)

19. Chen, C., et al. (2018) Learning to see in the dark. *arXiv:1805.01934*.

20. Ronneberger et al. (2015) U-Net: Convolutional networks for biomedical image segmentation. *arXiv: 1505.04597*.

21. That is, a short enough exposure time to enable practical handheld capture without motion blur but that renders images too dark to be useful.

Limitations aside, this work nevertheless provides a beguiling peek into how deep learning can adaptively correct images in photograph postprocessing pipelines with a level of sophistication not before seen from machines.

Summary

In this chapter, we introduced GANs and conveyed that this deep learning approach encodes exceptionally sophisticated representations within their latent spaces. These rich visual representations enable GANs to create novel images with particular, granular artistic styles. The outputs of GANs aren't purely aesthetic; they can be practical, too. They can, as examples, simulate data for training autonomous vehicles, hurry the pace of prototyping in the fields of fashion and architecture, and substantially augment the capacities of creative humans.[22]

In Chapter 11, after we get all of the prerequisite deep learning theory out of the way, you'll construct a GAN yourself to imitate sketches from the Quick, Draw! dataset (introduced at the end of Chapter 1). Take a gander at Figure 3.9 for a preview of what you'll be able to do.

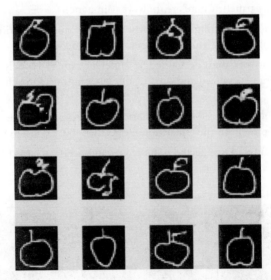

Figure 3.9   Novel "hand drawings" of apples produced by the GAN architecture we develop together in Chapter 11. Using this approach, you can produce machine-drawn "sketches" from across any of the hundreds of categories involved in the Quick, Draw! game.

---

22. Carter, S., and Nielsen, M. (2017, December 4). Using artificial intelligence to augment human intelligence. Distill. distill.pub/2017/aia

## 4

Game-Playing Machines

Alongside the generative adversarial networks introduced in Chapter 3, deep *reinforcement* learning has produced some of the most surprising artificial-neural-network advances, including the lion's share of the headline-grabbing "artificial intelligence" breakthroughs of recent years. In this chapter, we introduce what reinforcement learning is as well as how its fusion with deep learning has enabled machines to meet or surpass human-level performance on a diverse range of complex challenges, including Atari video games, the board game Go, and subtle physical-manipulation tasks.

Deep Learning, AI, and Other Beasts

Earlier in this book, we introduced deep learning with respect to vision (Chapter 1), language (Chapter 2), and the generation of novel "art" (Chapter 3). In doing this, we've loosely alluded to deep learning's relationship to the concept of artificial intelligence. At this stage, as we begin to cover deep reinforcement learning, it is worthwhile to define these terms more thoroughly as well as the terms' relationships to one another. As usual, we will be assisted by visual cues—in this case, the Venn diagram in Figure 4.1.

Artificial Intelligence

Artificial intelligence is the buzziest, vaguest, and broadest of the terms we cover in this section. Taking a stab at a technical definition regardless, a decent one is that AI involves a machine processing information from its surrounding environment and then factoring that information into decisions toward achieving some desired outcome. Perhaps given this, some consider the goal of AI to be the achievement of "general intelligence"— intelligence as it is generally referred to with respect to broad reasoning and problem-solving capabilities.[1] In practice and particularly in the popular press, "AI" is used to describe any cutting-edge machine capability. Presently, these capabilities include voice recognition, describing what's happening in a video, question-answering, driving a car,

---

1. Defining "intelligence" is not straightforward, and the great debate on it is beyond the scope of this book. A century-old definition of the term that we find amusing and that still today has some proponents among contemporary experts is that "intelligence is whatever IQ tests measure." See, for example, van der Mass, H., et al. (2014). Intelligence is what the intelligence test measures. Seriously. *Journal of Intelligence, 2,* 12–15.

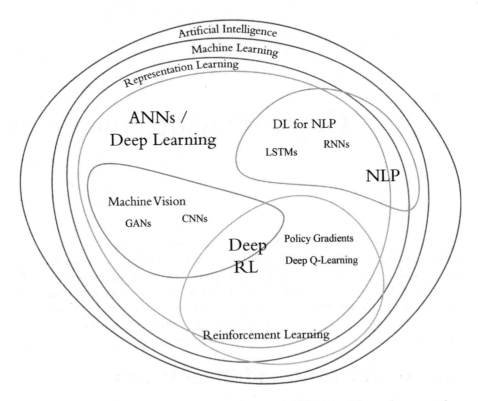

Figure 4.1   Venn diagram showing the relative positioning of the major concepts covered over the course of this book

industrial robots that mimic human exemplars in the factory, and dominating humans at "intuition-heavy" board games like Go. Once an AI capability becomes common-place (e.g., recognizing handwritten digits, which was cutting-edge in the 1990s; see Chapter 1), the "AI" moniker is typically dropped by the popular press for that capability such that the goalposts on the definition of AI are always moving.

Machine Learning

Machine learning is a subset of AI alongside other facets of AI like robotics. Machine learn-ing is a field of computer science concerned with setting up software in a manner so that the software can recognize patterns in data without the programmer needing to explicitly dictate how the software should carry out all aspects of this recognition. That said, the programmer would typically have some insight into or hypothesis about how the problem might be solved, and would thereby provide a rough model framework and relevant data such that the learning software is well prepared and well equipped to solve the problem. As depicted in Figure 1.12 and discussed time and again within the earlier chapters of this book, machine learning traditionally involves cleverly—albeit manually, and therefore laboriously—processing raw inputs to extract features that jibe well with data-modeling algorithms.

Representation Learning

Peeling back another layer of the Figure 4.1 onion, we find *representation learning*. This term was introduced at the start of Chapter 2, so we don't go into much detail again here. To recap briefly, representation learning is a branch of machine learning in which models are constructed in a way that—provided they are fed enough data— they learn features (or *representations*) automatically. These learned features may wind up being both more nuanced and more comprehensive than their manually curated cousins. The trade-off is that the learned features might not be as well understood nor as straight-forward to explain, although academic and industrial researchers alike are increasingly tackling these hitches.[2]

Artificial Neural Networks

Artificial neural networks (ANNs) dominate the field of representation learning today. As was touched on in earlier chapters and will be laid bare in Chapter 6, artificial neurons are simple algorithms inspired by biological brain cells, especially in the sense that individual neurons—whether biological or artificial—receive input from many other neurons, perform some computation, and then produce a single output. An artificial neural network, then, is a collection of artificial neurons arranged so that they send and receive information between each other. Data (e.g., images of handwritten digits) are fed into an ANN, which processes these data in some way with the goal of producing some desired result (e.g., an accurate guess as to what digits are represented by the handwriting).

Deep Learning

Of all the terms in Figure 4.1, *deep learning* is the easiest to define because it's so precise. We have mentioned a couple of times already in this book that a network composed of at least a few layers of artificial neurons can be called a deep learning network. As exemplified by the classic architectures in Figures 1.11 and 1.17; diagrammed simply in Figure 4.2; and fleshed out fully in Chapter 7, deep learning networks have a total of five or more layers with the following structure:

- A single *input* layer that is reserved for the data being fed into the network.
- Three or more *hidden* layers that learn representations from the input data. A general-purpose and frequently used type of hidden layer is the *dense* type, in which all of the neurons in a given layer can receive information from each of the neurons in the previous layer (it is apt, then, that a common synonym for "dense layer" is *fully connected layer*). In addition to this versatile hidden-layer type, there is a cornucopia of specialized types for particular use cases; we touch on the most popular ones as we make our way through this section.
- A single *output* layer that is reserved for the values (e.g., predictions) that the network yields.

---

2. For example, see Kindermans, P.-J., et al. (2018). Learning how to explain neural networks: PatternNet and PatternAttribution. *International Conference on Learning Representations*.

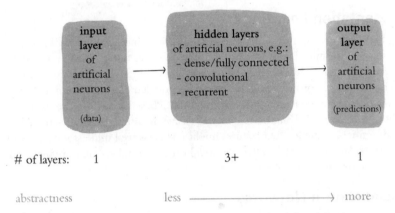

Figure 4.2   Generalization of deep learning model architectures

With each successive layer in the network being able to represent increasingly abstract, nonlinear recombinations of the previous layers, deep learning models with fewer than a dozen layers of artificial neurons are often sufficient for learning the representations that are of value for a given problem being solved with a given dataset. That said, deep learning networks with hundreds or even upwards of a thousand layers have in occasional circumstances been demonstrated to provide value.[3]

As rapidly improving accuracy benchmarks and countless competition wins since AlexNet's 2012 victory in the ILSVRC (Figure 1.15) have demonstrated, the deep learning approach to modeling excels at a broad range of machine learning tasks. Indeed, with deep learning driving so much of the contemporary progress in AI capabilities, the words "deep learning" and "artificial intelligence" are used essentially interchangeably by the popular press.

Let's move inside the deep learning ring of Figure 4.1 to explore classes of tasks that deep learning algorithms are leveraged for: machine vision, natural language processing, and reinforcement learning.

Machine Vision

Via analogy to the biological vision system, Chapter 1 introduced *machine vision*. There we focused on object recognition tasks such as distinguishing handwritten digits or breeds of dogs. Other prominent examples of applications that involve machine vision algorithms include self-driving cars, face-tagging suggestions, and phone unlocking via face recognition on smartphones. More broadly, machine vision is relevant to any AI that is going to need to recognize objects by their appearance at a distance or navigate a real-world environment.

Convolutional neural networks (ConvNets or CNNs for short) are a prominent type of deep learning architecture in contemporary machine vision applications. A CNN is any deep learning model architecture that features hidden layers of the *convolutional* type. We

---

3. For example, see He, K., et al. (2016). Identity mappings in deep residual networks. *arXiv:1603.05027*.

mentioned convolutional layers with respect to Ian Goodfellow's generative adversarial network results in Figure 3.2; we will detail and deploy them in Chapter 9.

Natural Language Processing

In Chapter 2, we covered language and natural language processing. Deep learning doesn't dominate natural language applications as comprehensively as it does machine vision applications, so our Venn diagram in Figure 4.1 shows NLP in both the deep learning region as well as the broader machine learning territory. As depicted by the timeline in Figure 2.3, however, deep learning approaches to NLP are beginning to overtake traditional machine learning approaches in the field with respect to both efficiency and accuracy. Indeed, in particular NLP areas like voice recognition (e.g., Amazon's Alexa or Google's Assistant), machine translation (including real-time voice translation over the phone), and aspects of Internet search engines (like predicting the characters or words that will be typed next by a user), deep learning already predominates. More generally, deep learning for NLP is relevant to any AI that interacts via natural language—be it spoken or typed—including to answer a complex series of questions automatically.

A type of hidden layer that is incorporated into many deep learning architectures in the NLP sphere is the *long short-term memory* (LSTM) cell, a member of the *recurrent neural network* (RNN) family. RNNs are applicable to any data that occur in a sequence such as financial time series data, inventory levels, traffic, and weather. We expound on RNNs, including LSTMs, in Chapter 8 when we incorporate them into predictive models involving natural language data. These language examples provide a firm foundation even if you're primarily seeking to apply deep learning techniques to the other classes of sequential data.

Three Categories of Machine Learning Problems

The one remaining section of the Venn diagram in Figure 4.1 involves reinforcement learning, which is the focus of the rest of this chapter. To introduce reinforcement learning, we contrast it with the two other principal categories of problems that machine learning algorithms are often leveraged to tackle: supervised and unsupervised learning problems.

Supervised Learning

In *supervised learning* problems, we have both an x variable and a y variable, where:

- x represents the data we're providing as input into our model.
- y represents an outcome we're building a model to predict. This y variable can also be called a *label*.

The goal with supervised learning is to have our model learn some function that uses x to approximate y. Supervised learning typically involves either of two types:

- *Regression*, where our y is a *continuous variable*. Examples include predicting the number of sales of a product, or predicting the future price of an asset like a home (an example we provide in Chapter 7) or a share in an exchange-listed company.

- *Classification*, where our y-values consist of labels that assign each instance of x to a particular category. In other words, y is a so-called *categorical variable*. Examples include identifying handwritten digits (you will code up models that do this in Chapter 9) or predicting whether someone who has reviewed a film loved it or loathed it (as you'll do in Chapter 8).

Unsupervised Learning

Unsupervised learning problems are distinguishable from supervised learning problems by the absence of a label y. Ergo, in unsupervised learning problems, we have some data x that we can put into a model, but we have no outcome y to predict. Rather, our goal with unsupervised learning is to have our model discover some hidden, underlying structure within our data. An often-used example is that of grouping news articles by their theme. Instead of providing a predefined list of categories that the news articles belong to (politics, sports, finance, etc.), we configure the model to group those with similar topics for us automatically. Other examples of unsupervised learning include creating a word-vector space (see Chapter 2) from natural language data (you'll do this in Chapter 8), or producing novel images with a generative adversarial network (as in Chapter 11).

Reinforcement Learning

Returning to Figure 4.1, we're now well positioned to cover *reinforcement learning* problems, which are markedly different from the supervised and unsupervised varieties. As illustrated lightheartedly in Figure 4.3, reinforcement learning problems are ones that we can frame as having an *agent* take a sequence of actions within some *environment*. The agent could, for example, be a human or an algorithm playing an Atari video game, or it could be a human or an algorithm driving a car. Perhaps the primary way in which reinforcement learning problems diverge from supervised or unsupervised ones is that the actions taken by the agent influence the information that the environment provides to the agent—that is, the agent receives direct feedback on the actions it takes. In supervised or unsupervised problems, in contrast, the model never impacts the underlying data; it simply consumes it.

Students of deep learning often have an innate desire to divide the supervised, unsupervised, and reinforcement learning paradigms into the traditional machine learning versus deep learning approaches. More specifically, they seem to want to associate supervised learning with traditional machine learning while associating unsupervised learning or reinforcement learning (or both) with deep learning. To be clear, there is no such association to be made. Both traditional machine learning and deep learning techniques can be applied to supervised, unsupervised, and reinforcement learning problems.

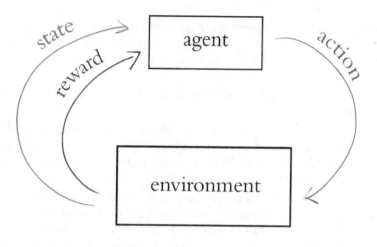

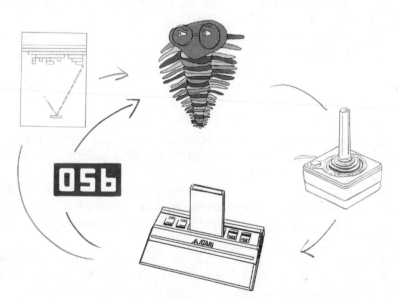

Figure 4.3   The reinforcement learning loop. The top diagram is a generalized version. The bottom diagram is specific to the example elaborated on in the text of an agent playing a video game on an Atari console. To our knowledge, trilobites can't actually play video games; we're using the trilobite as a symbolic representation of the reinforcement learning agent, which could be either a human or a machine.

Let's dive a bit further into the relationship between a reinforcement learning agent and its environment by exploring some examples. In Figure 4.3, the agent is represented by an anthropomorphized trilobite, but this agent could be either human or a machine. Where the agent is playing an Atari video game:

- The possible *actions* that can be taken are the buttons that can be pressed on the video game controller.[4]

- The *environment* (the Atari console) returns information back to the agent. This information comes in two delicious flavors: *state* (the pixels on the screen that represent the current condition of the environment) and *reward* (the point score in the game, which is what the agent is endeavoring to maximize via gameplay).

- If the agent is playing Pac-Man, then selecting the action of pressing the "up" button results in the environment returning an updated state where the pixels representing the video game character on the screen have moved upward. Prior to playing any of the game, a typical reinforcement learning algorithm would not even have knowledge of this simple relationship between the "up" button and the Pac-Man character moving upward; everything is learned from the ground up via trial and error.

- If the agent selects an action that causes Pac-Man to cross paths with a pair of delectable cherries, then the environment will return a *positive reward*: an increase in points. On the other hand, if the agent selects an action that causes Pac-Man to cross paths with a spooky ghost, then the environment will return a *negative reward*: a decrease in points.

In a second example, where the agent is driving a car,

- The available *actions* are much broader and richer than for Pac-Man. The agent can adjust the steering column, the accelerator, and the brakes to varying degrees ranging from subtle to dramatic.

- The *environment* in this case is the real world, consisting of roads, traffic, pedestrians, trees, sky, and so on. The *state* then is the condition of the vehicle's surroundings, as perceived by a human agent's eyes and ears, or by an autonomous vehicle's cameras and lidar.[5]

- The *reward*, in the case of an algorithm, could be programmed to be *positive* for, say, every meter of distance traveled toward a destination; it could be somewhat *negative* for minor traffic infractions, and severely negative in the event of a collision.

Deep Reinforcement Learning

At long last, we reach the *deep reinforcement learning* section near the center of the Venn diagram in Figure 4.3. A reinforcement learning algorithm earns its "deep" prefix when

---

4. We're not aware of video game-playing algorithms that literally press the buttons on the game console's controllers. They would typically interact with a video game directly via a software-based emulation. We go through the most popular open-source packages for doing this at the end of the chapter.

5. The laser-based equivalent of radar.

an artificial neural network is involved in it, such as to learn what actions to take when presented with a given state from the environment in order to have a high probability of obtaining a positive reward.[6] As you'll see in the examples coming up in the next section, the marriage of deep learning and reinforcement learning approaches has proved a prosperous one. This is because:

- Deep neural networks excel at processing the complex sensory input provided by real environments or advanced, simulated environments in order to distill relevant signals from a cacophony of incoming data. This is analogous to the functionality of the biological neurons of your brain's visual and auditory cortexes, which receive input from the eyes and ears, respectively.

- Reinforcement learning algorithms, meanwhile, shine at selecting an appropriate action from a vast scope of possibilities.

Taken together, deep learning and reinforcement learning are a powerful problem-solving combination. Increasingly complex problems tend to require increasingly large datasets for deep reinforcement learning agents to wade through vast noise as well as vast randomness in order to discover an effective policy for what actions it should take in a given circumstance. Because many reinforcement learning problems take place in a simulated environment, obtaining a sufficient amount of data is often not a problem: The agent can simply be trained on further rounds of simulations.

Although the theoretical foundations for deep reinforcement learning have been around for a couple of decades,[7] as with AlexNet for vanilla deep learning (Figure 1.17), deep reinforcement learning has in the past few years benefited from a confluence of three tail winds:

1. Exponentially larger datasets and much richer simulated environments
2. Parallel computing across many graphics processing units (GPUs) to model efficiently with large datasets as well as the breadth of associated possible states and possible actions
3. A research ecosystem that bridges academia and industry, producing a quickly developing body of new ideas on deep neural networks in general as well as on deep reinforcement learning algorithms in particular, to, for example, identify optimal actions across a wide variety of noisy states

Video Games

Many readers of this book recall learning a new video game as a child. Perhaps while at an arcade or staring at the family's heavy cathode-ray-tube television set, you quickly became aware that missing the ball in Pong or Breakout was an unproductive move. You

---

6. Earlier in this chapter (see Figure 4.2), we indicate that the "deep learning" moniker applies to an artificial neural network that has at least three hidden layers. While in general this is the case, when used by the reinforcement learning community, the term "deep reinforcement learning" may be used even if the artificial neural network involved in the model is shallow, that is, composed of as few as one or two hidden layers.

7. Tesauro, G. (1995). Temporal difference learning and TD-Gammon. *Communications of the Association for Computing Machinery, 38,* 58–68.

processed the visual information on the screen and, yearning for a score in excess of your friends', devised strategies to manipulate the controller effectively and achieve this aim. In recent years, researchers at a firm called DeepMind have been producing software that likewise learns how to play classic Atari games.

DeepMind was a British technology startup founded by Demis Hassabis (Figure 4.4), Shane Legg, and Mustafa Suleyman in London in 2010. Their stated mission was to "solve intelligence," which is to say they were interested in extending the field of AI by developing increasingly general-purpose learning algorithms. One of their early contributions was the introduction of deep Q-learning networks (DQNs; noted within Figure 4.1). Via this approach, a single model architecture was able to learn to play multiple Atari 2600 games well—from scratch, simply through trial and error.

In 2013, Volodymyr Mnih[8] and his DeepMind colleagues published[9] an article on their DQN agent, a deep reinforcement learning approach that you will come to understand intimately when you construct a variant of it yourself line by line in Chapter 10. Their agent received raw pixel values from its *environment*, a video game emulator,[10] as its *state* information—akin to the way human players of Atari games view a TV screen. In order to efficiently process this information, Mnih et al.'s DQN included a convolutional neural network (CNN), a common tactic for any deep reinforcement learning model that is fed visual data (this is why we elected to overlap "Deep RL" somewhat with "Machine Vision" in Figure 4.1). The handling of the flood of visual input from Atari games (in this case, a little over two million pixels per second) underscores how well suited deep learning in general is to filtering out pertinent features from noise. Further, playing Atari games within an emulator is a problem that is well suited to deep reinforcement learning in particular: While they provide a rich set of possible actions that are engineered to be challenging to master, there is thankfully no finite limit on the amount of training data available because the agent can engage in endless rounds of play.

Figure 4.4   Demis Hassabis cofounded DeepMind in 2010 after completing his PhD in cognitive neuroscience at University College London.

---

8. Mnih obtained his doctorate at the University of Toronto under the supervision of Geoff Hinton (Figure 1.16).

9. Mnih, V., et al. (2013). Playing Atari with deep reinforcement learning. *arXiv: 1312.5602*.

10. Bellemare, M., et al. (2012). The arcade learning environment: An evaluation platform for general agents. *arXiv: 1207.4708*.

During training, the DeepMind DQN was not provided any hints or strategies; it was provided only with state (screen pixels), reward (its point score, which it is programmed to maximize), and the range of possible actions (game-controller buttons) available in a given Atari game. The model was not altered for specific games, and yet it was able to outperform existing machine learning approaches in six of the seven games Mnih and his coworkers tested it on, even surpassing the performance of expert human players on three. Perhaps influenced by this conspicuous progress, Google acquired DeepMind in 2014 for the equivalent of half a billion U.S. dollars.

In a follow-up paper published in the distinguished journal *Nature*, Mnih and his teammates at now-Google DeepMind assessed their DQN algorithm across 49 Atari games.[11] The results are shown in Figure 4.5: It outperformed other machine learning approaches on all but three of the games (94 percent of them), and, astonishingly, it scored above human level on the majority of them (59 percent).[12]

Board Games

It might sound sensible that board games would serve as a logical prelude to video games given their analog nature and their chronological head start; however, the use of software emulators provided a simple and easy way to interact with video games digitally. Instead, the availability of these emulation tools provided the means, and so the principal advances in modern deep reinforcement learning initially took place in the realm of video games. Additionally, relative to Atari games, the complexity of some classical board games is much greater. There are myriad strategies and long-plays associated with chess expertise that are not readily apparent in Pac-Man or Space Invaders, for example. In this section, we provide an overview of how deep reinforcement learning strategies mastered the board games Go, chess, and shogi despite the data-availability and computational-complexity head winds.

AlphaGo

Invented several millennia ago in China, Go (illustrated in Figure 4.6) is a ubiquitous two-player strategy board game in Asia. The game has a simple set of rules based around the idea of capturing one's opponents' pieces (called *stones*) by encircling them with one's own.[13] This uncomplicated premise belies intricacy in practice, however. The larger board and the larger set of possible moves per turn make the game much more complex than, say, chess, for which we've had algorithms that can defeat the best human players for two decades.[14] There are a touch more than 2×10^{170} possible legal board positions in Go, which is far more than the number of atoms in the universe[15] and about a *googol* (10^{100}) more complex than chess.

---

11. Mnih, V., et al. (2015). Human-level control through deep reinforcement learning. *Nature, 518,* 529–33.
12. You can be entertained by watching the Google DeepMind DQN learn to master Space Invaders and Pong here: bit.ly/DQNpong.
13. Indeed, Go in Chinese translates literally to "encirclement board game."
14. IBM's Deep Blue defeated Garry Kasparov, arguably the world's greatest-ever chess player, in 1997. More on that storied match coming up shortly in this section.
15. There are an estimated 10^{80} atoms in the observable universe.

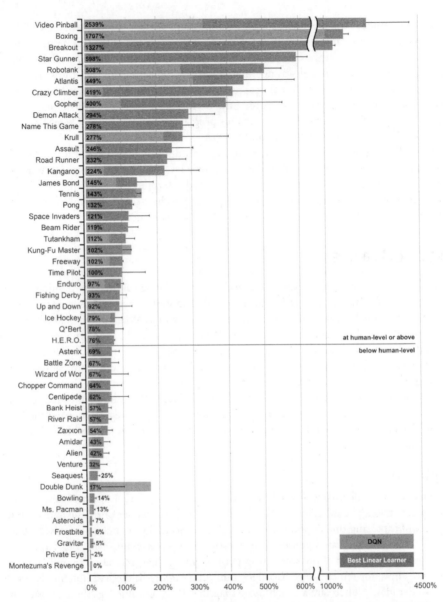

Figure 4.5   The normalized performance scores of Mnih and colleagues' (2015) DQN relative to a professional game tester: Zero percent represents random play, and 100% represents the pro's best performance. The horizontal line represents the authors' defined threshold of "human-level" play: the 75th percentile of professionals' scores.

Figure 4.6   The Go board game. One player uses the white stones while the other uses the black stones. The objective is to encircle the stones of your opponent, thereby capturing them.

An algorithm called *Monte Carlo tree search* (MCTS) can be employed to play uncomplicated games competently. In its purest form, MCTS involves selecting random moves[16] until the end of gameplay. By repeating this many times, moves that tended to lead to victorious game outcomes can be weighted as favorable options. Because of the extreme complexity and sheer number of possibilities within sophisticated games like Go, pure MCTS approach is impractical: There are simply too many options to search through and evaluate. Instead of pure MCTS, an alternative approach involves MCTS applied to a much more finite subset of actions that were curated by, for example, an established policy of optimal play. This curated approach has proved sufficient for defeating amateur human Go players but is uncompetitive against professionals. To bridge the gap from amateur- to professional-level capability, David Silver (Figure 4.7) and his colleagues at Google DeepMind devised a program called AlphaGo that combines MCTS with both supervised learning and deep reinforcement learning.[17]

Silver et al. (2016) used supervised learning on a historical database of expert human Go moves to establish something called a *policy network*, which provides a shortlist of possible moves for a given situation. Subsequently, this policy network was refined via *self-play* deep reinforcement learning, wherein both opponents are Go-playing agents of a comparable skill level. Through this self-play, the agent iteratively improves upon itself, and whenever it improves, it is pitted against its now-improved self, producing a positive-feedback loop of continuous advancement. Finally, the cherry atop the AlphaGo algorithm: a so-called *value network* that predicts the winner of the self-play games, thereby evaluating positions on the board and learning to identify strong moves. The combination of these policy and value networks (more on both of these in Chapter 10) reduces the breadth of search space for the MCTS.

---

16. Hence "Monte Carlo": The casino-dense district of Monaco evokes imagery of random outcomes.
17. Silver, D., et al. (2016). Mastering the game of Go with deep neural networks and tree search. *Nature, 529,* 484–9.

Figure 4.7   David Silver is a Cambridge- and Alberta-educated researcher at Google DeepMind. He has been instrumental in combining the deep learning and reinforcement learning paradigms.

AlphaGo was able to win the vast majority of games it played against other computer-based Go programs. Perhaps most strikingly, AlphaGo was also able to defeat Fan Hui, the then-reigning European Go champion, five games to zero. This marked the first time a computer defeated a professional human player in a full play of the game. As exemplified by the Elo ratings[18] in Figure 4.8, AlphaGo performed at or above the level of the best players in the world.

Following this success, AlphaGo was famously matched against Lee Sedol in March 2016 in Seoul, South Korea. Sedol has 18 world titles and is considered one of the all-time great players. The five-game match was broadcast and viewed live by 200 million people. AlphaGo won the match 4-1, launching DeepMind, Go, and the artificially intelligent future into the public imagination.[19]

AlphaGo Zero

Following AlphaGo, the folks at DeepMind took their work further and created a second-generation Go player: AlphaGo Zero. Recall that AlphaGo was initially trained in a supervised manner; that is, expert human moves were used to train the network first, and thereafter the network learned by reinforcement learning through self-play. Although this is a nifty approach, it doesn't exactly "solve intelligence" as DeepMind's founders would have liked. A better approximation of general intelligence would be a network that

---

18. Elo ratings enable the skill level of human and artificial game players alike to be compared. Derived from calculations of head-to-head wins and losses, an individual with a higher Elo score is more likely to win a game against an opponent with a lower score. The larger the score gap between the two players, the greater the probability that the player with the higher score will win.

19. There is an outstanding documentary on this Sedol match that gave us chills: Kohs, G. (2017). *AlphaGo*. United States: Moxie Pictures & Reel As Dirt.

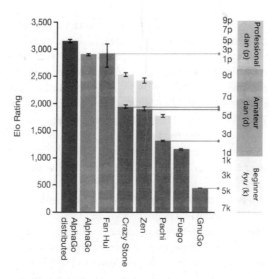

Figure 4.8   The Elo score of AlphaGo (blue) relative to Fan Hui (green) and several Go programs (red). The approximate human rank is shown on the right (see page 329 for the color image) .

could learn to play Go in a completely *de novo* setting—where the network is not supplied with any human input or domain knowledge, but improves by deep reinforcement learning alone. Enter AlphaGo Zero.

As we've alluded to before, the game of Go requires sophisticated look-ahead capabilities through vast search spaces. That is, there are so many *possible* moves and such a tiny fraction of them are *good* moves in the short- and longplay of the game that performing a search for the optimal move, keeping the likely future state of the game in mind, becomes exceedingly complex and computationally impractical. It is for this reason that it was thought that Go would be a final frontier for machine intelligence; indeed, it was thought that the achievements of AlphaGo in 2016 were a decade or more away.

Working off the momentum from the AlphaGo-Sedol match in Seoul, researchers at DeepMind created AlphaGo Zero, which learns to play Go far beyond the level of the original AlphaGo—while being revolutionary in several ways.[20] First and foremost, it is trained without any data from human gameplay. That means it learns purely by trial and error. Second, it uses only the stones on the board as inputs. Contrastingly, AlphaGo had received 15 supplementary, human-engineered features, which provided the algorithm key hints such as how many turns since a move was played or how many opponent stones would be captured. Third, a single (deep) neural network was used to evaluate the board and decide on a next move, rather than separate policy and value networks (as mentioned in the sidebar on page 61; more on these coming in Chapter 10). Finally, the tree search is simpler and relies on the neural network to evaluate positions and possible moves.

AlphaGo Zero played almost five million games of self-play over three days, taking an estimated 0.4s per move to "think." Within 36 hours, it had begun to outperform

---

20. Silver, D., et al. (2016). Mastering the game of Go without human knowledge. *Nature* 550, 354–359.

the model that beat Lee Sedol in Seoul (retroactively termed AlphaGo Lee), which—in stark contrast—took several months to train. At the 72-hour mark, the model was pitted against AlphaGo Lee in match conditions, where it handily won every single one of 100 games. Even more remarkable is that AlphaGo Zero achieved this on a single machine with four tensor processing units (TPUs)[21] whereas AlphaGo Lee was distributed over multiple machines and used 48 TPUs. (AlphaGo Fan, which beat Fan Hui, was distributed over 176 GPUs!) In Figure 4.9, the Elo score for AlphaGo Zero is shown over days of training time and compared to the scores for AlphaGo Master[22] and AlphaGo Lee. Shown on the right are the absolute Elo scores for a variety of iterations of AlphaGo and some other Go programs. AlphaGo Zero is far and away the superior model.

A startling discovery that emerged from this research was that the nature of the gameplay by AlphaGo Zero is qualitatively different from that of human players and (the human gameplay-trained) AlphaGo Lee. AlphaGo Zero began with random play but quickly learned professional *joseki*—corner sequences that are considered heuristics of distinguished play. After further training, however, the mature model tended to prefer novel *joseki* that were previously unknown to humankind. AlphaGo Zero did spontaneously learn a whole range of classical Go moves, implying a pragmatic alignment with these techniques. However, the model did this in an original manner: It did not learn the concept of *shicho* (ladder sequences), for example, until much later in its training, whereas this is one of the first concepts taught to novice human players. The authors additionally trained another iteration of the model with human gameplay data. This supervised model performed better initially; however, it began to succumb to the data-free model within

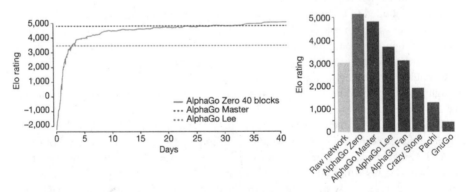

Figure 4.9   Comparing Elo scores between AlphaGo Zero and other AlphaGo variations or other Go programs. In the left-hand plot, the comparison is over days of AlphaGo Zero training.

---

21. Google built custom processor units for training neural networks, known as tensor processing units (TPUs). They took the existing architecture of a GPU and specifically optimized it for performing calculations that predominate the training of neural network models. At the time of writing, TPUs were accessible to the public via the Google Cloud Platform only.

22. AlphaGo Master is a hybrid between AlphaGo Lee and AlphaGo Zero; however, it uses the extra input features enjoyed by AlphaGo Lee and initializes training in a supervised manner. AlphaGo Master famously played online anonymously in January 2017 under the pseudonyms *Master* and *Magister*. It won all 60 of the games it played against some of the world's strongest Go players.

the first 24 hours of training and ultimately achieved a lower Elo score. Together, these results suggest that the data-free, self-learned model has a style of play distinct from that of human players—a dominating style that the supervised model fails to develop.

AlphaZero

Having trounced the Go community, the team at DeepMind shifted their focus to general game-playing neural networks. Although AlphaGo Zero is adept at playing Go, they wondered if a comparable network could learn to play multiple games expertly. To put this to the test, they added two new games to their repertoire: chess and shogi.[23]

Most readers are likely familiar with the game of chess, and shogi—referred to by some as Japanese chess—is similar. Both games are two-player strategy games, both take place on a grid-format board, both culminate in a checkmate of the opponent's king, and both consist of a range of pieces with different moving abilities. Shogi, however, is significantly more complex than chess, with a larger board size (9×9, relative to 8×8 in chess) and the fact that opponent pieces can be replaced anywhere on the board after their capture.

Historically, artificial intelligence has had a rich interaction with the game of chess. Over several decades, chess-playing computer programs have been developed extensively. The most famous is Deep Blue, conceived by IBM, which went on to beat the world champion Garry Kasparov in 1997.[24] It was heavily reliant on brute-force computing power[25] to execute complex searches through possible moves, and combined this with handcrafted features and domain-specific adaptations. Deep Blue was fine-tuned by analyzing thousands of master games (it was a supervised learning system!) and it was even tweaked between games.[26]

Although Deep Blue was an achievement two decades ago, the system was not generalizable; it could not perform any task other than chess. After AlphaGo Zero demonstrated that the game of Go could be learned by a neural network from first principles alone, given nothing but the board and the rules of the game, Silver and his DeepMind colleagues set out to devise a generalist neural network, a *single network architecture* that could dominate not only at Go but also at other board games.

Compared to Go, chess and shogi present pronounced obstacles. The rules of the games are position dependent (pieces can move differently based on where they are on the board) and asymmetrical (some pieces can move only in one direction).[27] Long-range actions are possible (such as the queen moving across the entire board), and games can result in draws.

---

23. Silver, D., et al. (2017). Mastering chess and shogi by self-play with a general reinforcement learning algorithm. *arXiv:1712.01815.*

24. Deep Blue lost its first match against Kasparov in 1996, and after significant upgrades went on to narrowly beat Kasparov in 1997. This was not the total domination of man by machine that AI proponents might have hoped for.

25. Deep Blue was the planet's 259th most powerful supercomputer at the time of the match against Kasparov.

26. This tweaking was a point of contention between IBM and Kasparov after his loss in 1997. IBM refused to release the program's logs and dismantled Deep Blue. Their computer system never received an official chess ranking, because it played so few games against rated chess masters.

27. This makes expanding the training data via synthetic augmentation—an approach used copiously for AlphaGo—more challenging.

AlphaZero feeds the board positions into a neural network and outputs a vector of move probabilities for each possible action, as well as a scalar[28] outcome value for that move. The network learns the parameters for these move probabilities and outcomes entirely from self-play deep reinforcement learning, as AlphaGo Zero did. An MCTS is then performed on the reduced space guided by these probabilities, returning a refined vector of probabilities over the possible moves. Whereas AlphaGo Zero optimizes the probability of winning (Go is a binary win/loss game), AlphaZero instead optimizes for the expected outcome. During self-play, AlphaGo Zero retains the best *player* to date and evaluates updated versions of itself against that player, continually replacing the player with the next best version. AlphaZero, in contrast, maintains a single network and at any given time is playing against the latest version of itself. AlphaZero was trained to play each of chess, shogi, and Go for a mere 24 hours. There were no game-specific modifications, with the exception of a manually configured parameter that regulates how frequently the model takes random, exploratory moves; this was scaled to the number of legal moves in each game.[29]

Across 100 competitive games, AlphaZero did not lose a single one against the 2016 Top Chess Engine Championship world champion Stockfish. In shogi, the Computer Shogi Association world champion, Elmo, managed to beat AlphaZero only eight times in 100 games. Its perhaps most worthy opponent, AlphaGo Zero, was able to defeat AlphaZero in 40 of their 100 games. Figure 4.10 shows the Elo scores for AlphaZero relative to these three adversaries.

Not only was AlphaZero superior, it was also efficient. AlphaZero's Elo score exceeded its greatest foes' after only two, four, and eight hours of training for shogi, chess, and Go, respectively. This is a sensationally rapid rate of learning, considering that in the case of Elmo and Stockfish, these computer programs represent the culmination of decades of research and fine-tuning in a focused, domain-specific manner. The generalizable AlphaZero algorithm is able to play all three games with aplomb: Simply switching out learned weights from otherwise identical neural network architectures imbues each with the same skills that have taken *years* to develop by other means. These results demonstrate that deep reinforcement learning is a strikingly powerful approach for developing general expert gameplay in an undirected fashion.

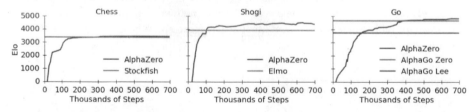

Figure 4.10   Comparing Elo scores between AlphaZero and each of its opponents in chess, shogi, and Go. AlphaZero rapidly outperformed all three opponents.

---

28. A single value.

29. This manually configured exploration parameter is called *epsilon*. It is detailed in Chapter 10.

Manipulation of Objects

As this chapter's title might suggest, thus far we've centered our coverage of deep rein-forcement learning on its game-playing applications. Although games offer a hot testbed for exploring the generalization of machine intelligence, in this section we spend a few moments expounding on practical, real-world applications of deep reinforcement learning.

One real-world example we mention earlier in this chapter is autonomous vehicles. As an additional example, here we provide an overview of research by Sergey Levine, Chelsea Finn (Figure 4.11), and labmates at the University of California, Berkeley.[30] These researchers trained a robot to perform a number of motor skills that require complex visual understanding and depth perception, such as screwing the cap back onto a bottle, removing a nail with a toy hammer, placing a hanger on a rack, and inserting a cube in a shape-fitting game (Figure 4.12).

Levine, Finn, and colleagues' algorithm maps raw visual input directly to the movement of the motors in the robot's arm. Their policy network was a seven-layer-deep convolutional neural network (CNN) consisting of fewer than 100,000 artificial neurons—a minuscule amount in deep learning terms, as you'll see when you train orders-of-magnitude larger networks later in this book. Although it would be tricky to elaborate further on this approach before we delve much into artificial-neural-network theory (in Part II, which is just around the corner), there are three take-away points we'd like to highlight on this elegant practical application of deep reinforcement learning. First, it is an "end-to-end" deep learning model in the sense that the model takes in raw images (pixels) as inputs and then outputs directly to the robot's motors. Second, the model

Figure 4.11   Chelsea Finn is a doctoral candidate at the University of California, Berkeley, in its AI Research Lab.

30. Levine, S., Finn, C., et al. (2016). End-to-end training of deep visuomotor policies. *Journal of Machine Learning Research*, 17, 1–40.

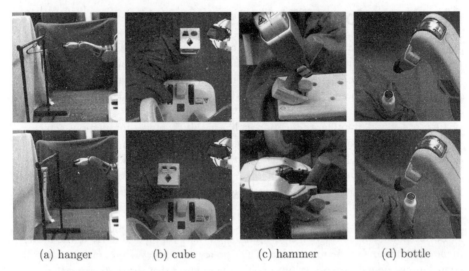

| (a) hanger | (b) cube | (c) hammer | (d) bottle |

Figure 4.12   Sample images from Levine, Finn, et al. (2016) exhibiting various object-manipulation actions the robot was trained to perform

generalizes neatly to a broad range of unique object–manipulation tasks. Third, it is an example of the *policy gradient* family of deep reinforcement learning approaches, rounding out the terms featured in the Venn diagram in Figure 4.1. Policy gradient methods are distinct from the DQN approach that is the focus of Chapter 10, but we touch on them then too.

Popular Deep Reinforcement Learning Environments

Over the past few sections, we talk a fair bit about software emulation of environments in which to train reinforcement learning models. This area of development is crucial to the ongoing progression of reinforcement learning; without environments in which our agents can play and explore (and gather data!), there would be no training of models. Here we introduce the three most popular environments, discussing their high-level attributes.

OpenAI Gym

OpenAI Gym[31] is developed by the nonprofit AI research company OpenAI.[32] The mission of OpenAI is to advance artificial general intelligence (more on that in the next section!) in a safe and equitable manner. To that end, the researchers at OpenAI have produced and open-sourced a number of tools for AI research, including the OpenAI

---

31. github.com/openai/gym
32. openai.com

Gym. This toolkit is designed to provide an interface for training reinforcement learning models, be they deep or otherwise.

As captured in Figure 4.13, the Gym features a diverse array of environments, including a number of Atari 2600 games,[33] multiple robotics simulators, a few simple text-based algorithmic games, and several robotics simulations using the MuJoCo physics engine.[34] In Chapter 10, you'll install OpenAI Gym in a single line of code and then employ an environment it provides to train the DQN agent that you build. OpenAI Gym is written in Python and is compatible with any deep learning computation library, including TensorFlow and PyTorch (we discuss the various deep learning libraries in Chapter 12; these are two particularly popular ones).

DeepMind Lab

DeepMind Lab[35] is another RL environment, this time from the developers at Google DeepMind (although they point out that DeepMind Lab is *not* an official Google product). As can be seen in Figure 4.14, the environment is built on top of id Software's Quake III Arena[36] and provides a sci-fi inspired three-dimensional world in which agents can explore. The agent experiences the environment from the first-person perspective, which is distinct from the Atari emulators available via OpenAI Gym.

There are a variety of levels available, which can be roughly divided into four categories:

1. Fruit-gathering levels, where the agent simply tries to find and collect rewards (apples and melons) while avoiding penalties (lemons).
2. Navigation levels with a static map, where the agent is tasked with finding a goal and remembering the layout of the map. The agent can either be randomly placed within a map at the start of each episode while the goal remains stationary, an arrangement that tests initial exploration followed by a reliance on memory to repeatedly find the goal; or the agent can start in the same place while the goal is moved for every episode, testing the agent's ability to explore.
3. Navigation levels with random maps, where the agent is required to explore a novel map in each episode, find the goal, and then repeatedly return to the goal as many times as possible within a time limit.
4. Laser-tag levels, where the agent is rewarded for hunting and attacking bots in an array of different scenes.

Installation of DeepMind Lab is not as straightforward as OpenAI Gym,[37] but it provides a rich, dynamic first-person environment in which to train agents, and the levels

---

33. OpenAI Gym uses the Arcade Learning Environment to emulate Atari 2600 games. This same framework is used in the Mnih et al. (2013) paper described in the "Video Games" section. You can find the framework yourself at github.com/mgbellemare/Arcade-Learning-Environment.

34. MuJoCo is an abbreviation of Multi-Joint dynamics with Contact. It is a physics engine that was developed by Emo Todorov for Roboti LLC.

35. Beattie, C. et al. (2016). DeepMind Lab. *arXiv:1612.03801*.

36. Quake III Arena. (1999). United States: id Software. github.com/id-Software/Quake-III-Arena

37. First the Github repository (github.com/deepmind/lab) is cloned, and then the software must be built using Bazel (bit.ly/installB). The DeepMind Lab repository provides detailed instructions (bit.ly/buildDML).

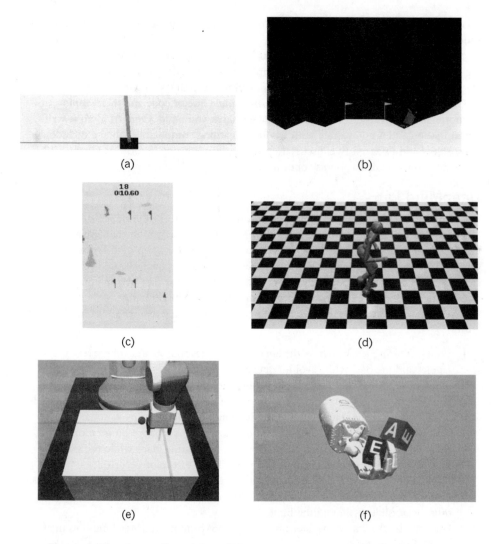

Figure 4.13 A sampling of OpenAI Gym environments: (a) CartPole, a classic control-theory problem; (b) LunarLander, a continuous-control task run inside a two-dimensional simulation; (c) Skiing, an Atari 2600 game; (d) Humanoid, a three-dimensional MuJuCo physics engine simulation of a bipedal person; (e) FetchPickAndPlace, one of several available simulations of real-world robot arms, in this case involving one called Fetch, with the goal of grasping a block and placing it in a target location; and (f) HandManipulateBlock, another practical simulation of a robotic arm, the Shadow Dexterous Hand.

Figure 4.14   A DeepMind Lab environment, in which positive-reward points are awarded for capturing scrumptious green apples

provide complex scenarios involving navigation, memory, strategy, planning, and fine-motor skills. These challenging environments can test the limits of what is tractable with contemporary deep reinforcement learning.

Unity ML-Agents

Unity is a sophisticated engine for two- and three-dimensional video games and digital simulations. Given the game-playing proficiency of reinforcement learning algorithms we chronicle earlier in this chapter, it may come as no surprise that the makers of a popular game engine are also in the business of providing environments to incorporate reinforcement learning into video games. The Unity ML-Agents plug-in[38] enables reinforcement learning models to be trained within Unity-based video games or simulations and, perhaps more fitting with the purpose of Unity itself, allows reinforcement learning models to guide the actions of agents within the game.

As with DeepMind Lab, installation of Unity ML-Agents is not a one-liner.[39]

Three Categories of AI

Of all deep learning topics, deep reinforcement learning is perhaps the one most closely tied to the popular perception of artificial intelligence as a system for replicating the cognitive, decision-making capacity of humans. In light of that, to wrap up this chapter, in this section we introduce three categories of AI.

---

38. github.com/Unity-Technologies/ml-agents
39. It requires the user to first install Unity (for download and installation instructions, see store.unity.com/download) and then clone the Github repository. Full instructions are available at the Unity ML-Agents Github repository (bit.ly/MLagents).

Artificial Narrow Intelligence

Artificial narrow intelligence (ANI) is machine expertise at a specific task. Many diverse examples of ANI exist today, and we've mentioned plenty already in this book, such as the visual recognition of objects, real-time machine translation between natural languages, automated financial-trading systems, AlphaZero, and self-driving cars.

Artificial General Intelligence

Artificial general intelligence (AGI) would involve a single algorithm that could perform well at all of the tasks described in the preceding paragraph: It would be able to recognize your face, translate this book into another language, optimize your investment portfolio, beat you at Go, and drive you safely to your holiday destination. Indeed, such an algorithm would be approximately indistinguishable from the intellectual capabilities of an individual human. There are countless hurdles to overcome in order for AGI to be realized; it is challenging to approximate when it will be achieved, if it will be achieved at all. That said, AI experts are happy to wave a finger in the air and speculate on timing. In a study conducted by the philosopher Vincent Müller and the influential futurist Nick Bostrom,[40] the median estimate across hundreds of professional AI researchers is that AGI will be attained in the year 2040.

Artificial Super Intelligence

Artificial super intelligence (ASI) is difficult to describe because it's properly mind-boggling. ASI would be an algorithm that is markedly more advanced than the intellectual capabilities of a human.[41] *If* AGI is possible, then ASI may be as well. Of course, there are even more hurdles on the road to ASI than to AGI, the bulk of which we can't foresee today. Citing the Müller and Bostrom survey again, however, AI experts' median estimate for the arrival of ASI is 2060, a rather hypothetical date that falls within the life-span of many earthlings alive today. In Chapter 12, at which point you'll be well-versed in deep learning both in theory and in practice, we discuss both how deep learning models could contribute to AGI as well as the present limitations associated with deep learning that would need to be bridged in order to attain AGI or, gasp, ASI.

Summary

The chapter began with an overview relating deep learning to the broader field of artificial intelligence. We then detailed deep reinforcement learning, an approach that blends deep learning with the feedback-providing reinforcement learning paradigm. As discussed via real-world examples ranging from the board game Go to the grasping of physical objects, such deep reinforcement learning enables machines to process vast amounts of data and take sensible sequences of actions on complex tasks, associating it with popular conceptions of AI.

---

40. Müller, V., and Bostrom, N. (2014). Future progress in artificial intelligence: A survey of expert opinion. In V. Müller (Ed.), *Fundamental Issues of Artificial Intelligence.* Berlin: Springer.
41. In 2015, the writer and illustrator Tim Urban provided a two-part series of posts that rivetingly covers ASI and the related literature. It's available at `bit.ly/urbanAI` for you to enjoy.

Essential Theory Illustrated

5

The (Code) Cart Ahead of the (Theory) Horse

In Part I, we provided a high-level overview of deep learning by demonstrating its use across a spectrum of cutting-edge applications. Along the way, we sprinkled in foundational deep learning concepts from its hierarchical, representation-learning nature through to its relationship to the field of artificial intelligence. Repeatedly, as we touched on a concept, we noted that in Part II of the book we would dive into the low-level theory and mathematics behind it. While we promise this *is* true, we are going to take this final opportunity to put the fun, hands-on coding cart ahead of the proverbial—in this case, theory-laden—horse.

In this chapter we do a line-by-line walk-through of a notebook of code featuring a neural network model. While you will need to bear with us because we have not yet detailed much of the theory underpinning the code, this serpentine approach will make the apprehension of theory in the subsequent chapters easier: Instead of being an abstract idea, each element of theory we introduce in this part of the book will be rooted in a tangible line of applied code.

Prerequisites

Working through the examples in this book will be easiest if you are familiar with the basics of the Unix command line. These are provided by Zed Shaw in Appendix A of his deceptively enjoyable *Learn Python the Hard Way*.[1]

Speaking of Python, since it is comfortably the most popular software language in the data science community (at time of writing, anyway), it's the language we selected for our example code throughout the book. Python's prevalence extends across the composition of stand-alone scripts through to the deployment of machine learning models into production systems. If you're new to Python or you're feeling a tad rusty, Shaw's book serves

---

1. Shaw, Z. (2013). *Learn Python the Hard Way, 3rd Ed*. New York: Addison-Wesley. This relevant appendix, Shaw's "Command Line Crash Course," is available online at `learnpythonthehardway.org/book/appendixa.html`.

as an appropriate general reference, while Daniel Chen's *Pandas for Everyone*[2] is ideal for learning how to apply the language to data modeling in particular.

Installation

Regardless of whether you're planning on executing our code notebooks via Unix, Linux, macOS, or Windows, we have made step-by-step installation instructions available in the GitHub repository that accompanies this book:

`github.com/the-deep-learners/deep-learning-illustrated`

If you'd prefer to view the completed notebooks instead of running them on your own machine, you are more than welcome to do that from the GitHub repo as well.

We elected to provide our code within the comfort of interactive Jupyter notebooks.[3] Jupyter is a common option today for writing and sharing scripts, particularly during exploratory phases in which a data scientist is experimenting with preprocessing, visualizing, and modeling her data. Our installation instructions suggest running Jupyter from within a Docker container.[4] This containerization ensures that you'll have all of the software dependencies you need to run our notebooks while simultaneously preventing these dependencies from clashing with software you already have installed on your system.

A Shallow Network in Keras

To kick off the code portion of our book, we will:

1. Detail a revered dataset of handwritten digits
2. Load these data into a Jupyter notebook
3. Use Python to prepare the data for modeling
4. Write a few lines of code in Keras, a high-level deep learning API, to construct an artificial neural network (in TensorFlow, behind the scenes) that predicts what digit a given handwritten sample represents

The MNIST Handwritten Digits

Back in Chapter 1 when we introduced the LeNet-5 machine vision architecture (Figure 1.11), we mentioned that one of the advantages Yann LeCun (Figure 1.9) and his colleagues had over previous deep learning practitioners was a superior dataset for training their model. This dataset of handwritten digits, called MNIST (see the samples in Figure 5.1), came up again in the context of being imitated by Ian Goodfellow's generative adversarial network (Figure 3.2a). The MNIST dataset is ubiquitous across

---

2. Chen, D. (2017). *Pandas for Everyone: Python Data Analysis.* New York: Addison-Wesley.
3. `jupyter.org`. We recommend familiarizing yourself with the hot keys to breeze through Jupyter notebooks with pizzazz.
4. `docker.com`

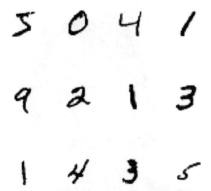

Figure 5.1 A sample of a dozen images from the MNIST dataset. Each image contains a single digit handwritten by either a high school student or a U.S. census worker.

deep learning tutorials, and for good reason. By modern standards, the dataset is small enough that it can be modeled rapidly, even on a laptop computer processor. In addition to their portable size, the MNIST digits are handy because they occupy a sweet spot with respect to how challenging they are to classify: The handwriting samples are sufficiently diverse and contain complex enough details that they are not *easy* for a machine-learning algorithm to identify with high accuracy, and yet by no means do they pose an insurmountable problem. However, as you will observe yourself as we make our way through Part II of this book, a well-designed deep-learning model can nearly faultlessly classify the handwriting as the appropriate digit.

The MNIST dataset was curated by LeCun (Figure 1.9), Corinna Cortes (Figure 5.2), and the Microsoft-AI-researcher-turned-musician Chris Burges in the 1990s.[5] It consists of 60,000 handwritten digits for training an algorithm, and 10,000 more for validating the algorithm's performance on previously unseen data. The data are a subset (a *modification*) of a larger body of handwriting samples collected from high school students and census workers by the U.S. National Institute of Standards and Technology (NIST).

As exemplified by Figure 5.3, every MNIST digit is a 28×28-pixel image.[6] Each pixel is 8-bit, meaning that the pixel darkness can vary from 0 (white) to 255 (black), with the intervening range of integers representing gradually darker shades of gray.

A Schematic Diagram of the Network

In our *Shallow Net in Keras* Jupyter notebook,[7] we create an artificial neural network to predict what digit a given handwritten MNIST image represents. As shown in the rough schematic diagram in Figure 5.4, this artificial neural network features one hidden layer of artificial neurons, for a total of three layers. Recalling Figure 4.2, with so few layers

---

5. yann.lecun.com/exdb/mnist/
6. Python uses zero indexing, so the first row and column are denoted with 0. The 28th row and 28th column of pixels are therefore both denoted with 27.
7. Within this book's GitHub repository, navigate into the *notebooks* directory.

Figure 5.2   The Danish computer scientist Corinna Cortes is head of research at Google's New York office. Among her countless contributions to both pure and applied machine learning, Cortes (with Chris Burges and Yann LeCun) curated the widely used MNIST dataset.

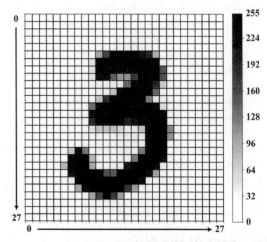

Figure 5.3   Each handwritten MNIST digit is stored as a 28×28-pixel grayscale image. See the Jupyter notebook titled *MNIST Digit Pixel by Pixel* that accompanies this book for the code we used to create this figure.

this ANN would not generally be considered a *deep* learning architecture; hence it is *shallow*.

The first layer of the network is reserved for inputting our MNIST digits. Because they are 28×28-pixel images, each one has a total of 784 values. After we load in the images, we'll flatten them from their native, two-dimensional 28×28 shape to a one-dimensional array of 784 elements.

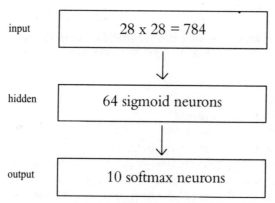

input	28 x 28 = 784

↓

hidden	64 sigmoid neurons

↓

output	10 softmax neurons

Figure 5.4 A rough schematic of the shallow artificial-neural-network architecture we're whipping up in this chapter. We detail the particular sigmoid and softmax flavors of artificial neurons in Chapter 6, respectively.

You could argue that collapsing the images from two dimensions to one will cause us to lose a lot of the meaningful structure of the handwritten digits. Well, if you argued that, you'd be right! Working with one-dimensional data, however, means we can use relatively unsophisticated neural network models, which is appropriate at this early stage in our journey. Later, in Chapter 9, you'll be in a position to appreciate more-complex models that can handle multidimensional inputs.

The pixel–data inputs will be passed through a single, hidden layer of 64 artificial neurons.[8] The number (64) and type (*sigmoid*) of these neurons aren't critical details at present; we begin to explain these model attributes in the next chapter. The key piece of information at this time is that, as we demonstrate in Chapter 1 (see Figures 1.18 and 1.19), the neurons in the hidden layer are responsible for learning representations of the input data so that the network can predict what digit a given image represents.

Finally, the information that is produced by the hidden layer will be passed to 10 neurons in the output layer. We detail how a *softmax* layer of neurons works in Chapter 7, but, in essence, we have 10 neurons because we have 10 categories of digit to classify. Each of these 10 neurons outputs a probability: one for each of the 10 possible digits that a given MNIST image could represent. As an example, a fairly well-trained network that is fed the image in Figure 5.3 might output that there is a 0.92 probability that the image is of a *three*, a 0.06 probability that it's a *two*, a 0.02 probability that it's an *eight*, and a probability of 0 for the other seven digits.

Loading the Data

At the top of the notebook we import our software dependencies, which is the unexciting but necessary step shown in Example 5.1.

8. "Hidden" layers are so called because they are not exposed; data impact them only indirectly, via the input layer or the output layer of neurons.

Example 5.1 Software dependencies for shallow net in Keras

```
import keras
from keras.datasets import mnist
from keras.models import Sequential
from keras.layers import Dense
from keras.optimizers import SGD
from matplotlib import pyplot as plt
```

We import Keras because that's the library we're using to fashion our neural network. We also import the MNIST dataset because these, of course, are the data we're working with in this example. The lines ending in Sequential, Dense, and SGD will make sense later; no need to worry about them at this stage. Finally, the matplotlib line will enable us to plot MNIST digits to our screen.

With these dependencies imported, we can conveniently load the MNIST data in a single line of code, as in Example 5.2.

Example 5.2 Loading MNIST data

```
(X_train, y_train), (X_valid, y_valid) = mnist.load_data()
```

Let's examine these data. As mentioned in Chapter 4, the mathematical notation x is used to represent the data we're feeding into a model as input, while y is used for the labeled output that we're training the model to predict. With this in mind, X_train stores the MNIST digits we'll be training our model on.[9] Executing X_train.shape yields the output (60000, 28, 28). This shows us that, as expected, we have 60,000 images in our training dataset, each of which is a 28×28 matrix of values. Running y_train.shape, we unsurprisingly discover we have 60,000 labels indicating what digit is contained in each of the 60,000 training images. y_train[0:12] outputs an array of 12 integers representing the first dozen labels, so we can see that the first handwritten digit in the training set (X_train[0]) is the number *five*, the second is a *zero*, the third is a *four*, and so on.

```
array([5, 0, 4, 1, 9, 2, 1, 3, 1, 4, 3, 5], dtype=uint8)
```

These happen to be the same dozen MNIST digits that were shown earlier in Figure 5.1, a figure we created by running the following chunk of code:

```
plt.figure(figsize=(5,5))
for k in range(12):
    plt.subplot(3, 4, k+1)
```

---

9. The convention is to use an uppercase letter like X when the variable being represented is a two-dimensional matrix or a data structure with even higher dimensionality. In contrast, a lowercase letter like x is used to represent a single value (a scalar) or a one-dimensional array.

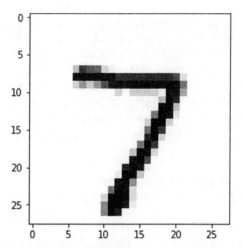

Figure 5.5   The first MNIST digit in the validation dataset (X_valid[0]) is a *seven*.

```
    plt.imshow(X_train[k], cmap='Greys')
    plt.axis('off')
plt.tight_layout()
plt.show()
```

Akin to the training data, by examining the shape of the validation data (X_valid.shape, y_valid.shape), we note that there are the expected 10,000 28×28-pixel validation images, each with a corresponding label: (10000, 28, 28), (10000,). Investigating the values that make up an individual image such as X_valid[0], we observe that the matrix of integers representing the handwriting is primarily zeros (whitespace). Tilting your head, you might even be able to make out that the digit in this example is a *seven* with the highest integers (e.g., 254, 255) representing the black core of the handwritten figure, and the outline of the figure (composed of intermediate integers) fading toward white. To corroborate that this is indeed the number *seven*, we both printed out the image using plt.imshow(X_valid[0], cmap='Greys') (output shown in Figure 5.5) and printed out its label using y_valid[0] (output was 7).

Reformatting the Data

The MNIST data now loaded, we come across the heading "Preprocess data" in the notebook. We won't, however, be preprocessing the images by applying functions to, say, extract features that provide hints to our artificial neural network. Instead, we will simply be rearranging the *shape* of the data so that they match up with the shapes of the input and output layers of the network.

Thus, we'll flatten our 28×28-pixel images into 784–element arrays. We employ the reshape() method, as shown in Example 5.3.

Example 5.3 Flattening two-dimensional images to one dimension

```
X_train = X_train.reshape(60000, 784).astype('float32')
X_valid = X_valid.reshape(10000, 784).astype('float32')
```

Simultaneously, we use `astype('float32')` to convert the pixel darknesses from integers into single-precision float values.[10] This conversion is preparation for the subsequent step, shown in Example 5.4, in which we divide all of the values by 255 so that they range from 0 to 1.[11]

Example 5.4 Converting pixel integers to floats

```
X_train /= 255
X_valid /= 255
```

Revisiting our example handwritten *seven* from Figure 5.5 by running `X_valid[0]`, we can verify that it is now represented by a one-dimensional array made up of float values as low as 0 and as high as 1.

That's all for reformatting our model inputs X. As shown in Example 5.5, for the labels y, we need to convert them from integers into one-hot encodings (shortly we demonstrate what these are via a hands-on example).

Example 5.5 Converting integer labels to one-hot

```
n_classes = 10
y_train = keras.utils.to_categorical(y_train, n_classes)
y_valid = keras.utils.to_categorical(y_valid, n_classes)
```

There are 10 possible handwritten digits, so we set `n_classes` equal to 10. In the other two lines of code we use a convenient utility function—`to_categorical`, which is provided within the Keras library—to transform both the training and the validation labels from integers into the one-hot format. Execute `y_valid` to see how the label *seven* is represented now:

```
array([0., 0., 0., 0., 0., 0., 0., 1., 0., 0.], dtype=float32)
```

Instead of using an integer to represent *seven*, we have an array of length 10 consisting entirely of 0s, with the exception of a 1 in the eighth position. In such a one-hot encoding, the label *zero* would be represented by a lone 1 in the first position, *one* by a lone 1 in

---

10. The data are initially stored as `uint8`, which is an unsigned integer from 0 to 255. This is more memory efficient, but it doesn't require much precision because there are only 256 possible values. Without specifying, Python would default to a 64-bit float, which would be overkill. Thus, by specifying a 32-bit float we can deliberately specify a lower-precision float that is sufficient for this use case.

11. Machine learning models tend to learn more efficiently when fed standardized inputs. Binary inputs would typically be a 0 or a 1, whereas distributions are often normalized to have a mean of 0 and a standard deviation of 1. As we've done here, pixel intensities are generally scaled to range from 0 to 1.

the second position, and so on. We arrange the labels with such one-hot encodings so that they line up with the 10 probabilities being output by the final layer of our artificial neural network. They represent the ideal output that we are striving to attain with our network: If the input image is a handwritten *seven*, then a perfectly trained network would output a probability of 1.00 that it is a *seven* and a probability of 0.00 for each of the other nine classes of digits.

Designing a Neural Network Architecture

From your authors' perspective, this is the most pleasurable bit of any script featuring deep learning code: architecting the artificial neural net itself. There are infinite possibilities here, and, as you progress through the book, you will begin to develop an intuition that guides the selection of the architectures you might experiment with for tackling a given problem. Referring to Figure 5.4, for the time being, we're keeping the architecture as elementary as possible in Example 5.6.

Example 5.6 Keras code to architect a shallow neural network

```
model = Sequential()
model.add(Dense(64, activation='sigmoid', input_shape=(784,)))
model.add(Dense(10, activation='softmax'))
```

In the first line of code, we instantiate the simplest type of neural network model object, the Sequential type[12] and—in a dash of extreme creativity—name the model model. In the second line, we use the add() method of our model object to specify the attributes of our network's hidden layer (64 sigmoid-type artificial neurons in the general-purpose, fully connected arrangement defined by the Dense() method)[13] as well as the shape of our input layer (one-dimensional array of length 784). In the third and final line we use the add() method again to specify the output layer and its parameters: 10 artificial neurons of the softmax variety, corresponding to the 10 probabilities (one for each of the 10 possible digits) that the network will output when fed a given handwritten image.

Training a Deep Learning Model

Later, we return to the model.summary() and model.compile() steps of the *Shallow Net in Keras* notebook, as well as its three lines of arithmetic. For now, we skip ahead to the model-fitting step (shown in Example 5.7).

Example 5.7 Keras code to train our shallow neural network

```
model.fit(X_train, y_train,
          batch_size=128, epochs=200,
          verbose=1,
          validation_data=(X_valid, y_valid))
```

---

12. So named because each layer in the network passes information to only the next layer in the *sequence* of layers.
13. Once more, these esoteric terms will become comprehensible over the coming chapters.

The critical aspects are:

1. The `fit()` method of our `model` object enables us to train our artificial neural network with the training images `X_train` as inputs and their associated labels `y_train` as the desired outputs.
2. As the network trains, the `fit()` method also provides us with the option to evaluate the performance of our network by passing our validation data `X_valid` and `y_valid` into the `validation_data` argument.
3. With machine learning, and especially with deep learning, it is commonplace to train our model on the same data multiple times. One pass through all of our training data (60,000 images in the current case) is called one *epoch* of training. By setting the `epochs` parameter to `200`, we cycle through all 60,000 training images 200 separate times.
4. By setting `verbose` to `1`, the `model.fit()` method will provide us with plenty of feedback as we train. At the moment, we'll focus on the `val_acc` statistic that is output following each epoch of training. *Validation accuracy* is the proportion of the 10,000 handwritten images in `X_valid` in which the network's highest probability in the output layer corresponds to the correct digit as per the labels in `y_valid`.

Following the first epoch of training, we observe that `val_acc` equals 0.1010.[14,15] That is, 10.1 percent of the images from the held-out validation dataset were correctly classified by our shallow architecture. Given that there are 10 classes of handwritten digits, we'd expect a random process to guess 10 percent of the digits correctly by chance, so this is not an impressive result. As the network continues to train, however, the results improve. After 10 epochs of training, it is correctly classifying 36.5 percent of the validation images—far better than would be expected by chance! And this is only the beginning: After 200 epochs, the network's improvement appears to be plateauing as it approaches 86 percent validation accuracy. Because we constructed an uninvolved, shallow neural-network architecture, this is not too shabby!

Summary

Putting the cart before the horse, in this chapter we coded up a shallow, elementary artificial neural network. With decent accuracy, it is able to classify the MNIST images. Over the remainder of Part II, as we dive into theory, unearth artificial-neural-network best practices, and layer up to authentic deep learning architectures, we should surely be able to classify inputs much more accurately, no? Let's see.

---

14. Artificial neural networks are *stochastic* (because of the way they're initialized as well as the way they learn), so your results will vary slightly from ours. Indeed, if you rerun the whole notebook (e.g., by clicking on the *Kernel* option in the Jupyter menu bar and selecting *Restart & Run All*), you should obtain new, slightly different results each time you do this.

15. By the end of Chapter 7, you'll have enough theory under your belt to study the output `model.fit()` in all its glory. For our immediate "cart before the horse" purposes, coverage of the *validation accuracy* metric alone suffices.

6

Artificial Neural Networks

Having received tantalizing exposure to applications of deep learning in the first part of this book and having coded up a functioning neural network in Chapter 5, the moment has come to delve into the nitty-gritty theory underlying these capabilities. We begin by dissecting artificial neurons, the units that—when wired together—constitute an artificial neural network.

Biological Neuroanatomy 101

As presented in the opening paragraphs of this book, ersatz neurons are inspired by biological ones. Given that, let's take a gander at Figure 6.1 for a précis of the first lecture in any neuroanatomy course: A given biological neuron receives input into its *cell body* from many (generally thousands) of *dendrites*, with each dendrite receiving signals of information from another neuron in the nervous system—a biological neural network. When the signal conveyed along a dendrite reaches the cell body, it causes a small change in the voltage of the cell body.[1] Some dendrites cause a small positive change in voltage, and the others cause a small negative change. If the cumulative effect of these changes causes the voltage to increase from its resting state of −70 millivolts to the critical threshold of −55 millivolts, the neuron will fire something called an *action potential* away from its cell body, down its axon, thereby transmitting a signal to other neurons in the network.

To summarize, biological neurons exhibit the following three behaviors in sequence:

1. Receive information from many other neurons
2. Aggregate this information via changes in cell voltage at the cell body
3. Transmit a signal if the cell voltage crosses a threshold level, a signal that can be received by many other neurons in the network

---

1. More precisely, it causes a change in the voltage *difference* between the cell's interior and its surroundings.

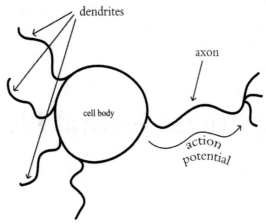

Figure 6.1   The anatomy of a biological neuron (see page 329 for the color image).

We've aligned the purple, red, and blue colors of the text here with the colors (indicating dendrites, cell body, and the axon, respectively) in Figure 6.1. We'll do this time and again throughout the book, including to discuss key equations and the variables they contain.

The Perceptron

In the late 1950s, the American neurobiologist Frank Rosenblatt (Figure 6.2) published an article on his *perceptron*, an algorithm influenced by his understanding of biological neurons, making it the earliest formulation of an artificial neuron.[2] Analogous to its living inspiration, the perceptron (Figure 6.3) can:

1. Receive input from multiple other neurons
2. Aggregate those inputs via a simple arithmetic operation called the *weighted sum*
3. Generate an output if this weighted sum crosses a threshold level, which can then be sent on to many other neurons within a network

The Hot Dog / Not Hot Dog Detector

Let's work through a lighthearted example to understand how the perceptron algorithm works. We're going to look at a perceptron that is specialized in distinguishing whether a given object is a hot dog or, well . . . not a hot dog.

A critical attribute of perceptrons is that they can only be fed binary information as inputs, and their output is also restricted to being binary. Thus, our hot dog-detecting

---

2. Rosenblatt, F. (1958). The perceptron: A probabilistic model for information storage and the organization in the brain. *Psychological Review, 65,* 386–408.

Figure 6.2   The American neurobiology and behavior researcher Frank Rosenblatt. He conducted much of his work out of the Cornell Aeronautical Laboratory, including physically constructing his Mark I Perceptron there. This machine, an early relic of artificial intelligence, can today be viewed at the Smithsonian Institution in Washington, D.C.

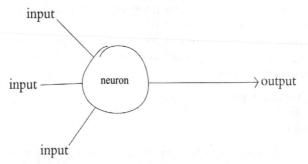

Figure 6.3   Schematic diagram of a perceptron, an early artificial neuron. Note the structural similarity to the biological neuron in Figure 6.1.

perceptron must be fed its particular three inputs (indicating whether the object involves ketchup, mustard, or a bun, respectively) as either a 0 or a 1. In Figure 6.4:

- The first input (a purple 1) indicates the object being presented to the perceptron involves ketchup.
- The second input (also a purple 1) indicates the object has mustard.
- The third input (a purple 0) indicates the object does *not* include a bun.

To make a prediction as to whether the object is a hot dog or not, the perceptron independently *weights* each of these three inputs.[3] The weights that we arbitrarily selected

---

3. If you are well accustomed to regression modeling, this should be a familiar paradigm.

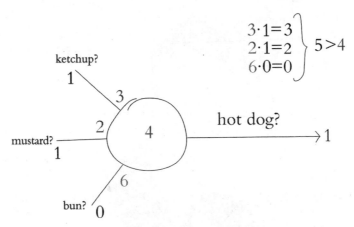

Figure 6.4   First example of a hot dog-detecting perceptron: In this instance, it predicts there is indeed a hot dog (see page 330 for the color image).

in this (entirely contrived) hot dog example indicate that the presence of a bun, with its weight of 6, is the most influential predictor of whether the object is a hot dog or not. The intermediate-weight predictor is ketchup with its weight of 3, and the least influential predictor is mustard, with a weight of 2.

Let's determine the weighted sum of the inputs: One input at a time (i.e., *elementwise*), we multiply the input by its weight and then sum the individual results. So first, let's calculate the weighted inputs:

1. For the *ketchup* input: $3 \times 1 = 3$
2. For *mustard*: $2 \times 1 = 2$
3. For *bun*: $6 \times 0 = 0$

With those three products, we can compute that the weighted sum of the inputs is 5: $3 + 2 + 0$. To generalize from this example, the calculation of the weighted sum of inputs is:

$$\sum_{i=1}^{n} w_i x_i \tag{6.1}$$

Where:

- w_i is the weight of a given input i (in our example, $w_1 = 3$, $w_2 = 2$, and $w_3 = 6$).
- x_i is the value of a given input i (in our example, $x_1 = 1$, $x_2 = 1$, and $x_3 = 0$).
- $w_i x_i$ represents the product of w_i and x_i—i.e., the weighted value of a given input i.
- $\sum_{i=1}^{n}$ indicates that we sum all of the individual weighted inputs $w_i x_i$, where n is the total number of inputs (in our example, we had three inputs, but artificial neurons can have any number of inputs).

The final step of the perceptron algorithm is to evaluate whether the weighted sum of the inputs is greater than the neuron's *threshold*. As with the earlier weights, we have again arbitrarily chosen a threshold value for our perceptron example: 4 (shown in the center of the neuron in Figure 6.4). The perceptron algorithm is:

$$\sum_{i=1}^{n} w_i x_i \quad \begin{matrix} > \textit{threshold}, \text{output } 1 \\ \leqslant \textit{threshold}, \text{output } 0 \end{matrix} \qquad (6.2)$$

Where:

- If the weighted sum of a perceptron's inputs is greater than its threshold, then it outputs a 1, indicating that the perceptron predicts the object is a hot dog.
- If the weighted sum is less than or equal to the threshold, the perceptron outputs a 0, indicating that it predicts there is *not* a hot dog.

Knowing this, we can wrap up our example from Figure 6.4: The weighted sum of 5 is greater than the neuron's threshold of 4, and so our hot dog-detecting perceptron outputs a 1.

Riffing on our first hot dog example, in Figure 6.5 the object evaluated by the perceptron now includes mustard only; there is no ketchup, and it is still without a bun. In this case the weighted sum of inputs comes out to 2. Because 2 is less than the perceptron's threshold, the neuron outputs 0, indicating that it predicts this object is *not* a hot dog.

In our third and final perceptron example, shown in Figure 6.6, the artificial neuron evaluates an object that involves neither mustard nor ketchup but *is* on a bun. The presence of a bun alone corresponds to the calculation of a weighted sum of 6. Because 6 is greater than the perceptron's threshold, the algorithm predicts that the object is a hot dog and outputs a 1.

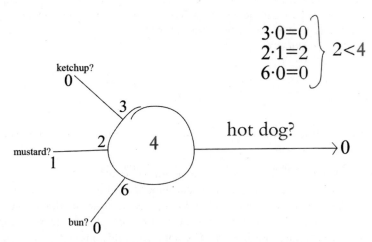

Figure 6.5   Second example of a hot dog-detecting perceptron: In this instance, it predicts there is not a hot dog.

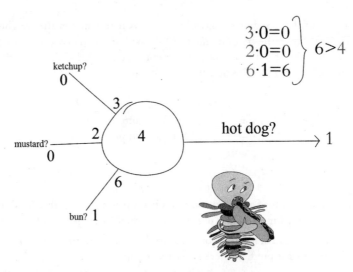

Figure 6.6   Third example of a hot dog-detecting perceptron: In this instance, it again predicts the object presented to it is a hot dog.

The Most Important Equation in This Book

To achieve the formulation of a simplified and universal perceptron equation, we must introduce a term called the *bias*, which we annotate as b and which is equivalent to the negative of an artificial neuron's threshold value:

$$b \equiv -threshold \tag{6.3}$$

Together, a neuron's bias and its weights constitute all of its *parameters*: the changeable variables that prescribe what the neuron will output in response to its inputs.

With the concept of a neuron's bias now available to us, we arrive at the most widely used perceptron equation:

$$\text{output} \begin{cases} 1 \text{ if } w \cdot x + b > 0 \\ 0 \text{ otherwise} \end{cases} \tag{6.4}$$

Notice that we made the following five updates to our initial perceptron equation (from Equation 6.2):

1. Substituted the bias b in place of the neuron's *threshold*
2. Flipped b onto the same side of the equation as all of the other variables
3. Used the array w to represent all of the w_i weights from w_1 through to w_n
4. Likewise, used the array x to represent all of the x_i values from x_1 through to x_n
5. Used the *dot product* notation $w \cdot x$ to abbreviate the representation of the weighted sum of neuron inputs (the longer form of this is shown in Equation 6.1: $\sum_{i=1}^{n} w_i x_i$)

Figure 6.7   The general equation for artificial neurons that we will return to time and again. It is the most important equation in this book.

Right at the heart of the perceptron equation in Equation 6.4 is $w \cdot x + b$, which we have cut out for emphasis and placed alone in Figure 6.7. *If there is one item you note down to remember from this chapter, it should be this three-variable formula, which is an equation that represents artificial neurons in general.* We refer to this equation many times over the course of this book.

To keep the arithmetic as undemanding as possible in our hot dog–detecting perceptron examples, all of the parameter values we made up—the perceptron's weights as well as its bias—were positive integers. These parameters could, however, be negative values, and, in practice, they would rarely be integers. Instead, parameters are configured as float values, which are less clunky.

Finally, while all of the parameters in these examples were fabricated by us, they would usually be learned through the training of artificial neurons on data. In Chapter 7, we cover how this training of neuron parameters is accomplished in practice.

Modern Neurons and Activation Functions

Modern artificial neurons—such as those in the hidden layer of the shallow architecture we built in Chapter 5 (look back to Figure 5.4 or to our *Shallow Net in Keras* notebook)—are not perceptrons. While the perceptron provides a relatively uncomplicated introduction to artificial neurons, it is not used widely today. The most obvious restriction of the perceptron is that it receives only binary inputs, and provides only a binary output. In many cases, we'd like to make predictions from inputs that are continuous variables and not binary integers, and so this restriction alone would make perceptrons unsuitable.

A less obvious (yet even more critical) corollary of the perceptron's binary-only restriction is that it makes learning rather challenging. Consider Figure 6.8, in which we use a new term, z, as shorthand for the value of the lauded $w \cdot x + b$ equation from Figure 6.7.

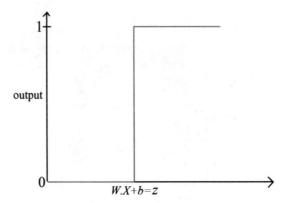

Figure 6.8 The perceptron's transition from outputting zero to outputting one happens suddenly, making it challenging to gently tune *w* and *b* to match a desired output.

When z is any value less than or equal to zero, the perceptron outputs its smallest possible output, 0. If z becomes positive to even the tiniest extent, the perceptron outputs its largest possible output, 1. This sudden and extreme transition is not optimal during training: When we train a network, we make slight adjustments to w and b based on whether it appears the adjustment will improve the network's output.[4] With the perceptron, the majority of slight adjustments to w and b would make no difference whatsoever to its output; z would generally be moving around at negative values much lower than 0 or at positive values much higher than 0. That behavior on its own would be unhelpful, but the situation is even worse: Every once in a while, a slight adjustment to w or b will cause z to cross from negative to positive (or vice versa), leading to a whopping, drastic swing in output from 0 all the way to 1 (or vice versa). Essentially, the perceptron has no finesse—it's either yelling or it's silent.

The Sigmoid Neuron

Figure 6.9 provides an alternative to the erratic behavior of the perceptron: a gentle curve from 0 to 1. This particular curve shape is called the *sigmoid* function and is defined by $\sigma(z) = \frac{1}{1+e^{-z}}$, where:

- z is equivalent to $w \cdot x + b$.
- e is the mathematical constant beginning in 2.718. It is perhaps best known for its starring role in the natural exponential function.
- σ is the Greek letter *sigma*, the root word for "sigmoid."

The sigmoid function is our first example of an artificial neuron *activation function*. It may be ringing a bell for you already, because it was the neuron type that we selected for the hidden layer of our *Shallow Net in Keras* from Chapter 5. As you'll see as this section progresses, the sigmoid function is the canonical activation function—so much so that the Greek letter σ (sigma) is conventionally used to denote *any* activation function.

---

4. *Improve* here means providing output more closely in line with the true output y given some input x. We discuss this further in Chapter 7.

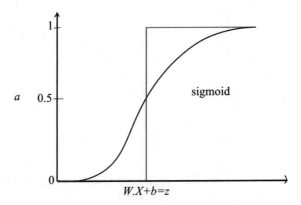

Figure 6.9   The sigmoid activation function

The output from any given neuron's activation function is referred to simply as its *activation*, and throughout this book, we use the variable term *a*—as shown along the vertical axis in Figure 6.9—to denote it.

In our view, there is no need to memorize the sigmoid function (or indeed any of the activation functions). Instead, we believe it's easier to understand a given function by playing around with its behavior interactively. With that in mind, feel free to join us in the *Sigmoid Function* Jupyter notebook from the book's GitHub repository as we work through the following lines of code.

Our only dependency in the notebook is the constant *e*, which we load using the statement `from math import e`. Next is the fun bit, where we define the sigmoid function itself:

```
def sigmoid(z):
    return 1/(1+e**-z)
```

As depicted in Figure 6.9 and demonstrated by executing `sigmoid(.00001)`, near-0 inputs into the sigmoid function will lead it to return values near `0.5`. Increasingly large positive inputs will result in values that approach 1. As an extreme example, an input of `10000` results in an output of `1.0`. Moving more gradually with our inputs—this time in the negative direction—we obtain outputs that gently approach 0: As examples, `sigmoid(-1)` returns `0.2689`, while `sigmoid(-10)` returns `4.5398e-05`.[5]

Any artificial neuron that features the sigmoid function as its activation function is called a *sigmoid neuron*, and the advantage of these over the perceptron should now be tangible: Small, gradual changes in a given sigmoid neuron's parameters *w* or *b* cause small, gradual changes in *z*, thereby producing similarly gradual changes in the neuron's activation, *a*. Large negative or large positive values of *z* illustrate an exception: At extreme *z* values, sigmoid neurons—like perceptrons—will output 0's (when *z* is negative) or 1's (when *z* is positive). As with the perceptron, this means that subtle updates to the weights

---

5. The `e` in `4.5398e-05` should not be confused with the base of the natural logarithm. Used in code outputs, it refers to an *exponent*, so the output is the equivalent of 4.5398×10^{-5}.

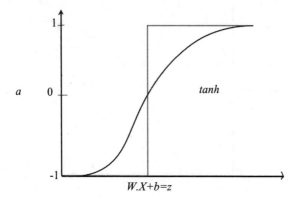

Figure 6.10   The tanh activation function

and biases during training will have little to no effect on the output, and thus learning will stall. This situation is called neuron *saturation* and can occur with most activation functions. Thankfully, there are tricks to avoid saturation, as you'll see in Chapter 7.

The Tanh Neuron

A popular cousin of the sigmoid neuron is the *tanh* (pronounced "tanch" in the deep learning community) neuron. The tanh activation function is pictured in Figure 6.10 and is defined by $\sigma(z) = \frac{e^z - e^{-z}}{e^z + e^{-z}}$. The shape of the tanh curve is similar to the sigmoid curve, with the chief distinction being that the sigmoid function exists in the range $[0:1]$, whereas the tanh neuron's output has the range $[-1:1]$. This difference is more than cosmetic. With negative z inputs corresponding to negative a activations, $z = 0$ corresponding to $a = 0$, and positive z corresponding to positive a activations, the output from tanh neurons tends to be centered near 0. As we cover further in Chapters 6 through 7, these 0-centered a outputs usually serve as the inputs x to other artificial neurons in a network, and such 0-centered inputs make (the dreaded!) neuron saturation less likely, thereby enabling the entire network to learn more efficiently.

ReLU: Rectified Linear Units

The final neuron we detail in this book is the *rectified linear unit*, or ReLU neuron, whose behavior we graph in Figure 6.11. The ReLU activation function, whose shape diverges glaringly from the sigmoid and tanh sorts, was inspired by properties of biological neurons[6] and popularized within artificial neural networks by Vinod Nair and Geoff Hinton (Figure 1.16).[7] The shape of the ReLU function is defined by $a = max(0, z)$.

---

6. The action potentials of biological neurons have only a "positive" firing mode; they have no "negative" firing mode. See Hahnloser, R., & Seung, H. (2000). Permitted and forbidden sets in symmetric threshold-linear networks. *Advances in Neural Information Processing Systems, 13.*

7. Nair, V., & Hinton, G. (2010). Rectified linear units improve restricted Boltzmann machines. *Proceedings of the International Conference on Machine Learning.*

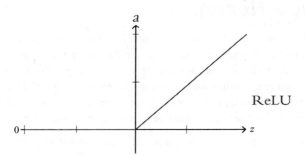

Figure 6.11   The ReLU activation function

This function is uncomplicated:

- If z is a positive value, the ReLU activation function returns z (unadulterated) as $a = z$.

- If $z = 0$ or z is negative, the function returns its floor value of 0, that is, the activation $a = 0$.

The ReLU function is one of the simplest functions to imagine that is *nonlinear*. That is, like the sigmoid and tanh functions, its output a does not vary uniformly linearly across all values of z. The ReLU is in essence *two* distinct linear functions combined (one at negative z values returning 0, and the other at positive z values returning z, as is visible in Figure 6.11) to form a straightforward, nonlinear function overall. This non-linear nature is a critical property of all activation functions used within deep learning architectures. As demonstrated via a series of captivating interactive applets in Chapter 4 of Michael Nielsen's *Neural Networks and Deep Learning* e-book, these nonlinearities permit deep learning models to approximate any continuous function.[8] This universal ability to approximate some output y given some input x is one of the hallmarks of deep learning—the characteristic that makes the approach so effective across such a breadth of applications.

The relatively simple shape of the ReLU function's particular brand of nonlinearity works to its advantage. As you'll see in Chapter 7, learning appropriate values for w and b within deep learning networks involves partial derivative calculus, and these calculus operations are more computationally efficient on the linear portions of the ReLU function relative to its efficiency on the curves of, say, the sigmoid and tanh functions.[9] As a testament to its utility, the incorporation of ReLU neurons into AlexNet (Figure 1.17) was one of the factors behind its trampling of existing machine vision benchmarks in 2012 and shepherding in the era of deep learning. Today, ReLU units are the most widely used neuron within the hidden layers of deep artificial neural networks, and they appear in the majority of the Jupyter notebooks associated with this book.

---

8. neuralnetworksanddeeplearning.com/chap4.html
9. In addition, there is mounting research that suggests ReLU activations encourage *parameter sparsity*—that is, less-elaborate neural-network-level functions that tend to generalize to validation data better. More on model generalization coming up in Chapter 7.

Choosing a Neuron

Within a given hidden layer of an artificial neural network, you are able to choose any activation function you fancy. With the constraint that you should select a nonlinear function if you'd like to be able to approximate any continuous function with your deep learning model, you're nevertheless left with quite a bit of room for choice. To assist your decision-making process, let's rank the neuron types we've discussed in this chapter, ordering them from those we recommend least through to those we recommend most:

1. The *perceptron*, with its binary inputs and the aggressive step of its binary output, is not a practical consideration for deep learning models.
2. The *sigmoid* neuron is an acceptable option, but it tends to lead to neural networks that train less rapidly than those composed of, say, tanh or ReLU neurons. Thus, we recommend limiting your use of sigmoid neurons to situations where it would be helpful to have a neuron provide output within the range of $[0, 1]$.[10]
3. The tanh neuron is a solid choice. As we covered earlier, the 0-centered output helps deep learning networks learn rapidly.
4. Our preferred neuron is the ReLU because of how efficiently these neurons enable learning algorithms to perform computations. In our experience they tend to lead to well-calibrated artificial neural networks in the shortest period of training time.

In addition to the neurons covered in this chapter, there is a veritable zoo of activation functions available and the list is ever growing. At time of writing, some of the "advanced" activation functions provided by Keras[11] are the *leaky ReLU*, the *parametric ReLU*, and the *exponential linear unit*—all three of which are derivations from the ReLU neuron. We encourage you to check these activations out in the Keras documentation and read about them on your own time. Furthermore, you are welcome to swap out the neurons we use in any of the Jupyter notebooks in this book to compare the results. We'd be pleasantly surprised if you discover that they provide efficiency or accuracy gains in your neural networks that are far beyond the performance of ours.

Up to this section, we detailed the mathematics behind the neural units that make up artificial neural networks, including deep learning models. We also summarized the pros and cons of the most established neuron types, providing you with guidance on which ones you might select for your own deep learning models. In the coming section, we cover how artificial neurons are networked together in order to learn features from raw data and approximate complex functions.

---

10. In Chapters 6 and 8, you will encounter a couple of these situations—most notably, with a sigmoid neuron as the sole neuron in the output layer of a binary-classifier network.
11. See keras.io/layers/advanced-activations for documentation.

Artificial Neural Networks

In the previous section, we examined the intricacies of artificial neurons. The theme of the coming section, is the natural extension of that: We cover how individual neural units are linked together to form artificial neural networks, including deep learning networks.

The Input Layer

In our *Shallow Net in Keras* Jupyter notebook (a schematic of which is available in Figure 5.4), we crafted an artificial neural network with the following layers:

1. An *input* layer consisting of 784 neurons, one for each of the 784 pixels in an MNIST image
2. A *hidden* layer composed of 64 sigmoid neurons
3. An *output* layer consisting of 10 softmax neurons, one for each of the 10 classes of digits

Of these three, the input layer is the most straightforward to detail. We start with it and then move on to discussion of the hidden and output layers.

Neurons in the input layer don't perform any calculations; they are simply placeholders for input data. This placeholding is essential because the use of artificial neural networks involves performing computations on matrices that have predefined dimensions. At least one of these predefined dimensions in the network architecture corresponds directly to the shape of the input data.

Dense Layers

There are many kinds of hidden layers, but as mentioned in Chapter 4, the most general type is the *dense layer*, which can also be called a *fully connected layer*. Dense layers are found in many deep learning architectures, including the majority of the models we go over in this book. Their definition is uncomplicated: Each of the neurons in a given dense layer receive information from *every one* of the neurons in the preceding layer of the network. In other words, a dense layer is fully connected to the layer before it!

While they might not be as specialized nor as efficient as the other flavors of hidden layers we dig into in Part III, dense layers are broadly useful, because they can nonlinearly recombine the information provided by the preceding layer of the network.[12] Reviewing the TensorFlow Playground demo from the end of Chapter 1, we're now better positioned to appreciate the deep learning model we built. Breaking it down layer by layer, the network in Figures 1.18 and 1.19 has the following layers:

---

12. This statement assumes that the dense layer is made up of neurons with a nonlinear activation function like the sigmoid, tanh, and ReLU neurons introduced in Chapter 6, which should be a safe assumption.

1. An *input layer with two neurons*: one for storing the vertical position of a given dot within the grid on the far right, and the other for storing the dot's horizontal position.
2. A *hidden layer composed of eight ReLU neurons*. Visually, we can see that this is a dense layer because each of the eight neurons in it is connected to (i.e., is receiving information from) both of the input-layer neurons, for a total of 16 (= 8 × 2) incoming connections.
3. Another *hidden layer composed of eight ReLU neurons*. We can again discern that this is a dense layer because each of its eight neurons receives input from each of the eight neurons in the preceding layer, for a total of 64 (= 8 × 8) inbound connections. Note in Figure 1.19 how the neurons in this layer are nonlinearly recombining the straight-edge features provided by the neurons in the first hidden layer to produce more-elaborate features like curves and circles.[13]
4. A third *dense hidden layer*, this one *consisting of four ReLU neurons* for a total of 32 (= 4 × 8) connecting inputs. This layer nonlinearly recombines the features from the previous hidden layer to learn more-complex features that begin to look directly relevant to the binary (orange versus blue) classification problem shown in the grid on the right in Figure 1.18.
5. A fourth and final *dense hidden layer*. With its *two ReLU neurons*, it receives a total of 8 (= 2 × 4) inputs from the previous layer. The neurons in this layer devise such elaborate features via nonlinear recombination that they visually approximate the overall boundary dividing blue from orange on the far-right grid.
6. An *output layer made up of a single sigmoid neuron*. Sigmoid is the typical choice of neuron for a binary classification problem like this one. As shown in Figure 6.9, the sigmoid function outputs activations that range from 0 up to 1, allowing us to obtain the network's estimated probability that a given input x is a positive case (a blue dot in the current example). Like the hidden layers, the *output layer is dense*, too: Its neuron receives information from both neurons of the final hidden layer for a total of 2 (= 1 × 2) connections.

In summary, *every* layer within the networks provided by the TensorFlow Playground is a dense layer. We can call such a network a *dense network*, and we'll experiment with these versatile creatures for the remainder of Part II.[14]

---

13. By returning to `playground.tensorflow.org` you can observe these features closely by hovering over these neurons with your mouse.

14. Elsewhere, you may find dense networks referred to as *feedforward neural networks* or *multilayer perceptrons* (MLPs). We prefer not to use the former term because other model architectures, such as convolutional neural networks (formally introduced in Chapter 9), are feedforward networks (that is, any network that doesn't include a loop) as well. Meanwhile, we prefer not to use the latter term because MLPs, confusingly, don't involve the perceptron neural units we cover in Chapter 6.

A Hot Dog-Detecting Dense Network

Let's further strengthen your comprehension of dense networks by returning to two old flames of ours from Chapter 6: a frivolous hot dog-detecting binary classifier and the mathematical notation we used to define artificial neurons. As shown in Figure 6.12, our hot dog classifier is no longer a single neuron; in this chapter, it is a dense network of artificial neurons. More specifically, with this network architecture, the following differences apply:

- We have reduced the number of input neurons down to two for simplicity.
  - The first input neuron, x_1, represents the volume of ketchup (in, say, milliliters, which abbreviates to mL) on the object being considered by the network. (We are no longer working with perceptrons, so we are no longer restricted to binary inputs only.)
  - The second input neuron, x_2, represents milliliters of mustard.
- We have two dense hidden layers.
  - The first hidden layer has three ReLU neurons.
  - The second hidden layer has two ReLU neurons.
- The output neuron is denoted by y in the network. This is a binary classification problem, so—as outlined in the previous section—this neuron should be sigmoid. As in our perceptron examples in Chapter 6, $y = 1$ corresponds to the presence of a hot dog and $y = 0$ corresponds to the presence of some other object.

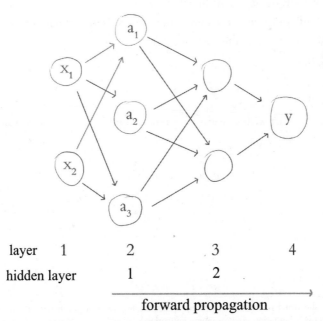

Figure 6.12 A dense network of artificial neurons, highlighting the inputs to the neuron labeled a_1

Forward Propagation Through the First Hidden Layer

Having described the architecture of our hot dog-detecting network, let's turn our attention to its functionality by focusing on the neuron labeled a_1.[15] This particular neuron, like its siblings a_2 and a_3, receives input regarding a given object's "ketchup-y-ness" and "mustard-y-ness" from x_1 and x_2, respectively. Despite receiving the same data as a_2 and a_3, a_1 treats these data uniquely by having its own unique parameters. Remembering Figure 6.7, "the most important equation in this book"—$w \cdot x + b$—you may grasp this behavior more concretely. Breaking this equation down for the neuron labeled a_1, we consider that it has two inputs from the preceding layer: x_1 and x_2. This neuron also has two weights: w_1 (which applies to the importance of the ketchup measurement x_1) and w_2 (which applies to the importance of the mustard measurement x_2). With these five pieces of information we can calculate z, the weighted input to that neuron:

$$z = w \cdot x + b$$
$$z = (w_1 x_1 + w_2 x_2) + b \tag{6.5}$$

In turn, with the z value for the neuron labeled a_1, we can calculate the activation a it outputs. Because the neuron labeled a_1 is a ReLU neuron, we use the equation introduced with respect to Figure 6.11:

$$a = max(0, z) \tag{6.6}$$

To make this computation of the output of neuron a_1 tangible, let's concoct some numbers and work through the arithmetic together:

- x_1 is 4.0 mL of ketchup for a given object presented to the network
- x_2 is 3.0 mL of mustard for that same object
- $w_1 = -0.5$
- $w_2 = 1.5$
- $b = -0.9$

To calculate z let's start with Equation 6.5 and then fill in our contrived values:

$$z = w \cdot x + b$$
$$= w_1 x_1 + w_1 x_2 + b$$
$$= -0.5 \times 4.0 + 1.5 \times 3.0 - 0.9 \tag{6.7}$$
$$= -2 + 4.5 - 0.9$$
$$= 1.6$$

---

15. We're using a shorthand notation for conveniently identifying neurons in this chapter. See Appendix A for a more precise and formal notation used for neural networks.

Finally, to compute a—the activation output of the neuron labeled a_1—we can leverage Equation 6.6:

$$\begin{aligned} a &= max(0, z) \\ &= max(0, 1.6) \\ &= 1.6 \end{aligned} \qquad (6.8)$$

As suggested by the right-facing arrow along the bottom of Figure 6.12, executing the calculations through an artificial neural network from the input layer (the x values) through to the output layer (y) is called *forward propagation*. Just now, we detailed the process for forward propagating through a single neuron in the first hidden layer of our hot dog-detecting network. To forward propagate through the remaining neurons of the first hidden layer—that is, to calculate the a values for the neurons labeled a_2 and a_3— we would follow the same process as we did for the neuron labeled a_1. The inputs x_1 and x_2 are identical for all three neurons, but despite being fed the same measurements of ketchup and mustard, each neuron in the first hidden layer will output a different activation a because the parameters w_1, w_2, and b vary for each of the neurons in the layer.

Forward Propagation Through Subsequent Layers

The process of forward propagating through the remaining layers of the network is essentially the same as propagating through the first hidden layer, but for clarity's sake, let's work through an example together. In Figure 6.13, we assume that we've already

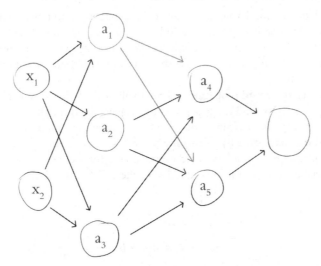

Figure 6.13   Our hot dog-detecting network from Figure 6.12, now highlighting the activation output of neuron a_1, which is provided as an input to both neuron a_4 and neuron a_5

calculated the activation value a for each of the neurons in the first hidden layer. Return-ing our focus to the neuron labeled a_1, the activation it outputs ($a_1 = 1.6$) becomes one of the three inputs into the neuron labeled a_4 (and, as highlighted in the figure, this same activation of $a = 1.6$ is also fed as one of the three inputs into the neuron labeled a_5).

To provide an example of forward propagation through the second hidden layer, let's compute a for the neuron labeled a_4. Again, we employ the all-important equation $w \cdot x + b$. For brevity's sake, we've combined it with the ReLU activation function:

$$a = max(0, z)$$
$$= max(0, (w \cdot x + b)) \tag{6.9}$$
$$= max(0, (w_1 x_1 + w_2 x_2 + w_3 x_3 + b))$$

This is sufficiently similar to Equations 6.7 and 6.8 that it would be superfluous to walk through the arithmetic again with feigned values. As we propagate through the second hidden layer, the only twist is that the layer's inputs (i.e., x in the equation $w \cdot x + b$) do not come from outside the network; instead they are provided by the first hidden layer. Thus, in Equation 6.9:

- x_1 is the value $a = 1.6$, which we obtained earlier from the neuron labeled a_1
- x_2 is the activation output a (whatever it happens to equal) from the neuron labeled a_2
- x_3 is likewise a unique activation a from the neuron labeled a_3

In this manner, the neuron labeled a_4 is able to nonlinearly recombine the information provided by the three neurons of the first hidden layer. The neuron labeled a_5 also non-linearly recombines this information, but it would do it in its own distinctive way: The unique parameters w_1, w_2, w_3, and b for this neuron would lead it to output a unique a activation of its own.

Having illustrated forward propagation through all of the hidden layers of our hot dog-detecting network, let's round the process off by propagating through the output layer. Figure 6.14 highlights that our single output neuron receives its inputs from the neurons labeled a_4 and a_5. Let's begin by calculating z for this output neuron. The formula is identical to Equation 6.5, which we used to calculate z for the neuron labeled a_1, except that the (contrived, as usual) values we plug in to the variables are different:

$$z = w \cdot x + b$$
$$= w_1 x_1 + w_2 x_2 + b$$
$$= 1.0 \times 2.5 + 0.5 \times 2.0 - 5.5 \tag{6.10}$$
$$= 3.5 - 5.5$$
$$= -2.0$$

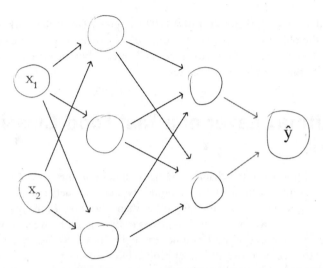

Figure 6.14 Our hot dog-detecting network, with the activations providing input to the output neuron ŷ highlighted

The output neuron is sigmoid, so to compute its activation a we pass its z value through the sigmoid function from Figure 6.9:

$$\begin{aligned}
a &= \sigma(z) \\
&= \frac{1}{1 + e^{-z}} \\
&= \frac{1}{1 + e^{-(-2.0)}} \\
&\approx 0.1192
\end{aligned} \tag{6.11}$$

We are lazy, so we didn't work out the final line of this equation manually. Instead, we used the *Sigmoid Function* Jupyter notebook that we created in Chapter 6. By executing the line sigmoid(-2.0) within it, our machine did the heavy lifting for us and kindly informed us that a comes out to about 0.1192.

The activation a computed by the sigmoid neuron in the output layer is a special case, because it is the final output of our entire hot dog-detecting neural network. Because it's so special, we assign it a distinctive designation: $\hat{y}$. This variable is a version of the letter y that wears an object called a *caret* to keep its head warm, and so we call it "why hat." The value represented by $\hat{y}$ is the network's guess as to whether a given object is a hot dog or not a hot dog, and we can express this in probabilistic language. Given the inputs x_1 and x_2 that we fed into the network—that is, 4.0 mL of ketchup and 3.0 mL of mustard—the network estimates that there is an 11.92 percent chance that an object with those particular condiment measurements is a hot dog.[16] If the object presented to the network was

---

16. Don't say we didn't warn you from the start that this was a silly example! If we're lucky, its outlandishness will make it memorable.

indeed a hot dog ($y = 1$), then this $\hat{y}$ of 0.1192 was pretty far off the mark. On the other hand, if the object was truly not a hot dog ($y = 0$), then the $\hat{y}$ is quite good. We formalize the evaluation of $\hat{y}$ predictions in Chapter 7, but the general notion is that the closer $\hat{y}$ is to the true value y, the better.

The Softmax Layer of a Fast Food-Classifying Network

As demonstrated thus far in the chapter, the sigmoid neuron suits us well as an output neuron if we're building a network to distinguish two classes, such as a blue dot versus an orange dot, or a hot dog versus something other than a hot dog. In many other circumstances, however, you have more than two classes to distinguish between. For example, the MNIST dataset consists of the 10 numerical digits, so our *Shallow Net in Keras* from Chapter 6 had to accommodate 10 output probabilities—one representing each digit.

When concerned with a multiclass problem, the solution is to use a softmax layer as the output layer of our network. Softmax is in fact the activation function that we specified for the output layer in our *Shallow Net in Keras* Jupyter notebook (Example 5.6), but we initially suggested you not concern yourself with that detail. Now, a couple of chapters later, the time to unravel softmax has arrived.

In Figure 6.15, we provide a new architecture that builds upon our binary hot dog classifier. The schematic is the same—right down to its volumes-of-ketchup-and-mustard inputs—except that instead of having a single output neuron, we now have three. This multiclass output layer is still dense, so each of the three neurons receives information from both of the neurons in the final hidden layer. Continuing on with our proclivity for fast food, let's say that now:

- y_1 represents hot dogs.
- y_2 is for burgers.
- y_3 is for pizza.

Note that with this configuration, there can be no alternatives to hot dogs, burgers, or pizza. The assumption is that all objects presented to the network belong to one of these three classes of fast food, and *one* of the classes only.

Because the sigmoid function applies solely to binary problems, the output neurons in Figure 6.15 take advantage of the softmax activation function. Let's use code from our *Softmax Demo* Jupyter notebook to elucidate how this activation function operates. The only dependency is the `exp` function, which calculates the natural exponential of whatever value it's given. More specifically, if we pass some value x into it with the command `exp(x)`, we will get back e^x. The effect of this exponentiation will become clear as we move through the forthcoming example. We import the `exp` function into the notebook by using `from math import exp`.

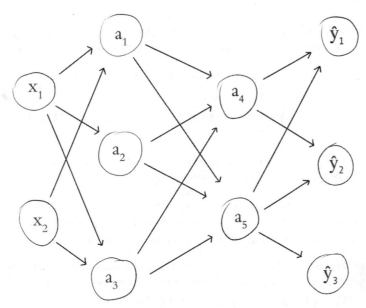

Figure 6.15 Our food-detecting network, now with three softmax neurons in the output layer

To concoct a particular example, let's say that we presented a slice of pizza to the network in Figure 6.15. This pizza slice has negligible amounts of ketchup and mustard on it, and so x_1 and x_2 are near-0 values. Provided these inputs, we use forward propagation to pass information through the network toward the output layer. Based on the information that the three neurons receive from the final hidden layer, they individually use our old friend $w \cdot x + b$ to calculate three unique (and, for the purposes of this example, contrived) z values:

- z for the neuron labeled $\hat{y}_1$, which represents hot dogs, comes out to –1.0.
- For the neuron labeled $\hat{y}_2$, which represents burgers, z is 1.0.
- For the pizza neuron $\hat{y}_3$, z comes out to 5.0.

These values indicate that the network estimates that the object presented to it is most likely to be pizza and least likely to be a hot dog. Expressed as z, however, it isn't straightforward to intuit *how much* more likely the network predicts the object to be pizza relative to the other two classes. This is where the softmax function comes in.

After importing our dependency, we create a list named z to store our three z values:

```
z = [-1.0, 1.0, 5.0]
```

Applying the softmax function to this list involves a three-step process. The first step is to calculate the exponential of each of the z values. More explicitly:

- `exp(z[0])` comes out to 0.3679 for hot dog.[17]
- `exp(z[1])` gives us 2.718 for burger.
- `exp(z[2])` gives us the much, much larger (exponentially so!) 148.4 for pizza.

The second step of the softmax function is to sum up our exponentials:

```
total = exp(z[0]) + exp(z[1]) + exp(z[2])
```

With this `total` variable we can execute the third and final step, which provides proportions for each of our three classes relative to the sum of all of the classes:

- `exp(z[0])/total` outputs a $\hat{y}_1$ value of 0.002428, indicating that the network estimates there's a ~0.2 percent chance that the object presented to it is a hot dog.
- `exp(z[1])/total` outputs a $\hat{y}_2$ value of 0.01794, indicating an estimated ~1.8 percent chance that it's a burger.
- `exp(z[2])/total` outputs a $\hat{y}_3$ value of 0.9796, for an estimated ~98.0 percent chance that the object is pizza.

Given this arithmetic, the etymology of the "softmax" name should now be discernible: The function returns z with the highest value (the *max*), but it does so *softly*. That is, instead of indicating that there's a 100 percent chance the object is pizza and a 0 percent chance it's either of the other two fast food classes (that would be a *hard* max function), the network hedges its bets, to an extent, and provides a likelihood that the object is each of the three classes. This leaves us to make the decision about how much confidence we would require to accept a neural network's guess.[18]

The use of the softmax function with a single neuron is a special case of softmax that is mathematically equivalent to using a sigmoid neuron.

---

17. Recall that Python uses zero indexing, so `z[0]` corresponds to the z of neuron $\hat{y}_1$.
18. Confidence thresholds may vary based on your particular application, but typically we'd simply accept whichever class has the highest likelihood. This class can, for example, be identified with the `argmax()` (argument maximum) function in Python, which returns the index position (i.e., the class label) of the largest value.

Revisiting Our Shallow Network

With the knowledge of dense networks that you've developed over the course of this chapter, we can return to our *Shallow Net in Keras* notebook and understand the model summary within it. Example 5.6 shows the three lines of Keras code we use to architect a shallow neural network for classifying MNIST digits. As detailed in Chapter 5, over those three lines of code we instantiate a model object and add layers of artificial neurons to it. By calling the `summary()` method on the model, we see the model-summarizing table provided in Figure 6.16. The table has three columns:

- `Layer (type)`: the name and type of each of our layers
- `Output Shape`: the dimensionality of the layer
- `Param #`: the number of parameters (weights w and biases b) associated with the layer

Layer (type)	Output Shape	Param #
dense_1 (Dense)	(None, 64)	50240
dense_2 (Dense)	(None, 10)	650

Total params: 50,890
Trainable params: 50,890
Non-trainable params: 0

Figure 6.16   A summary of the model object from our *Shallow Net in Keras* Jupyter notebook

The input layer performs no calculations and never has any of its own parameters, so no information on it is displayed directly. The first row in the table, therefore, corresponds to the first hidden layer of the network. The table indicates that this layer:

- Is called dense_1; this is a default name because we did not designate one explicitly
- Is a Dense layer, as we specified in Example 5.6
- Is composed of 64 neurons, as we further specified in Example 5.6

- Has 50,240 parameters associated with it, broken down into the following:
  - 50,176 weights, corresponding to each of the 64 neurons in this dense layer receiving input from each of the 784 neurons in the input layer (64 × 784)
  - Plus 64 biases, one for each of the neurons in the layer
  - Giving us a total of 50,240 parameters:
    $n_{parameters} = n_{w} + n_{b} = 50176 + 64 = 50240$

The second row of the table in Figure 6.16 corresponds to the model's output layer. The table tells us that this layer:

- Is called dense_2
- Is a Dense layer, as we specified it to be
- Consists of 10 neurons—again, as we specified
- Has 650 parameters associated with it, as follows:
  - 640 weights, corresponding to each of the 10 neurons receiving input from each of the 64 neurons in the hidden layer (64 × 10)
  - Plus 10 biases, one for each of the output neurons

From the parameter counts for each layer, we can calculate for ourselves the Total params line displayed in Figure 6.16:

$$n_{total} = n_1 + n_2$$
$$= 50240 + 650 \qquad (6.12)$$
$$= 50890$$

All 50,890 of these parameters are Trainable params because—during the subsequent model.fit() call in the *Shallow Net in Keras* notebook—they are permitted to be tuned during model training. This is the norm, but as you'll see in Part III, there are situations when it is fruitful to freeze some of the parameters in a model, rendering them Non-trainable params.

Summary

In this chapter, we detailed how artificial neurons are networked together to approximate an output y given some inputs x. In the remaining chapters of Part II, we detail how a network learns to improve its approximations of y by using training data to tune the parameters of its constituent artificial neurons. Simultaneously, we broaden our coverage of best practices for designing and training artificial neural networks so that you can include additional hidden layers and form a high-caliber deep learning model.

Key Concepts

As we move through the chapters of the book, we will gradually add terms to this list of key concepts. If you keep these foundational concepts fresh in your mind, you should have little difficulty understanding subsequent chapters and, by book's end, possess a firm grip on deep learning theory and application. The critical concepts thus far are as follows.

- parameters:
  - weight w
  - bias b
- activation a
- artificial neurons:
  - sigmoid
  - tanh
  - ReLU
- input layer
- hidden layer
- output layer
- layer types:
  - dense (fully connected)
  - softmax
- forward propagation

7

Deep Networks

In the preceding chapters, we described artificial neurons comprehensively and we walked through the process of forward propagating information through a network of neurons to output a prediction, such as whether a given fast food item is a hot dog, a juicy burger, or a greasy slice of pizza. In those culinary examples from Chapter 6, we fabricated numbers for the neuron parameters—the neuron weights and biases. In real-world applications, however, these parameters are not typically concocted arbitrarily: They are learned by training the network on data.

In this chapter, you will become acquainted with two techniques—called *gradient descent* and *backpropagation*—that work in tandem to learn artificial neural network parameters. As usual in this book, our presentation of these methods is not only theoretical: We provide pragmatic best practices for implementing the techniques. The chapter culminates in the application of these practices to the construction of a neural network with more than one hidden layer.

Cost Functions

In Chapter 7, you discovered that, upon forward propagating some input values all the way through an artificial neural network, the network provides its estimated output, which is denoted $\hat{y}$. If a network were perfectly calibrated, it would output $\hat{y}$ values that are exactly equal to the true label y. In our binary classifier for detecting hot dogs, for example (Figure 6.14), $y = 1$ indicated that the object presented to the network is a hot dog, while $y = 0$ indicated that it's something else. In an instance where we have in fact presented a hot dog to the network, therefore, ideally it would output $\hat{y} = 1$.

In practice, the gold standard of $\hat{y} = y$ is not always attained and so may be an excessively stringent definition of the "correct" $\hat{y}$. Instead, if $y = 1$ we might be quite pleased to see a $\hat{y}$ of, say, 0.9997, because that would indicate that the network has an extremely high confidence that the object is a hot dog. A $\hat{y}$ of 0.9 might be considered acceptable, $\hat{y} = 0.6$ to be disappointing, and $\hat{y} = 0.1192$ (as computed in Equation 6.11) to be awful.

To quantify the spectrum of output-evaluation sentiments from "quite pleased" all the way down to "awful," machine learning algorithms often involve *cost functions* (also known as *loss functions*). The two such functions that we cover in this book are called quadratic cost and cross-entropy cost. Let's cover them in turn.

Quadratic Cost

Quadratic cost is one of the simplest cost functions to calculate. It is alternatively called *mean squared error*, which handily describes all that there is to its calculation:

$$C = \frac{1}{n} \sum_{i=1}^{n} (y_i - \hat{y}_i)^2 \qquad (7.1)$$

For any given instance i, we calculate the difference (the *error*) between the true label y_i and the network's estimated $\hat{y}_i$. We then *square* this difference, for two reasons:

1. Squaring ensures that whether y is greater than $\hat{y}$ or vice versa, the difference between the two is stated as a positive value.
2. Squaring penalizes large differences between y and $\hat{y}$ much more severely than small differences.

Having obtained a *squared error* for each instance i by using $(y_i - \hat{y}_i)^2$, we can then calculate the *mean* cost C across all n of our instances by:

1. Summing up cost across all instances using $\sum_{i=1}^{n}$
2. Dividing by however many instances we have using $\frac{1}{n}$

By taking a peek inside the *Quadratic Cost* Jupyter notebook from the book's GitHub repo, you can play around with Equation 7.1 yourself. At the top of the notebook, we define a function to calculate the squared error for an instance i:

```
def squared_error(y, yhat):
    return (y - yhat)**2
```

By plugging a true y of 1 and the ideal yhat of 1 in to the function by using `squared_error(1, 1)`, we observe that—as desired—this perfect estimate is associated with a cost of 0. Likewise, minor deviations from the ideal, such as a yhat of 0.9997, correspond to an extremely small cost: 9.0e-08.[1] As the difference between y and yhat increases, we witness the expected exponential increase in cost: Holding y steady at 1 but lowering yhat from 0.9 to 0.6, and then to 0.1192, the cost climbs increasingly rapidly from 0.01 to 0.16 and then to 0.78. As a final bit of amusement in the notebook, we note that had y truly been 0, our yhat of 0.1192 would be associated with a small cost: 0.0142.

Saturated Neurons

While quadratic cost serves as a straightforward introduction to loss functions, it has a vital flaw. Consider Figure 7.1, in which we recapitulate the tanh activation function from Figure 6.10. The issue presented in the figure, called *neuron saturation*, is common across all activation functions, but we'll use tanh as our lone exemplar. A neuron is

---

1. 9.0e-08 is equivalent to 9.0×10^{-8}.

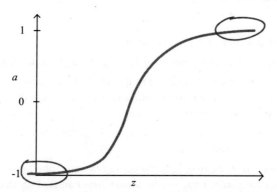

Figure 7.1   Plot reproducing the tanh activation function shown in Figure 6.10, drawing attention to the high and low values of z at which a neuron is saturated

considered saturated when the combination of its inputs and parameters (interacting as per "the most important equation," $z = w \cdot x + b$, which is captured in Figure 6.10) produces extreme values of z—the areas encircled in the plot in Figure 7.1. In these areas, changes in z (via adjustments to the neuron's underlying parameters w and b) cause only teensy-weensy changes in the neuron's activation a.[2]

Using methods that we cover later in this chapter—namely, gradient descent and backpropagation—a neural network is able to learn to approximate y through the tuning of the parameters w and b associated with all of its constituent neurons. In a saturated neuron, where changes to w and b lead to only minuscule changes in a, this learning slows to a crawl: If adjustments to w and b make no discernible impact on a given neuron's activation a, then these adjustments cannot have any discernible impact downstream (via forward propagation) on the network's $\hat{y}$, its estimate of y.

Cross-Entropy Cost

One of the ways[3] to minimize the impact of saturated neurons on learning speed is to use *cross-entropy cost* in lieu of quadratic cost. This alternative loss function is configured to enable efficient learning anywhere within the activation function curve of Figure 7.1. Because of this, it is a far more popular choice of cost function and it is the selection that predominates the remainder of this book.[4]

You need not preoccupy yourself with the equation for cross-entropy cost, but for the sake of completeness, here it is:

$$C = -\frac{1}{n} \sum_{i=1}^{n} [y_i \ln \hat{y}_i + (1 - y_i) \ln(1 - \hat{y}_i)] \tag{7.2}$$

---

2. Recall from Chapter 6 that $a = \sigma(z)$, where σ is some activation function—in this example, the tanh function.
3. More methods for attenuating saturated neurons and their negative effects on a network are covered in Chapter 7.
4. Cross-entropy cost is well suited to neural networks solving classification problems, and such problems dominate this book. For regression problems (covered in Chapter 7), quadratic cost is a better option than cross-entropy cost.

The most pertinent aspects of the equation are:

- Like quadratic cost, divergence of $\hat{y}$ from y corresponds to increased cost.
- Analogous to the use of the square in quadratic cost, the use of the natural logarithm ln in cross-entropy cost causes larger differences between $\hat{y}$ and y to be associated with exponentially larger cost.
- Cross-entropy cost is structured so that the larger the difference between $\hat{y}$ and y, *the faster the neuron is able to learn.*[5]

To make it easier to remember that the greater the cost, the more quickly a neural network incorporating cross-entropy cost learns, here's an analogy that would absolutely never involve any of your esteemed authors: Let's say you're at a cocktail party leading the conversation of a group of people that you've met that evening. The strong martini you're holding has already gone to your head, and you go out on a limb by throwing a risqué line into your otherwise charming repartee. Your audience reacts with immediate, visible disgust. With this response clearly indicating that your quip was well off the mark, you learn pretty darn quickly. It's exceedingly unlikely you'll be repeating the joke anytime soon.

Anyway, that's plenty enough on disasters of social etiquette. The final item to note on cross-entropy cost is that, by including $\hat{y}$, the formula provided in Equation 7.2 applies to only the output layer. Recall from Chapter 7 (specifically the discussion of Figure 6.14) that $\hat{y}$ is a special case of a: It's actually just another plain old a value—except that it's being calculated by neurons in the output layer of a neural network. With this in mind, Equation 7.2 could be expressed with a_i substituted in for $\hat{y}_i$ so that the equation generalizes neatly beyond the output layer to neurons in any layer of a network:

$$C = -\frac{1}{n}\sum_{i=1}^{n}[y_i \ln a_i + (1 - y_i)\ln(1 - a_i)] \tag{7.3}$$

To cement all of this theoretical chatter about cross-entropy cost, let's interactively explore our aptly named *Cross Entropy Cost* Jupyter notebook. There is only one dependency in the notebook: the `log` function from the *NumPy* package, which enables us to compute the natural logarithm ln shown twice in Equation 7.3. We load this dependency using `from numpy import log`.

Next, we define a function for calculating cross-entropy cost for an instance i:

```
def cross_entropy(y, a):
    return -1*(y*log(a) + (1-y)*log(1-a))
```

5. To understand how the cross-entropy cost function in Equation 7.2 enables a neuron with larger cost to learn more rapidly, we require a touch of partial-derivative calculus. (Because we endeavor to minimize the use of advanced mathematics in this book, we've relegated this calculus-focused explanation to this footnote.) Central to the two computational methods that enable neural networks to learn—gradient descent and backpropagation—is the comparison of the rate of change of cost C relative to neuron parameters like weight w. Using partial-derivative notation, we can represent these relative rates of change as $\frac{\partial C}{\partial w}$. The cross-entropy cost function is deliberately structured so that, when we calculate its derivative, $\frac{\partial C}{\partial w}$ is related to $(\hat{y} - y)$. Thus, the larger the difference between the ideal output y and the neuron's estimated output $\hat{y}$, the greater the rate of change of cost C with respect to weight w.

Table 7.1   Cross-entropy costs associated with selected example inputs

y	a	C
1	0.9997	0.0003
1	0.9	0.1
1	0.6	0.5
1	0.1192	2.1
0	0.1192	0.1269
1	1−0.1192	0.1269

Plugging the same values in to our `cross_entropy()` function as we did the `squared_error()` function earlier in this chapter, we observe comparable behavior. As shown in Table 7.1, by holding y steady at 1 and gradually decreasing a from the nearly ideal estimate of 0.9997 downward, we get exponential increases in cross-entropy cost. The table further illustrates that—again, consistent with the behavior of its quadratic cousin—cross-entropy cost would be low, with an a of 0.1192, if y happened to in fact be 0. These results reiterate for us that the chief distinction between the quadratic and cross-entropy functions is not the particular cost value that they calculate per se, but rather it is the rate at which they learn within a neural net—especially if saturated neurons are involved.

Optimization: Learning to Minimize Cost

Cost functions provide us with a quantification of how incorrect our model's estimate of the ideal y is. This is most helpful because it arms us with a metric we can leverage to reduce our network's incorrectness.

As alluded to a couple of times in this chapter, the primary approach for minimizing cost in deep learning paradigms is to pair an approach called gradient descent with another one called backpropagation. These approaches are *optimizers* and they enable the network to *learn*. This learning is accomplished by adjusting the model's parameters so that its estimated $\hat{y}$ gradually converges toward the target of y, and thus the cost decreases. We cover gradient descent first and move on to backpropagation immediately afterward.

Gradient Descent

Gradient descent is a handy, efficient tool for adjusting a model's parameters with the aim of minimizing cost, particularly if you have a lot of training data available. It is widely used across the field of machine learning, not only in deep learning.

In Figure 7.2, we use a nimble trilobite in a cartoon to illustrate how gradient descent works. Along the horizontal axis in each frame is some parameter that we've denoted as p. In an artificial neural network, this parameter would be either a neuron's weight w or bias b. In the top frame, the trilobite finds itself on a hill. Its goal is to *descend* the gradient, thereby finding the location with the minimum cost, C. But there's a twist: The trilobite

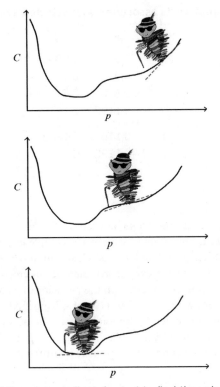

Figure 7.2   A trilobite using gradient descent to find the value of a parameter p
associated with minimal cost, C

is blind! It cannot see whether deeper valleys lie far away somewhere, and so it can only use its cane to investigate the slope of the terrain in its immediate vicinity.

The dashed orange line in Figure 7.2 indicates the blind trilobite's calculation of the slope at the point where it finds itself. According to that slope line, if the trilobite takes a step to the left (i.e., to a slightly lower value of p), it would be moving to a location with smaller cost. On the hand, if the trilobite takes a step to the right (a slightly *higher* value of p), it would be moving to a location with *higher* cost. Given the trilobite's desire to descend the gradient, it chooses to take a step to the left.

By the middle frame, the trilobite has taken several steps to the left. Here again, we see it evaluating the slope with the orange line and discovering that, yet again, a step to the left will bring it to a location with lower cost, and so it takes another step left. In the lower frame, the trilobite has succeeded in making its way to the location—the value of the parameter p—corresponding to the minimum cost. From this position, if it were to take a step to the left *or* to the right, cost would go up, so it gleefully remains in place.

In practice, a deep learning model would not have only one parameter. It is not uncommon for deep learning networks to have millions of parameters, and some industrial applications have billions of them. Even our *Shallow Net in Keras*—one of the smallest models we build in this book—has 5,89 parameters (see Figure 7.5).

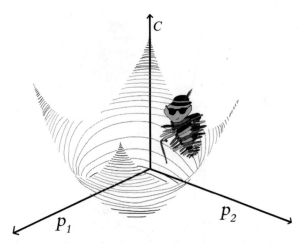

Figure 7.3 A trilobite exploring along two model parameters—p_1 and p_2—in order to minimize cost via gradient descent. In a mountain-adventure analogy, p_1 and p_2 could be thought of as latitude and longitude, and altitude represents cost.

Although it's impossible for the human mind to imagine a billion-dimensional space, the two-parameter cartoon shown in Figure 7.3 provides a sense of how gradient descent scales up to minimize cost across multiple parameters simultaneously. Across however many trainable parameters there are in a model, gradient descent iteratively evaluates slopes[6] to identify the adjustments to those parameters that correspond to the steepest reduction in cost. With two parameters, as in the trilobite cartoon in Figure 7.3, for example, this procedure can be likened to a blind hike through the mountains, where:

- Latitude represents one parameter, say p_1.
- Longitude represents the other parameter, p_2.
- Altitude represents cost—the lower the altitude, the better!

The trilobite randomly finds itself at a location in the mountains. From that point, it feels around with its cane to identify the direction of the step it can take that will reduce its altitude the most. It then takes that single step. Repeating this process many times, the trilobite may eventually find itself at the latitude and longitude coordinates that correspond to the lowest-possible altitude (the minimum cost), at which point the trilobite's surreal alpine adventure is complete.

Learning Rate

For conceptual simplicity, in Figure 7.4, let's return to a blind trilobite navigating a single-parameter world instead of a two-parameter world. Now let's imagine that we have a ray-gun that can shrink or enlarge trilobites. In the middle panel, we've used our ray-gun to make our trilobite very small. The trilobite's steps will then be correspondingly small, and so it will take our intrepid little hiker a long time to find its way to the

---

6. Using partial-derivative calculus.

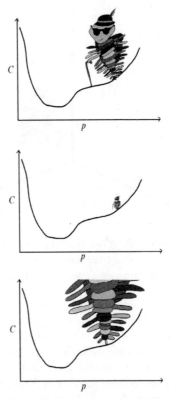

Figure 7.4 The learning rate (η) of gradient descent expressed as the size of a trilobite. The middle panel has a small learning rate, and the bottom panel, a large one.

legendary valley of minimum cost. On the other hand, consider the bottom panel, in which we've used our ray-gun to make the trilobite very large. The situation here is even worse! The trilobite's steps will now be so large that it will step right over the valley of minimum cost, and so it never has any hope of finding it.

In gradient descent terminology, step size is referred to as *learning rate* and denoted with the Greek letter η (eta, pronounced "ee-ta"). Learning rate is the first of several model *hyperparameters* that we cover in this book. In machine learning, including deep learning, hyperparameters are aspects of the model that we configure before we begin training the model. So hyperparameters such as η are preset while, in contrast, parameters—namely, w and b—are learned during training.

Getting your hyperparameters right for a given deep learning model often requires some trial and error. For the learning rate η, it's something like the fairy tale of "Goldilocks and the Three Bears": Too small and too large are both inadequate, but there's a sweet spot in the middle. More specifically, as we portray in Figure 7.4, if η is too small, then it will take many, many iterations of gradient descent (read: an unnecessarily long time) to reach the minimal cost. On the other hand, selecting a value for η

that is too large means we might never reach minimal cost at all: The gradient descent algorithm will act erratically as it jumps right over the parameters associated with minimal cost.

Coming up in Chapter 7, we have a clever trick waiting for you that will circumnavigate the need for you to manually select a given neural network's η hyperparameter. In the interim, however, here are our rules of thumb on the topic:

- Begin with a learning rate of about 0.01 or 0.001.

- If your model is able to learn (i.e., if cost decreases consistently epoch over epoch) but training happens very slowly (i.e., each epoch, the cost decreases only a small amount), then increase your learning rate by an order of magnitude (e.g., from 0.01 to 0.1). If the cost begins to jump up and down erratically epoch over epoch, then you've gone too far, so rein in your learning rate.

- At the other extreme, if your model is unable to learn, then your learning rate may be too high. Try decreasing it by orders of magnitude (e.g., from 0.001 to 0.0001) until cost decreases consistently epoch over epoch. For a visual, interactive way to get a handle on the erratic behavior of a model when its learning rate is too high, you can return to the TensorFlow Playground example from Figure 1.18 and dial up the value within the "Learning rate" dropdown box.

Batch Size and Stochastic Gradient Descent

When we introduced gradient descent, we suggested that it is efficient for machine learning problems that involve a large dataset. In the strictest sense, we outright lied to you. The truth is that if we have a very large quantity of training data, *ordinary* gradient descent would not work at all because it wouldn't be possible to fit all of the data into the memory (RAM) of our machine.

Memory isn't the only potential snag; compute power could cause us headaches, too. A relatively large dataset might squeeze into the memory of our machine, but if we tried to train a neural network containing millions of parameters with all those data, vanilla gradient descent would be highly *in*efficient because of the computational complexity of the associated high-volume, high-dimensional calculations.

Thankfully, there's a solution to these memory and compute limitations: the *stochastic* variant of gradient descent. With this variation, we split our training data into *minibatches*—small subsets of our full training dataset—to render gradient descent both manageable and productive.

Although we didn't focus on it at the time, when we trained the model in our *Shallow Net in Keras* notebook back in Chapter 5 we were already using stochastic gradient descent by setting our `optimizer` to `SGD` in the `model.compile()` step. Further, in the subsequent line of code when we called the `model.fit()` method, we set `batch_size` to `128` to specify the size of our mini-batches—the number of training data points that we use for a given iteration of SGD. Like the learning rate η presented earlier in this chapter, *batch size* is also a model hyperparameter.

Let's work through some numbers to make the concepts of batches and stochastic gradient descent more tangible. In the MNIST dataset, there are 60,000 training images.

With a batch size of 128 images, we then have $\lceil 468.75 \rceil = 469$ batches[7,8] of gradient descent per epoch:

$$
\begin{aligned}
\text{number of batches} &= \left\lceil \frac{\text{size of training dataset}}{\text{batch size}} \right\rceil \\
&= \left\lceil \frac{60,000 \text{ images}}{128 \text{ images}} \right\rceil \\
&= \lceil 468.75 \rceil \\
&= 469
\end{aligned}
\tag{7.4}
$$

Before carrying out any training, we initialize our network with random values for each neuron's parameters w and b.[9] To begin the first epoch of training:

1. We shuffle and divide the training images into mini-batches of 128 images each. These 128 MNIST images provide 784 pixels each, which all together constitute the inputs x that are passed into our neural network. It's this shuffling step that puts the *stochastic* (which means *random*) in "stochastic gradient descent."
2. By forward propagation, information about the 128 images is processed by the network, layer through layer, until the output layer ultimately produces $\hat{y}$ values.
3. A cost function (e.g., cross-entropy cost) evaluates the network's $\hat{y}$ values against the true y values, providing a cost C for this particular mini-batch of 128 images.
4. To minimize cost and thereby improve the network's estimates of y given x, the gradient descent part of stochastic gradient descent is performed: Every single w and b parameter in the network is adjusted proportional to how much each contributed to the error (i.e., the cost) in this batch (note that the adjustments are scaled by the learning rate hyperparameter η).[10]

These four steps constitute a *round of training*, as summarized by Figure 7.5.

Figure 7.6 captures how rounds of training are repeated until we run out of training images to sample. The sampling in step 1 is done *without replacement*, meaning that at the end of an epoch each image has been seen by the algorithm only once, and yet between different epochs the mini-batches are sampled randomly. After a total of 468 rounds, the final batch contains only 96 samples.

This marks the end of the first epoch of training. Assuming we've set our model up to train for further epochs, we begin the next epoch by replenishing our pool with all 6,training images. As we did through the previous epoch, we then proceed through a further 469 rounds of stochastic gradient descent.[11] Training continues in this way until the total desired number of epochs is reached.

---

7. Because 60,000 is not perfectly divisible by 128, that 469th batch would contain only $0.75 \times 128 = 96$ images.
8. The square brackets we use here and in Equation 7.4 that appear to be missing the horizontal element from the bottom are used to denote the calculation of an integer-value ceiling. The whole-integer ceiling of 468.75, for example, is 469.
9. We delve into the particulars of parameter initialization with random values in Chapter 7.
10. This error-proportional adjustment is calculated during backpropagation. We haven't covered backpropagation explicitly yet, but it's coming up in the next section, so hang on tight!
11. Because we're sampling randomly, the order in which we select training images for our 469 mini-batches is completely different for every epoch.

Round of Training:

1. Sample a mini-batch of x values

2. Forward propagate x through network
   to estimate y with $\hat{y}$

3. Calculate cost C by comparing y and $\hat{y}$

4. Descend gradient of C to adjust w and b, enabling
   x to better predict y

Figure 7.5 An individual round of training with stochastic gradient descent. Although mini-batch size is a hyperparameter that can vary, in this particular case, the mini-batch consists of 128 MNIST digits, as exemplified by our hike-loving trilobite carrying a small bag of data.

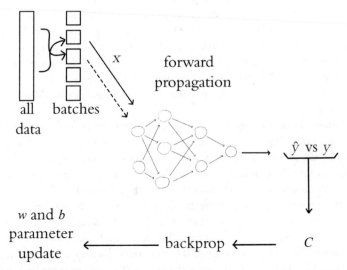

Figure 7.6 An outline of the overall process for training a neural network with stochastic gradient descent. The entire dataset is shuffled and split into batches. Each batch is forward propagated through the network; the output $\hat{y}$ is compared to the ground truth y and the cost C is calculated; backpropagation calculates the gradients; and the model parameters w and b are updated. The next batch (indicated by a dashed line) is forward propagated, and so on until all of the batches have moved through the network. Once all the batches have been used, a single epoch is complete and the process starts again with a reshuffling of the full training dataset.

The total *number of epochs* that we set our network to train for is yet another hyperparameter, by the way. This hyperparameter, though, is one of the easiest to get right:

- If the cost on your validation data is going down epoch over epoch, and if your final epoch attained the lowest cost yet, then you can try training for additional epochs.

- Once the cost on your validation data begins to creep upward, that's an indicator that your model has begun to *overfit* to your training data because you've trained for too many epochs. (We elaborate much more on overfitting in Chapter 7.)

- There are methods[12] you can use to automatically monitor training and validation cost and stop training early if things start to go awry. In this way, you could set the number of epochs to be arbitrarily large and know that training will continue until the validation cost stops improving—and certainly before the model begins overfitting!

Escaping the Local Minimum

In all of the examples of gradient descent thus far in the chapter, our hiking trilobite has encountered no hurdles on its journey toward minimum cost. There are no guarantees that this would be the case, however. Indeed, such smooth sailing is unusual.

Figure 7.7 shows the mountaineering trilobite exploring the cost of some new model that is being used to solve some new problem. With this new problem, the relationship between the parameter p and cost C is more complex. To have our neural network estimate y as accurately as possible, gradient descent needs to identify the parameter values associated with the lowest-attainable cost. However, as our trilobite makes its way from its random starting point in the top panel, gradient descent leads it to getting trapped in a *local minimum*. As shown in the middle panel, while our intrepid explorer is in the local minimum, a step to the left or a step to the right both lead to an increase in cost, and so the blind trilobite stays put, completely oblivious of the existence of a deeper valley—the *global minimum*—lying yonder.

All is not lost, friends, for stochastic gradient descent comes to the rescue here again. The sampling of mini-batches can have the effect of smoothing out the cost curve, as exemplified by the dashed curve shown in the bottom panel of Figure 7.7. This smoothing happens because the estimate is noisier when estimating the gradient from a smaller mini-batch (versus from the entire dataset). Although the actual gradient in the local minimum truly is zero, estimates of the gradient from small subsets of the data don't provide the complete picture and might give an inaccurate reading, causing our trilobite to take a step left thinking there is a gradient when there really isn't one. This noisiness and inaccuracy is paradoxically a good thing! The incorrect gradient may result in a step that is large enough for the trilobite to escape the local valley and continue making its way down the mountain. Thus, by estimating the gradient many times on these mini-batches, the noise is smoothed out and we are able to avoid local minima. In summary, although each mini-batch on its own lacks complete information about the cost curve, in the long run—over a large number of mini-batches—this tends to work to our advantage.

---

12. See keras.io/callbacks/#earlystopping.

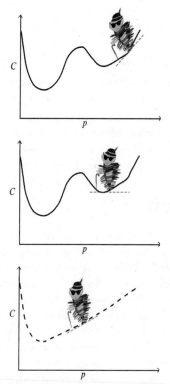

Figure 7.7   A trilobite applying vanilla gradient descent from a random starting point (top panel) is ensnared by a local minimum of cost (middle panel). By turning to stochastic gradient descent in the bottom panel, the daring trilobite is able to bypass the local minimum and make its way toward the global minimum.

Like the learning rate hyperparameter η, there is also a Goldilocks-style sweet spot for batch size. If the batch size is too large, the estimate of the gradient of the cost function is far more accurate. In this way, the trilobite has a more exacting impression of the gradient in its immediate vicinity and is able to take a step (proportional to η) in the direction of the steepest possible descent. However, the model is at risk of becoming trapped in local minima as described in the preceding paragraph.[13] Besides that, the model might not fit in memory on your machine, and the compute time per iteration of gradient descent could be very long.

On the other hand, if the batch size is too small, each gradient estimate may be excessively noisy (because a very small subset of the data is being used to estimate the gradient of the entire dataset) and the corresponding path down the mountain will be unnecessarily circuitous; training will take longer because of these erratic gradient descent steps. Furthermore, you're not taking advantage of the memory and compute resources on your

---

13. It's worth noting that the learning rate η plays a role here. If the size of the local minimum was *smaller* than the step size, the trilobite would likely breeze right past the local minimum, akin to how we step over cracks in the sidewalk.

machine.[14] With that in mind, here are our rules of thumb for finding the batch-size sweet spot:

- Start with a batch size of 32.
- If the mini-batch is too large to fit into memory on your machine, try decreasing your batch size by powers of 2 (e.g., from 32 to 16).
- If your model trains well (i.e., cost is going down consistently) but each epoch is taking very long and you are aware that you have RAM to spare,[15] you could experiment with increasing your batch size. To avoid getting trapped in local minima, we don't recommend going beyond 128.

Backpropagation

Although stochastic gradient descent operates well on its own to adjust parameters and minimize cost in many types of machine learning models, for deep learning models in particular there is an extra hurdle: We need to be able to efficiently adjust parameters *through multiple layers* of artificial neurons. To do this, stochastic gradient descent is partnered up with a technique called *backpropagation*.

Backpropagation—or backprop for short—is an elegant application of the "chain rule" from calculus.[16] As shown along the bottom of Figure 7.6 and as suggested by its very name, backpropagation courses through a neural network in the opposite direction of forward propagation. Whereas forward propagation carries information about the input x through successive layers of neurons to approximate y with $\hat{y}$, backpropagation carries information about the cost C *backwards* through the layers in reverse order and, with the overarching aim of reducing cost, adjusts neuron parameters throughout the network.

Although the nitty-gritty of backpropagation has been relegated to Appendix B, it's worth understanding (in broad strokes) what the backpropagation algorithm does: Any given neural network model is randomly initialized with parameter (w and b) values (such initialization is detailed in Chapter 7). Thus, prior to any training, when the first x value is fed in, the network outputs a random guess at $\hat{y}$. This is unlikely to be a good guess, and the cost associated with this random guess will probably be high. At this point, we need to update the weights in order to minimize the cost—the very essence of machine learning. To do this within a neural network, we use backpropagation to calculate the *gradient* of the cost function with respect to each weight in the network.

---

14. Stochastic gradient descent with a batch size of 1 is known as *online learning*. It's worth noting that this is not the fastest method in terms of compute. The matrix multiplication associated with each round of mini-batch training is highly optimized, and so training can be several orders of magnitude quicker when using moderately sized mini-batches relative to online learning.

15. On a Unix-based operating system, including macOS, RAM usage may be assessed by running the top or htop command within a Terminal window.

16. To elucidate the mathematics underlying backpropagation, a fair bit of partial-derivative calculus is necessary. While we encourage the development of an in-depth understanding of the beauty of backprop, we also appreciate that calculus might not be the most appetizing topic for everyone. Thus, we've placed our content on backprop mathematics in Appendix B.

Recall from our mountaineering analogies earlier that the cost function represents a hiking trail, and our trilobite is trying to reach basecamp. At each step along the way, the trilobite finds the gradient (or the slope) of the cost function and moves *down* that gradient. That movement corresponds to a weight update: By adjusting the weight in proportion to the cost function's gradient *with respect to that weight*, backprop adjusts that weight in a direction that reduces the cost.

Reflecting back on the "most important equation" from Figure 6.7 ($w \cdot x + b$), and remembering that neural networks are stacked with information forward propagating through their layers, we can grasp that any given weight in the network contributes to the final $\hat{y}$ output, and thus the cost C. Using backpropagation, we move layer-by-layer backwards through the network, starting at the cost in the output layer, and we find the gradients of every single parameter. A given parameter's gradient can then be used to adjust the parameter up or down (by an increment corresponding to the learning rate η)—whichever of the two directions is associated with a reduction in cost.

We appreciate that this is not the lightest section of this book. If there's only one thing you take away, let it be this: Backpropagation uses cost to calculate the relative contribution by every single parameter to the total cost, and then it updates each parameter accordingly. In this way, the network iteratively reduces cost and, well . . . learns!

Tuning Hidden-Layer Count and Neuron Count

As with learning rate and batch size, the number of hidden layers you add to your neural network is also a hyperparameter. And as with the previous two hyperparameters, there is yet again a Goldilocks sweet spot for your network's count of layers. Throughout this book, we've reiterated that with each additional hidden layer within a deep learning network, the more abstract the representations that the network can represent. That is the primary advantage of adding layers.

The *dis*advantage of adding layers is that backpropagation becomes less effective: As demonstrated by the plot of learning speed across the layers of a five-hidden-layer network in Figure 7.8, backprop is able to have its greatest impact on the parameters of the hidden layer of neurons closest to the output $\hat{y}$.[17] The farther a layer is from $\hat{y}$, the more diluted the effect of that layer's parameters on the overall cost. Thus, the fifth layer, which is closest to the output $\hat{y}$, learns most rapidly because those weights are associated with larger gradients. In contrast, the third hidden layer, which is several layers away from the output layer's cost calculation, learns about an order of magnitude more slowly than the fifth hidden layer.

Given the above, our rules of thumb for selecting the number of hidden layers in a network are:

---

17. If you're curious as to how we made Figure 7.8, check out our *Measuring Speed of Learning* Jupyter notebook.

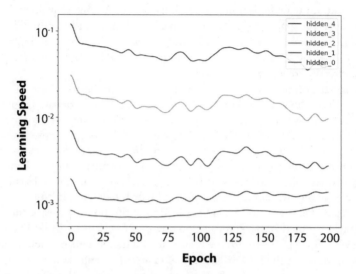

Figure 7.8 The speed of learning over epochs of training for a deep learning network with five hidden layers. The fifth hidden layer, which is closest to the output $\hat{y}$, learns about an order of magnitude more quickly than the third hidden layer.

- The more abstract the ground-truth value y you'd like to estimate with your network, the more helpful additional hidden layers may be. With that in mind, we recommend starting off with about two to four hidden layers.

- If reducing the number of layers does not increase the cost you can achieve on your validation dataset, then do it. Following the problem-solving principle called *Occam's razor*, the simplest network architecture that can provide the desired result is the best; it will train more quickly and require fewer compute resources.

- On the other hand, if increasing the number of layers decreases the validation cost, then you should pile up those layers!

Not only is network depth a model hyperparameter, but the number of neurons in a given layer is, too. If you have many layers in your network, then there are many layers you could be fine-tuning your neuron count in. This may seem intimidating at first, but it's nothing to be too concerned about: A few too many neurons, and your network will have a touch more computational complexity than is necessary; a touch too few neurons, and your network's accuracy may be held back imperceptibly.

As you build and train more and more deep learning models for more and more problems, you'll begin to develop a sense for how many neurons might be appropriate in a given layer. Depending on the particular data you're modeling, there may be lots of low-level features to represent, in which case you might want to have more neurons in the network's early layers. If there are lots of higher-level features to represent, then you may benefit from having additional neurons in its later layers. To determine this empirically, we generally experiment with the neuron count in a given layer by varying it by powers of 2. If doubling the number of neurons from 64 to 128 provides an appreciable improvement in model accuracy, then go for it. Rehashing Occam's razor, however, consider this: If halving the number of neurons from 64 to 32 doesn't detract from model accuracy, then that's probably the way to go because you're reducing your model's computational complexity with no apparent negative effects.

An Intermediate Net in Keras

To wrap up this chapter, let's incorporate the new theory we've covered into a neural network to see if we can outperform our previous *Shallow Net in Keras* model at classifying handwritten digits.

The first few stages of our *Intermediate Net in Keras* Jupyter notebook are identical to those of its *Shallow Net* predecessor. We load the same Keras dependencies, load the MNIST dataset in the same way, and preprocess the data in the same way. As shown in Example 7.1, the situation begins to get interesting when we design our neural network architecture.

Example 7.1 Keras code to architect an intermediate-depth neural network

```
model = Sequential()
model.add(Dense(64, activation='relu', input_shape=(784,)))
model.add(Dense(64, activation='relu'))
model.add(Dense(10, activation='softmax'))
```

The first line of this code chunk, `model = Sequential()`, is the same as before (refer to Example 5.6); this is our instantiation of a neural network model object. It's in the second line that we begin to diverge. In it, we specify that we'll substitute the sigmoid activation function in the first hidden layer with our most-highly-recommended neuron from Chapter 6, the `relu`. Other than this activation function swap, the first hidden layer remains the same: It still consists of **64** neurons, and the dimensionality of the **784**-neuron input layer is unchanged.

The other significant change in Example 7.1 relative to the shallow architecture of Example 5.6 is that we specify a second hidden layer of artificial neurons. By calling the `model.add()` method, we nearly effortlessly add a second `Dense` layer of 64 `relu` neurons, providing us with the notebook's namesake: an intermediate-depth neural network. With a call to `model.summary()`, you can see from Figure 7.9 that this additional layer corresponds to an additional 4,160 trainable parameters relative to our shallow architecture (refer to Figure 7.5). We can break these parameters down into:

- 4,096 weights, corresponding to each of the 64 neurons in the second hidden layer densely receiving input from each of the 64 neurons in the first hidden layer ($64 \times 64 = 4,096$)

- Plus 64 biases, one for each of the neurons in the second hidden layer

- Giving us a total of 4,160 parameters: $n_{parameters} = n_w + n_b = 4,096 + 64 = 4,160$

In addition to changes to the model architecture, we've also made changes to the parameters we specify when compiling our model, as shown in Example 7.2.

Example 7.2 Keras code to compile our intermediate-depth neural network

```
model.compile(loss='categorical_crossentropy',
              optimizer=SGD(lr=0.1),
              metrics=['accuracy'])
```

Layer (type)	Output Shape	Param #
dense_1 (Dense)	(None, 64)	50240
dense_2 (Dense)	(None, 64)	4160
dense_3 (Dense)	(None, 10)	650

Total params: 55,050
Trainable params: 55,050
Non-trainable params: 0

Figure 7.9   A summary of the model object from our *Intermediate Net in Keras* Jupyter notebook

With these lines from Example 7.2, we:

- Set our loss function to cross-entropy cost by using `loss='categorical_crossentropy'` (in *Shallow Net in Keras*, we used quadratic cost by using `loss='mean_squared_error'`)

- Set our cost-minimizing method to stochastic gradient descent by using `optimizer=SGD`

- Specify our SGD learning rate hyperparameter η by setting `lr=0.1`[18]
- Indicate that, in addition to the Keras default of providing feedback on `loss`, by setting `metrics=['accuracy']`, we'd also like to receive feedback on model accuracy[19]

Finally, we train our intermediate net by running the code in Example 7.3.

Example 7.3 Keras code to train our intermediate-depth neural network

```
model.fit(X_train, y_train,
          batch_size=128, epochs=20,
          verbose=1,
          validation_data=(X_valid, y_valid))
```

Relative to the way we trained our shallow net (see Example 5.7), the only change we've made is reducing our `epochs` hyperparameter from 200 down by an order of magnitude

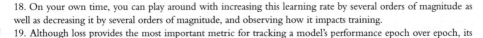
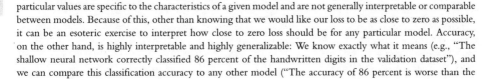

```
Epoch 1/20
60000/60000 [==============================] - 1s 15us/step - loss: 0.4744 - acc: 0.8637 - val_loss: 0.2686 - val_acc: 0.9234
Epoch 2/20
60000/60000 [==============================] - 1s 12us/step - loss: 0.2414 - acc: 0.9289 - val_loss: 0.2004 - val_acc: 0.9404
Epoch 3/20
60000/60000 [==============================] - 1s 12us/step - loss: 0.1871 - acc: 0.9452 - val_loss: 0.1578 - val_acc: 0.9521
Epoch 4/20
60000/60000 [==============================] - 1s 12us/step - loss: 0.1538 - acc: 0.9551 - val_loss: 0.1435 - val_acc: 0.9574
```

Figure 7.10   The performance of our intermediate-depth neural network over its first four epochs of training

to 20. As you'll see, our much-more-efficient intermediate architecture required far fewer epochs to train.

Figure 7.10 provides the results of the first three epochs of training the network. Recalling that our shallow architecture plateaued as it approached 86 percent accuracy on the validation dataset after 200 epochs, our intermediate-depth network is clearly superior: The `val_acc` field shows that we attained 92.34 percent accuracy *after a single epoch of training*. This accuracy climbs to more than 95 percent by the third epoch and appears to plateau around 97.6 percent by the twentieth. My, how far we've come already!

---

18. On your own time, you can play around with increasing this learning rate by several orders of magnitude as well as decreasing it by several orders of magnitude, and observing how it impacts training.

19. Although loss provides the most important metric for tracking a model's performance epoch over epoch, its particular values are specific to the characteristics of a given model and are not generally interpretable or comparable between models. Because of this, other than knowing that we would like our loss to be as close to zero as possible, it can be an esoteric exercise to interpret how close to zero loss should be for any particular model. Accuracy, on the other hand, is highly interpretable and highly generalizable: We know exactly what it means (e.g., "The shallow neural network correctly classified 86 percent of the handwritten digits in the validation dataset"), and we can compare this classification accuracy to any other model ("The accuracy of 86 percent is worse than the accuracy of our deep neural network").

Let's break down the verbose `model.fit()` output shown in Figure 7.10 in further detail:

- The progress bar shown next fills in over the course of the 469 "rounds of training" (Figure 7.5):
  60000/60000 [==============================]
- `1s 15us/step` indicates that all 469 rounds in the first epoch required 1 second to train, at an average rate of 15 microseconds per round.
- `loss` shows the average cost on our training data for the epoch. For the first epoch this is 0.4744, and, epoch over epoch, this cost is reliably minimized via stochastic gradient descent (SGD) and backpropagation, eventually diminishing to 0.0332 by the twentieth epoch.
- `acc` is the classification accuracy on training data for the epoch. The model correctly classified 86.37 percent for the first epoch, increasing to more than 99 percent by the twentieth. Because a model can overfit to the training data, one shouldn't be overly impressed by high accuracy on the training data.
- Thankfully, our cost on the validation dataset (`val_loss`) does generally decrease as well, eventually plateauing as it approaches 0.08 over the final five epochs of training.
- Corresponding to the decreasing cost of the validation data is an increase in accuracy (`val_acc`). As mentioned, validation accuracy plateaued at about 97.6 percent, which is a vast improvement over the 86 percent of our shallow net.

Starting from an appreciation of how a neural network with fixed parameters processes information, we developed an understanding of the cooperating methods—cost functions, stochastic gradient descent, and backpropagation—that enable network parameters to be learned so that we can approximate any y that has a continuous relationship to some input x. Along the way, we introduced several network hyperparameters, including learning rate, mini-batch size, and number of epochs of training—as well as our rules of thumb for configuring each of these. The chapter concluded by applying your newfound knowledge to develop an intermediate-depth neural network that greatly outperformed our previous, shallow network on the same handwritten-digit-classification task. Up next, we have techniques for improving the stability of artificial neural networks as they deepen, enabling you to architect and train a bona fide deep learning model for the first time.

In the forthcoming section, we arranged these neural units together as the nodes of a network, enabling the forward propagation of some input x through the network to produce some output $\hat{y}$. Most recently, in Chapter 7, we described how to quantify the inaccuracies of a network (compare $\hat{y}$ to the true y with a cost function) as well as how to minimize these inaccuracies (adjust the network parameters w and b via optimization with stochastic gradient descent and backpropagation).

In this chapter, we cover common barriers to the creation of high-performing neural networks and techniques that overcome them. We apply these ideas directly in code while architecting our first deep neural n etwork.[20] Combining this additional network depth with our newfound best practices, we'll see if we can outperform the handwritten-digit classification accuracy of our simpler, shallower architectures from previous chapters.

Weight Initialization

In Chapter 7, we introduced the concept of neuron saturation (see Figure 7.1), where very low or very high values of z diminish the capacity for a given neuron to learn. At the time, we offered cross-entropy cost as a solution. Although cross-entropy does effectively attenuate the effects of neuron saturation, pairing it with thoughtful *weight initialization* will reduce the likelihood of saturation occurring in the first place. As mentioned in a footnote in Chapter 1, modern weight initialization provided a significant leap forward in deep learning capability: It is one of the landmark theoretical advances between LeNet-5 (Figure 1.11) and AlexNet (Figure 1.17) that dramatically broadened the range of problems artificial neural networks could reliably solve. In this section, we play around with several weight initializations to help you develop an intuition around how they're so impactful.

While describing neural network training in Chapter 7, we mentioned that the parameters w and b are initialized with random values such that a network's starting approxi-mation of y will be far off the mark, thereby leading to a high initial cost C. We haven't needed to dwell on this much, because, in the background, Keras by default constructs TensorFlow models that are initialized with sensible values for w and b. It's neverthe-less worthwhile discussing this initialization, not only to be aware of another method for avoiding neuron saturation but also to fill in a gap in your understanding of how neural network training works. Although Keras does a sensible job of choosing default values—and that's a key benefit of using Keras in the first place—it's certainly possible, and sometimes even necessary, to change these defaults to suit your problem.

---

20. Recall from Chapter 4 that a neural network earns the *deep* moniker if it consists of at least three hidden layers.

To make this section interactive, we encourage you to check out our accompanying Jupyter notebook, *Weight Initialization*. As shown in the following chunk of code, our library dependencies are NumPy (for numerical operations), matplotlib (for generating plots), and a handful of Keras methods, which we will detail as we work through them in this section.

```
import numpy as np
import matplotlib.pyplot as plt
from keras import Sequential
from keras.layers import Dense, Activation
from keras.initializers import Zeros, RandomNormal
from keras.initializers import glorot_normal, glorot_uniform
```

In this notebook, we simulate 784 pixel values as inputs to a single dense layer of artificial neurons. The inspiration behind our simulation of these 784 inputs comes of course from our beloved MNIST digits (Figure 5.3). For the number of neurons in the dense layer (256), we picked a number large enough so that, when we make some plots later on, they have ample data:

```
n_input = 784
n_dense = 256
```

Now for the impetus of this section: the initialization of the network parameters w and b. Before we begin passing training data into our network, we'd like to start with reasonably scaled parameters. This is for two reasons.

1. Large w and b values tend to correspond to larger z values and therefore saturated neurons (see Figure 7.1 for a plot on neuron saturation).
2. Large parameter values would imply that the network has a strong opinion about how x is related to y, but before any training on data has occurred, any such strong opinions are wholly unmerited.

Parameter values of zero, on the other hand, imply the weakest opinion on how x is related to y. To bring back the fairy tale yet again, we're aiming for a Goldilocks-style, middle-of-the-road approach that starts training from a balanced and *learnable* beginning. With that in mind, when we design our neural network architecture, we select the Zeros() method for initializing the neurons of our dense layer with $b = 0$:

```
b_init = Zeros()
```

Following the line of thinking from the preceding paragraph to its natural conclusion, we might be tempted to think that we should also initialize our network weights w
with zeros as well. In fact, this would be a training disaster: If all weights and biases were
identical, many neurons in the network would treat a given input x identically, giving
stochastic gradient descent a minimum of heterogeneity for identifying individual parameter adjustments that might reduce the cost C. It would be more productive to initialize
weights with a range of different values so that each neuron treats a given x uniquely,
thereby providing SGD with a wide variety of starting points for approximating y. By
chance, some of the initial neuron outputs may contribute in part to a sensible mapping
from x to y. Although this contribution will be weak at first, SGD can experiment with
it to determine whether it might contribute to a reduction in the cost C between the
predicted $\hat{y}$ and the target y.

As worked through earlier (e.g., in discussion of Figures 6.16 and 7.9), the vast majority
of the parameters in a typical network are weights; relatively few are biases. Thus, it's
acceptable (indeed, it's the most common practice) to initialize biases with zeros, and the
weights with a range of values *near* zero. One straightforward way to generate random
values near zero is to sample from the standard normal distribution[21] as in Example 7.4.

**Example 7.4 Weight initialization with values sampled from standard normal
distribution**

```
w_init = RandomNormal(stddev=1.0)
```

To observe the impact of the weight initialization we've chosen, in Example 7.5 we
design a neural network architecture for our single dense layer of sigmoid neurons.

Example 7.5 Architecture for a single dense layer of sigmoid neurons

```
model = Sequential()
model.add(Dense(n_dense,
                input_dim=n_input,
                kernel_initializer=w_init,
                bias_initializer=b_init))
model.add(Activation('sigmoid'))
```

As in all of our previous examples, we instantiate a model by using `Sequential()`. We
then use the `add()` method to create a single `Dense` layer with the following parameters:

- 256 neurons (n_dense)
- 784 inputs (n_input)
- `kernel_initializer` set to `w_init` to initialize the network weights via our desired approach, in this case sampling from the standard normal distribution
- `bias_initializer` set to `b_init` to initialize the biases with zeros

---

21. The *normal* distribution is also known as the Gaussian distribution or, colloquially, as the "bell curve" because
of its bell-like shape. The *standard normal* distribution in particular is a normal distribution with a mean of 0 and
standard deviation of 1.

For simplicity when updating it later in this section, we add the sigmoid activation function to the layer separately by using `Activation('sigmoid')`.

With our network set up, we use the NumPy `random()` method to generate 784 "pixel values," which are floats randomly sampled from the range $[0.0, 1.0)$:

```
x = np.random.random((1,n_input))
```

We subsequently use the `predict()` method to forward propagate x through the single layer and output the activations **a**:

```
a = model.predict(x)
```

With our final line of code, we use a histogram to visualize the **a** activations:[22]

```
_ = plt.hist(np.transpose(a))
```

Your result will look slightly different from ours because of the `random()` method we used to generate our input values, but your outputs should look approximately like those shown in Figure 7.11.

As expected given Figure 6.9, the **a** activations output from our sigmoid layer of neurons is constrained to a range from 0 to 1. What is undesirable about these activations, however, is that they are chiefly pressed up against the extremes of the range: Most of them are either immediately adjacent to 0 or immediately adjacent to 1. This indicates that with the normal distribution from which we sampled to initialize the layer's weights w, we ended up encouraging our artificial neurons to produce large z values. This is unwelcome for two reasons mentioned earlier in this section:

1. It means the vast majority of the neurons in the layer are saturated.
2. It implies that the neurons have strong opinions about how x would influence y *prior* to any training on data.

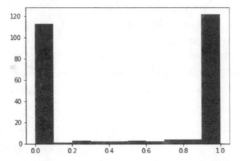

Figure 7.11   Histogram of the *a* activations output by a layer of sigmoid neurons, with weights initialized using a standard normal distribution

---

22. In case you're wondering, the leading underscore (_ =) keeps the Jupyter notebook tidier by outputting the plot only, instead of the plot *as well as* an object that stores the plot.

Thankfully, this ickiness can be resolved by initializing our network weights with values sampled from alternative distributions.

Xavier Glorot Distributions

In deep learning circles, popular distributions for sampling weight-initialization values were devised by Xavier Glorot and Yoshua Bengio[23] (portrait provided in Figure 1.10). These *Glorot distributions*, as they are typically called,[24] are tailored such that sampling from them will lead to neurons initially outputting small *z* values. Let's examine them in action. Replacing the standard-normal-sampling code (Example 7.4) of our *Weight Initialization* notebook with the line in Example 7.6, we sample from the *Glorot normal distribution*[25] instead.

Example 7.6 Weight initialization with values sampled from Glorot normal distribution

```
w_init = glorot_normal()
```

By restarting and rerunning the notebook,[26] you should now observe a distribution of the activations **a** similar to the histogram shown in Figure 7.12.

In stark contrast to Figure 7.11, the **a** activations obtained from our layer of sigmoid neurons is now normally distributed with a mean of ~0.5 and few (if any) values at the

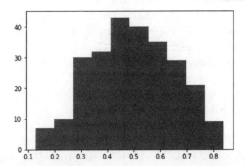

Figure 7.12   Histogram of the *a* activations output by a layer of sigmoid neurons, with weights initialized using the Glorot normal distribution

---

23. Glorot, X., & Bengio, Y. (2010). Understanding the difficulty of training deep feedforward neural networks. *Proceedings of Machine Learning Research, 9,* 249–56.

24. Some folks also refer to them as *Xavier distributions*.

25. The Glorot normal distribution is a truncated normal distribution. It is centered at 0 with a standard deviation of $\sqrt{\frac{2}{n_{in}+n_{out}}}$, where n_{in} is the number of neurons in the preceding layer and n_{out} is the number of neurons in the subsequent layer.

26. Select *Kernel* from the Jupyter notebook menu bar and choose *Restart & Run All*. This ensures you start completely fresh and don't reuse old parameters from the previous run.

extremes of the sigmoid range (i.e., less than 0.1 or greater than 0.9). This is a good starting point for a neural network because now:

1. Few, if any, of the neurons are saturated.
2. It implies that the neurons generally have weak opinions about how x would influence y, which—prior to any training on data—is sensible.

> As demonstrated in this section, one of the potentially confusing aspects of weight initialization is that, if we would like the a values returned by a layer of artificial neurons to be normally distributed (and we do!), we should *not* sample our initial weights from a standard normal distribution.

In addition to the Glorot normal distribution, there is also the *Glorot uniform distribution*.[27] The impact of selecting one of these Glorot distributions over the other when initializing your model weights is generally unnoticeable. You're welcome to rerun the notebook while sampling values from the Glorot uniform distribution by setting w_init equal to glorot_uniform(). Your histogram of activations should come out more or less indistinguishable from Figure 7.12.

By swapping out the sigmoid activation function in Example 7.5 with tanh (Activation('tanh')) or ReLU (Activation('relu')) in the *Weight Initialization* notebook, you can observe the consequences of initializing weights with values sampled from a standard normal distribution relative to a Glorot distribution across a range of activations. As shown in Figure 7.13, regardless of the chosen activation function, weight initialization with the standard normal leads to a activation outputs that are extreme relative to those obtained when initializing with Glorot.

To be sure you're aware of the parameter initialization approach used by Keras, you can delve into the library's documentation on a layer-by-layer basis, but, as we've suggested here, its default configuration is typically to initialize biases with 0 and to initialize weights with a Glorot distribution.

> Glorot initialization is probably the most popular technique for initializing weights, but there are other sensible options such as He initialization[28] and LeCun initialization.[29] In our experience, the difference in outcome when selecting between these weight-initialization techniques is minimal to imperceptible.

---

27. The Glorot uniform distribution is on the range $[-l, l]$ where $l = \sqrt{\frac{6}{n_{in}+n_{out}}}$.

28. He, Y., et al. (2015). Delving deep into rectifiers: Surpassing human-level performance on ImageNet classification. *arXiv: 1502.01852* .

29. LeCun, Y., et al. (1998). Efficient backprop. In G. Montavon et al. (Eds.) *Neural Networks: Tricks of the Trade. Lecture Notes in Computer Science,* 7700 (pp. 355–65). Berlin: Springer.

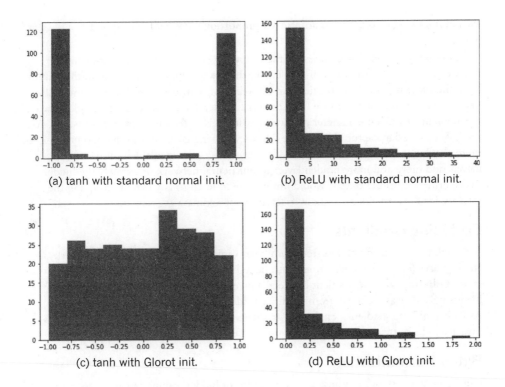

Figure 7.13   The activations output by a dense layer of 256 neurons, while varying activation function (tanh or ReLU) and weight initialization (standard normal or Glorot uniform). Note that while the distributions in (b) and (d) appear comparable at first glance, the standard normal initialization produced large activation values (reaching toward 40) while all the activations resulting from Glorot initialization are below 2.

Unstable Gradients

Another issue associated with artificial neural networks, and one that becomes especially perturbing as we add more hidden layers, is *unstable gradients*. Unstable gradients can either be vanishing or explosive in nature. We cover both varieties in turn here, and then discuss a solution to these issues called batch normalization.

Vanishing Gradients

Recall that using the cost C between the network's predicted $\hat{y}$ and the true y, as depicted in Figure 7.6, backpropagation works its way from the output layer toward the input layer, adjusting network parameters with the aim of minimizing cost. As exemplified by the mountaineering trilobite in Figure 7.2, each of the parameters is adjusted in proportion to its *gradient* with respect to cost: If, for example, the gradient of a parameter (with respect to the cost) is large and positive, this implies that the parameter contributes a *large* amount to the cost, and so *decreasing* it proportionally would correspond to a decrease in cost.[30]

In the hidden layer that is closest to the output layer, the relationship between its parameters and cost is the most direct. The farther away a hidden layer is from the output layer, the more muddled the relationship between its parameters and cost becomes. The impact of this is that, as we move from the final hidden layer toward the first hidden layer, the gradient of a given parameter relative to cost tends to flatten; it gradually *vanishes*. As a result of this, and as captured by Figure 7.8, the farther a layer is from the output layer, the more slowly it tends to learn. Because of this *vanishing gradient* problem, if we were to naïvely add more and more hidden layers to our neural network, eventually the hidden layers farthest from the output would not be able to learn to any extent, crippling the capacity for the network as a whole to learn to approximate y given x.

Exploding Gradients

Although they occur much less frequently than vanishing gradients, certain network architectures (e.g., the recurrent nets introduced in Chapter 8) can induce *exploding gradients*. In this case, the gradient between a given parameter relative to cost becomes increasingly *steep* as we move from the final hidden layer toward the first hidden layer. As with vanishing gradients, exploding gradients can inhibit an entire neural network's capacity to learn by saturating the neurons with extreme values.

Batch Normalization

During neural network training, the distribution of hidden parameters in a layer may gradually move around; this is known as *internal covariate shift*. In fact, this is sort of the point of training: We want the parameters to change in order to learn things about the underlying data. But as the distribution of the weights in a layer changes, the inputs to the next layer might be *shifted* away from an ideal (i.e., normal, as in Figure 7.12) distribution. Enter *batch normalization* (or *batch norm* for short).[31] Batch norm takes the a activations output from the preceding layer, subtracts the batch mean, and divides by the batch standard deviation. This acts to recenter the distribution of the a values with a mean of 0 and a standard deviation of 1 (see Figure 7.14). Thus, if there are any extreme values in the preceding layer, they won't cause exploding or vanishing gradients in the next layer. In addition, batch norm has the following positive effects:

- It allows layers to learn more independently from each other, because large values in one layer won't excessively influence the calculations in the next layer.

- It allows for selection of a higher learning rate—because there are no extreme values in the normalized activations—thus enabling faster learning.

- The layer outputs are normalized to the *batch* mean and standard deviation, and that adds a noise element (especially with smaller batch sizes), which, in turn,

---

30. The change is directly proportional to the negative magnitude of the gradient, scaled by the learning rate η.
31. Ioffe, S., & Szegedy, C. (2015). Batch normalization: Accelerating deep network training by reducing internal covariate shift. *arXiv: 1502.03167.*

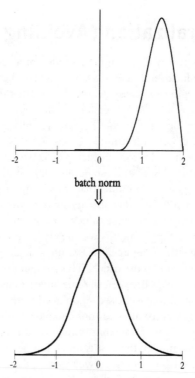

Figure 7.14 Batch normalization transforms the distribution of the activations output by a given layer of neurons toward a standard normal distribution.

contributes to regularization. (Regularization is covered in the next section, but suffice it to say here that regularization helps a network generalize to data it hasn't encountered previously, which is a good thing.)

Batch normalization adds two extra learnable parameters to any given layer it is applied to: γ (gamma) and β (beta). In the final step of batch norm, the outputs are linearly transformed by multiplying by γ and adding β, where γ is analogous to the standard deviation, and β to the mean. (You may notice this is the exact inverse of the operation that normalized the output values in the first place!) However, the output values were originally normalized by the *batch* mean and *batch* standard deviation, whereas γ and β are learned by SGD. We initialize the batch norm layer with $\gamma = 1$ and $\beta = 0$, and thus at the start of training this linear transformation makes no changes; batch norm is allowed to normalize the outputs as intended. As the network learns, though, it may determine that *denormalizing* any given layer's activations is optimal for reducing cost. In this way, if batch norm is not helpful the network will *learn* to stop using it on a layer-by-layer basis. Indeed, because γ and β are continuous variables, the network can decide *to what degree* it would like to denormalize the outputs, depending on what works best to minimize the cost. Pretty neat!

Model Generalization (Avoiding Overfitting)

In Chapter 7, we mention that after training a model for a certain number of epochs the cost calculated on the validation dataset—which may have been decreasing nicely over earlier epochs—could begin to increase despite the fact that the cost calculated on the *training* dataset is still decreasing. This situation—when training cost continues to go down while validation cost goes up—is formally known as *overfitting*.

We illustrate the concept of overfitting in Figure 7.15. Notice we have the same data points scattered along the x and y axes in each panel. We can imagine that there is some underlying distribution that describes these points, and we show a sampling from that distribution. Our goal is to generate a model that explains the relationship between x and y but, perhaps most importantly, one that also *approximates* the original distribution; in this way, the model will be able to generalize to new data points drawn from the distribution and not just model the sampling of points we already have.

In the first panel (top left) of Figure 7.15, we use a single-parameter model, which is limited to fitting a straight line to the data.[32] This straight line *underfits* the data: The cost (represented by the vertical gaps between the line and the data points) is high, and the model would not generalize well to new data points. In other words, the line *misses* most of the points because this kind of model is not complex enough. In the next panel (top right), we use a model with two parameters, which fits a parabola-shaped curve to the data.[33] With this parabolic model, the cost is much lower relative to the linear model, and it appears the model would also generalize well to new data—great!

In the third panel (bottom left) of Figure 7.15, we use a model with too many parameters—more parameters than we have data points. With this approach we reduce the cost associated with our training data points to nil: There is no perceptible gap between the curve and the data. In the last panel (bottom right), however, we show new data points from the original distribution in green, which were unseen by the model during training and so can be used to validate the model. Despite eliminating *training* cost entirely, the model fits these validation data poorly and so it results in a significant validation cost. The many-parameter model, dear friends, is overfit: It is a perfect model for the training data, but it doesn't actually capture the relationship between x and y well; rather, it has learned the exact features of the training data too closely, and it subsequently performs poorly on unseen data.

Consider how in three lines of code in Example 5.6, we created a shallow neural network architecture with more than 50,000 parameters (Figure 7.5). Given this, it should not be surprising that deep learning architectures regularly have millions of parameters.[34] Working with datasets that have such a large number of parameters but with perhaps only thousands of training samples could be a recipe for severe overfitting.[35] Because we yearn to capitalize on deep, sophisticated network architectures even if we don't have oodles

---

32. This models a linear relationship, the simplest form of regression between two variables.
33. Recall the quadratic function from high school algebra.
34. Indeed, as early as Chapter 9, you'll encounter models with tens of millions of parameters.
35. This circumstance can be annotated as $n \gg p$, indicating the *n*umber of samples is much greater than the parameter count.

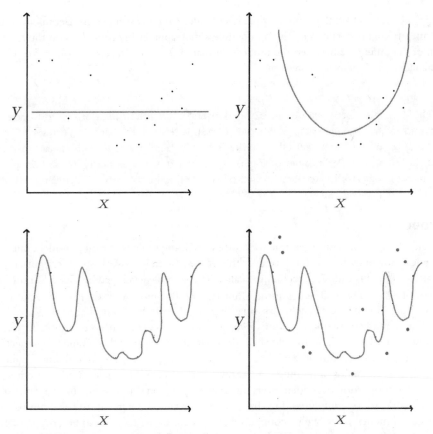

Figure 7.15   Fitting *y* given *x* using models with varying numbers of parameters. Top left: A single-parameter model underfits the data. Top right: A two-parameter model fits a parabola that suits the relationship between *x* and *y* well. Bottom left: A many-parameter model overfits the data, generalizing poorly to new data points (shown in green in the bottom-right panel).

of data at hand, thankfully we can rely on techniques specifically designed to reduce overfitting. In this section, we cover three of the best-known such techniques: L1/L2 regularization, dropout, and data augmentation.

L1 and L2 Regularization

In branches of machine learning other than deep learning, the use of *L1* or *L2 regularization* to reduce overfitting is prevalent. These techniques—which are alternately known as *LASSO*[36] *regression* and *ridge regression*, respectively—both penalize models for including parameters by adding the parameters to the model's cost function. The larger a

---

36. Least absolutely shrinkage and selection operator

given parameter's size, the more that parameter adds to the cost function. Because of this, parameters are not retained by the model unless they appreciably contribute to the reduction of the difference between the model's estimated $\hat{y}$ and the true y. In other words, extraneous parameters are pared away.

> The distinction between L1 and L2 regularization is that L1's additions to cost correspond to the absolute value of parameter sizes, whereas L2's additions correspond to the *square* of these. The net effect of this is that L1 regularization tends to lead to the inclusion of a smaller number of larger-sized parameters in the model, while L2 regularization tends to lead to the inclusion of a larger number of smaller-sized parameters.

Dropout

L1 and L2 regularization work fine to reduce overfitting in deep learning models, but deep learning practitioners tend to favor the use of a neural-network-specific regularization technique instead. This technique, called *dropout*, was developed by Geoff Hinton (Figure 1.16) and his colleagues at the University of Toronto[37] and was made famous by its incorporation in their benchmark-smashing AlexNet architecture (Figure 1.17).

Hinton and his coworkers' intuitive yet powerful concept for preventing overfitting is captured by Figure 7.16. In a nutshell, dropout simply *pretends* that a randomly selected proportion of the neurons in each layer *don't exist* during each round of training. To illustrate this, three rounds of training[38] are shown in the figure. For each round, we remove a specified proportion of hidden layers by random selection. For the first hidden layer of the network, we've configured it to drop out one-third (33.3 percent) of the neurons. For the second hidden layer, we've configured 50 percent of the neurons to be dropped out. Let's cover the three training rounds shown in Figure 7.16:

1. In the top panel, the second neuron of the first hidden layer and the first neuron of the second hidden layer are randomly dropped out.
2. In the middle panel, it is the first neuron of the first hidden layer and the second one of the second hidden layer that are selected for dropout. There is no "memory" of which neurons have been dropped out on previous training rounds, and so it is by chance alone that the neurons dropped out in the second round are distinct from those dropped out in the first.
3. In the bottom panel, the third neuron of the first hidden layer is dropped out for the first time. For the second consecutive round of training, the second neuron of the second hidden layer is also randomly selected.

Instead of reining in parameter sizes toward zero (as with batch normalization), dropout doesn't (directly) constrain how large a given parameter value can become. Dropout is nevertheless an effective regularization technique, because it prevents any

---

37. Hinton, G., et al. (2012). Improving neural networks by preventing co-adaptation of feature detectors. *arXiv:1207.0580.*

38. If the phrase *round of training* is not immediately familiar, refer to Figure 8.5 for a refresher.

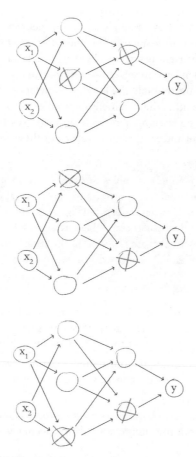

Figure 7.16   Dropout, a technique for reducing model overfitting, involves the removal of randomly selected neurons from a network's hidden layers in each round of training. Three rounds of training with dropout are shown here.

single neuron from becoming excessively influential within the network: Dropout makes it challenging for some very specific aspect of the training dataset to create an overly specific forward-propagation pathway through the network because, on any given round of training, neurons along that pathway could be removed. In this way, the model doesn't become overreliant on certain features of the data to generate a good prediction.

When validating a neural network model that was trained using dropout, or indeed when making real-world inferences with such a network, we must take an extra step first. During validation or inference, we would like to leverage the power of the full network, that is, its total complement of neurons. The snag is that, during training, we only ever used a subset of the neurons to forward propagate x through the network and estimate $\hat{y}$. If we were to naïvely carry out this forward propagation with suddenly *all* of the neurons, our $\hat{y}$ would emerge befuddled: There are now too many parameters, and the totals after all the mathematical operations would be larger than expected. To compensate for the additional neurons, we must correspondingly adjust our neuron parameters downward. If we had, say, dropped out half of the neurons in a hidden layer during training, then we would need to multiply the layer's parameters by 0.5 prior to validation or inference. As a second example, for a hidden layer in which we dropped out 33.3 percent of the neurons during training, we then must multiply the layer's parameters by 0.667 prior to validation.[39] Thankfully, Keras handles this parameter-adjustment process for us automatically. When working in other deep learning libraries (e.g., low-level TensorFlow), however, you may need to be mindful and remember to carry out these adjustments yourself.

If you're familiar with creating ensembles of statistical models (e.g., a single random forest out of multiple random decision trees), then it may already be evident to you that dropout produces such an ensemble. During each round of training, a random subnetwork is created, and its parameter values are tuned. Later, at the conclusion of training, all of these subnetworks are reflected in the parameter values throughout the final network. In this way, the final network is an aggregated *ensemble* of its constituent subnetworks.

As with learning rate and mini-batch size (discussed in Chapter 7), network architecture options pertaining to dropout are hyperparameters. Here are our rules of thumb for choosing which layers to apply dropout to and how much of it to apply:

- If your network is overfitting to your training data (i.e., your validation cost increases while your training cost goes down), then dropout is warranted somewhere in the network.

- Even if your network isn't obviously overfitting to your training data, adding some dropout to the network may improve validation accuracy—especially in later epochs of training.

- Applying dropout to *all* of the hidden layers in your network may be overkill. If your network has a fair bit of depth, it may be sufficient to apply dropout solely to later layers in the network (the earliest layers may be harmlessly identifying features). To test this out, you could begin by applying dropout only to the final hidden layer and observing whether this is sufficient for curtailing overfitting; if not, add dropout to the next deepest layer, test it, and so on.

- If your network is struggling to reduce validation cost or to recapitulate low validation costs attained when less dropout was applied, then you've added too much dropout—pare it back! As with other hyperparameters, there is a Goldilocks zone for dropout, too.

- With respect to *how much* dropout to apply to a given layer, each network behaves uniquely and so some experimentation is required. In our experience, dropping out 20 percent up to 50 percent of the hidden-layer neurons in machine vision applications tends to provide the highest validation accuracies. In natural language

---

39. Put another way, if the probability of a given neuron being retained during training is p, then we multiply that neuron's parameters by p prior to carrying out model validation or inference.

applications, where individual words and phrases can convey particular significance, we have found that dropping out a smaller proportion—between 20 percent and 30 percent of the neurons in a given hidden layer—tends to be optimal.

Data Augmentation

In addition to regularizing your model's parameters to reduce overfitting, another approach is to increase the size of your training dataset. If it is possible to inexpensively collect additional high-quality training data for the particular modeling problem you're working on, then you should do so! The more data provided to a model during training, the better the model will be able to generalize to unseen validation data.

In many cases, collecting fresh data is a pipe dream. It may nevertheless be possible to generate new training data from existing data by augmenting it, thereby artificially expanding your training dataset. With the MNIST digits, for example, many different types of transforms would yield training samples that constitute suitable handwritten digits, such as:

- Skewing the image
- Blurring the image
- Shifting the image a few pixels
- Applying random noise to the image
- Rotating the image slightly

Indeed, as shown on the personal website of Yann LeCun (see Figure 1.9 for a portrait), many of the record-setting MNIST validation dataset classifiers took advantage of such artificial training dataset expansion.[40],[41]

Fancy Optimizers

So far in this book we've used only one optimization algorithm: stochastic gradient descent. Although SGD performs well, researchers have devised shrewd ways to improve it.

Momentum

The first SGD improvement is to consider *momentum*. Here's an analogy of the principle: Let's imagine it's winter and our intrepid trilobite is skiing down a snowy gradient-mountain. If a local minimum is encountered (as in the middle panel of Figure 7.7), the momentum of the trilobite's movement down the slippery hill will keep it moving, and the minimum will be easily bypassed. In this way, the gradients on *previous* steps have influenced the current step.

We calculate momentum in SGD by taking a moving average of the gradients for each parameter and using that to update the weights in each step. When using momentum, we have the additional hyperparameter β (beta), which ranges from 0 to 1, and which controls how many previous gradients are incorporated in the moving average. Small β

---

40. yann.lecun.com/exdb/mnist
41. We will use Keras data-augmentation tools on actual images of hot dogs in Chapter 9.

values permit older gradients to contribute to the moving average, something that can be unhelpful; the trilobite wouldn't want the steepest part of the hill to guide its speed as it approaches the lodge for its après-ski drinks. Typically we'd use larger β values, with $\beta = 0.9$ serving as a reasonable default.

Nesterov Momentum

Another version of momentum is called *Nesterov momentum*. In this approach, the moving average of the gradients is *first* used to update the weights and find the gradients at whatever that position may be; this is equivalent to a quick peek at the position where momentum might take us. We then use the gradients from this sneak-peek position to execute a gradient step *from our original position*. In other words, our trilobite is suddenly aware of its speed down the hill, so it's taking that into account, guessing where its own momentum might be taking it, and then adjusting its course before it even gets there.

AdaGrad

Although both momentum approaches improve SGD, a shortcoming is that they both use a single learning rate η for all parameters. Imagine, if you will, that we could have an individual learning rate for each parameter, thus enabling those parameters that have already reached their optimum to slow or halt learning, while those that are far from their optima can keep going. Well, you're in luck! That's exactly what can be achieved with the other optimizers we'll discuss in this section: AdaGrad, AdaDelta, RMSProp, and Adam.

The name *AdaGrad* comes from "adaptive gradient."[42] In this variation, every parameter has a unique learning rate that scales depending on the importance of that feature. This is especially useful for sparse data where some features occur only rarely: When those features do occur, we'd like to make larger updates of their parameters. We achieve this individualization by maintaining a matrix of the sum of squares of the past gradients for each parameter, and dividing the learning rate by its square root. AdaGrad is the first introduction to the parameter ϵ (epsilon), which is a doozy: Epsilon is a smoothing factor to avoid divide-by-zero errors and can safely be left at its default value of $\epsilon = 1 \times 10^{-8}$.[43]

A significant benefit of AdaGrad is that it minimizes the need to tinker with the learning rate hyperparameter η. You can generally just set-it-and-forget-it at its default of $\eta = 0.01$. A considerable downside of AdaGrad is that, as the matrix of past gradients increases in size, the learning rate is increasingly divided by a larger and larger value, which eventually renders the learning rate impractically small and so learning essentially stops.

AdaDelta and RMSProp

AdaDelta resolves the gradient-matrix-size shortcoming of AdaGrad by maintaining a *moving average* of previous gradients in the same manner that momentum does.[44]

---

42. Duchi, J., et al. (2011). Adaptive subgradient methods for online learning and stochastic optimization. *Journal of Machine Learning Research, 12,* 2121–59.
43. AdaGrad, AdaDelta, RMSProp, and Adam all use ϵ for the same purpose, and it can be left at its default across all of these methods.
44. Zeiler, M.D. (2012). ADADELTA: An adaptive learning rate method. *arXiv:1212.5701.*

AdaDelta also eliminates the η term, so a learning rate doesn't need to be configured at all.[45]

RMSProp (root mean square propagation) was developed by Geoff Hinton (see Figure 1.16 for a portrait) at about the same time as AdaDelta.[46] It works similarly except it retains the learning rate η parameter. Both RMSProp and AdaDelta involve an extra hyperparameter ρ (rho), or decay rate, which is analogous to the β value from momentum and which guides the size of the window for the moving average. Recommended values for the hyperparameters are $\rho = 0.95$ for both optimizers, and setting $\eta = 0.001$ for RMSProp.

Adam

The final optimizer we discuss in this section is also the one we employ most often in the book. *Adam*—short for adaptive moment estimation—builds on the optimizers that came before it.[47] It's essentially the RMSProp algorithm with two exceptions:

1. An extra moving average is calculated, this time of past gradients for each parameter (called the average first moment of the gradient,[48] or simply the mean) and this is used to inform the update instead of the actual gradients at that point.
2. A clever bias trick is used to help prevent these moving averages from skewing toward zero at the start of training.

Adam has two β hyperparameters, one for each of the moving averages that are calculated. Recommended defaults are $\beta_1 = 0.9$ and $\beta_2 = 0.999$. The learning rate default with Adam is $\eta = 0.001$, and you can generally leave it there.

Because RMSProp, AdaDelta, and Adam are so similar, they can be used interchangeably in similar applications, although the bias correction may help Adam later in training. Even though these newfangled optimizers are in vogue, there is still a strong case for simple SGD with momentum (or Nesterov momentum), which in some cases performs better. As with other aspects of deep learning models, you can experiment with optimizers and observe what works best for your particular model architecture and problem.

A Deep Neural Network in Keras

We can now sound the trumpet, because we're reached a momentous milestone! With the additional theory we've covered in this chapter, you have enough knowledge under your

---

45. This is achieved through a crafty mathematical trick that we don't think is worth expounding on here. You may notice, however, that Keras and TensorFlow still have a learning rate parameter in their implementations of AdaDelta. In those cases, it is recommended to leave η at 1, that is, no scaling and therefore no functional learning rate as you have come to know it in this book.

46. This optimizer remains unpublished. It was first proposed in Lecture 6e of Hinton's Coursera Course "Neural Networks for Machine Learning" (www.cs.toronto.edu/~hinton/coursera/lecture6/lec6.pdf).

47. Kingma, D.P., & Ba, J. (2014). Adam: A method for stochastic optimization. *arXiv:1412.6980*.

48. The other moving average is of the squares of the gradient, which is the second moment of the gradient, or the variance.

belt to competently design and train a deep learning model. If you'd like to follow along interactively as we do so, pop into the accompanying *Deep Net in Keras* Jupyter notebook. Relative to our shallow and intermediate-depth model notebooks (refer to Example 5.1), we have a pair of additional dependencies—namely, dropout and batch normalization—as provided in Example 7.7.

Example 7.7 Additional dependencies for deep net in Keras

```
from keras.layers import Dropout
from keras.layers.normalization import BatchNormalization
```

We load and preprocess the MNIST data in the same way as previously. As shown in Example 7.8, it's the neural network architecture cell where we begin to diverge.

Example 7.8 Deep net in Keras model architecture

```
model = Sequential()

model.add(Dense(64, activation='relu', input_shape=(784,)))
model.add(BatchNormalization())

model.add(Dense(64, activation='relu'))
model.add(BatchNormalization())

model.add(Dense(64, activation='relu'))
model.add(BatchNormalization())
model.add(Dropout(0.2))

model.add(Dense(10, activation='softmax'))
```

As before, we instantiate a `Sequential` model object. After we add our first hidden layer to it, however, we also add a `BatchNormalization()` layer. In doing this we are not adding an actual layer replete with neurons, but rather we're adding the batch-norm transformation for the activations *a* from the layer before (the first hidden layer). As with the first hidden layer, we also add a `BatchNormalization()` layer atop the second hidden layer of neurons. Our output layer is identical to the one used in the shallow and intermediate-depth nets, but to create an honest-to-goodness *deep* neural network, we are further adding a third hidden layer of neurons. As with the preceding hidden layers, the third hidden layer consists of **64** batch-normalized `relu` neurons. We are, however, supplementing this final hidden layer with `Dropout`, set to remove one-fifth (0.2) of the layer's neurons during each round of training.

As captured in Example 7.9, the only other change relative to our intermediate-depth network is that we use the Adam optimizer (`optimizer='adam'`) in place of ordinary SGD optimization.

Example 7.9 Deep net in Keras model compilation

```
model.compile(loss='categorical_crossentropy',
              optimizer='adam',
              metrics=['accuracy'])
```

Note that we need not supply any hyperparameters to the Adam optimizer, because Keras automatically includes all the sensible defaults we detailed in the preceding section. For all of the other optimizers we covered, Keras (and TensorFlow, for that matter) has implementations that can easily be dropped in in place of ordinary SGD or Adam. You can refer to the documentation for those libraries online to see exactly how it's done.

When we call the fit() method on our model,[49] we discover that our digestion of all the additional theory in this chapter paid off: With our intermediate-depth network, our validation accuracy plateaued around 97.6 percent, but our deep net attained 97.87 percent validation accuracy following 15 epochs of training (see Figure 7.17), shaving away 11 percent of our already-small error rate. To squeeze even more juice out of the error-rate lemon than that, we're going to need machine-vision-specific neuron layers such as those introduced in the upcoming Chapter 9.

Regression

In Chapter 4, when discussing supervised learning problems, we mentioned that these can involve either classification or regression. In this book, nearly all our models are used for classifying inputs into one category or another. In this section, however, we depart from that tendency and highlight how to adapt neural network models to regression tasks—that is, any problem where you'd like to predict some continuous variable. Examples of regression problems include predicting the future price of a stock, forecasting how many centimeters of rain may fall tomorrow, and modeling how many sales to expect of a particular product. In this section, we use a neural network and a classic dataset to estimate the price of housing near Boston, Massachusetts, in the 1970s.

Our dependencies, as shown in our *Regression in Keras* notebook, are provided in Example 7.10. The only unfamiliar dependency is the boston_housing dataset, which is conveniently bundled into the Keras library.

```
Epoch 15/20
60000/60000 [==============================] - 1s 23us/step - loss: 0.0288 - acc: 0.9906 - val_loss: 0.0865 - val_acc: 0.9787
Epoch 16/20
60000/60000 [==============================] - 1s 22us/step - loss: 0.0246 - acc: 0.9919 - val_loss: 0.0880 - val_acc: 0.9767
```

Figure 7.17   Our deep neural network architecture peaked at a 97.87 percent validation following 15 epochs of training, besting the accuracy of our shallow and intermediate-depth architectures. Because of the randomness of network initialization and training, you may obtain a slightly lower or a slightly higher accuracy with the identical architecture.

---

49. This model.fit() step is exactly the same as for our *Intermediate Net in Keras* notebook, that is, Example 7.3.

Example 7.10 Regression model dependencies

```
from keras.datasets import boston_housing
from keras.models import Sequential
from keras.layers import Dense, Dropout
from keras.layers.normalization import BatchNormalization
```

Loading the data is as simple as with the MNIST digits:

```
(X_train, y_train), (X_valid, y_valid) = boston_housing.load_data()
```

Calling the `shape` parameter of X_train and X_valid, we find that there are 404 training cases and 102 validation cases. For each case—a distinct area of the Boston suburbs—we have 13 predictor variables related to building age, mean number of rooms, crime rate, the local student-to-teacher ratio, and so on.[50] The median house price (in thousands of dollars) for each area is provided in the y variables. As an example, the first case in the training set has a median house price of $15,200.[51]

The network architecture we built for house-price prediction is provided in Example 7.11.

Example 7.11 Regression model network architecture

```
model = Sequential()

model.add(Dense(32, input_dim=13, activation='relu'))
model.add(BatchNormalization())

model.add(Dense(16, activation='relu'))
model.add(BatchNormalization())
model.add(Dropout(0.2))

model.add(Dense(1, activation='linear'))
```

Reasoning that with only 13 input values and a few hundred training cases we would gain little from a deep neural network with oodles of neurons in each layer, we opted for a two-hidden-layer architecture consisting of merely 32 and 16 neurons per layer. We applied batch normalization and a touch of dropout to avoid overfitting to the particular cases of the training dataset. *Most critically*, in the output layer we set the `activation` argument to `linear`—the option to go with when you'd like to predict a continuous variable, as we do when performing regression. The linear activation function outputs z directly so that the network's $\hat{y}$ can be any numeric value (representing, e.g., dollars,

---

50. You can read more about the data by referring to the article they were originally published in: Harrison, D., & Rubinfeld, D. L. (1978). Hedonic prices and the demand for clean air. *Journal of Environmental Economics and Management, 5*, 81–102.
51. Running y_train[0] returns 15.2.

centimeters) instead of being squashed into a probability between 0 and 1 (as happens when you use the sigmoid or softmax activation functions).

When compiling the model (see Example 7.12), another regression-specific adjustment we made is using mean squared error (MSE) in place of cross-entropy (loss='mean_squared_error'). While we've used cross-entropy cost exclusively so far in this book, that cost function is specifically designed for classification problems, in which $\hat{y}$ is a probability. For regression problems, where the output is inherently *not* a probabilty, we use MSE instead.[52]

Example 7.12 Compiling a regression model

```
model.compile(loss='mean_squared_error', optimizer='adam')
```

You may have noticed that we left out the accuracy metric when compiling this time around. This is deliberate: There's no point in calculating accuracy, because this metric (the percentage of cases classified correctly) isn't relevant to continuous variables as it is with categorical ones.[53]

Fitting our model (as in Example 7.13) is one step that is no different from classification.

Example 7.13 Fitting a regression model

```
model.fit(X_train, y_train,
          batch_size=8, epochs=32, verbose=1,
          validation_data=(X_valid, y_valid))
```

We trained for 32 epochs because, in our experience with this particular model, training for longer produced no lower validation losses. We didn't spend any time optimizing the batch-size hyperparameter, so there could be small accuracy gains to be made by varying it.

During our particular run of the regression model, our lowest validation loss (25.7) was attained in the 22nd epoch. By our final (32nd) epoch, this loss had risen considerably to 56.5 (for comparison, we had a validation loss of 56.6 after just one epoch). In Chapter 8, we demonstrate how to save your model parameters after each epoch of training so that the best-performing epoch can be reloaded later, but for the time being we're stuck with the relatively crummy parameters from the final epoch. In any event, if you'd like to see specific examples of model house-price inferences given some particular input data, you can do this by running the code provided in Example 7.14.[54]

---

52. There are other cost functions applicable to regression problems, such as mean absolute error (MAE) and Huber loss, although these aren't covered in this book. MSE should serve you well enough.

53. It's also helpful to remember that, generally, accuracy is used only to set our minds at ease about how well our models are performing. The model itself learns from the cost, not the accuracy.

54. Note that we had to use the NumPy reshape method to pass in the 13 predictor variables of the 43rd case as a row-oriented array of values ([1, 13]) as opposed to as a column.

Example 7.14 Predicting the median house price in a particular suburb of Boston

```
model.predict(np.reshape(X_valid[42], [1, 13]))
```

This returned for us a predicted median house price ($\hat{y}$) of $20,880 for the 43rd Boston suburb in the validation dataset. The actual median price (y; which can be output by calling y_valid[42]) is $14,100.

TensorBoard

When evaluating the performance of your model epoch over epoch, it can be tedious and time-consuming to read individual results numerically, as we did after running the code in Example 7.13 particularly if the model has been training for many epochs. Instead, TensorBoard (Figure 7.18) is a convenient, graphical tool for:

- Visually tracking model performance in real time
- Reviewing historical model performances
- Comparing the performance of various model architectures and hyperparameter settings applied to fitting the same data

TensorBoard comes automatically with the TensorFlow library, and instructions for getting it up and running are available via the TensorFlow site.[55] It's generally straightforward to set up. Provided here, for example, is a procedure that adapts our *Deep Net in Keras* notebook for TensorBoard use on a Unix-based operating system, including macOS:

1. As shown in Example 7.15 change your Python code as follows:[56]
   a. Import the TensorBoard dependency from keras.callbacks.
   b. Instantiate a TensorBoard object (we'll call it tensorboard), and specify a new, unique directory name (e.g., deep-net) that you'd like to create and have TensorBoard log data written into for this particular run of model-fitting:
   ```
   tensorboard = TensorBoard(log_dir='logs/deep-net')
   ```
   c. Pass the TensorBoard object as a callback parameter to the fit() method:
   ```
   callbacks = [tensorboard]
   ```
2. In your terminal, run the following:[57]
   ```
   tensorboard --logdir='logs/deep-net' --port 6006
   ```
3. Navigate to localhost:6006 in your favorite web browser.

---

55. tensorflow.org/guide/summaries_and_tensorboard
56. This is also laid out in our *Deep Net in Keras with TensorBoard* notebook.
57. Note: We specified the same logging directory location that the TensorBoard object was set to use in step 1b. Since we specified a relative path and not an absolute path for our logging directory, we need to be mindful to run the tensorboard command from the same directory as our *Deep Net in Keras with TensorBoard* notebook.

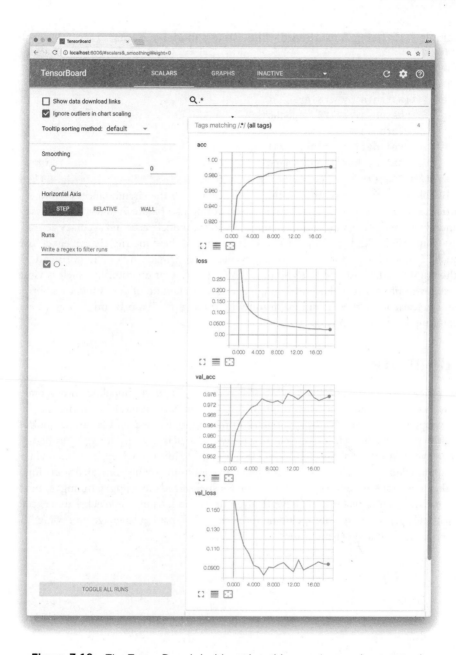

Figure 7.18 The TensorBoard dashboard enables you to, epoch over epoch, visually track your model's cost (`loss`) and accuracy (`acc`) across both your training data and your validation (`val`) data.

Example 7.15 Using TensorBoard while itting a model in Keras

```
from keras.callbacks import TensorBoard
tensorboard = TensorBoard('logs/deep-net')
model.fit(X_train, y_train,
          batch_size=128, epochs=20,
          verbose=1,
          validation_data=(X_valid, y_valid),
          callbacks=[tensorboard])
```

By following these steps or an analogous procedure for the circumstances of your
particular operating system, you should see something like Figure 7.18 in your browser
window. From there, you can visually track any given model's cost and accuracy across
both your training and validation datasets in real time as these metrics change epoch over
epoch. This kind of performance tracking is one of the primary uses of TensorBoard,
although the dashboard interface also provides heaps of other functionality, such as visual
breakdowns of your neural network graph and the distribution of your model weights.
You can learn about these additional features by reading the TensorBoard docs and
exploring the interface on your own.

Summary

Over the course of the chapter, we discussed common pitfalls in modeling with neural
networks and covered strategies for minimizing their impact on model performance.
We wrapped up the chapter by applying all of the theory learned thus far in the book to
construct our first bona fide deep learning network, which provided us with our best-yet
accuracy on MNIST handwritten-digit classification. While such deep, dense neural nets
are applicable to generally approximating any given output y when provided some input
x, they may not be the most efficient option for specialized modeling. Coming up next
in Part III, we introduce neural network layers and deep learning approaches that excel
at particular, specialized tasks, including machine vision, natural language processing, the
generation of art, and playing games.

Key Concepts

Here are the essential foundational concepts thus far. New terms from the current chapter are highlighted in purple.

- parameters:
  - weight w
  - bias b
- activation a
- artificial neurons:
  - sigmoid
  - tanh
  - ReLU
  - linear
- input layer
- hidden layer
- output layer
- layer types:
  - dense (fully connected)
  - softmax
- cost (loss) functions:
  - quadratic (mean squared error)
  - cross-entropy

- forward propagation
- backpropagation
- unstable (especially vanishing) gradients
- Glorot weight initialization
- batch normalization
- dropout
- optimizers:
  - stochastic gradient descent
  - Adam
- optimizer hyperparameters:
  - learning rate η
  - batch size

III

Interactive Applications of Deep Learning

## 8

Natural Language Processing

In Chapter 2, we introduced computational representations of language, particularly highlighting *word vectors* as a potent approach for quantitatively capturing word meaning. In the present chapter, we cover code that will enable you to create your own word vectors as well as to provide them as an input into a deep learning model.

The natural language processing models you build in this chapter will incorporate neural network layers we've applied already: dense layers from Chapters 5 through 7, and convolutional layers from Chapter 8. Our NLP models will also incorporate new layer types—ones from the family of recurrent neural networks. RNNs natively handle information that occurs in sequences such as natural language, but they can, in fact, handle *any* sequential data—such as financial time series or temperatures at a given geographic location—so they're quite versatile. The chapter concludes with a section on deep learning networks that process data via multiple parallel streams—a concept that dramatically widens the scope for creativity when you design your model architectures and, as you'll see, can also improve model accuracy.

Preprocessing Natural Language Data

There are steps you can take to preprocess natural language data such that the modeling you carry out downstream may be more accurate. Common natural language preprocessing options include:

- *Tokenization*: This is the splitting of a document (e.g., a book) into a list of discrete elements of language (e.g., words), which we call *tokens*.

- Converting all characters *to lowercase*: A capitalized word at the beginning of a sentence (e.g., *She*) has the same meaning as when it's used later in a sentence (*she*). By converting all characters in a corpus to lowercase, we disregard any use of capitalization.

- Removing *stop words*: These are frequently occurring words that tend to contain relatively little distinctive meaning, such as *the*, *at*, *which*, and *of*. There is no universal consensus on the precise list of stop words, but depending on your application it may be sensible to ensure that certain words are (or aren't!) considered to be stop words. For example, in this chapter, we'll build a model to classify movie reviews as positive or negative. Some lists of stop words include negations like *didn't*, *isn't*, and *wouldn't* that might be critical for our model to identify the sentiment of a movie review, so these words probably shouldn't be removed.

- Removing *punctuation*: Punctuation marks generally don't add much value to a natural language model and so are often removed.

- *Stemming*:[1] Stemming is the truncation of words down to their *stem*. For example, the words *house* and *housing* both have the stem *hous*. With smaller datasets in particular, stemming can be productive because it pools words with similar meanings into a single token. There will be more examples of this stemmed token's context, enabling techniques like word2vec or GloVe to more accurately identify an appropriate location for the token in word-vector space (see Figures 2.5 and 2.6).

- Handling *n-grams*: Some words commonly co-occur in such a way that the combination of words is better suited to being considered a single concept than several separate concepts. As examples, *New York* is a *bigram* (an *n*-gram of length two), and *New York City* is a *trigram* (an *n*-gram of length three). When chained together, the words *new*, *york*, and *city* have a specific meaning that might be better captured by a single token (and therefore a single location in word-vector space) than three separate ones.

Depending on the particular task that we've designed our model for, as well as the dataset that we're feeding into it, we may use all, some, or none of these data preprocessing steps. As you consider applying any preprocessing step to your particular problem, you can use your intuition to weigh whether it might ultimately be valuable to your downstream task. We've already mentioned some examples of this:

- Stemming may be helpful for a small corpus but unhelpful for a large one.

- Likewise, converting all characters to lowercase is likely to be helpful when you're working with a small corpus, but, in a larger corpus that has many more examples of individual uses of words, the distinction of, say, *general* (an adjective meaning "widespread") versus *General* (a noun meaning the commander of an army) may be valuable.

- Removing punctuation would not be an advantage in all cases. Consider, for example, if you were building a question-answering algorithm, which could use question marks to help it identify questions.

- Negations may be helpful as stop words for some classifiers but probably not for a sentiment classifier, for example. Which words you include in your list of stop words could be crucial to your particular application, so be careful with this one. In many instances, it will be best to remove only a limited number of stop words.

If you're unsure whether a given preprocessing step may be helpful or not, you can investigate the situation empirically by incorporating the step and observing whether it impacts the accuracy of your deep learning model downstream. As a general rule, the larger a corpus becomes, the fewer preprocessing steps that will be helpful. With a small corpus, you're likely to be concerned about encountering words that are rare or that are outside the vocabulary of your training dataset. By pooling several rare words into a single

---

1. *Lemmatization*, a more sophisticated alternative to stemming, requires the use of a reference vocabulary. For our purposes in this book, stemming is a sufficient approach for considering multiple related words as a single token.

common token, you'll be more likely to train a model effectively on the meaning of the group of related words. As the corpus becomes larger, however, rare words and out-of-vocabulary words become less and less of an issue. With a very large corpus, then, it is likely to be helpful to *avoid* pooling several words into a single common token. That's because there will be enough instances of even the less-frequently-occurring words to effectively model their unique meaning as well as to model the relatively subtle nuances between related words (that might otherwise have been pooled together).

To provide practical examples of these preprocessing steps in action, we invite you to check out our *Natural Language Preprocessing* Jupyter notebook. It begins by loading a number of dependencies:

```
import nltk
from nltk import word_tokenize, sent_tokenize
from nltk.corpus import stopwords
from nltk.stem.porter import *
nltk.download('gutenberg')
nltk.download('punkt')
nltk.download('stopwords')

import string

import gensim
from gensim.models.phrases import Phraser, Phrases
from gensim.models.word2vec import Word2Vec

from sklearn.manifold import TSNE

import pandas as pd
from bokeh.io import output_notebook, output_file
from bokeh.plotting import show, figure
%matplotlib inline
```

Most of these dependencies are from *nltk* (the Natural Language Toolkit) and *gensim* (another natural language library for Python). We explain our use of each individual dependency when we apply it in the example code that follows.

Tokenization

The dataset we used in this notebook is a small corpus of out-of-copyright books from *Project Gutenberg*.[2] This corpus is available within nltk so it can be easily loaded using this code:

```
from nltk.corpus import gutenberg
```

---

2. Named after the printing-press inventor Johannes Gutenberg, Project Gutenberg is a source of tens of thousands of electronic books. These books are classic works of literature from across the globe whose copyright has now expired, making them freely available. See gutenberg.org.

This wee corpus consists of a mere 18 literary works, including Jane Austen's *Emma*, Lewis Carroll's *Alice in Wonderland*, and three plays by a little-known fellow named William Shakespeare. (Execute `gutenberg.fileids()` to print the names of all 18 documents.) By running `len(gutenberg.words())`, you can see that the corpus comes out to 2.6 million words—a manageable quantity that means you'll be able to run all of the code examples in this section on a laptop.

To tokenize the corpus into a list of sentences, one option is to use nltk's `sent_tokenize()` method:

```
gberg_sent_tokens = sent_tokenize(gutenberg.raw())
```

Accessing the first element of the resulting list by running `gberg_sent_tokens[0]`, you can see that the first book in the Project Gutenberg corpus is *Emma*, because this first element contains the book's title page, chapter markers, and first sentence, all (erroneously) blended together with newline characters (\n):

```
'[Emma by Jane Austen 1816]\n\nVOLUME I\n\nCHAPTER I\n\n\nEmma Wood-
house, handsome, clever, and rich, with a comfortable home\nand happy
disposition, seemed to unite some of the best blessings\nof existence;
and had lived nearly twenty-one years in the world\nwith very little to
distress or vex her.'
```

A stand-alone sentence is found in the second element, which you can view by executing `gberg_sent_tokens[1]`:

```
"She was the youngest of the two daughters of a most affectionate,
\nindulgent father; and had, in consequence of her sister's mar-
riage,\nbeen mistress of his house from a very early period."
```

You can further tokenize this sentence down to the word level using nltk's `word_tokenize()` method:

```
word_tokenize(gberg_sent_tokens[1])
```

This prints a list of words with all whitespace, including newline characters, stripped out (see Figure 8.1). The word *father*, for example, is the 15th word in the second sentence, as you can see by running this line of code:

```
word_tokenize(gberg_sent_tokens[1])[14]
```

Although the `sent_tokenize()` and `word_tokenize()` methods may come in handy for working with your own natural language data, with this Project Gutenberg corpus, you can instead conveniently employ its built-in `sents()` method to achieve the same aims in a single step:

```
gberg_sents = gutenberg.sents()
```

This command produces `gberg_sents`, a tokenized list of lists. The higher-level list consists of individual sentences, and each sentence contains a lower-level list of words within

```
['She',
 'was',
 'the',
 'youngest',
 'of',
 'the',
 'two',
 'daughters',
 'of',
 'a',
 'most',
 'affectionate',
 ',',
 'indulgent',
 'father',
 ';',
 'and',
 'had',
 ',',
 'in',
 'consequence',
 'of',
 'her',
 'sister',
 "'",
 's',
 'marriage',
 ',',
 'been',
 'mistress',
 'of',
 'his',
 'house',
 'from',
 'a',
 'very',
 'early',
 'period',
 '.']
```

Figure 8.1   The second sentence of Jane Austen's classic *Emma* tokenized to the word level

it. Appropriately, the sents() method also separates the title page and chapter markers into their own individual elements, as you can observe with a call to gberg_sents[0:2]:

```
[['[', 'Emma', 'by', 'Jane', 'Austen', '1816', ']'],
 ['VOLUME', 'I'],
 ['CHAPTER', 'I']]
```

Because of this, the first actual sentence of *Emma* is now on its own as the fourth element of gberg_sents, and so to access the 15th word (*father*) in the second actual sentence, we now use gberg_sents[4][14].

Converting All Characters to Lowercase

For the remaining natural language preprocessing steps, we begin by applying them iteratively to a single sentence. As we wrap up the section later on, we'll apply the steps across the entire 18-document corpus.

Looking back at Figure 8.1, we see that this sentence begins with the capitalized word *She*. If we'd like to disregard capitalization so that this word is considered to be identical to *she*, then we can use the Python `lower()` method from the `string` library, as shown in Example 8.1.

Example 8.1 Converting a sentence to lowercase

```
[w.lower() for w in gberg_sents[4]]
```

This line returns the same list as in Figure 8.1 with the exception that the first element in the list is now `she` instead of `She`.

Removing Stop Words and Punctuation

Another potential inconvenience with the sentence in Figure 8.1 is that it's littered with both stop words and punctuation. To handle these, let's use the + operator to concatenate together nltk's list of English stop words with the `string` library's list of punctuation marks:

```
stpwrds = stopwords.words('english') + list(string.punctuation)
```

If you examine the `stpwrds` list that you've created, you'll see that it contains many common words that often don't contain much particular meaning, such as *a*, *an*, and *the*.[3] However, it also contains words like *not* and other negative words that could be critical if we were building a sentiment classifier, such as in the sentence, "This film was *not* good."

In any event, to remove all of the elements of `stpwrds` from a sentence we could use a *list comprehension*[4] as we do in Example 8.2, which incorporates the lowercasing we used in Example 8.1.

Example 8.2 Removing stop words and punctuation with a list comprehension

```
[w.lower() for w in gberg_sents[4] if w.lower() not in stpwrds]
```

Relative to Figure 8.1, running this line of code returns a much shorter list that now contains only words that each tend to convey a fair bit of meaning:

```
['youngest',
 'two',
 'daughters',
 'affectionate',
 'indulgent',
 'father',
 'consequence',
 'sister',
 'marriage',
 'mistress',
```

---

3. These three particular words are called *articles*, or *determiners*.
4. See `bit.ly/listComp` if you'd like an introduction to list comprehensions in Python.

```
'house',
'early',
'period']
```

Stemming

To stem words, you can use the Porter algorithm[5] provided by nltk. To do this, you create an instance of a `PorterStemmer()` object and then add its `stem()` method to the list
comprehension you began in Example 8.2, as shown in Example 8.3.

Example 8.3 Adding word stemming to our list comprehension

```
[stemmer.stem(w.lower()) for w in gberg_sents[4]
  if w.lower() not in stpwrds]
```

This outputs the following:

```
['youngest',
 'two',
 'daughter',
 'affection',
 'indulg',
 'father',
 'consequ',
 'sister',
 'marriag',
 'mistress',
 'hous',
 'earli',
 'period']
```

This is similar to our previous output of the sentence except that many of the words have
been stemmed:

1. *daughters* to *daughter* (allowing the plural and singular terms to be treated identically)
2. *house* to *hous* (allowing related words like *house* and *housing* to be treated as the same)
3. *early* to *earli* (allowing differing tenses such as *early*, *earlier*, and *earliest* to be treated as
   the same)

These stemming examples may be advantageous with a corpus as small as ours, because
there are relatively few examples of any given word. By pooling similar words together,
we obtain more occurrences of the pooled version, and so it may be assigned to a more
accurate location in vector space (Figure 2.6). With a very large corpus, however, where
you have many more examples of rarer words, there might be an advantage to treating
plural and singular variations on a word differently, treating related words as unique, and
retaining multiple tenses; the nuances could prove to convey valuable meaning.

---

5. Porter, M. F. (1980). An algorithm for suffix stripping. *Program, 14,* 130–7.

Handling *n*-grams

To treat a bigram like *New York* as a single token instead of two, we can use the
`Phrases()` and `Phraser()` methods from the gensim library. As demonstrated in
Example 8.4, we use them in this way:

1. `Phrases()` to train a "detector" to identify how often any given pair of words
   occurs together in our corpus (the technical term for this is *bigram collocation*) relative
   to how often each word in the pair occurs by itself
2. `Phraser()` to take the bigram collocations detected by the `Phrases()` object and
   then use this information to create an object that can efficiently be passed over our
   corpus, converting all bigram collocations from two consecutive tokens into a single
   token

Example 8.4 Detecting collocated bigrams

```
phrases = Phrases(gberg_sents)
bigram = Phraser(phrases)
```

By running `bigram.phrasegrams`, we output a dictionary of the count and *score* of each
bigram. The topmost lines of this dictionary are provided in Figure 8.2.

Each bigram in Figure 8.2 has a count and a score associated with it. The bigram *two
daughters*, for example, occurs a mere 19 times across our Gutenberg corpus. This bigram
has a fairly low score (12.0), meaning the terms *two* and *daughters* do not occur together
very frequently relative to how often they occur apart. In contrast, the bigram *Miss Taylor*
occurs more often (48 times), and the terms *Miss* and *Taylor* occur much more frequently
together relative to how often they occur on their own (score of 453.8).

```
{(b'two', b'daughters'): (19, 11.966813731181546),
 (b'her', b'sister'): (195, 17.7960829227865),
 (b"'", b's'): (9781, 31.066242737744524),
 (b'very', b'early'): (24, 11.01214147275924),
 (b'Her', b'mother'): (14, 13.529425062715127),
 (b'long', b'ago'): (38, 63.22343628984788),
 (b'more', b'than'): (541, 29.023584433996874),
 (b'had', b'been'): (1256, 22.306024648925288),
 (b'an', b'excellent'): (54, 39.063874851750626),
 (b'Miss', b'Taylor'): (48, 453.75918026073305),
 (b'very', b'fond'): (28, 24.134280468850747),
 (b'passed', b'away'): (25, 12.35053642325912),
 (b'too', b'much'): (173, 31.376002029426687),
 (b'did', b'not'): (935, 11.728416217142811),
 (b'any', b'means'): (27, 14.096964108090186),
 (b'wedding', b'-'): (15, 17.4695197740113),
 (b'Her', b'father'): (18, 13.129571562488772),
 (b'after', b'dinner'): (21, 21.5285481168817),
```

Figure 8.2 A dictionary of bigrams detected within our corpus

Scanning over the bigrams in Figure 8.2, notice that they are marred by capitalized words and punctuation marks. We'll resolve those issues in the next section, but in the meantime let's explore how the `bigram` object we've created can be used to convert bigrams from two consecutive tokens into one. Let's tokenize a short sentence by using the `split()` method on a string of characters wherever there's a space, as follows:

```
tokenized_sentence = "Jon lives in New York City".split()
```

If we print `tokenized_sentence`, we output a list of unigrams only: `['Jon', 'lives', 'in', 'New', 'York', 'City']`. If, however, we pass the list through our gensim `bigram` object by using `bigram[tokenized_sentence]`, the list then contains the bigram *New York*: `['Jon', 'lives', 'in', 'New_York', 'City']`.

After you've identified bigrams across your corpus by running it through the `bigram` object, you can detect trigrams (such as *New York City*) by passing this new, bigram-filled corpus through the `Phrases()` and `Phraser()` methods. This could be repeated again to identify 4-grams (and then again to identify 5-grams, and so on); however, there are diminishing returns from this. Bigrams (or at most trigrams) should suffice for the majority of applications. By the way, if you go ahead and detect trigrams with the Project Gutenberg corpus, *New York City* is unlikely to be detected. Our corpus of classic literature doesn't mention it often enough.

Preprocessing the Full Corpus

Having run through some examples of preprocessing steps on individual sentences, we now compose some code to preprocess the entire Project Gutenberg corpus. This will also enable us to collocate bigrams on a cleaned-up corpus that no longer contains capital letters or punctuation.

Later on in this chapter, we'll use a corpus of film reviews that was curated by Andrew Maas and his colleagues at Stanford University to predict the sentiment of the reviews with NLP models.[6] During their data preprocessing steps, Maas and his coworkers decided to leave in stop words because they are "indicative of sentiment."[7] They also decided not to stem words because they felt their corpus was sufficiently large that their word-vector-based NLP model "learns similar representations of words of the same stem when the data suggest it." Said another way, words that have a similar meaning should find their way to a similar location in word-vector space (Figure 2.6) during model training.

Following their lead, we'll also forgo stop-word removal and stemming when preprocessing the Project Gutenberg corpus, as in Example 8.5.

---

6. Maas, A., et al. (2011). Learning word vectors for sentiment analysis. *Proceedings of the 49th Annual Meeting of the Association for Computational Linguistics*, 142–50.

7. This is in line with our thinking, as we mentioned earlier in the chapter.

Example 8.5 Removing capitalization and punctuation from Project Gutenberg corpus

```
lower_sents = []
for s in gberg_sents:
    lower_sents.append([w.lower() for w in s if w.lower()
                        not in list(string.punctuation)])
```

In this example, we begin with an empty list we call `lower_sents`, and then we append preprocessed sentences to it using a `for` loop.[8] For preprocessing each sentence within the loop, we used a variation on the list comprehension from Example 8.2, in this case removing only punctuation marks while converting all characters to lowercase.

With punctuation and capitals removed, we can set about detecting collocated bigrams across the corpus afresh:

```
lower_bigram = Phraser(Phrases(lower_sents))
```

Relative to Example 8.4, this time we created our gensim `lower_bigram` object in a single line by chaining the `Phrases()` and `Phraser()` methods together. The top of the output of a call to `lower_bigram.phrasegrams` is provided in Figure 8.3: Comparing these bigrams with those from Figure 8.2, we do indeed observe that they are all in lowercase (e.g., *miss taylor*) and bigrams that included punctuation marks are nowhere to be seen.

```
{(b'two', b'daughters'): (19, 11.080802900992637),
 (b'her', b'sister'): (201, 16.93971298099339),
 (b'very', b'early'): (25, 10.516998773665177),
 (b'her', b'mother'): (253, 10.70812618607742),
 (b'long', b'ago'): (38, 59.226442015336005),
 (b'more', b'than'): (562, 28.529926612065935),
 (b'had', b'been'): (1260, 21.583193129694834),
 (b'an', b'excellent'): (58, 37.41859680854167),
 (b'sixteen', b'years'): (15, 131.42913000977515),
 (b'miss', b'taylor'): (48, 420.4340982546865),
 (b'mr', b'woodhouse'): (132, 104.19907841850323),
 (b'very', b'fond'): (30, 24.185726346489627),
 (b'passed', b'away'): (25, 11.751473221742694),
 (b'too', b'much'): (177, 30.36309017383541),
 (b'did', b'not'): (977, 10.846196223896685),
 (b'any', b'means'): (28, 14.294148100212627),
 (b'after', b'dinner'): (22, 18.60737125272944),
 (b'mr', b'weston'): (162, 91.63290824201266),
```

Figure 8.3   Sample of a dictionary of bigrams detected within our lowercased and punctuation-free corpus

8. If you're preprocessing a large corpus, we'd recommend using optimizable and parallelizable functional programming techniques in place of our simple (and therefore simple-to-follow) for loop.

Examining the results in Figure 8.3 further, however, it appears that the default min-imum thresholds for both count and score are far too liberal. That is, word pairs like *two daughters* and *her sister* should not be considered bigrams. To attain bigrams that we thought were more sensible, we experimented with more conservative count and score thresholds by increasing them by powers of 2. Following this approach, we were generally satisfied by setting the optional `Phrases()` arguments to a *min(imum) count* of 32 and to a score *threshold* of 64, as shown in Example 8.6.

Example 8.6 Detecting collocated bigrams with more conservative thresholds

```
lower_bigram = Phraser(Phrases(lower_sents,
                        min_count=32, threshold=64))
```

Although it's not perfect,[9] because there are still a few questionable bigrams like *great deal* and *few minutes*, the output from a call to `lower_bigram.phrasegrams` is now largely defensible, as shown in Figure 8.4.

Armed with our well-appointed `lower_bigram` object from Example 8.6, we can at last use a `for` loop to iteratively append for ourselves a corpus of cleaned-up sentences, as in Example 8.7.

Example 8.7 Creating a "clean" corpus that includes bigrams

```
clean_sents = []
for s in lower_sents:
    clean_sents.append(lower_bigram[s])
```

```
{(b'miss', b'taylor'): (48, 156.44059469941823),
 (b'mr', b'woodhouse'): (132, 82.04651843976633),
 (b'mr', b'weston'): (162, 75.87438262077481),
 (b'mrs', b'weston'): (249, 160.68485093258923),
 (b'great', b'deal'): (182, 93.36368125424357),
 (b'mr', b'knightley'): (277, 161.74131790625913),
 (b'miss', b'woodhouse'): (173, 229.03802722366902),
 (b'years', b'ago'): (56, 74.31594785893046),
 (b'mr', b'elton'): (214, 121.3990121932397),
 (b'dare', b'say'): (115, 89.94000515807346),
 (b'frank', b'churchill'): (151, 1316.4456593286038),
 (b'miss', b'bates'): (113, 276.39588291692513),
 (b'drawing', b'room'): (49, 84.91494947493561),
 (b'mrs', b'goddard'): (58, 143.57843432545658),
 (b'miss', b'smith'): (58, 73.03442128232508),
 (b'few', b'minutes'): (86, 204.16834974753786),
 (b'john', b'knightley'): (58, 83.03755747111268),
 (b'don', b't'): (830, 250.30957446808512),
```

Figure 8.4 Sample of a more conservatively thresholded dictionary of bigrams

---

9. These are statistical approximations, of course!

```
['sixteen',
 'years',
 'had',
 'miss_taylor',
 'been',
 'in',
 'mr_woodhouse',
 's',
 'family',
 'less',
 'as',
 'a',
 'governess',
 'than',
 'a',
 'friend',
 'very',
 'fond',
 'of',
 'both',
 'daughters',
 'but',
 'particularly',
 'of',
 'emma']
```

Figure 8.5   Clean, preprocessed sentence from the Project Gutenberg corpus

As an example, Figure 8.5 shows the seventh element of our clean corpus (`clean_sents[6]`), a sentence that includes the bigrams *miss taylor* and *mr woodhouse*.

Creating Word Embeddings with word2vec

With the cleaned corpus of natural language `clean_sents` now available to us, we are well positioned to embed words from the corpus into word-vector space (Figure 2.6). As you'll see in this section, such word embeddings can be produced with a single line of code. This single line of code, however, should not be executed blindly, and it has quite a few optional arguments to consider carefully. Given this, we'll cover the essential theory behind word vectors before delving into example code.

The Essential Theory Behind word2vec

In Chapter 2, we provided an intuitive understanding of what word vectors are. We also discussed the underlying idea that because you can "know a word by the company it keeps" then a given word's meaning can be well represented as the average of the words that tend to occur around it. word2vec is an unsupervised learning technique[10]—that is, it is applied to a corpus of natural language without making use of any labels that may or

---

10. See Chapter 4 for a recap of the differences between the supervised, unsupervised, and reinforcement learning problems.

may not happen to exist for the corpus. This means that any dataset of natural language could be appropriate as an input to word2vec.[11]

When running word2vec, you can choose between two underlying model architectures—*skip-gram* (SG) or *continuous bag of words* (CBOW; pronounced *see*-bo)—either of which will typically produce roughly comparable results despite maximizing probabilities from "opposite" perspectives. To make sense of this, reconsider our toy-sized corpus from Figure 2.5:

```
you shall know a word by the company it keeps
```

In it, we are considering word to be the *target* word, and the three words to the right of it as well as the three words to the left of it are considered to be *context* words. (This corresponds to a *window size* of three words—one of the primary hyperparameters we must take into account when applying word2vec.) With the SG architecture, context words are predicted given the target word.[12] With CBOW, it is the inverse: The target word is predicted based on the context words.[13]

To understand word2vec more concretely, let's focus on the CBOW architecture in greater detail (although we equally could have focused on SG instead). With CBOW, the target word is predicted to be the average of all the context words considered *jointly*. "Jointly" means "all at once": The particular position of context words isn't taken into consideration, nor whether the context word occurs before or after the target word. That the CBOW architecture has this attribute is right there in the "bag of words" part of its name:

- We take all the context words within the windows to the right and the left of the target word.

- We (figuratively!) throw all of these context words into a bag. If it helps you remember that the sequence of words is irrelevant, you can even imagine shaking up the bag.

- We calculate the average of all the context words contained in the bag, using this average to estimate what the target word could be.

If we were concerned about syntax—the grammar of language (see Figure 2.9 for a refresher on the elements of natural language)—then word order would matter. But because with word2vec we're concerned only with semantics—the *meaning* of words—it turns out that the order of context words is, on average, irrelevant.

Having considered the intuitiveness of the "BOW" component of the CBOW moniker, let's also consider the "continuous" part of it: The target word and context

---

11. Mikolov, T., et al. (2013). Efficient estimation of word representations in vector space. *arXiv:1301.3781*.
12. In more technical machine learning terms, the cost function of the skip-gram architecture is to maximize the log probability of any possible context word from a corpus given the current target word.
13. Again, in technical ML jargon, the cost function for CBOW is maximizing the log probability of any possible target word from a corpus given the current context words.

Table 8.1   Comparison of word2vec architectures

Architecture	Predicts	Relative Strengths
Skip-gram (SG)	Context words given target word	Better for a smaller corpus; represents rare words well
CBOW	Target word given context words	Multiple times faster; represents frequent words slightly better

word windows slide *continuously* one word at a time from the first word of the corpus all the way through to the final word. At each position along the way, the target word is estimated given the context words. Via stochastic gradient descent, the location of words within vector space can be shifted, and thereby these target-word estimates can gradually be improved.

In practice, and as summarized in Table 8.1, the SG architecture is a better choice when you're working with a small corpus. It represents rare words in word-vector space well. In contrast, CBOW is much more computationally efficient, so it is the better option when you're working with a very large corpus. Relative to SG, CBOW also represents frequently occurring words slightly better.[14]

Although word2vec is comfortably the most widely used approach for embedding words from a corpus of natural language into vector space, it is by no means the only approach. A major alternative to word2vec is GloVe—global vectors for word representation—which was introduced by the prominent natural language researchers Jeffrey Pennington, Richard Socher, and Christopher Manning.[15] At the time—in 2014—the three were colleagues working together at Stanford University.

GloVe and word2vec differ in their underlying methodology: word2vec uses predictive models, while GloVe is count based. Ultimately, both approaches tend to produce vector-space embeddings that perform similarly in downstream NLP applications, with some research suggesting that word2vec may provide modestly better results in select cases. One potential advantage of GloVe is that it was designed to be parallelized over multiple processors or even multiple machines, so it might be a good option if you're looking to create a word-vector space with many unique words and a very large corpus.

---

14. Regardless of whether you use the SG or CBOW architecture, an additional option you have while running word2vec is the training method. For this, you have two different options: *hierarchical softmax* and *negative sampling*. The former involves normalization and is better suited to rare words. The latter, on the other hand, forgoes normalization, making it better suited to common words and low-dimensional word-vector spaces. For our purposes in this book, the differences between these two training methods are insignificant and we don't cover them further.

15. Pennington, J., et al. (2014). GloVe: Global vectors for word representations. *Proceedings of the Conference on Empirical Methods in Natural Language Processing.*

The contemporary leading alternative to both word2vec and GloVe is fastText.[16,17,18,19] This approach was developed by researchers at Facebook. A major benefit of fastText is that it operates on a *subword* level—its "word" vectors are actually subcomponents of words. This enables fastText to work around some of the issues related to rare words and out-of-vocabulary words addressed in the preprocessing section at the outset of this chapter.

Evaluating Word Vectors

However you create your word vectors—be it with word2vec or an alternative approach—there are two broad perspectives you can consider when evaluating the quality of word vectors: *intrinsic* and *extrinsic* evaluations.

Extrinsic evaluations involve assessing the performance of your word vectors within whatever your downstream NLP application of interest is—your sentiment-analysis classifier, say, or perhaps your named-entity recognition tool. Although extrinsic evaluations can take longer to carry out because they require you to carry out all of your downstream processing steps—including perhaps training a computationally intensive deep learning model—you can be confident that it's worthwhile to retain a change to your word vectors if they relate to an appreciable improvement in the accuracy of your NLP application.

In contrast, intrinsic evaluations involve assessing the performance of your word vectors not on your final NLP application, but rather on some specific intermediate subtask. One common such task is assessing whether your word vectors correspond well to arithmetical analogies like those shown in Figure 2.7. For example, if you start at the word-vector location for king, subtract man, and add woman, do you end up near the word-vector location for queen?[20]

Relative to extrinsic evaluations, intrinsic tests are quick. They may also help you better understand (and therefore troubleshoot) intermediate steps within your broader NLP process. The limitation of intrinsic evaluations, however, is that they may not ultimately lead to improvements in the accuracy of your NLP application downstream unless you've identified a reliable, quantifiable relationship between performance on the intermediate test and your NLP application.

Running word2vec

As mentioned earlier, and as shown in Example 8.8, word2vec can be run in a single line of code—albeit with quite a few arguments.

---

16. The open-source fastText library is available at `fasttext.cc`.
17. Joulin, A., et al. (2016). Bag of tricks for efficient text classification. *arXiv: 1607.01759*.
18. Bojanowski, P., et al. (2016). Enriching word vectors with subword information. *arXiv: 1607.04606*.
19. Note that the lead author of the landmark word2vec paper, Tomas Mikolov, is the final author of both of these landmark fastText papers.
20. A test set of 19,500 such analogies was developed by Tomas Mikolov and his colleagues in their 2013 word2vec paper. This test set is available at `download.tensorflow.org/data/questions-words.txt`.

Example 8.8 Running word2vec

```
model = Word2Vec(sentences=clean_sents, size=64,
                 sg=1, window=10, iter=5,
                 min_count=10, workers=4)
```

Here's a breakdown of each of the arguments we passed into the Word2Vec() method from the gensim library:

- **sentences**: Pass in a list of lists like clean_sents as a corpus. Elements in the higher-level list are sentences, whereas elements in the lower-level list can be word-level tokens.

- **size**: The number of dimensions in the word-vector space that will result from running word2vec. This is a hyperparameter that can be varied and evaluated extrinsically or intrinsically. Like other hyperparameters in this book, there is a Goldilocks sweet spot. You can home in on an optimal value by specifying, say, 32 dimensions and varying this value by powers of 2. Doubling the number of dimensions will double the computational complexity of your downstream deep learning model, but if doing this results in markedly higher model accuracy then this extrinsic evaluation suggests that the extra complexity could be worthwhile. On the other hand, halving the number of dimensions halves computational complexity downstream: If this can be done without appreciably decreasing your NLP model's accuracy, then it should be. By performing a handful of intrinsic inspections (which we'll go over shortly), we found 64 dimensions to provide more sensible word vectors than 32 dimensions for this particular case. Doubling this figure to 128, however, provided no noticeable improvement.

- **sg**: Set to 1 to choose the skip-gram architecture, or leave at the 0 default to choose CBOW. As summarized in Table 8.1, SG is generally better suited to small datasets like our Gutenberg corpus.

- **window**: For SG, a window size of 10 (for a total of 20 context words) is a good bet, so we set this hyperparameter to 10. If we were using CBOW, then a window size of 5 (for a total of 10 context words) could be near the optimal value. In either case, this hyperparameter can be experimented with and evaluated extrinsically or intrinsically. Small adjustments to this hyperparameter may not be perceptibly impactful, however.

- **iter**: By default, the gensim Word2Vec() method iterates over the corpus fed into it (i.e., slides over all of the words) five times. Multiple iterations of word2vec is analogous to multiple epochs of training a deep learning model. With a small corpus like ours, the word vectors improve over several iterations. With a very large corpus, on the other hand, it might be cripplingly computationally expensive to run even two iterations—and, because there are so many examples of words in a very large corpus anyway, the word vectors might not be any better.

- **min_count**: This is the minimum number of times a word must occur across the corpus in order to fit it into word-vector space. If a given target word occurs only once or a few times, there are a limited number of examples of its contextual words to consider, and so its location in word-vector space may not be reliable. Because of this, a minimum count of about 10 is often reasonable. The higher the count, the smaller the vocabulary of words that will be available to your downstream NLP task. This is yet another hyperparameter that can be tuned, with extrinsic evaluations likely being more illuminating than intrinsic ones because the size of the vocabulary you have to work with could make a considerable impact on your downstream NLP application.

- **workers**: This is the number of processing cores you'd like to dedicate to training. If the CPU on your machine has, say, eight cores, then eight is the largest number of parallel worker threads you can have. In this case, if you choose to use fewer than eight cores, you're leaving compute resources available for other tasks.

In our GitHub repository, we saved our model using the **save()** method of word2vec objects:

```
model.save('clean_gutenberg_model.w2v')
```

Instead of running word2vec yourself, then, you're welcome to load up our word vectors using this code:

```
model = gensim.models.Word2Vec.load('clean_gutenberg_model.w2v')
```

If you do choose the word vectors we created, then the following examples will produce the same outputs.[21] We can see the size of our vocabulary by calling len(model.wv.vocab). This tells us that there are 10,329 words (well, more specifically, tokens) that occur at least 10 times within our clean_sents corpus.[22] One of the words in our vocabulary is *dog*. As shown in Figure 8.6, we can output its location in 64-dimensional word-vector space by running model.wv['dog'].

```
array([ 0.38401067,  0.01232518, -0.37594706, -0.00112308,  0.38663676,
        0.01287549,  0.398965  ,  0.0096426 , -0.10419296, -0.02877572,
        0.3207022 ,  0.27838793,  0.62772304,  0.34408906,  0.23356602,
        0.24557391,  0.3398472 ,  0.07168821, -0.18941355, -0.10122284,
       -0.35172758,  0.4038952 , -0.12179806,  0.096336  ,  0.00641343,
        0.02332107,  0.7743452 ,  0.03591069, -0.20103034, -0.1688079 ,
       -0.01331445, -0.29832968,  0.08522387, -0.02750671,  0.32494134,
       -0.14266558, -0.4192913 , -0.09291836, -0.23813559,  0.38258648,
        0.11036541,  0.005807  , -0.16745028,  0.34308755, -0.20224966,
       -0.77683043,  0.05146591, -0.5883941 , -0.0718769 , -0.18120563,
        0.00358319, -0.29351747,  0.153776  ,  0.48048878,  0.22479494,
        0.5465321 ,  0.29695514,  0.00986911, -0.2450937 , -0.19344331,
        0.3541134 ,  0.3426432 , -0.10496043,  0.00543602], dtype=float32)
```

Figure 8.6 The location of the token "dog" within the 64-dimensional word-vector space we generated using a corpus of books from Project Gutenberg

---

21. Every time word2vec is run, the initial locations of every word of the vocabulary within word-vector space are assigned randomly. Because of this, the same data and arguments provided to Word2Vec() will nevertheless produce unique word vectors every time, but the semantic relationships should be similar.
22. Vocabulary size is equal to the number of tokens from our corpus that had occurred at least 10 times, because we set min_count=10 when calling Word2Vec() in Example 8.8.

As a rudimentary intrinsic evaluation of the quality of our word vectors, we can use the `most_similar()` method to confirm that words with similar meanings are found in similar locations within our word-vector space.[23] For example, to output the three words that are most similar to *father* in our word-vector space, we can run this code:

```
model.wv.most_similar('father', topn=3)
```

This outputs the following:

```
[('mother', 0.8257375359535217),
 ('brother', 0.7275018692016602),
 ('sister', 0.7177823781967163)]
```

This output indicates that *mother, brother,* and *sister* are the most similar words to *father* in our word-vector space. In other words, within our 64-dimensional space, the word that is closest[24] to *father* is the word *mother*. Table 8.2 provides some additional examples of the words most similar to (i.e., closest to) particular words that we've picked from our word-vector vocabulary, all five of which appear pretty reasonable given our small Gutenberg corpus.[25]

Suppose we run the following line of code:

```
model.wv.doesnt_match("mother father sister brother dog".split())
```

We get the output `dog`, indicating that *dog* is the least similar relative to all the other possible word pairs. We can also use the following line to observe that the similarity score between *father* and *dog* is a mere `0.44`:

```
model.wv.similarity('father', 'dog')
```

Table 8.2   The words most similar to select test words from our Project Gutenberg vocabulary

Test Word	Most Similar Word	Cosine Similarity Score
father	mother	0.82
dog	puppy	0.78
eat	drink	0.83
day	morning	0.76
ma_am	madam	0.85

23. Technically speaking, the similarity between two given words is computed here by calculating the cosine similarity.

24. That is, has the shortest Euclidean distance in that 64-dimensional vector space.

25. Note that the final test word in Table 8.2—*ma'am*—is only available because of the bigram collocation (see Examples 8.6 and 8.7).

This similarity score of 0.44 is much lower than the similarity between *father* and any of *mother*, *brother*, or *sister*, and so it's unsurprising that *dog* is relatively distant from the other four words within our word-vector space.

As a final little intrinsic test, we can compute word-vector analogies as in Figure 2.7. For example, to calculate $v_{father} - v_{man} + v_{woman}$, we can execute this code:

```
model.wv.most_similar(positive=['father', 'woman'], negative=['man'])
```

The top-scoring word comes out as `mother`, which is the correct answer to the analogy. Suppose we likewise execute this code:

```
model.wv.most_similar(positive=['husband', 'woman'], negative=['man'])
```

In this case, the top-scoring word comes out as `wife`, again the correct answer, thereby suggesting that our word-vector space may generally be on the right track.

A given dimension within an n-dimensional word-vector space does not necessarily represent any specific factor that relates words. For example, although the real-world differences in meaning of gender or verb tense are represented by some vector direction (i.e., some movement along some combination of dimensions) within the vector space, this meaningful vector direction may only by chance be aligned—or perhaps correlated—with a particular axis of the vector space.

This contrasts with some other approaches that involve n-dimensional vector spaces, where the axes are intended to represent some specific explanatory variable. One such approach that many people are familiar with is principal component analysis (PCA), a technique for identifying linearly uncorrelated (i.e., orthogonal) vectors that contribute to variance in a given dataset. A corollary of this difference between information stored as points in PCA versus in word-vector space is that in PCA, the first principal components contribute most of the variance, and so you can focus on them and ignore later principal components; but in a word-vector space, all of the dimensions may be important and need to be taken into consideration. In this way, approaches like PCA are useful for dimensionality reduction because we do not need to consider all of the dimensions.

Plotting Word Vectors

Human brains are not well suited to visualizing anything in greater than three dimensions. Thus, plotting word vectors—which could have dozens or even hundreds of dimensions—in their native format is out of the question. Thankfully, we can use techniques for *dimensionality reduction* to approximately map the locations of words from high-dimensional word-vector space down to two or three dimensions. Our recommended approach for such dimensionality reduction is *t-distributed stochastic neighbor embedding* (t-SNE; pronounced *tee*-snee), which was developed by Laurens van der Maaten in collaboration with Geoff Hinton (Figure 1.16).[26]

Example 8.9 provides the code from our *Natural Language Preprocessing* notebook for reducing our 64-dimensional Project Gutenberg-derived word-vector space down to two dimensions, and then storing the resulting x and y coordinates within a Pandas DataFrame. There are two arguments for the `TSNE()` method (from the *scikit-learn* library) that we need to focus on:

- `n_components` is the number of dimensions that should be returned, so setting this to 2 results in a two-dimensional output, whereas 3 would result in a three-dimensional output.

- `n_iter` is the number of iterations over the input data. As with word2vec (Example 8.8), iterations are analogous to the epochs associated with training a neural network. More iterations corresponds to a longer training time but may improve the results (although only up to a point).

Example 8.9 t-SNE for dimensionality reduction

```
tsne = TSNE(n_components=2, n_iter=1000)
X_2d = tsne.fit_transform(model.wv[model.wv.vocab])
coords_df = pd.DataFrame(X_2d, columns=['x','y'])
coords_df['token'] = model.wv.vocab.keys()
```

Running t-SNE as in Example 8.9 may take some time on your machine, so you're welcome to use our results if you're feeling impatient by running the following code:[27,28]

```
coords_df = pd.read_csv('clean_gutenberg_tsne.csv')
```

Whether you ran t-SNE to produce `coords_df` on your own or you loaded in ours, you can check out the first few lines of the DataFrame by using the `head()` method:

```
coords_df.head()
```

Our output from executing `head()` is shown in Figure 8.7.

Example 8.10 provides code for creating a static scatterplot (Figure 8.8) of the two-dimensional data we created with t-SNE (in Example 8.9).

Example 8.10 Static two-dimensional scatterplot of word-vector space

```
_ = coords_df.plot.scatter('x', 'y', figsize=(12,12),
                           marker='.', s=10, alpha=0.2)
```

---

26. van der Maaten, L., & Hinton, G. (2008). Visualizing data using t-SNE. *Journal of Machine Learning Research, 9*, 2579–605.

27. We created this CSV after running t-SNE on our word-vectors using this command:
`coords_df.to_csv('clean_gutenberg_tsne.csv', index=False)`

28. Note that because t-SNE is stochastic, you will obtain a unique result every time you run it.

	x	y	token
0	62.494060	8.023034	emma
1	8.142986	33.342200	by
2	62.507140	10.078477	jane
3	12.477635	17.998343	volume
4	25.736960	30.876250	i

Figure 8.7   This is a Pandas DataFrame containing a two-dimensional representation of the word-vector space we created from the Project Gutenberg corpus. Each unique token has an *x* and *y* coordinate.

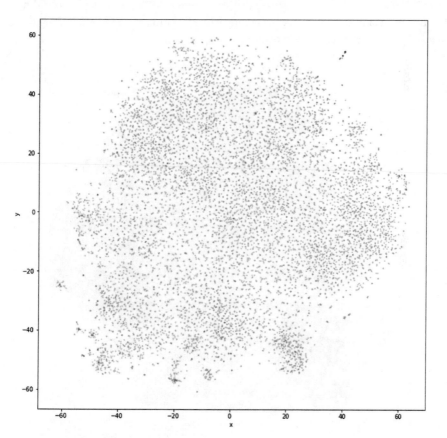

Figure 8.8   Static two-dimensional word-vector scatterplot

On its own, the scatterplot displayed in Figure 8.8 may look interesting, but there's little actionable information we can take away from it. Instead, we recommend using the *bokeh* library to create a highly interactive—and actionable—plot, as with the code provided in Example 8.11.[29]

Example 8.11 Interactive bokeh plot of two-dimensional word-vector data

```
output_notebook()
subset_df = coords_df.sample(n=5000)
p = figure(plot_width=800, plot_height=800)
_ = p.text(x=subset_df.x, y=subset_df.y, text=subset_df.token)
show(p)
```

The code in Example 8.11 produces the interactive scatterplot in Figure 8.9 using the x and y coordinates generated using t-SNE.

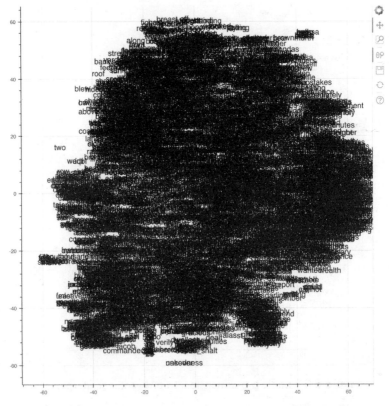

Figure 8.9   Interactive bokeh two-dimensional word-vector plot

---

29. In Example 8.11, we used the Pandas `sample()` method to reduce the dataset down to 5,000 tokens, because we found that using more data than this corresponded to a clunky user experience when using the bokeh plot interactively.

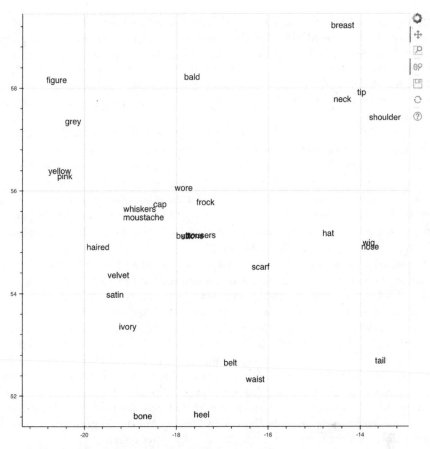

Figure 8.10   Clothing words from the Project Gutenberg corpus, revealed by zooming in to a region of the broader bokeh plot from Figure 8.9

By toggling the *Wheel Zoom* button in the top-right corner of the plot, you can use your mouse to zoom into locations within the cloud so that the words become legible. For example, as shown in Figure 8.10, we identified a region composed largely of items of clothing, with related clusters nearby, including parts of the human anatomy, colors, and fabric types. Exploring in this way provides a largely subjective intrinsic evaluation of whether related terms—and particularly synonyms—cluster together as you'd expect them to. Doing similar, you may also notice particular shortcomings of your natural-language preprocessing steps, such as the inclusion of punctuation marks, bigrams, or other tokens that you may prefer weren't included within your word-vector vocabulary.

The Area under the ROC Curve

Our apologies for interrupting the fun, interactive plotting of word vectors. We need to take a brief break from natural language-specific content here to introduce a metric that will come in handy in the next section of the chapter, when we will evaluate the performance of deep learning NLP models.

Up to this point in the book, most of our models have involved multiclass outputs: When working with the MNIST digits, for example, we used 10 output neurons to represent each of the 10 possible digits that an input image could represent. In the remaining sections of this chapter, however, our deep learning models will be *binary classifiers*: They will distinguish between only two classes. More specifically, we will build binary classifiers to predict whether the natural language of film reviews corresponds to a favorable review or negative one.

Unlike artificial neural networks tasked with multiclass problems, which require as many output neurons as classes, ANNs that are acting as binary classifiers require only a single output neuron. This is because there is no extra information associated with having two output neurons. If a binary classifier is provided some input x and it calculates some output $\hat{y}$ for one of the classes, then the output for the other class is simply $1 - \hat{y}$. As an example, if we feed a movie review into a binary classifier and it outputs that the probability that this review is a positive one is 0.85, then it must be the case that the probability of the review being negative is $1 - 0.85 = 0.15$.

Because binary classifiers have a single output, we can take advantage of metrics for evaluating our model's performance that are sophisticated relative to the excessively black-and-white *accuracy* metric that dominates multiclass problems. A typical accuracy calculation, for example, would contend that if $\hat{y} > 0.5$, then the model is predicting that the input x belongs to one class, whereas if it outputs anything less than 0.5, it belongs to the other class. To illustrate why having a specific binary threshold like this is overly simplistic, consider a situation where inputting a movie review results in a binary classifier outputting $\hat{y} = 0.48$: A typical accuracy calculation threshold would hold that—because this $\hat{y}$ is lower than 0.5—it is being classed as a negative review. If a second film review corresponds to an output of $\hat{y} = 0.51$, the model has barely any more confidence that this review is positive relative to the first review. Yet, because 0.51 is greater than the 0.5 accuracy threshold, the second review is classed as a positive review.

The starkness of the accuracy metric threshold can hide a fair bit of nuance in the quality of our model's output, and so when evaluating the performance of binary classifiers, we prefer a metric called the *area under the curve of the receiver operating characteristic*. The ROC AUC, as the metric is known for short, has its roots in the Second World War, when it was developed to assess the performance of radar engineers' judgment as they attempted to identify the presence of enemy objects.

We like the ROC AUC for two reasons:
1. It blends together two useful metrics—*true positive rate* and *false positive rate*—into a single summary value.
2. It enables us to evaluate the performance of our binary classifier's output across the full range of $\hat{y}$, from 0.0 to 1.0. This contrasts with the accuracy metric, which evaluates the performance of a binary classifier at a single threshold value only— usually $\hat{y} = 0.5$.

The Confusion Matrix

The first step toward understanding how to calculate the ROC AUC metric is to understand the so-called *confusion matrix*, which—as you'll see—isn't actually all that confusing. Rather, the matrix is a straightforward 2×2 table of how confused a model (or, as back in

Table 8.3   A confusion matrix

		actual *y*	
		1	0
predicted *y*	1	True positive	False positive
	0	False negative	True negative

WWII, a person) is while attempting to act as a binary classifier. You can see an example of a confusion matrix in Table 8.3.

To bring the confusion matrix to life with an example, let's return to the hot dog / not hot dog binary classifier that we've used to construct silly examples over many of the preceding chapters:

- When we provide some input x to a model and it *predicts* that the input represents a hot dog, then we're dealing with the first row of the table, because the *predicted* $y = 1$. In that case,

  - True positive: If the input is *actually* a hot dog (i.e., *actual* $y = 1$), then the model correctly classified the input.

  - False positive: If the input is actually *not* a hot dog (i.e., *actual* $y = 0$), then the model is *confused*.

- When we provide some input x to a model and it predicts that the input does *not* represent a hot dog, then we're dealing with the second row of the table, because *predicted* $y = 0$. In that case,

  - False negative: If the input is *actually* a hot dog (i.e., *actual* $y = 1$), then the model is also confused in this circumstance.

  - True negative: If the input is actually *not* a hot dog (i.e., *actual* $y = 0$), then the model correctly classified the input.

Calculating the ROC AUC Metric

Briefed on the confusion matrix, we can now move forward and calculate the ROC AUC metric itself, using a toy-sized example. Let's say, as shown in Table 8.4, we provide four inputs to a binary-classification model. Two of these inputs are actually hot dogs ($y = 1$), and two of them are not hot dogs ($y = 0$). For each of these inputs, the model outputs some predicted $\hat{y}$, all four of which are provided in Table 8.4.

To calculate the ROC AUC metric, we consider each of the $\hat{y}$ values output by the model as the binary-classification threshold in turn. Let's start with the lowest $\hat{y}$, which is 0.3 (see the "0.3 threshold" column in Table 8.5). At this threshold, only the first input

Table 8.4   Four hot dog / not hot dog predictions

y	*ŷ*
0	0.3
1	0.5
0	0.6
1	0.9

Table 8.5   Four hot dog / not hot dog predictions, now with intermediate ROC AUC calculations

y	ŷ	0.3 threshold	0.5 threshold	0.6 threshold
0 (not hot dog)	0.3	0 (TN)	0 (TN)	0 (TN)
1 (hot dog)	0.5	1 (TP)	0 (FN)	0 (FN)
0 (not hot dog)	0.6	1 (FP)	1 (FP)	0 (TN)
1 (hot dog)	0.9	1 (TP)	1 (TP)	1 (TP)

True Positive Rate = $\frac{TP}{TP+FN}$		$\frac{2}{2+0}=1.0$	$\frac{1}{1+1}=0.5$	$\frac{1}{1+1}=0.5$
False Positive Rate = $\frac{FP}{FP+TN}$		$\frac{1}{1+1}=0.5$	$\frac{1}{1+1}=0.5$	$\frac{0}{0+2}=0.0$

is classed as *not* a hot dog, whereas the second through fourth inputs (all with $\hat{y} > 0.3$) are all classed as hot dogs. We can compare each of these four predicted classifications with the confusion matrix in Table 8.3:

1. True negative (TN): This is actually not a hot dog ($y = 0$) and was correctly predicted as such.
2. True positive (TP): This is actually a hot dog ($y = 1$) and was correctly predicted as such.
3. False positive (FP): This is actually not a hot dog ($y = 0$) but it was erroneously predicted to be one.
4. True positive (TP): Like input 2, this is actually a hot dog ($y = 1$) and was correctly predicted as such.

The same process is repeated with the classification threshold set to 0.5 and yet again with the threshold set to 0.6, allowing us to populate the remaining columns of Table 8.5. As an exercise, it might be wise to work through these two columns, comparing the classifications at each threshold with the actual y values and the confusion matrix (Table 8.3) to ensure that you have a good handle on these concepts. Finally, note that the highest $\hat{y}$ value (in this case, 0.9) can be skipped as a potential threshold, because at such a high threshold we'd be considering all four instances to not be hot dogs, making it a ceiling instead of a classification boundary.

The next step toward computing the ROC AUC metric is to calculate both the true positive rate (TPR) and the false positive rate (FPR) at each of the three thresholds. Equations 8.1 and 8.2 use the "0.3 threshold" column to provide examples of how to calculate the true positive rate and false positive rate, respectively.

$$
\begin{aligned}
True\ Positive\ Rate &= \frac{(TP\ count)}{(TP\ count)\ +\ (FN\ count)} \\
&= \frac{2}{2+0} \\
&= \frac{2}{2} \\
&= 1.0
\end{aligned}
\tag{8.1}
$$

$$False\ Positive\ Rate = \frac{(FP\ count)}{(FP\ count)\ +\ (TN\ count)}$$
$$= \frac{1}{1+1}$$
$$= \frac{1}{2}$$
$$= 0.5$$

(8.2)

Shorthand versions of the arithmetic for calculating TPR and FPR for the thresholds 0.5 and 0.6 are also provided for your convenience at the bottom of Table 8.5. Again, perhaps you should test if you can compute these values yourself on your own time.

The final stage in calculating ROC AUC is to create a plot like the one we provide in Figure 8.11. The points that make up the shape of the receiver operating characteristic (ROC) curve are the false positive rate (horizontal, x-axis coordinate) and true positive rate (vertical, y-axis coordinate) at each of the available thresholds (which in this case is three) in Table 8.5, plus two extra points in the bottom-left and top-right corners of the plot. Specifically, these five points (shown as orange dots in Figure 8.11) are:

1. (0, 0) for the bottom-left corner
2. (0, 0.5) from the 0.6 threshold
3. (0.5, 0.5) from the 0.5 threshold
4. (0.5, 1) from the 0.3 threshold
5. (1, 1) for the top-right corner

In this toy-sized example, we only used four distinct $\hat{y}$ values, so there are only five points that determine the shape of the ROC curve, making the curve rather step shaped. When there are many available predictions providing many distinct $\hat{y}$ values—as is typically the case in real-world examples—the ROC curve has many more points, and so it's much less step shaped and much more, well, curve shaped. The area under the curve (AUC) of the ROC curve is exactly what it sounds like: In Figure 8.11, we've shaded this area in orange and, in this example, the AUC constitutes 75 percent of all the possible area and so the ROC AUC metric comes out to 0.75.

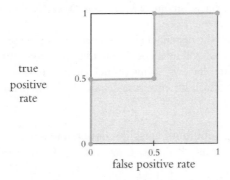

Figure 8.11 The (orange-shaded) area under the curve of the receiving operator characteristic, determined using the TPRs and FPRs from Table 8.5

A binary classifier that works as well as chance will generate a straight diagonal running from the bottom-left corner of the plot to its top-right corner, so an ROC AUC of 0.5 indicates that the classifier works as well as flipping a coin. A perfect ROC AUC is 1.0, which is attained by having FPR = 0 and TPR = 1 across all of the available $\hat{y}$ thresholds. When you're designing a binary classifier to perform well on the ROC AUC metric, the goal is thus to minimize FPR and maximize TPR across the range of $\hat{y}$ thresholds. That said, for most problems you encounter, attaining a perfect ROC AUC of 1.0 is not possible: There is usually some noise—perhaps a lot of noise—in the data that makes perfection unattainable. Thus, when you're working with any given dataset, there is some (typically unknown!) maximum ROC AUC score, such that no matter how ideally suited your model is to act as a binary classifier for the problem, there's an ROC AUC ceiling that no model can crack through.

Over the remainder of this chapter we use the illuminating ROC AUC metric, alongside the simpler accuracy and cost metrics you are already acquainted with, to evaluate the performance of the binary-classifying deep learning models that we design and train.

Natural Language Classification with Familiar Networks

In this section, we tie together concepts that were introduced in this chapter—natural language preprocessing best practices, the creation of word vectors, and the ROC AUC metric—with the deep learning theory from previous chapters. As we already alluded to earlier, the natural language processing model you'll experiment with over the remainder of the chapter will be a binary classifier that predicts whether a given film review is a positive one or a negative one. We begin by classifying natural language documents using types of neural networks that you're already familiar with—dense and convolutional—before moving along to networks that are specialized to handle data that occur in a sequence.

Loading the IMDb Film Reviews

As a performance baseline, we'll initially train and test a relatively simple dense network. All of the code for doing this is provided within our *Dense Sentiment Classifier* Jupyter notebook.

Example 8.12 provides the dependencies we need for our dense sentiment classifier. Many of these dependencies will be recognizable from previous chapters, but others (e.g., for loading a dataset of film reviews, saving model parameters as we train, calculating ROC AUC) are new. As usual, we cover the details of these dependencies as we apply them later on.

Example 8.12 Loading sentiment classifier dependencies

```
import keras
from keras.datasets import imdb # new!
from keras.preprocessing.sequence import pad_sequences # new!
```

```
from keras.models import Sequential
from keras.layers import Dense, Flatten, Dropout
from keras.layers import Embedding # new!
from keras.callbacks import ModelCheckpoint # new!
import os # new!
from sklearn.metrics import roc_auc_score, roc_curve # new!
import pandas as pd
import matplotlib.pyplot as plt # new!
%matplotlib inline
```

It's a good programming practice to put as many hyperparameters as you can at the top of your file. This makes it easier to experiment with these hyperparameters. It also makes it easier for you (or, indeed, your colleagues) to understand what you were doing in the file when you return to it (perhaps much) later. With this in mind, we place all of our hyperparameters together in a single cell within our Jupyter notebook. The code is provided in Example 8.13.

Example 8.13 Setting dense sentiment classifier hyperparameters

```
# output directory name:
output_dir = 'model_output/dense'

# training:
epochs = 4
batch_size = 128

# vector-space embedding:
n_dim = 64
n_unique_words = 5000
n_words_to_skip = 50
max_review_length = 100
pad_type = trunc_type = 'pre'

# neural network architecture:
n_dense = 64
dropout = 0.5
```

Let's break down the purpose of each of these variables:

- output_dir: A directory name (ideally, a unique one) in which to store our model's parameters after each epoch, allowing us to return to the parameters from any epoch of our choice at a later time.
- epochs: The number of epochs that we'd like to train for, noting that NLP models often overfit to the training data in fewer epochs than machine vision models.

- `batch_size`: As before, the number of training examples used during each round of model training (see Figure 7.5).

- `n_dim`: The number of dimensions we'd like our word-vector space to have.

- `n_unique_words`: With word2vec earlier in this chapter, we included tokens in our word-vector vocabulary only if they occurred at least a certain number of times within our corpus. An alternative approach—the one we take here—is to sort all of the tokens in our corpus by the number of times they occur, and then only use a certain number of the most popular words. Andrew Maas and his coworkers[30] opted to use the 5,000 most popular words across their film-review corpus and so we'll do the same.[31]

- `n_words_to_skip`: Instead of removing a manually curated list of stop words from their word-vector vocabulary, Maas et al. made the assumption that the 50 most frequently occurring words across their film-review corpus would serve as a decent list of stop words. We followed their lead and did the same.[32]

- `max_review_length`: Each movie review must have the same length so that TensorFlow knows the shape of the input data that will be flowing through our deep learning model. For this model, we selected a review length of 100 words.[33] Any reviews longer than 100 are truncated. Any reviews shorter than 100 are padded with a special *padding character* (analogous to the zero padding that can be used in machine vision, as in Figure 9.3).

- `pad_type`: By selecting `'pre'`, we add padding characters to the start of every review. The alternative is `'post'`, which adds them to the end. With a dense net-work like the one in this notebook, it shouldn't make much difference which of these options we pick. Later in this chapter, when we're working with specialized, sequential-data layer types,[34] it's generally best to use `'pre'` because the content at the end of the document is more influential in the model and so we want the largely uninformative padding characters to be at the beginning of the document.

- `trunc_type`: As with `pad_type`, our truncation options are `'pre'` or `'post'`. The former will remove words from the beginning of the review, whereas the latter will remove them from the end. By selecting `'pre'`, we're making (a bold!) assumption that the end of film reviews tend to include more information on review sentiment than the beginning.

- `n_dense`: The number of neurons to include in the dense layer of our neural network architecture. We waved our finger in the air to select 64, so some

---

30. We mentioned Maas et al. (2011) earlier in this chapter. They put together the movie-review corpus we're using in this notebook.

31. This 5,000-word threshold may not be optimal, but we didn't take the time to test lower or higher values. You are most welcome to do so yourself!

32. Note again that following Maas et al.'s lead may not be the optimal choice. Further, note that this means we'll actually be including the 51st most popular word through to the 5050th most popular word in our word-vector vocabulary.

33. You are free to experiment with lengthier or shorter reviews.

34. For example, RNN, LSTM.

experimentation and optimization are warranted at your end if you feel like it. For simplicity's sake, we also are using a single layer of dense neurons, but you could opt to have several.

- **dropout**: How much dropout to apply to the neurons in the dense layer. Again, we did not take the time to optimize this hyperparameter (set at 0.5) ourselves.

Loading in the film review data is a one-liner, provided in Example 8.14.

Example 8.14 Loading IMDb ilm review data

```
(x_train, y_train), (x_valid, y_valid) = \
    imdb.load_data(num_words=n_unique_words, skip_top=n_words_to_skip)
```

This dataset from Maas et al. (2011) is made up of the natural language of reviews from the publicly available Internet Movie Database (IMDb; imdb.com). It consists of 50,000 reviews, half of which are in the training dataset (x_train), and half of which are for model validation (x_valid). When submitting their review of a given film, users also provide a star rating, with a maximum of 10 stars. The labels (y_train and y_valid) are binary, based on these star ratings:

- Reviews with a score of four stars or fewer are considered to be a negative review ($y = 0$).
- Reviews with a score of seven stars or more, meanwhile, are classed as a positive review ($y = 1$).
- Moderate reviews—those with five or six stars—are not included in the dataset, making the binary classification task easier for any model.

By specifying values for the num_words and skip_top arguments when calling imdb.load_data(), we are limiting the size of our word-vector vocabulary and removing the most common (stop) words, respectively.

In our *Dense Sentiment Classifier* notebook, we have the convenience of loading our IMDb film-review data via the Keras imdb.load_data() method. When you're working with your own natural language data, you'll likely need to preprocess many aspects of the data yourself. In addition to the general preprocessing guidance we provided earlier in this chapter, Keras provides a number of convenient text preprocessing utilities, as documented online at keras.io/preprocessing/text. In particular, the Tokenizer() class may enable you to carry out all of the preprocessing steps you need in a single line of code, including

- Tokenizing a corpus to the word level (or even the character level)
- Setting the size of your word-vector vocabulary (with num_words)
- Filtering out punctuation
- Converting all characters to lowercase
- Converting tokens into an integer index

Examining the IMDb Data

Executing `x_train[0:6]`, we can examine the first six reviews from the training dataset, the first two of which are shown in Figure 8.12. These reviews are natively in an integer-index format, where each unique token from the dataset is represented by an integer. The first few integers are special cases, following a general convention that is widely used in NLP:

- 0: Reserved as the padding token (which we'll soon add to the reviews that are shorter than `max_review_length`).
- 1: Would be the *starting token*, which would indicate the beginning of a review. As per the next bullet point, however, the starting token is among the top 50 most common tokens and so is shown as "unknown."
- 2: Any tokens that occur very frequently across the corpus (i.e., they're in the top 50 most common words) or rarely (i.e., they're below the top 5,050 most common words) will be outside of our word-vector vocabulary and so are replaced with this *unknown token*.
- 3: The most frequently occurring word in the corpus.
- 4: The second-most frequently occurring word.
- 5: The third-most frequently occurring, and so on.

Using the following code from Example 8.15, we can see the length of the first six reviews in the training dataset.

Example 8.15 Printing the number of tokens in six reviews

```
for x in x_train[0:6]:
    print(len(x))
```

They are rather variable, ranging from 43 tokens up to 550 tokens. Shortly, we'll handle these discrepancies, standardizing all reviews to the same length.

The film reviews are fed into our neural network model in the integer-index format of Figure 8.12 because this is a memory-efficient way to store the token information. It would require appreciably more memory to feed the tokens in as character strings, for example. For us humans, however, it is uninformative (and, frankly, uninteresting) to examine reviews in the integer-index format. To view the reviews as natural language, we create an index of words as follows, where PAD, START, and UNK are customary for representing padding, starting, and unknown tokens, respectively:

```
word_index = keras.datasets.imdb.get_word_index()
word_index = {k:(v+3) for k,v in word_index.items()}
word_index["PAD"] = 0
word_index["START"] = 1
word_index["UNK"] = 2
index_word = {v:k for k,v in word_index.items()}
```

```
array([ [2, 2, 2, 2, 2, 530, 973, 1622, 1385, 65, 458, 4468, 66, 3941, 2,
173, 2, 256, 2, 2, 100, 2, 838, 112, 50, 670, 2, 2, 2, 480, 284, 2, 150,
2, 172, 112, 167, 2, 336, 385, 2, 2, 172, 4536, 1111, 2, 546, 2, 2, 447,
2, 192, 50, 2, 2, 147, 2025, 2, 2, 2, 2, 1920, 4613, 469, 2, 2, 71, 87,
2, 2, 2, 530, 2, 76, 2, 2, 1247, 2, 2, 2, 515, 2, 2, 2, 626, 2, 2, 2, 62,
386, 2, 2, 316, 2, 106, 2, 2, 2223, 2, 2, 480, 66, 3785, 2, 2, 130, 2, 2,
2, 619, 2, 2, 124, 51, 2, 135, 2, 2, 1415, 2, 2, 2, 2, 215, 2, 77, 52, 2,
2, 407, 2, 82, 2, 2, 2, 107, 117, 2, 2, 256, 2, 2, 2, 3766, 2, 723, 2, 7
1, 2, 530, 476, 2, 400, 317, 2, 2, 2, 1029, 2, 104, 88, 2, 381, 2, 29
7, 98, 2, 2071, 56, 2, 141, 2, 194, 2, 2, 2, 226, 2, 2, 134, 476, 2, 480,
2, 144, 2, 2, 2, 51, 2, 2, 224, 92, 2, 104, 2, 226, 65, 2, 2, 1334, 88,
2, 2, 283, 2, 2, 4472, 113, 103, 2, 2, 2, 2, 2, 178, 2],
        [2, 194, 1153, 194, 2, 78, 228, 2, 2, 1463, 4369, 2, 134, 2, 2, 71
5, 2, 118, 1634, 2, 394, 2, 2, 119, 954, 189, 102, 2, 207, 110, 3103, 2,
2, 69, 188, 2, 2, 2, 2, 2, 249, 126, 93, 2, 114, 2, 2300, 1523, 2, 647,
2, 116, 2, 2, 2, 2, 229, 2, 340, 1322, 2, 118, 2, 2, 130, 4901, 2, 2, 100
2, 2, 89, 2, 952, 2, 2, 2, 455, 2, 2, 2, 2, 1543, 1905, 398, 2, 1649, 2,
2, 2, 163, 2, 3215, 2, 2, 1153, 2, 194, 775, 2, 2, 349, 2637, 148, 60
5, 2, 2, 2, 123, 125, 68, 2, 2, 2, 349, 165, 4362, 98, 2, 2, 228, 2, 2,
2, 1157, 2, 299, 120, 2, 120, 174, 2, 220, 175, 136, 50, 2, 4373, 228, 2,
2, 2, 656, 245, 2350, 2, 2, 2, 131, 152, 491, 2, 2, 2, 2, 1212, 2, 2, 2,
371, 78, 2, 625, 64, 1382, 2, 2, 168, 145, 2, 2, 1690, 2, 2, 2, 1355, 2,
2, 2, 52, 154, 462, 2, 89, 78, 285, 2, 145, 95],
```

Figure 8.12   The first two film reviews from the training dataset of Andrew Maas and colleagues' (2011) IMDb dataset. Tokens are in an integer-index format.

Then we can use the code in Example 8.16 to view the film review of our choice—in this case, the first review from the training data.

Example 8.16 Printing a review as a character string

```
' '.join(index_word[id] for id in x_train[0])
```

The resulting string should look identical to the output shown in Figure 8.13.

Remembering that the review in Figure 8.13 contains the tokens that are fed into our neural network, we might nevertheless find it enjoyable to read the full review without all of the UNK tokens. In some cases of debugging model results, it might indeed even be practical to be able to view the full review. For example, if we're being too aggressive or conservative with either our n_unique_words or n_words_to_skip thresholds, it might become apparent by comparing a review like the one in Figure 8.13 with a full

```
"UNK UNK UNK UNK UNK brilliant casting location scenery story direction e
veryone's really suited UNK part UNK played UNK UNK could UNK imagine bei
ng there robert UNK UNK UNK amazing actor UNK now UNK same being director
UNK father came UNK UNK same scottish island UNK myself UNK UNK loved UNK
fact there UNK UNK real connection UNK UNK UNK UNK witty remarks througho
ut UNK UNK were great UNK UNK UNK brilliant UNK much UNK UNK bought UNK U
NK UNK soon UNK UNK UNK released UNK UNK UNK would recommend UNK UNK ever
yone UNK watch UNK UNK fly UNK UNK amazing really cried UNK UNK end UNK U
NK UNK sad UNK UNK know what UNK say UNK UNK cry UNK UNK UNK UNK must UNK
been good UNK UNK definitely UNK also UNK UNK UNK two little UNK UNK play
ed UNK UNK UNK norman UNK paul UNK were UNK brilliant children UNK often
left UNK UNK UNK UNK list UNK think because UNK stars UNK play them UNK g
rown up UNK such UNK big UNK UNK whole UNK UNK these children UNK ama
zing UNK should UNK UNK UNK what UNK UNK done don't UNK think UNK whole s
tory UNK UNK lovely because UNK UNK true UNK UNK someone's life after UNK
UNK UNK UNK UNK us UNK"
```

Figure 8.13   The first film review from the training dataset, now shown as a character string

```
"START this film was just brilliant casting location scenery story direct
ion everyone's really suited the part they played and you could just imag
ine being there robert redford's is an amazing actor and now the same bei
ng director norman's father came from the same scottish island as myself
so i loved the fact there was a real connection with this film the witty
remarks throughout the film were great it was just brilliant so much that
i bought the film as soon as it was released for retail and would recomme
nd it to everyone to watch and the fly fishing was amazing really cried a
t the end it was so sad and you know what they say if you cry at a film i
t must have been good and this definitely was also congratulations to the
two little boy's that played the part's of norman and paul they were just
brilliant children are often left out of the praising list i think becaus
e the stars that play them all grown up are such a big profile for the wh
ole film but these children are amazing and should be praised for what th
ey have done don't you think the whole story was so lovely because it was
true and was someone's life after all that was shared with us all"
```

Figure 8.14   The first film review from the training dataset, now shown in full as a character string

one. With our index of words (index_words) already available to us, we simply need to download the full reviews:

```
(all_x_train,_),(all_x_valid,_) = imdb.load_data()
```

Then we modify Example 8.16 to execute join() on the full-review list of our choice (i.e., all_x_train or all_x_valid), as provided in Example 8.17.

Example 8.17 Print full review as character string

```
' '.join(index_word[id] for id in all_x_train[0])
```

Executing this outputs the full text of the review of our choice—again, in this case, the first training review—as shown in Figure 8.14.

Standardizing the Length of the Reviews

By executing Example 8.15 earlier, we discovered that there is variability in the length of the film reviews. In order for the Keras-created TensorFlow model to run, we need to specify the size of the inputs that will be flowing into the model during training. This enables TensorFlow to optimize the allocation of memory and compute resources. Keras provides a convenient **pad_sequences()** method that enables us to both pad and truncate documents of text in a single line. Here we standardize our training and validation data in this way, as shown in Example 8.18.

Example 8.18 Standardizing input length by padding and truncating

```
x_train = pad_sequences(x_train, maxlen=max_review_length,
                        padding=pad_type, truncating=trunc_type, value=0)
x_valid = pad_sequences(x_valid, maxlen=max_review_length,
                        padding=pad_type, truncating=trunc_type, value=0)
```

```
'PAD PAD PAD PAD PAD PAD PAD PAD PAD PAD PAD PAD PAD PAD PAD PAD PAD PAD
PAD PAD PAD PAD PAD PAD PAD PAD PAD PAD PAD PAD PAD PAD PAD PAD PAD PAD P
AD PAD PAD PAD PAD PAD PAD PAD PAD PAD PAD PAD PAD PAD PAD PAD PAD PAD PA
D PAD PAD UNK begins better than UNK ends funny UNK UNK russian UNK crew
UNK UNK other actors UNK UNK those scenes where documentary shots UNK UNK
spoiler part UNK message UNK UNK contrary UNK UNK whole story UNK UNK doe
s UNK UNK UNK UNK'
```

Figure 8.15   The sixth film review from the training dataset, padded with the PAD token at the beginning so that—like all the other reviews—it has a length of 100 tokens

Now, when printing reviews (e.g., with x_train[0:6]) or their lengths (e.g., with the code from Example 8.15), we see that all of the reviews have the same length of 100 (because we set max_review_length =100). Examining x_train[5]—which previously had a length of only 43 tokens—with code similar to Example 8.16, we can observe that the beginning of the review has been padded with 57 PAD tokens (see Figure 8.15).

Dense Network

With sufficient NLP theory behind us, as well as our data loaded and preprocessed, we're at long last prepared to make use of a neural network architecture to classify film reviews by their sentiment. A baseline dense network model for this task is shown in Example 8.19.

Example 8.19 Dense sentiment classifier architecture

```
model = Sequential()
model.add(Embedding(n_unique_words, n_dim,
                    input_length=max_review_length))
model.add(Flatten())
model.add(Dense(n_dense, activation='relu'))
model.add(Dropout(dropout))
# model.add(Dense(n_dense, activation='relu'))
# model.add(Dropout(dropout))
model.add(Dense(1, activation='sigmoid'))
```

Let's break the architecture down line by line:

- We're using a Keras Sequential() method to invoke a sequential model, as we have for all of the models so far in this book.
- As with word2vec, the Embedding() layer enables us to create word vectors from a corpus of documents—in this case, the 25,000 movie reviews of the IMDb training dataset. Relative to independently creating word vectors with word2vec (or GloVe, etc.) as we did earlier in this chapter, training your word vectors via backpropagation as a component of your broader NLP model has a potential advantage: The locations that words are assigned to within the vector space reflect not only word similarity but also the relevance of the words to the ultimate, specific purpose of the model (e.g., binary classification of IMDb reviews by sentiment). The size of the word-vector vocabulary and the number of dimensions of the vector space are specified by n_unique_words and n_dim, respectively. Because the embedding layer

is the first hidden layer in our network, we must also pass into it the shape of our input layer: We do this with the `input_length` argument.

- As in Chapter 9, the `Flatten()` layer enables us to pass a many-dimensional output (here, a two-dimensional output from the embedding layer) into a one-dimensional dense layer.

- Speaking of `Dense()` layers, we used a single one consisting of `relu` activations in this architecture, with `Dropout()` applied to it.

- We opted for a fairly shallow neural network architecture for our baseline model, but you can trivially deepen it by adding further `Dense()` layers (see the lines that are commented out).

- Finally, because there are only two classes to classify, we require only a single output neuron (because, as discussed earlier in this chapter, if one class has the probability p then the other class has the probability $1 - p$). This neuron is `sigmoid` because we'd like it to output probabilities between 0 and 1 (refer to Figure 6.9).

In addition to training word vectors on natural language data alone (e.g., with word2vec or GloVe) or training them with an embedding layer as part of a deep learning model, pretrained word vectors are also available online.

As with using a ConvNet trained on the millions of images in ImageNet (Chapter 10), this natural language transfer learning is powerful, because these word vectors may have been trained on extremely large corpuses (e.g., all of Wikipedia, or the English-language Internet) that provide large, nuanced vocabularies that would be expensive to train yourself. Examples of pretrained word vectors are available at `github.com/Kyubyong/wordvectors` and `nlp.stanford.edu/projects/glove`. The fast-Text library also offers subword embeddings in 157 languages; these can be downloaded from `fasttext.cc`.

In this book, we don't cover substituting pretrained word vectors (be they downloaded or trained separately from your deep learning model, as we did with `Word2Vec()` earlier in this chapter) in place of the embedding layer, because there are many different permutations on how you might like to do this. For a neat tutorial from François Chollet, the creator of Keras, go to `bit.ly/preTrained`.

Executing `model.summary()`, we discover that our fairly simple NLP model has quite a few parameters, as shown in Figure 8.16:

- In the embedding layer, the 320,000 parameters come from having 5,000 words, each one with a location specified in a 64-dimensional word-vector space ($64 \times 5,000 = 320,000$).

- Flowing out of the embedding layer through the flatten layer and into the dense layer are 6,400 values: Each of our film-review inputs consists of 100 tokens, with each token specified by 64 word-vector-space coordinates ($64 \times 100 = 6,400$).

- Each of the 64 neurons in the dense hidden layer receives input from each of the 6,400 values flowing out of the flatten layer, for a total of $64 \times 6,400 = 409,600$

```
Layer (type)                   Output Shape              Param #
=================================================================
embedding_1 (Embedding)        (None, 100, 64)           320000
_____
flatten_1 (Flatten)            (None, 6400)              0
_____
dense_1 (Dense)                (None, 64)                409664
_____
dropout_1 (Dropout)            (None, 64)                0
_____
dense_2 (Dense)                (None, 1)                 65
=================================================================
Total params: 729,729
Trainable params: 729,729
Non-trainable params: 0
```

Figure 8.16   Dense sentiment classifier model summary

weights. And, of course, each of the 64 neurons has a bias, for a total of 409,664 parameters in the layer.

- Finally, the single neuron of the output layer has 64 weights—one for the activation output by each of the neurons in the preceding layer—plus its bias, for a total of 65 parameters.

- Summing up the parameters from each of the layers, we have a grand total of 730,000 of them.

As shown in Example 8.20, we compile our dense sentiment classifier with a line of code that should already be familiar from recent chapters, except that—because we have a single output neuron within a binary classifier—we use binary_crossentropy cost in place of the categorical_crossentropy cost we used for our multiclass MNIST classifiers.

Example 8.20 Compiling our sentiment classifier

```
model.compile(loss='binary_crossentropy', optimizer='adam',
              metrics=['accuracy'])
```

With the code provided in Example 8.21, we create a ModelCheckpoint() object that will allow us to save our model parameters after each epoch during training. By doing this, we can return to the parameters from our epoch of choice later on during model evaluation or to make inferences in a production system. If the output_dir directory doesn't already exist, we use the makedirs() method to make it.

Example 8.21 Creating an object and directory for checkpointing model parameters after each epoch

```
modelcheckpoint = ModelCheckpoint(filepath=output_dir+
                                  "/weights.{epoch:02d}.hdf5")
if not os.path.exists(output_dir):
    os.makedirs(output_dir)
```

```
Train on 25000 samples, validate on 25000 samples
Epoch 1/4
25000/25000 [==============================] - 2s 80us/step - loss: 0.5612 - acc: 0.6892 - val_loss: 0.3630 - val_acc: 0.8398
Epoch 2/4
25000/25000 [==============================] - 2s 69us/step - loss: 0.2851 - acc: 0.8841 - val_loss: 0.3486 - val_acc: 0.8447
Epoch 3/4
25000/25000 [==============================] - 2s 70us/step - loss: 0.1158 - acc: 0.9646 - val_loss: 0.4252 - val_acc: 0.8337
Epoch 4/4
25000/25000 [==============================] - 2s 70us/step - loss: 0.0237 - acc: 0.9961 - val_loss: 0.5304 - val_acc: 0.8340
```

Figure 8.17   Training the dense sentiment classifier

Like the compile step, the model-fitting step (Example 8.22 for our sentiment classifier should be familiar except, perhaps, for our use of the `callbacks` argument to pass in
the `modelcheckpoint` object.[35]

Example 8.22 Fitting our sentiment classifier

```
model.fit(x_train, y_train,
          batch_size=batch_size, epochs=epochs, verbose=1,
          validation_data=(x_valid, y_valid),
          callbacks=[modelcheckpoint])
```

As shown in Figure 8.17, we achieve our lowest validation loss (0.349 and highest validation accuracy (84.5 percent in the second epoch. In the third and fourth epochs, the
model is heavily overfit, with accuracy on the training set considerably higher than on
the validation set. By the fourth epoch, training accuracy stands at 99.6 percent while
validation accuracy is much lower, at 83.4 percent.

To evaluate the results of the best epoch more thoroughly, we use the Keras `load_`
`weights()` method to load the parameters from the second epoch (`weights.02.hdf5`
back into our model, as in Example 8.23.[36,37]

Example 8.23 Loading model parameters

```
model.load_weights(output_dir+"/weights.02.hdf5")
```

We can then calculate validation set $\hat{y}$ values for the best epoch by passing the
`predict_proba()` method on the `x_valid` dataset, as shown in Example 8.24.

Example 8.24 Predicting $\hat{y}$ for all validation data

```
y_hat = model.predict_proba(x_valid)
```

---

35. This isn't our first use of the `callbacks` argument. We previously used this argument, which can take in a list
of multiple different callbacks, to provide data on model training progress to TensorBoard (see Chapter 7).

36. Although the method is called `load_weights()`, it loads in *all* model parameters, including biases. Because
weights typically constitute the vast majority of parameters in a model, deep learning practitioners often call
parameter files "weights" files.

37. Earlier versions of Keras used zero indexing for epochs, but more recent versions index starting at 1.

With y_hat[0], for example, we can now see the model's prediction of the sentiment of the first movie review in the validation set. For this review, $\hat{y} = 0.09$, indicating the model estimates that there's a 9 percent chance the review is positive and, therefore, a 91 percent chance it's negative. Executing y_valid[0] informs us that $\hat{y} = 0$ for this review—that is, it is in fact a negative review—so the model's $\hat{y}$ is pretty good! If you're curious about what the content of the negative review was, you can run a slight modification on Example 8.17 to access the full text of the all_x_valid[0] list item, as shown in Example 8.25.

Example 8.25 Printing a full validation review

```
' '.join(index_word[id] for id in all_x_valid[0])
```

Examining individual scores can be interesting, but we get a much better sense of our model's performance by looking at all of the validation results together. We can plot a histogram of all the validation $\hat{y}$ values by running the code in Example 8.26.

Example 8.26 Plotting a histogram of validation data $\hat{y}$ values

```
plt.hist(y_hat)
_ = plt.axvline(x=0.5, color='orange')
```

The histogram output is provided in Figure 8.18. The plot shows that the model often has a strong opinion on the sentiment of a given review: Some 8,000 of the 25,000 re-views (~32 percent of them) are assigned a $\hat{y}$ of less than 0.1, and ~6,500 (~26 percent) are given a $\hat{y}$ greater than 0.9.

The vertical orange line in Figure 8.18 marks the 0.5 threshold above which reviews are considered by a simple accuracy calculation to be positive. As discussed earlier in the chapter, such a simple threshold can be misleading, because a review with a $\hat{y}$ just below 0.5 is not predicted by the model to have much difference in sentiment relative to a review with a $\hat{y}$ just above 0.5. To obtain a more nuanced assessment of our model's performance as a binary classifier, we can use the roc_auc_score() method from the

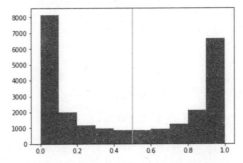

Figure 8.18 Histogram of validation data $\hat{y}$ values for the second epoch of our dense sentiment classifier

scikit-learn metrics library to straightforwardly calculate the ROC AUC score across the validation data, as shown in Example 8.27.

Example 8.27 Calculating ROC AUC for validation data

```
pct_auc = roc_auc_score(y_valid, y_hat)*100.0
"{:0.2f}".format(pct_auc)
```

Printing the output in an easy-to-read format with the `format()` method, we see that the percentage of the area under the receiver operating characteristic curve is (a fairly high) 92.9 percent.

To get a sense of where the model breaks down, we can create a DataFrame of y and $\hat{y}$ validation set values, using the code in Example 8.28.

Example 8.28 Creating a ydf DataFrame of *y* and *ŷ* values

```
float_y_hat = []
for y in y_hat:
    float_y_hat.append(y[0])
ydf = pd.DataFrame(list(zip(float_y_hat, y_valid)),
                   columns=['y_hat', 'y'])
```

Printing the first 10 rows of the resulting ydf DataFrame with `ydf.head(10)`, we see the output shown in Figure 8.19.

Querying the ydf DataFrame as we do in Examples 8.29 and 8.30 and then examining the individual reviews these queries surface by varying the list index in

	y_hat	y
0	0.089684	0
1	0.982754	1
2	0.746905	1
3	0.543328	0
4	0.997054	1
5	0.833994	1
6	0.766254	1
7	0.008032	0
8	0.812743	0
9	0.729463	1

Figure 8.19   DataFrame of *y* and *ŷ* values for the IMDb validation data

```
"START wow another kevin costner hero movie postman tin cup waterworld bo
dyguard wyatt earp robin hood even that baseball movie seems like he make
s movies specifically to be the center of attention the characters are al
most always the same the heroics the flaws the greatness the fall the red
emption yup within the 1st 5 minutes of the movie we're all supposed to b
e in awe of his character and it builds up more and more from there br br
and this time the story story is just a collage of different movies you d
on't need a spoiler you've seen this movie several times though it had di
fferent titles you'll know what will happen way before it happens this is
like mixing an officer and a gentleman with but both are easily better mo
vies watch to see how this kind of movie should be made and also to see h
ow an good but slightly underrated actor russell plays the hero"
```

Figure 8.20   An example of a false positive: This negative review was misclassified as positive by our model.

Example 8.25, you can get a sense of the kinds of reviews that cause the model to make its largest errors.

Example 8.29 Ten cases of negative validation reviews with high $\hat{y}$ scores

```
ydf[(ydf.y == 0) & (ydf.y_hat > 0.9)].head(10)
```

Example 8.30 Ten cases of positive validation reviews with low $\hat{y}$ scores

```
ydf[(ydf.y == 0) & (ydf.y_hat > 0.9)].head(10)
```

An example of a false positive—a negative review ($y = 0$) with a very high model score ($\hat{y} = 0.97$)—that was identified by running the code in Example 8.29 is provided in Figure 8.20.[38] And an example of a false negative—a positive review ($y = 1$) with a very low model score ($\hat{y} = 0.06$)—that was identified by running the code in Example 8.30 is provided in Figure 8.21.[39] Carrying out this kind of post hoc anal-ysis of our model, one potential shortcoming that surfaces is that our dense classifier is not specialized to detect patterns of multiple tokens occurring in a sequence that might predict film-review sentiment. For example, it might be handy for patterns like the token-pair *not-good* to be easily detected by the model as predictive of negative sentiment.

Convolutional Networks

As covered in Chapter 9, convolutional layers are particularly adept at detecting spatial patterns. In this section, we use them to detect spatial patterns among words—like the *not-good* sequence—and see whether they can improve upon the performance of our dense network at classifying film reviews by their sentiment. All of the code for this ConvNet can be found in our *Convolutional Sentiment Classifier* notebook.

---

38. We output this particular review—the 387th in the validation dataset—by running the following code:
` '.join(index_word[id] for id in all_x_valid[386])`.
39. Run ` '.join(index_word[id] for id in all_x_valid[224])` to print out this same review yourself.

```
"START finally a true horror movie this is the first time in years that i
had to cover my eyes i am a horror buff and i recommend this movie but it
is quite gory i am not a big wrestling fan but kane really pulled the who
le monster thing off i have to admit that i didn't want to see this movie
my 17 year old dragged me to it but am very glad i did during and after t
he movie i was looking over my shoulder i have to agree with others about
the whole remake horror movies enough is enough i think that is why this
movie is getting some good reviews it is a refreshing change and takes yo
u back to the texas chainsaw first one michael myers and jason and no cgi
crap"
```

Figure 8.21   An example of a false negative: This positive review was misclassified as negative by our model.

The dependencies for this model are identical to those of our dense sentiment classifier (see Example 8.12), except that it has three new Keras layer types, as provided in Example 8.31.

Example 8.31 Additional CNN dependencies

```
from keras.layers import Conv1D, GlobalMaxPooling1D
from keras.layers import SpatialDropout1D
```

The hyperparameters for our convolutional sentiment classifier are provided in Example 8.32.

Example 8.32 Convolutional sentiment classifier hyperparameters

```
# output directory name:
output_dir = 'model_output/conv'

# training:
epochs = 4
batch_size = 128

# vector-space embedding:
n_dim = 64
n_unique_words = 5000
max_review_length = 400
pad_type = trunc_type = 'pre'
drop_embed = 0.2 # new!

# convolutional layer architecture:
n_conv = 256 # filters, a.k.a. kernels
k_conv = 3 # kernel length

# dense layer architecture:
n_dense = 256
dropout = 0.2
```

Relative to the hyperparameters from our dense sentiment classifier (see Example 8.13):

- We have a new, unique directory name (`'conv'`) for storing model parameters after each epoch of training.
- Our number of epochs and batch size remain the same.
- Our vector-space embedding hyperparameters remain the same, except that
  - We quadrupled `max_review_length` to 400. We did this because, despite the fairly dramatic increase in input volume as well as an increase in our number of hidden layers, our convolutional classifier will still have far fewer parameters relative to our dense sentiment classifier.
  - With `drop_embed`, we'll be adding dropout to our embedding layer.
- Our convolutional sentiment classifier will have two hidden layers after the embedding layer:
  - A convolutional layer with 256 filters (n_conv), each with a single dimension (a *length*) of 3 (k_conv). When working with two-dimensional images in Chapter 9, our convolutional layers had filters with two dimensions. Natural language—be it written or spoken—has only one dimension associated with it (the dimension of time) and so the convolutional layers used in this chapter will have one-dimensional filters.
  - A dense layer with 256 neurons (n_dense) and `dropout` of 20 percent.

The steps for loading the IMDb data and standardizing the length of the reviews are identical to those in our *Dense Sentiment Classifier* notebook (see Examples 8.14 and 8.18). The model architecture is of course rather different, and is provided in Example 8.33.

Example 8.33 Convolutional sentiment classifier architecture

```
model = Sequential()

# vector-space embedding:
model.add(Embedding(n_unique_words, n_dim,
                    input_length=max_review_length))
model.add(SpatialDropout1D(drop_embed))

# convolutional layer:
model.add(Conv1D(n_conv, k_conv, activation='relu'))
# model.add(Conv1D(n_conv, k_conv, activation='relu'))
model.add(GlobalMaxPooling1D())

# dense layer:
model.add(Dense(n_dense, activation='relu'))
model.add(Dropout(dropout))

# output layer:
model.add(Dense(1, activation='sigmoid'))
```

Breaking the model down:

- Our embedding layer is the same as before, except that it now has dropout applied to it.

- We no longer require `Flatten()`, because the `Conv1D()` layer takes in both dimensions of the embedding layer output.

- We use `relu` activation within our one-dimensional convolutional layer. The layer has 256 unique filters, each of which is free to specialize in activating when it passes over a particular three-token sequence. The activation map for each of the 256 filters has a length of 398, for a 256×398 output shape.[40]

- If you fancy it, you're welcome to add additional convolutional layers, by, for example, uncommenting the second `Conv1D()` line.

- *Global max-pooling* is common for dimensionality reduction within deep learning NLP models. We use it here to squash the activation map from 256×398 to 256×1. By applying it, only the magnitude of largest activation for a given convolutional filter is retained by the maximum-calculating operation, and we lose any temporal-position-specific information the filter may have output to its 398-element-long activation map.

- Because the activations output from the global max-pooling layer are one-dimensional, they can be fed directly into the dense layer, which consists (again) of `relu` neurons and dropout is applied.

- The output layer remains the same.

- The model has a grand total of 435,000 parameters (see Figure 8.22), several hundred thousand fewer than our dense sentiment classifier. Per epoch, this model will

```
Layer (type)                    Output Shape              Param #
=================================================================
embedding_1 (Embedding)         (None, 400, 64)           320000
_____
spatial_dropout1d_1 (Spatial    (None, 400, 64)           0
_____
conv1d_1 (Conv1D)               (None, 398, 256)          49408
_____
global_max_pooling1d_1 (Glob    (None, 256)               0
_____
dense_1 (Dense)                 (None, 256)               65792
_____
dropout_1 (Dropout)             (None, 256)               0
_____
dense_2 (Dense)                 (None, 1)                 257
=================================================================
Total params: 435,457
Trainable params: 435,457
Non-trainable params: 0
```

Figure 8.22 Convolutional sentiment classifier model summary

---

40. As described in Chapter 9, when a two-dimensional filter convolves over an image, we lose pixels around the perimeter if we don't pad the image first. In this natural language model, our one-dimensional convolutional filter has a length of three, so, on the far left of the movie review, it begins centered on the second token and, on the far right, it ends centered on the second-to-last token. Because we didn't pad the movie reviews at both ends before feeding them into the convolutional layer, we thus lose a token's worth of information from each end: $400 - 1 - 1 = 398$. We're not upset about this loss.

nevertheless take longer to train because the convolutional operation is relatively computationally expensive.

A critical item to note about this model architecture is that the convolutional filters are not detecting simply triplets of *words*. Rather, they are detecting triplets of *word vectors*. Following from our discussion in Chapter 2, contrasting discrete, one-hot word representations with the word-vector representations that gently smear meaning across a high-dimensional space (see Table 2.1), all of the models in this chapter become specialized in associating word *meaning* with review sentiment—as opposed to merely associating individual words with review sentiment. As an example, if the network learns that the token pair *not-good* is associated with a negative review, then it should also associate the pair *not-great* with negative reviews, because *good* and *great* have similar meanings (and thus should occupy a similar location in word-vector space).

The compile, checkpoint, and model-fitting steps are the same as for our dense sentiment classifier (see Examples 8.20, 8.21, and 8.22, respectively). Model-fitting progress is shown in Figure 8.23. The epoch with the lowest validation loss (0.258) and highest validation accuracy (89.6 percent) was the third epoch. Loading the model parameters from that epoch back in (with the code from Example 8.23 but specifying weights.03.hdf5), we then predict $\hat{y}$ for all validation data (exactly as in Example 8.24). Creating a histogram (Figure 8.24) of these $\hat{y}$ values (with the same code as in Example 8.26), we can see visually that our CNN has a stronger opinion of review sentiment than our dense network did (refer to Figure 8.18): There are about a thousand more reviews with $\hat{y} < 0.1$ and several thousand more with $\hat{y} > 0.9$. Calculating ROC AUC (with the code from Example 8.27), we output a very high score of 96.12 percent, indicating that the CNN's confidence was not misplaced: It is a marked improvement over the already high ~93 percent score of the dense net.

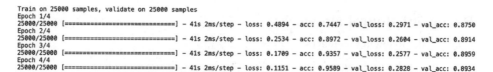

Figure 8.23 Training the convolutional sentiment classifier

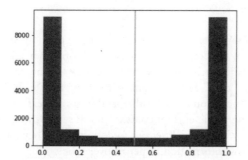

Figure 8.24 Histogram of validation data $\hat{y}$ values for the third epoch of our convolutional sentiment classifier

Networks Designed for Sequential Data

Our ConvNet classifier outperformed our dense net—perhaps in large part because its convolutional layer is adept at learning patterns of words that predict some outcome, such as whether a film review is favorable or negative. The filters within convolutional layers tend to excel at learning short sequences like triplets of words (recall that we set k = 3 in Example 8.32), but a document of natural language like a movie review might contain much longer sequences of words that, when considered all together, would enable the model to accurately predict some outcome. To handle long sequences of data like this, there exists a family of deep learning models called recurrent neural networks (RNNs), which include specialized layer types like *long short-term memory units* (LSTMs) and *gated recurrent units* (GRUs). In this section, we cover the essential theory of RNNs and apply several variants of them to our movie-review classification problem. We also introduce *attention*—an especially sophisticated approach to modeling natural language data that is setting new benchmarks across NLP applications.

As mentioned at the start of the chapter, the RNN family, including LSTMs and GRUs, is well suited to handling not only natural language data but also any input data that occur in a one-dimensional sequence. This includes price data (e.g., financial time series, stock prices), sales figures, temperatures, and disease rates (epidemiology). While RNN applications other than NLP are beyond the scope of this textbook, we collate resources for modeling quantitative data over time at jonkrohn.com/resources under the heading *Time Series Prediction*.

Recurrent Neural Networks

Consider the following sentences:

> Jon and Grant are writing a book together. They have really enjoyed writing it.

The human mind can track the concepts in the second sentence quite easily. You already know that "they" in the second sentence refers to your authors, and "it" refers to the book we're writing. Although this task is easy for you, however, it is not so trivial for a neural network.

The convolutional sentiment classifier we built in the previous section was able to consider a word only in the context of the two words on either side of it (k_conv = 3, as in Example 8.32). With such a small window of text, that neural network had no capacity to assess what "they" or "it" might be referring to. Our human brains can do it because our thoughts loop around each other, and we revisit earlier ideas in order to inform our understanding of the current context. In this section we introduce the concept of recurrent neural networks, which set out to do just that: They have loops built into their structure that allow information to persist over time.

The high-level structure of a recurrent neural network (RNN) is shown in Figure 8.25. On the left, the dotted line indicates the *loop* that passes information

Recurrent Neural Network   RNN unpacked

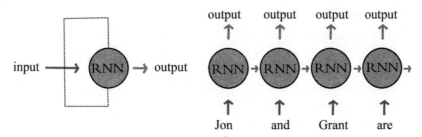

Figure 8.25 Schematic diagram of a recurrent neural network

between steps in the network. As in a dense network, where there is a neuron for each input, so too is there a neuron for each input here. We can observe this more easily on the right, where the schematic of the RNN is unpacked. There is a recurrent module for each word in the sentence (only the first four words are shown here for b revity).[41] However, each module receives an additional input from the previous module, and in doing so the network is able to pass along information from earlier timesteps in the sequence. In the case of Figure 8.25, each word is represented by a distinct timestep in the RNN sequence, so the network might be able to learn that "Jon" and "Grant" were writing the book, thereby associating these terms with the word "they" that occurs later in the sequence.

Recurrent neural networks are, computationally, more complex to train than exclusively "feedforward" neural networks like the dense nets and CNNs we've used so far in the book. As depicted in Figure 7.6, feedforward networks involve backpropagating cost from the output layer back toward the input layer. If a network includes a recurrent layer (such as SimpleRNN, LSTM, or GRU), then the cost must be backpropagated not only back toward the input layer, but back over the timesteps of the recurrent layer (from later timesteps back toward earlier timesteps), as well. Note that, in the same way that the gradient of learning vanishes as we backpropagate over later hidden layers toward earlier ones (see Figure 7.8), so, too, does the gradient vanish as we backpropagate over later timesteps within a recurrent layer toward earlier ones. Because of this, later timesteps in a sequence have more influence within the model than earlier ones do.[42]

---

41. This is also why we have to pad shorter sentences during preprocessing: The RNN expects a sequence of a particular length, and so if the sequence is not long enough we add PAD tokens to make up the difference.
42. If you suspect that the beginning of your sequences (e.g., the words at the beginning of a movie review) is generally more relevant to the problem you're solving with your model (sentiment classification) than the end (the words at the end of the review), you can reverse the sequence before passing it as an input into your network. In that way, within your network's recurrent layers, the beginning of the sequence will be backpropagated over before the end is.

Implementing an RNN in Keras

Adding a recurrent layer to a neural network architecture to create an RNN is straightforward in Keras, as we illustrate in our *RNN Sentiment Classifier* Jupyter notebook. For the sake of brevity and readability, please note that the following code cells are identical across all the Jupyter notebooks in this chapter, including the *Dense* and *Convolutional Sentiment Classifier* notebooks that we've already covered:

- Loading dependencies (Example 8.12), except that there are often one or two additional dependencies in a given notebook. We'll note these additions separately—typically when we present the notebook's neural network architecture.
- Loading IMDb film review data (Example 8.14).
- Standardizing review length (Example 8.18).
- Compiling the model (Example 8.20).
- Creating the `ModelCheckpoint()` object and directory (Example 8.21).
- Fitting the model (Example 8.22).
- Loading the model parameters from the best epoch (Example 8.23), with the critical exception that the particular epoch we select to load varies depending on which epoch has the lowest validation loss.
- Predicting $\hat{y}$ for all validation data (Example 8.24).
- Plotting a histogram of $\hat{y}$ (Example 8.26).
- Calculating ROC AUC (Example 8.27).

The code cells that vary are those in which we:

1. Set hyperparameters
2. Design the neural network architecture

The hyperparameters for our RNN are as shown in Example 8.34.

Example 8.34 RNN sentiment classifier hyperparameters

```
# output directory name:
output_dir = 'model_output/rnn'

# training:
epochs = 16 # way more!
batch_size = 128

# vector-space embedding:
n_dim = 64
n_unique_words = 10000
max_review_length = 100 # lowered due to vanishing gradient over time
pad_type = trunc_type = 'pre'
drop_embed = 0.2
```

```
# RNN layer architecture:
n_rnn = 256
drop_rnn = 0.2
```

Changes relative to our previous sentiment classifier notebooks are:

- We quadrupled epochs of training to 16 because overfitting didn't occur in the early epochs.

- We lowered `max_review_length` back down to 100, although even this is excessive for a simple RNN. We can backpropagate over about 100 timesteps (i.e., 100 tokens or words in a natural language model) with an LSTM (covered in the next section) before the gradient of learning vanishes completely, but the gradient in a plain old RNN vanishes completely after about 10 timesteps. Thus, `max_review_length` could probably be lowered to less than 10 before we would notice a reduction in this model's performance.

- For all of the RNN-family architectures in this chapter, we experimented with doubling the word-vector vocabulary to 10000 tokens. This seemed to provide improved results for these architectures, although we didn't test it rigorously.

- We set `n_rnn = 256`, so we could say that this recurrent layer has 256 *units*, or, alternatively, we could say it has 256 *cells*. In the same way that having 256 convolutional filters enabled our CNN model to specialize in detecting 256 unique triplets of word meaning,[43] this setting enables our RNN to detect 256 unique sequences of word meaning that may be relevant to review sentiment.

Our RNN model architecture is provided in Example 8.35.

Example 8.35 RNN sentiment classifier architecture

```
from keras.layers import SimpleRNN

model = Sequential()
model.add(Embedding(n_unique_words, n_dim,
                    input_length=max_review_length))
model.add(SpatialDropout1D(drop_embed))
model.add(SimpleRNN(n_rnn, dropout=drop_rnn))
model.add(Dense(1, activation='sigmoid'))
```

In place of a convolutional layer or a dense layer (or both) within the hidden layers of this model, we have a Keras `SimpleRNN()` layer, which has a `dropout` argument; as a result, we didn't need to add dropout in a separate line of code. Unlike putting a dense layer after a convolutional layer, it is relatively uncommon to add a dense layer after a recurrent layer, because it provides little performance advantage. You're welcome to try it by adding in a `Dense()` hidden layer anyway.

---

43. "Word meaning" here refers to a location in word-vector space.

The results of running this model (which are shown in full in our *RNN Sentiment Classifier* notebook) were not encouraging. We found that the training loss, after going down steadily over the first half-dozen epochs, began to jump around after that. This indicates that the model is struggling to learn patterns even within the training data, which—relative to the validation data—it should be readily able to do. Indeed, all of the models fit so far in this book have had training losses that reliably attenuated epoch over epoch.

As the training loss bounced around, so too did the validation loss. We observed the lowest validation loss in the seventh epoch (0.504), which corresponded to a validation accuracy of 77.6 percent and an ROC AUC of 84.9 percent. All three of these metrics are our worst yet for a sentiment classifier model. This is because, as we mentioned earlier in this section, RNNs are only able to backpropagate through ~10 time steps before the gradient diminishes so much that parameter updates become negligibly small. Because of this, simple RNNs are rarely used in practice: More-sophisticated recurrent layer types like LSTMs, which can backpropagate through ~100 time steps, are far more common.[44]

Long Short-Term Memory Units

As stated at the end of the preceding section, simple RNNs are adequate if the space between the relevant information and the context where it's needed is small (fewer than 10 timesteps); however, if the task requires a broader context (which is often the case in NLP tasks), there is another recurrent layer type that is well suited to it: long short-term memory units, or LSTMs.

LSTMs were introduced by Sepp Hochreiter and Jürgen Schmidhuber in 1997,[45] but they are more widely used in NLP deep learning applications today than ever before. The basic structure of an LSTM layer is the same as the simple recurrent layers captured in Figure 8.25. LSTMs receive input from the sequence of data (e.g., a particular token from a natural language document), and they also receive input from the previous time point in the sequence. The difference is that inside each cell in a simple recurrent layer (e.g., `SimpleRNN()` in Keras), you'll find a single neural network activation function such as a tanh function, which transforms the RNN cell's inputs to generate its output. In contrast, the cells of an LSTM layer contain a far more complex structure, as depicted in Figure 8.26.

This schematic can appear daunting, and, admittedly, we agree that a full step-by-step breakdown of each component inside of an LSTM cell is unnecessarily detailed for this book.[46] That said, there are a few key points that we should nevertheless touch on here. The first is the *cell state* running across the top of the LSTM cell. Notice that the cell

---

44. The only situation we could think of where a simple RNN would be practical is one where your sequences only had 10 or fewer consecutive timesteps of information that are relevant to the problem you're solving with your model. This might be the case with some time series forecasting models or if you only had very short strings of natural language in your dataset.

45. Hochreiter, S., & Schmidhuber, J. (1997). Long short-term memory. *Neural Computation, 9,* 1735–80.

46. For a thorough exposition of LSTM cells, we recommend Christopher Olah's highly visual explainer, which is available at `bit.ly/colahLSTM`.

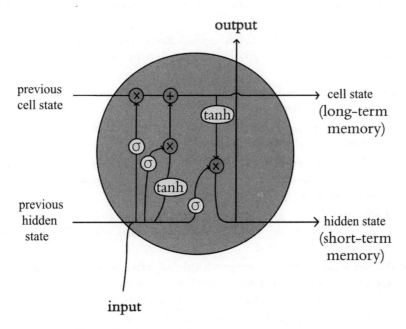

Figure 8.26   Schematic diagram of an LSTM

state does not pass through any nonlinear activation functions. In fact, the cell state only undergoes some minor linear transformations, but otherwise it simply passes through from cell to cell. Those two linear transformations (a multiplication and an addition operation) are points where a cell in an LSTM layer can add information to the cell state, information that will be passed onto the next cell in the layer. In either case, there is a sigmoid activation (represented by σ in the figure) *before* the information is added to the cell state. Because a sigmoid activation produces values between 0 and 1, these sigmoids act as "gates" that decide whether new information (from the current timestep) is added to the cell state or not.

The new information at the current timestep is a simple concatenation of the current timestep's input and the hidden state from the preceding timestep. This concatenation has two chances to be incorporated into the cell state—either linearly or following a nonlinear tanh activation—and in either case it's those sigmoid gates that decide whether the information is combined.

After the LSTM has determined what information to add to the cell state, another sigmoid gate decides whether the information from the current input is added to the final cell state, and this results in the output for the current timestep. Notice that, under a different name ("hidden state"), the output is also sent into the next LSTM module (which represents the next timestep in the sequence), where it is combined with the next timestep's input to begin the whole process again, and that (alongside the hidden state) the final cell state is also sent to the module representing the next timestep.

We know this might be a lot to come to grips with. Another way to distill this LSTM content is:

- The cell state enables information to persist along the length of the sequence, through each timestep in a given LSTM cell. It is the *long*-term memory of the LSTM.

- The hidden state is analogous to the recurrent connections in a simple RNN and represents the *short*-term memory of the LSTM.

- Each module represents a particular point in the sequence of data (e.g., a particular token from a natural language document).

- At each timestep, several decisions are made (using those sigmoid gates) about whether the information at that particular timestep in the sequence is relevant to the local (hidden state) and global (cell state) contexts.

- The first two sigmoid gates determine whether the information from the current timestep is relevant to the global context (the cell state) and how it will be combined into that stream.

- The final sigmoid gate determines whether the information from the current timestep is relevant to the local context (i.e., whether it is added to the hidden state, which doubles as the output for the current timestep).

We recommend taking a moment to reconsider Figure 8.26 and see if you can follow how information moves through an LSTM cell. This task should be easier if you keep in mind that the sigmoid gates decide whether information is let through or not. Regardless, the primary take-aways from this section are:

- Simple RNN cells pass only one type of information (the hidden state) between timesteps and contain only one activation function.

- LSTM cells are markedly more complex: They pass two types of information between timesteps (hidden state *and* cell state) and contain five activation functions.

Implementing an LSTM with Keras

Despite all of their additional computational complexity, as demonstrated within our *LSTM Sentiment Classifier* notebook, implementing LSTMs with Keras is a breeze. As shown in Example 8.36, we selected the same hyperparameters for our LSTM as we did for our simple RNN, except:

- We changed the output directory name.

- We updated variable names to n_lstm and drop_lstm.

- We reduced the number of epochs of training to 4 because the LSTM begins to overfit to the training data much earlier than the simple RNN.

Example 8.36 LSTM sentiment classifier hyperparameters

```
# output directory name:
output_dir = 'model_output/LSTM'

# training:
```

```
epochs = 4
batch_size = 128

# vector-space embedding:
n_dim = 64
n_unique_words = 10000
max_review_length = 100
pad_type = trunc_type = 'pre'
drop_embed = 0.2

# LSTM layer architecture:
n_lstm = 256
drop_lstm = 0.2
```

Our LSTM model architecture is also the same as our RNN architecture, except that we replaced the SimpleRNN() layer with LSTM(); see Example 8.37.

Example 8.37 LSTM sentiment classifier architecture

```
from keras.layers import LSTM

model = Sequential()
model.add(Embedding(n_unique_words, n_dim,
                    input_length=max_review_length))
model.add(SpatialDropout1D(drop_embed))
model.add(LSTM(n_lstm, dropout=drop_lstm))
model.add(Dense(1, activation='sigmoid'))
```

The results of training the LSTM are provided in full in our *LSTM Sentiment Classifier* notebook. To summarize, training loss decreased steadily epoch over epoch, suggesting that model-fitting proceeded more conventionally than with our simple RNN. The results are not a slam dunk, however. Despite its relative sophistication, our LSTM performed only as well as our baseline dense model. The LSTM's epoch with the lowest validation loss is the second one (0.349); it had a validation accuracy of 84.8 percent and an ROC AUC of 92.8 percent.

Bidirectional LSTMs

Bidirectional LSTMs (or Bi-LSTMs, for short) are a clever variation on standard LSTMs. Whereas the latter involve backpropagation in only one direction (typically backward over timesteps, such as from the end of a movie review toward the beginning), *bidirectional* LSTMs involve backpropagation in *both* directions (backward *and forward* over timesteps) across some one-dimensional input. This extra backpropagation doubles computational complexity, but if accuracy is paramount to your application, it is often worth it: Bi-LSTMs are a popular choice in modern NLP applications because their ability to learn patterns both before and after a given token within an input document facilitates high-performing models.

Converting our LSTM architecture (Example 8.37) into a Bi–LSTM architecture is painless. We need only *wrap* our `LSTM()` layer within the `Bidirectional()` wrapper, as shown in Example 8.38.

Example 8.38 Bidirectional LSTM sentiment classifier architecture

```
from keras.layers import LSTM
from keras.layers.wrappers import Bidirectional # new!

model = Sequential()
model.add(Embedding(n_unique_words, n_dim,
                    input_length=max_review_length))
model.add(SpatialDropout1D(drop_embed))
model.add(Bidirectional(LSTM(n_lstm, dropout=drop_lstm)))
model.add(Dense(1, activation='sigmoid'))
```

The straightforward conversion from LSTM to Bi-LSTM yielded substantial performance gains, as the results of model-fitting show (provided in full in our *Bi LSTM Sentiment Classifier* notebook). The epoch with the lowest validation loss (0.331) was the fourth, which had validation accuracy of 86.0 percent and an ROC AUC of 93.5 percent, making it our second-best model so far as it trails behind only our convolutional architecture.

Stacked Recurrent Models

Stacking multiple RNN-family layers (be they `SimpleRNN()`, `LSTM`, or another type) is not *quite* as straightforward as stacking dense or convolutional layers in Keras—although it certainly isn't difficult: It requires only specifying an extra argument when the layer is defined.

As we've discussed, recurrent layers take in an ordered sequence of inputs. The *recurrent* nature of these layers comes from their processing each timestep in the sequence and passing along a hidden state as an input to the next timestep in the sequence. Upon reaching the final timestep in the sequence, the output of a recurrent layer is the *final* hidden state.

So in order to stack recurrent layers, we use the argument `return_sequences=True`. This asks the recurrent layer to return the hidden states for each step in the layer's sequence. The resulting output now has three dimensions, matching the dimensions of the input sequence that was fed into it. The default behavior of a recurrent layer is to pass only the final hidden state to the next layer. This works perfectly well if we're passing this information to, say, a dense layer. If, however, we'd like the subsequent layer in our network to be another recurrent layer, that subsequent recurrent layer must receive a sequence as its input. Thus, to pass the array of hidden states from across all individual timesteps in the sequence (as opposed to only the single final hidden state value) to this subsequent recurrent layer, we set the optional `return_sequences` argument to `True`.[47]

---

47. There is also a `return_state` argument (which, like `return_sequences`, defaults to `False`) that asks the network to return the final cell state in addition to the final hidden state. This optional argument is not used as often, but it is useful when we'd like to initialize a recurrent layer's cell state with that of another layer, as we do in "encoder-decoder" models (introduced in the next section).

To observe this in action, check out the two-layer Bi-LSTM model shown in Example 8.39. (Notice that in this example we still leave the final recurrent layer with its default `return_sequences=False` so that only the final hidden state of this final recurrent layer is returned for use further downstream in the network.)

Example 8.39 Stacked recurrent model architecture

```
from keras.layers import LSTM
from keras.layers.wrappers import Bidirectional

model = Sequential()
model.add(Embedding(n_unique_words, n_dim,
                     input_length=max_review_length))
model.add(SpatialDropout1D(drop_embed))
model.add(Bidirectional(LSTM(n_lstm_1, dropout=drop_lstm,
                             return_sequences=True))) # new!
model.add(Bidirectional(LSTM(n_lstm_2, dropout=drop_lstm)))
model.add(Dense(1, activation='sigmoid'))
```

As you've discovered a number of times since Chapter 1 of this book, additional layers within a neural network model can enable it to learn increasingly complex and abstract representations. In this case, the abstraction facilitated by the supplementary Bi-LSTM layer translated to performance gains. The stacked Bi-LSTM outperformed its unstacked cousin by a noteworthy margin, with an ROC AUC of 94.9 percent and validation accuracy of 87.8 percent in its best epoch (the second, with its validation loss of 0.296). The full results are provided in our *Stacked Bi LSTM Sentiment Classifier* notebook.

The performance of our stacked Bi-LSTM architecture, despite being considerably more sophisticated than our convolutional architecture *and* despite being designed specifically to handle sequential data like natural language, nevertheless lags behind the accuracy of our ConvNet model. Perhaps some hyperparameter experimentation and fine-tuning would yield better results, but ultimately our hypothesis is that because the IMDb film review dataset is so small, our LSTM models don't have an opportunity to demonstrate their potential. We opine that a much larger natural language dataset would facilitate effective backpropagation over the many timesteps associated with LSTM layers.[48]

A relative of the LSTM within the family of RNNs is the gated recurrent unit (GRU).[49] GRUs are slightly less computationally intensive than LSTMs because they involve only three activation functions, and yet their performance often approaches the performance of LSTMs. If a bit more compute isn't a deal breaker for you, we see

---

48. If you'd like to test our hypothesis yourself, we provide appropriate sentiment analysis dataset suggestions in Chapter 12.

49. Cho, K., et al. (2014). Learning phrase representations using RNN encoder-decoder for statistical machine translation. *arXiv:1406.1078*.

little advantage in choosing a GRU over an LSTM. If you're interested in trying a GRU in Keras anyway, it's as easy as importing the `GRU()` layer type and dropping it into a model architecture where you might otherwise place an `LSTM()` layer. Check out our *GRU Sentiment Classifier* notebook for a hands-on example.

Seq2seq and Attention

Natural language techniques that involve so-called *sequence-to-sequence* (seq2seq; pronounced "seek-to-seek") models take in an input sequence and generate an output sequence as their product. *Neural machine translation* (NMT) is a quintessential class of seq2seq models, with Google Translate's machine-translation algorithm serving as an example of NMT being used in a production system.[50]

NMTs consist of an *encoder-decoder* structure, wherein the encoder processes the input sequence and the decoder generates the output sequence. The encoder and decoder are both RNNs, and so during the encoding step there exists a hidden state that is passed between units of the RNN. At the end of the encoding phase, the final hidden state is passed to the decoder; this final state can be referred to as the "context." In this way, the decoder *starts* with a context for what is happening in the input sequence. Although this idea is sound in theory, the context is often a bottleneck: It's difficult for models to handle really long sequences, and so the context loses its punch.

Attention was developed to overcome the computational bottleneck associated with context.[51] In a nutshell, instead of passing a single hidden state vector (the final one) from the encoder to the decoder, with attention we pass the full sequence of hidden states to the decoder. Each of these hidden states is associated with a single step in the input sequence, although the decoder might need the context from multiple steps in the input to inform its behavior at any given step during decoding. To achieve this, for each step in the sequence the decoder calculates a score for each of the hidden states from the encoder. Each encoder hidden state is multiplied by the softmax of its score.[52] This serves to amplify the most relevant contexts (they would have high scores, and thus higher softmax probabilities) while muting the ones that aren't relevant; in essence, attention weights the available contexts for a given timestep. The weighted hidden states are summed, and this new context vector is used to predict the output for each timestep in the decoder sequence. Following this approach, the model selectively reviews what it knows about the input sequence and uses only the relevant information where necessary to inform the output. It's *paying attention* to the most relevant elements of the whole sentence!

If this book were dedicated solely to NLP, we'd have at least a chapter covering seq2seq and attention. As it stands, we'll have to leave it to you to further explore these techniques, which are raising the bar of the performance of many NLP applications.

---

50. Google Translate has incorporated NMT since 2016. You can read more about it at bit.ly/translateNMT.
51. Bahdanau, D., et al. (2014). Neural machine translation by jointly learning to align and translate. *arXiv:1409.0473*.
52. Recall from Chapter 6 that the softmax function takes a vector of real numbers and generates a probability distribution with the same number of classes as the input vector.

Transfer Learning in NLP

Machine vision practitioners have for a number of years been helped along by the ready availability of nuanced models that have been pretrained on large, rich datasets. As covered in the "Transfer Learning" section near the end of Chapter 9, casual users can download model architectures with pretrained weights and rapidly scale up their particular vision application to a state-of-the-art model. Well, more recently, such transfer learning has become readily available for NLP, too.[53]

First came ULMFiT (*universal language model fine-tuning*), wherein tools were described and open-sourced that enabled others to use a lot of what the model learns during pretraining.[54] In this way, models can be fine-tuned on task-specific data, thus requiring less training time and fewer data to attain high-accuracy results.

Shortly thereafter, ELMo (*embeddings from language models*) was revealed to the world.[55] In this update to the standard word vectors we introduced in this chapter, the word embeddings are dependent not only on the word itself but also on the context in which the word occurs. In place of a fixed word embedding for each word in the dictionary, ELMo looks at each word in the sentence before assigning each word a specific embedding. The ELMo model is pretrained on a very large corpus; if you had to train it yourself, it would likely strain your compute resources, but you can now nevertheless use it as a component in your own NLP models.

The final transfer learning development we'll mention is the release of BERT (*bi-directional encoder representations from transformers*) from Google.[56] Perhaps even more so than ULMFiT and ELMo, pretrained BERT models tuned to particular NLP tasks have been associated with the achievement of new state-of-the-art benchmarks across a broad range of applications, while requiring much less training time and fewer data to get there.

Non-sequential Architectures: The Keras Functional API

To solve a given problem, there are countless ways that the layer types we've already covered in this book can be recombined to form deep learning model architectures. For example, see our *Conv LSTM Stack Sentiment Classifier* notebook, wherein we were extra creative in designing a model that involves a convolutional layer passing its

---

53. When we introduced Keras `Embedding()` layers earlier in this chapter, we touched on transfer learning with word vectors. The transfer learning approaches covered in this section—ULMFiT, ELMo, and BERT—are closer in spirit to the transfer learning of machine vision, because (analogous to the hierarchical visual features that are represented by a deep CNN; see Figure 1.17) they allow for the hierarchical representation of the elements of natural language (e.g., subwords, words, and context, as in Figure 2.9). Word vectors, in contrast, have no hierarchy; they capture only the word level of language.

54. Howard, J., and Ruder, S. (2018). Universal language model fine-tuning for text classification. *arXiv:1801.06146*.

55. Peters, M.E., et al. (2018). Deep contextualized word representations. *arXiv:1802.05365*.

56. Devlin, J., et al. (2018). BERT: Pre-training of deep bidirectional transformers for language understanding. *arXiv: 0810.04805*.

activations into a Bi–LSTM layer.[57] Thus far, however, our creativity has been constrained by our use of the Keras `Sequential()` model, which requires each layer to flow directly into a following one.

Although sequential models constitute the vast majority of deep learning models, there are times when non-sequential architectures—which permit infinite model-design possibilities and are often more complex—could be warranted.[58] In such situations, we can take advantage of the Keras *functional API*, which makes use of the `Model` class instead of the `Sequential` models we've worked with so far in this book.

As an example of a non-sequential architecture, we decided to riff on our highest-performing sentiment classifier, the convolutional model, to see if we could squeeze more juice out of the proverbial lemon. As diagrammed in Figure 8.27, our idea was to have three parallel streams of convolutional layers—each of which takes in word vectors from an `Embedding()` layer. As in our *Convolutional Sentiment Classifier* notebook,

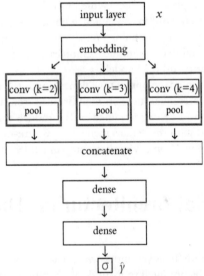

Figure 8.27   A non-sequential model architecture: Three parallel streams of convolutional layers—each with a unique filter length ($k = 2$, $k = 3$, or $k = 4$)—receive input from a word-embedding layer. The activations of all three streams are concatenated together and passed into a pair of sequentially stacked dense hidden layers en route to the sigmoid output neuron.

---

57. This conv-LSTM model approached the validation accuracy and ROC AUC of our Stacked Bi-LSTM architecture, but each epoch trained in 82 percent less time.

58. Popular aspects of non-sequential models include having multiple model inputs or outputs (potentially at different levels within the architecture; e.g., a model could have an additional input or an additional output midway through the architecture), sharing the activations of a single layer with multiple other layers, and creating directed acyclic graphs.

one of these streams would have a filter length of three tokens. One of the others will have a filter length of *two*—so it will specialize in learning word-vector pairs that appear to be relevant to classifying a film review as having positive or negative sentiment. The third convolutional stream will have a filter length of *four* tokens, so it will specialize in detecting relevant quadruplets of word meaning.

The hyperparameters for our three-convolutional-stream model are provided in Example 8.40 as well as in our *Multi ConvNet Sentiment Classifier* Jupyter notebook.

Example 8.40 Multi-ConvNet sentiment classifier hyperparameters

```
# output directory name:
output_dir = 'model_output/multiconv'

# training:
epochs = 4
batch_size = 128

# vector-space embedding:
n_dim = 64
n_unique_words = 5000
max_review_length = 400
pad_type = trunc_type = 'pre'
drop_embed = 0.2

# convolutional layer architecture:
n_conv_1 = n_conv_2 = n_conv_3 = 256
k_conv_1 = 3
k_conv_2 = 2
k_conv_3 = 4

# dense layer architecture:
n_dense = 256
dropout = 0.2
```

The novel hyperparameters are associated with the three convolutional layers. All three convolutional layers have **256** filters, but mirroring the diagram in Figure 8.27, the layers form parallel streams—each with a unique filter length (k that ranges from **2** up to **4**.

The Keras code for our multi-ConvNet model architecture is provided in Example 8.41.

Example 8.41 Multi-ConvNet sentiment classifier architecture

```
from keras.models import Model
from keras.layers import Input, concatenate
```

```
# input layer:
input_layer = Input(shape=(max_review_length,),
                     dtype='int16', name='input')

# embedding:
embedding_layer = Embedding(n_unique_words, n_dim,
                            name='embedding')(input_layer)
drop_embed_layer = SpatialDropout1D(drop_embed,
                                    name='drop_embed')(embedding_layer)

# three parallel convolutional streams:
conv_1 = Conv1D(n_conv_1, k_conv_1,
                activation='relu', name='conv_1')(drop_embed_layer)
maxp_1 = GlobalMaxPooling1D(name='maxp_1')(conv_1)

conv_2 = Conv1D(n_conv_2, k_conv_2,
                activation='relu', name='conv_2')(drop_embed_layer)
maxp_2 = GlobalMaxPooling1D(name='maxp_2')(conv_2)

conv_3 = Conv1D(n_conv_3, k_conv_3,
                activation='relu', name='conv_3')(drop_embed_layer)
maxp_3 = GlobalMaxPooling1D(name='maxp_3')(conv_3)

# concatenate the activations from the three streams:
concat = concatenate([maxp_1, maxp_2, maxp_3])

# dense hidden layers:
dense_layer = Dense(n_dense,
                    activation='relu', name='dense')(concat)
drop_dense_layer = Dropout(dropout, name='drop_dense')(dense_layer)
dense_2 = Dense(int(n_dense/4),
                activation='relu', name='dense_2')(drop_dense_layer)
dropout_2 = Dropout(dropout, name='drop_dense_2')(dense_2)

# sigmoid output layer:
predictions = Dense(1, activation='sigmoid', name='output')(dropout_2)

# create model:
model = Model(input_layer, predictions)
```

This architecture may look a little alarming if you haven't seen the Keras `Model` class used before, but as we break it down line-by-line here, it should lose any intimidating aspects it might have:

- With the `Model` class, we specify the `Input()` layer independently, as opposed to specifying it as the shape argument of the first hidden layer. We specified the data type (dtype) explicitly: 16-bit integers (int16) can range up to 32,767, which will accommodate the maximum index of the words we input.[59] As with all of the layers in this model, we specify a recognizable name argument so that when we print the model later (using model.summary()) it will be easy to make sense of everything.

- Every layer is assigned to a unique variable name, such as input_layer, embedding_layer, and conv_2. We will use these variable names to specify the flow of data within our model.

- The most noteworthy aspect of using the Model class, which will be familiar to developers who have worked with functional programming languages, is the variable name within the second set of parentheses following any layer call. This specifies which layer's outputs are flowing into a given layer. For example, (input_layer) in the second set of parentheses of the embedding_layer indicates that the output of the input layer flows into the embedding layer.

- The Embedding() and SpatialDropout1D layers take the same arguments as before in this chapter.

- The output of the SpatialDropout1D layer (with a variable named drop_embed_layer) is the input to three separate, parallel convolutional layers: conv_1, conv_2, and conv_3.

- As per Figure 8.27, each of the three convolutional streams includes a Conv1D layer (with a unique k_conv filter length) and a GlobalMaxPooling1D layer.

- The activations output by the GlobalMaxPooling1D layer of each of the three convolutional streams are concatenated into a single array of activation values by the concatenate() layer, which takes in a list of inputs ([maxp_1, maxp_2, maxp_3]) as its only argument.

- The concatenated convolutional-stream activations are provided as input to two Dense() hidden layers, each of which has a Dropout() layer associated with it. (The second dense layer has one-quarter as many neurons as the first, as specified by n_dense/4.)

- The activations output by the sigmoid output neuron ($\hat{y}$) are assigned to the variable name predictions.

- Finally, the Model class ties all of the model's layers together by taking two arguments: the variable name of the input layer (i.e., input_layer) and the output layer (i.e., predictions).

Our elaborate parallel network architecture ultimately provided us with a modest bump in capability to give us the best-performing sentiment classifier in this chapter (see Table 8.6). As detailed in our *Multi ConvNet Sentiment Classifier* notebook, the lowest validation loss was attained in the second epoch (0.262), and this epoch was associated with a validation accuracy of 89.4 percent and an ROC AUC of 96.2 percent—a tenth of a percent better than our Sequential convolutional model.

---

59. The index goes up to only 5,500, because of the n_unique_words and n_words_to_skip hyperparameters we selected.

Table 8.6   Comparison of the performance of our sentiment classifier model architectures

Model	ROC AUC (%)
Dense	92.9
Convolutional	96.1
Simple RNN	84.9
LSTM	92.8
Bi-LSTM	93.5
Stacked Bi-LSTM	94.9
GRU	93.0
Conv-LSTM	94.5
Multi-ConvNet	96.2

Summary

In this chapter, we discussed methods for preprocessing natural language data, ways to create word vectors from a corpus of natural language, and the procedure for calculating the area under the receiver operating characteristic curve. In the second half of the chapter, we applied this knowledge to experiment with a wide range of deep learning NLP models for classifying film reviews as favorable or negative. Some of these models involved layer types you were familiar with from earlier chapters (i.e., dense and convolutional layers), while later ones involved new layer types from the RNN family (LSTMs and GRUs) and, for the first time in this book, a non-sequential model architecture.

A summary of the results of our sentiment-classifier experiments are provided in Table 8.6. We hypothesize that, had our natural language dataset been much larger, the Bi-LSTM architectures might have outperformed the convolutional ones.

Key Concepts

Here are the essential foundational concepts thus far. New terms from the current chapter are highlighted in purple.

- parameters:
  - weight w
  - bias b
- activation a
- artificial neurons:
  - sigmoid
  - tanh
  - ReLU
  - linear
- input layer
- hidden layer
- output layer
- layer types:
  - dense (fully connected)
  - softmax
  - convolutional
  - max-pooling
  - flatten
  - embedding
  - RNN
  - (bidirectional-)LSTM
  - concatenate

- cost (loss) functions:
  - quadratic (mean squared error)
  - cross-entropy
- forward propagation
- backpropagation
- unstable (especially vanishing) gradients
- Glorot weight initialization
- batch normalization
- dropout
- optimizers:
  - stochastic gradient descent
  - Adam
- optimizer hyperparameters:
  - learning rate η
  - batch size
- word2vec

9

Machine Vision

Welcome to Part III, dear reader. Previously, we provided a high-level overview of particular applications of deep learning (Part I). With the foundational, low-level theory we've covered since (in Part II), you're now well positioned to work through specialized content across a range of application areas, primarily via hands-on example code. In this chapter, for example, you'll discover convolutional neural networks and apply them to machine vision tasks.

Convolutional Neural Networks

A *convolutional neural network*—also known as a ConvNet or a CNN—is an artificial neural network that features one or more *convolutional layers* (also called *conv* layers). This layer type enables a deep learning model to efficiently process spatial patterns. As you'll see firsthand in this chapter, this property makes convolutional layers especially effective in computer vision applications.

The Two-Dimensional Structure of Visual Imagery

In our previous code examples involving handwritten MNIST digits, we converted the image data into one-dimensional arrays of numbers so that we could feed them into a dense hidden layer. More specifically, we began with 28×28-pixel grayscale images and converted them into 784-element one-dimensional arrays.[1] Although this step was necessary in the context of a dense, fully connected network—we needed to flatten the 784 pixel values so that each one could be fed into a neuron of the first hidden layer—the collapse of a two-dimensional image into one dimension corresponds to a substantial loss of meaningful visual image structure. When you draw a digit with a pen on paper, you

---

1. Recall that the pixel values were divided by 255 in order to scale everything to $[0:1]$.

don't conceptualize it as a continuous linear sequence of pixels running from top-left to bottom-right. If, for example, we printed an MNIST digit for you here as a 784-pixel long stream in shades of gray, we'd be willing to wager that you couldn't identify the digit. Instead, humans perceive visual information in a two-dimensional form,[2] and our ability to recognize what we're looking at is inherently tied to the spatial relationships between the shapes and colors we perceive.

Computational Complexity

In addition to the loss of two-dimensional structure when we collapse an image, a second consideration when piping images into a dense network is computational complexity. The MNIST images are very small—28×28 pixels with only one *channel* (there is only one color "channel" because MNIST digits are monochromatic; to render images in full color, in contrast, at least three channels—usually red, green, and blue—are required). Passing MNIST image information into a dense layer, that corresponds to 785 parameters per neuron: 784 weights for each of the pixels, plus the neuron's bias. If we were handling a moderately sized image, however—say, a 200×200-pixel, full-color RGB[3] image— then the number of parameters increases dramatically. In that case, we'd have three color channels, each with 40,000 pixels, corresponding to a total of 120,001 parameters per neuron in a dense layer.[4] With a modest number of neurons in the dense layer—let's say 64—that corresponds to nearly 8 million parameters associated with the first hidden layer of our network alone.[5] Furthermore, the image is *only* 200×200 pixels—that's barely 0.4MP,[6] whereas most modern smartphones have 12MP or greater camera sensors. Generally, machine vision tasks don't need to run on high-resolution images in order to be successful, but the point should be clear: Images can contain a very large number of data points, and using these in a naïve, fully connected manner will explode the neural network's compute power requirements.

Convolutional Layers

Convolutional layers consist of sets of *kernels*, which are also known as *filters*. Each of these kernels is a small window (called a *patch*) that scans across the image (in more technical terms, the filter *convolves*), from top left to bottom right (see Figure 9.1 for an illustration of this *convolutional operation*).

Kernels are made up of weights, which—as in dense layers—are learned through back-propagation. Kernels can range in size, but a typical size is 3×3, and we use that in the examples in this chapter.[7] For the monochromatic MNIST digits, this 3×3-pixel window would consist of $3 \times 3 \times 1$ weights—nine weights, for a total of 10 parameters (like an artificial neuron in a dense layer, every convolutional filter has a bias term b). For

---

2. Well . . . three-dimensional, but let's ignore depth for the purposes of this discussion.
3. The *red*, *green*, and *blue* channels required for a full-color image.
4. 200 pixels × 200 pixels × 3 color channels + 1 bias = 120,001 parameters.
5. 64 neurons × 120,001 parameters per neuron = 7,680,064 parameters.
6. Megapixels.
7. Another typical size is 5×5, with kernels larger than that used infrequently.

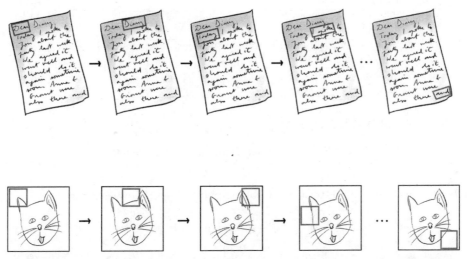

Figure 9.1   When reading a page of a book written in English, we begin in the top-left corner and read to the right. Every time we reach the end of a row of text, we progress to the next row. In this way, we eventually reach the bottom-right corner, thereby reading all of the words on the page. Analogously, the kernel in a convolutional layer begins on a small window of pixels in the top-left corner of a given image. From the top row downward, the kernel scans from left to right, until it eventually reaches the bottom-right corner, thereby scanning all of the pixels in the image.

comparison, if we happened to be working with full-color RGB images, then a kernel covering the same number of pixels would have three times as many weights—$3 \times 3 \times 3$ of them, for a total of 27 weights and 28 parameters.

As depicted in Figure 9.1, the kernel occupies discrete positions across an image as it convolves. Sticking with the 3×3 kernel size for this explanation, during forward propagation a multidimensional variation of the "most important equation in this book"— $w \cdot x + b$ (introduced in Figure 6.7)—is calculated at each position that the kernel occupies as it convolves over the image. Referring to the 3×3 window of pixels and the 3×3 kernel in Figure 9.2 as inputs x and weights w, respectively, we can demonstrate the calculation of the weighted sum $w \cdot x$ in which products are calculated elementwise based on the alignment of vertical and horizontal locations. It's helpful to imagine the kernel superimposed over the pixel values. The math is presented here:

$$
\begin{aligned}
w \cdot x = {}& .01 \times .53 + .09 \times .34 + .22 \times .06 \\
& + -1.36 \times .37 + .34 \times .82 + -1.59 \times .01 \\
& + .13 \times .62 + -.69 \times .91 + 1.02 \times .34 \\
= {}& -0.3917
\end{aligned}
\tag{9.1}
$$

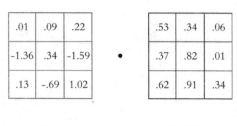

kernel weights   pixel input

Figure 9.2   A 3×3 kernel and a 3×3-pixel window

Next, using Equation 6.1, we add some bias term b (say, -0.19) to arrive at z:

$$z = w \cdot x + b$$
$$= -0.39 + b$$
$$= -0.39 + 0.20 \tag{9.2}$$
$$= -0.19$$

With z, we can at last calculate an activation value a by passing z through the activation function of our choice, say the tanh function or the ReLU function.

Note that the fundamental operation hasn't changed relative to the artificial neuron mathematics of Chapter 6. Convolutional kernels have weights, inputs, and a bias; a weighted sum of these is produced using our most important equation; and the resulting z is passed through some nonlinear function to produce an activation. What has changed is that there isn't a weight for *every* input, but rather a discrete kernel with 3×3 weights. These weights do not change as the kernel convolves; instead they're *shared* across all of the inputs. In this way, a convolutional layer can have orders of magnitude fewer weights than a fully connected layer. Another important point is that, like the inputs, the outputs from this kernel (all of the activations) are also arranged in a two–dimensional array. We'll delve more into this in a moment, but first . . .

Multiple Filters

Typically, we have multiple filters in a given convolutional layer. Each filter enables the network to learn a representation of the data at a given layer in a unique way. For example, analogous to Hubel and Wiesel's simple cells in the biological visual system (Figure 1.5), if the first hidden layer in our network is a convolutional layer, it might contain a kernel that responds optimally to vertical lines. Thus, whenever it convolves (slides over) a vertical line in an input image, it produces a large activation (a) value. Additional kernels in this layer can learn to represent other simple spatial features such as horizontal lines and color transitions (for examples, see the bottom–left panel of Figure 1.17). This is how these kernels came to be known as *filters*; they scan over the image and filter out the location of specific features, producing high activations when they come across the pattern, shape, and/or color they are specially tuned to detect. One could say that they function as highlighters, producing a two–dimensional array of activations that indicate *where* that filter's particular feature exists in the original image. For this reason, the output from a kernel is referred to as an *activation map*.

Analogous to the hierarchical representations of the biological visual system (Figure 1.6), subsequent convolutional layers receive these activation maps as their inputs. As the network gets deeper, the filters in the layers react to increasingly complex combinations of these simple features, learning to represent increasingly abstract spatial patterns and eventually building a hierarchy from simple lines and colors up to complex textures and shapes (see the panels along the bottom of Figure 1.17). In this way, later layers within the network have the capacity to recognize whole objects or even, say, to distinguish an image of a Great Dane from that of a Yorkshire Terrier.

The number of filters in the layer, like the number of neurons in a dense layer, is a hyperparameter that we configure ourselves. As with the other hyperparameters covered already in this book, there is a Goldilocks sweet spot for filter number. Here are our rules of thumb for homing in on it for your particular problem:

- Having a larger number of kernels facilitates the identification of more-complex features, so consider the complexity of the data and the problem you're solving. Of course, more kernels comes with the cost of computation efficiency.

- If a network has multiple convolutional layers, the optimal number of kernels for a given layer could vary quite a bit from layer to layer. Keep in mind that early layers identify simple features, whereas later layers identify complex recombinations of these simple features, so let this guide where you stack your network. As we'll see when we get into coded examples of CNNs later in this chapter, a common approach for machine vision is to have many more kernels in later convolutional layers relative to early convolutional layers.

- As always, strive to minimize computational complexity: Consider using the smallest number of kernels that facilitates a low cost on your validation data. If doubling the number of kernels (say, from 32 to 64 to 128) in a given layer significantly decreases your model's validation cost, then consider using the higher value. If halving the number of kernels (say, from 32 to 16 to 8) in a given layer doesn't increase your model's validation cost, then consider using the smaller value.

A Convolutional Example

Convolutional layers are a nontrivial departure from the simpler fully connected layers of Part II, so, to help you make sense of the way the pixel values and weights combine to produce feature maps, across Figures 9.3 through 9.5 we've created a detailed contrived example with accompanying math. To begin, imagine we're convolving over a single RGB image that's 3×3 pixels in size. In Python, those data are stored in a [3,3,3] array as shown at the top of Figure 9.3.[8]

---

8. We admit that the RGB example of the tree has far more than nine pixels, but we struggled to identify a compelling color image that was 3×3.

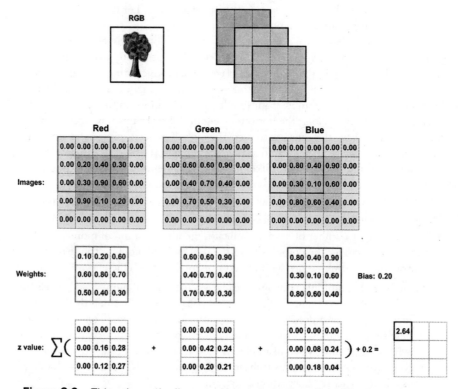

Figure 9.3   This schematic diagram demonstrates how the activation values in a feature map are calculated in a convolutional layer.

Shown in the middle of the figure are the 3×3 arrays for each of the three channels: red, green, and blue. Note that the image has been padded with zeros on all four sides. We'll discuss more about padding shortly, but for now all you need to know is this: Padding is used to ensure that the resulting feature map has the same dimensions as the input data. Below the arrays of pixel values you'll find the weight matrices for each of the channels. We chose a kernel size of 3×3, and given that there are three channels in the input image the weights matrix will be an array with dimensions $[3,3,3]$, shown here individually. The bias term is 0.2. The current position of the filter is indicated by an overlay on each array of pixel values, and the z value (determined by calculating the weighted sum from Equation 9.1 across all three color channels, and then adding the bias as in Equation 9.2) is given at the bottom right of the figure. Finally, all of these z values are summed to create the first entry in the feature map at the bottom right.

Proceeding to Figure 9.4, the image arrays are now shown with the filter in its next position, one pixel to the right. Exactly as in Figure 9.3, the z value is calculated following Equations 9.1 and 9.2. This z-value can then fill the second position in the activation map, as shown again at the bottom right of the figure.

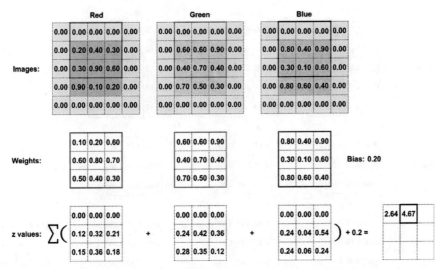

Figure 9.4 A continuation of the convolutional example from Figure 9.3, now showing the activation for the next filter position

This process is repeated for every possible filter position, and the z-value that was calculated for each of these nine positions is shown in the bottom-right corner of Figure 9.5. To convert this 3×3 map of z-values into a corresponding 3×3 activation map, we pass each z-value through an activation function, such as the ReLU function. Because a single convolutional layer nearly always has multiple filters, each producing its own two-dimensional activation map, activation maps have an additional *depth* dimension, analogous to the depth provided by the three the channels of an RGB image. Each of these kernel "channels" in the activation map represents a feature that that particular kernel specializes in recognizing, such as an edge (a straight line) at a particular orientation.[9] Figure 9.6 shows how the calculation of activation values a from the input image build up a three-dimensional activation map. The convolutional layer that produced the activation map shown in Figure 9.6 has 16 kernels, thus resulting in an activation map with a depth of 16 "channels" (we'll call these *slices* going forward).

In Figure 9.6, the kernel filter is positioned over the top-left corner of the input image. This corresponds to 16 activation values in the top-left corner of the activation map: one activation a for each of the 16 kernels. By convolving over all of the pixel windows in the input image from left to right and from top to bottom, all of the values

---

9. Figure 1.17 shows real-world examples of the features individual kernels become specialized to detect across a range of convolutional-layer depths. In the first convolutional layer, for example, the majority of the kernels have a speciality in detecting an edge at a particular orientation.

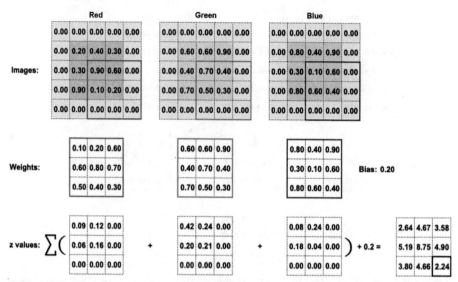

Figure 9.5   Finally, the activation for the last filter position has been calculated, and the activation map is complete.

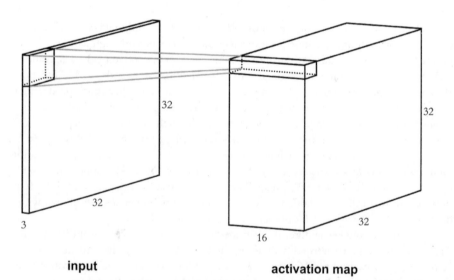

input

activation map

Figure 9.6   A graphical representation of the input array (left; represented here is a three-channel RGB image of size 32×32 with the kernel patch currently focused on the first—i.e., top-left—position) and the activation map (right). There are 16 kernels, resulting in an activation map with a depth of 16. Each position a given kernel occupies as it convolves over the input image corresponds to one a value in the resulting activation map.

in the activation map are filled in.[10] If the first of the 16 filters is tuned to respond op-timally to vertical lines, then the first slice of the activation map will highlight all the physical regions of the input image that contain vertical lines. If the second filter is tuned to respond optimally to *horizontal* lines, then the second slice of the activation map will highlight regions of the image that contain horizontal lines. In this way, all 16 filters in the activation map can together represent the spatial location of 16 different spatial features.[11]

At this point, students of deep learning often wonder where the weights for a given convolutional kernel come from. In our examples in this section, all of the parameter values have been contrived. In real-world convolutional layers, however, the kernel weights and biases are initialized with random values (as usual, per Chapter 7) and then learned through backpropagation, akin to the way weights and biases are learned in dense layers. As suggested by the hierarchical abstraction theme of Chapter 1, the earliest convolutional layers in a deep CNN tend to become tuned to simple features like straight lines at particular orientations, whereas deeper layers might specialize in representing, say, a face, a clock, or a dog. A four-minute video by Jason Yosinski and his colleagues (available at `bit.ly/DeepViz`) vividly demonstrates the specializations of convolutional kernels by ConvNet layer depth.[12] We highly recommend checking it out.

Now that we've described the general principles underscoring convolutional layers in deep learning, it's a good time to review the basic features:

- They allow deep learning models to learn to recognize features in a position invari-ant manner; a single kernel can identify its cognate feature anywhere in the input data.

- They remain faithful to the two-dimensional structure of images, allowing features to be identified within their spacial context.

- They significantly reduce the number of parameters required for modeling image data, yielding higher computational efficiency.

- Ultimately, they perform machine vision tasks (e.g., image classification) more accurately.

---

10. Note that regardless of whether an input image is monochromatic (with only one color channel) or full-color (with three), there is only *one* activation map output for each convolutional kernel. If there is one color channel, we calculate the weighted sum of inputs for that single channel as in Equation 9.1. If there are three color channels, we calculate the total weighted sum of inputs across all three channels as in Figures 9.3, 9.4, and 9.5. Either way (after adding the kernel's bias and passing the resulting z-value through an activation function), we produce only one activation value for each position that each kernel convolves over.

11. If you are interested in an interactive demonstration of convolutional-filter calculations, we highly recommend one created by Andrej Karpathy (see Figure 12.6 for a portrait). It's available at `bit.ly/CNNdemo` under the *Convolution Demo* heading.

12. Yosinski, J., et al. (2015). Understanding neural networks through deep visualization. *Proceedings of the International Conference on Machine Learning*.

Convolutional Filter Hyperparameters

In contrast with dense layers, convolutional layers are inherently *not* fully connected. That is, there isn't a weight mapping every single pixel to every single neuron in the first hidden layer. Instead, there are a handful of hyperparameters that dictate the number of weights and biases associated with a given convolutional layer. These include:

- Kernel size
- Stride length
- Padding

Kernel Size

In all of the examples covered so far in this chapter, the *kernel size* (also known as *filter size* or *receptive field*[13]) has been 3 pixels wide and 3 pixels tall. This is a common size that is found to be effective across a broad range of machine vision applications in contemporary ConvNet architectures. A kernel size of 5×5 pixels is also popular, and 7×7 is about as expansive as they ever get. If the kernel is too large with respect to the image, there would be too many competing features in the receptive field and it would be challenging for the convolutional layer to learn effectively, but if the receptive field is too small (e.g., 2×2) it wouldn't be able to tune to any structures, and that isn't helpful either.

Stride Length

Stride refers to the size of the step that the kernel takes as it moves over the image. Across our convolutional-layer example (Figures 9.3 to 9.5) we use a stride length of 1 pixel, which is a frequently used option. Another common choice is a 2-pixel stride and, less often, a stride of 3. Anything much larger is likely to be suboptimal, because the kernel might skip regions of the image that are of value to the model. On the other hand, increasing the stride will yield an increase in speed because there are fewer calculations that need to be carried out. As ever in deep learning, it's about finding a balance—that Goldilocks sweet spot—between these effects. We recommend a stride of 1 or 2, while avoiding anything larger than 3.

Padding

Next is *padding*, which plays handily with stride to keep the calculations of a convolutional layer in order. Let's suppose you had a 28×28 MNIST digit and a 5×5 kernel. With a stride of 1, there are 24×24 "positions" for the kernel to move through before it bumps up against the edges of the image, so the activation map output by the layer is slightly smaller than the input. If you'd like to produce an activation map that is the exact same size as the input image, you can simply pad the image with zeros around the edges (Figures 9.3, 9.4, and 9.5 contain an example of a zero-padded image). In the case of the 28×28 image and the 5×5 kernel, padding with two zeros on each edge will produce a 28×28 activation map. This can be calculated with the following equation:

$$\text{Activation map} = \frac{D - F + 2P}{S} + 1 \tag{9.3}$$

---

13. The term *receptive field* is borrowed directly from the study of biological visual systems like the eye.

Where:

- D is the size of the image (either width or height, depending on whether you're calculating the width or height of the activation map).
- F is the size of the filter.
- P is the amount of padding.
- S is the stride length.

Thus, with our padding of 2, we can calculate that the output volume is 28×28:

$$\text{Activation map} = \frac{D - F + 2P}{S} + 1$$

$$\text{Activation map} = \frac{28 - 5 + 2 \times 2}{1} + 1$$

$$\text{Activation map} = 28$$

Given the interconnected nature of kernel size, stride, and padding, one has to make sure these hyperparameters align when designing CNN architectures. That is, the hyperparameters must combine to produce a valid activation map size—specifically, an integer value. Take, for example, a kernel size of 5×5 with a stride of 2 and no padding. Using Equation 9.3, this would result in a 12.5×12.5 activation map:

$$\text{Activation map} = \frac{D - F + 2P}{S} + 1$$

$$\text{Activation map} = \frac{28 - 5 + 0 \times 2}{2} + 1$$

$$\text{Activation map} = 12.5$$

There is no such thing as a partial activation value, so a convolutional layer with these dimensions would simply not be computable.

Pooling Layers

Convolutional layers frequently work in tandem with another layer type that is a staple in machine vision neural networks: *pooling layers*. This layer type serves to reduce the overall count of parameters in a network as well as to reduce complexity, thereby speeding up computation and helping to avoid overfitting.

As discussed in the preceding section, a convolutional layer can have any number of kernels. Each of these kernels produces an activation map (whose dimensions are defined by Equation 9.3), such that the output from a convolutional layer is a three-dimensional array of activation maps, with the depth dimension of the output corresponding to the number of filters in that convolutional layer. The pooling layer reduces these activation maps spatially, while leaving the depth of the activation maps intact.

Like convolutional layers, any given pooling layer has a filter size and a stride length. Also like a convolutional layer, the pooling layer slides over its input. At each position it occupies, the pooling layer applies a data-reducing operation. Pooling layers most often use the `max` operation, and these are termed *max-pooling layers*: They retain the largest value (the *maximum* activation) within the receptive field while discarding the other values (see Figure 9.7).[14] Typically, a pooling layer has a filter size of 2 × 2 and a stride length of 2.[15] In this case, at each position the pooling layer evaluates four activations, retaining only the maximum value, and thereby downsampling the activations by a factor of 4. Because this pooling operation happens independently for each depth slice in the three-dimensional array, a 28 × 28 activation map with a depth of 16 slices would be reduced to a 14 × 14 activation map but it would retain its full complement of 16 slices.

An alternative approach to pooling for reducing computational complexity is to use a convolutional layer with a larger stride (see how stride relates to the output size in Equation 9.3). This can be handy for some specialized machine vision tasks (e.g., the generative adversarial networks you'll build later in Chapter 11) that tend to perform better without pooling layers. Finally, you might be wondering what happens in a pooling layer during backpropagation: The network keeps track of the index of the max value in each forward pass, such that the gradient for that particular weight is backpropagated correctly and is used to update the correct parameters.

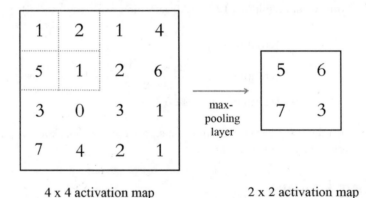

4 x 4 activation map   2 x 2 activation map

Figure 9.7 An example of a max-pooling layer being passed a 4×4 activation map. Like a convolutional layer, the pooling layer slides from left to right and from top to bottom over the matrix of values input into it. With a 2×2-sized filter, the layer retains only the largest of four input values (e.g., the orange "5" in the 2×2 hatch-marked top-left corner). With a 2×2 stride, the resulting output from this max-pooling layer has one-quarter of the volume of its input: a 2×2 activation map.

---

14. Other pooling variants (e.g., *average pooling*, *L2-norm pooling*) exist but are much less common relative to max-pooling, which typically suits machine vision applications sufficiently accurately while requiring minimal computational resources (it is, for example, more computationally expensive to calculate an average than a maximum).
15. Max-pooling with a filter size of 2 × 2 with a stride of 2 is our default recommendation. Both, however, are hyperparameters that you can experiment with, if desired.

LeNet-5 in Keras

All the way back at Figure 1.11, as we introduced the hierarchical nature of deep learning, we discussed the machine vision architecture called LeNet-5. In this section, we use Keras to construct an MNIST digit-classifying model that is inspired by this landmark architecture. However, we afford Yann LeCun and his colleagues' 1998 model some modern twists:

- Because computation is much cheaper today, we opt to use more kernels in our convolutional layers. More specifically, we include 32 and 64 filters in the first and second convolutional layers, respectively, whereas the original LeNet-5 had only 6 and 16 in each.

- Also thanks to cheap compute, we are subsampling activations only once (with a max-pooling layer), whereas LeNet-5 did twice.[16]

- We leverage innovations like ReLU activations and dropout, which had not yet been invented at the time of LeNet-5.

If you'd like to follow along interactively, please make your way to our *LeNet in Keras* Jupyter notebook. As shown in Example 9.1, relative to our previous notebook (*Deep Net in Keras*, covered in Chapter 7), we have three additional dependencies.

Example 9.1 Dependencies for LeNet in Keras

```
import keras
from keras.datasets import mnist
from keras.models import Sequential
from keras.layers import Dense, Dropout
from keras.layers import Conv2D, MaxPooling2D # new!
from keras.layers import Flatten # new!
```

Two of these dependencies—Conv2D and MaxPooling2D—are for implementing convolutional and max-pooling layers, respectively. The Flatten layer, meanwhile, enables us to collapse many-dimensional arrays down to one dimension. We'll explain why that's necessary shortly when we build our model architecture.

Next, we load our MNIST data in precisely the same way we did for all of the previous notebooks involving handwritten digit classification (see Example 5.2). Previously, however, we reshaped the image data from its native two-dimensional representation to a one-dimensional array so that we could feed it into a dense network (see Example 5.3). The first hidden layer in our LeNet-5-inspired network will be convolutional, so we can leave the images in the 28×28-pixel format, as in Example 9.2.[17]

---

16. There is a general trend in deep learning to use pooling layers less frequently, presumably due to increasingly inexpensive computation costs.

17. For any arrays passed into a Keras Conv2D() layer, a fourth dimension is expected. Given the monochromatic nature of the MNIST digits, we use 1 as the fourth-dimension argument passed into reshape(). If our data were full-color images we would have three color channels, and so this argument would be 3.

Example 9.2 Retaining two-dimensional image shape

```
X_train = X_train.reshape(60000, 28, 28, 1).astype('float32')
X_valid = X_valid.reshape(10000, 28, 28, 1).astype('float32')
```

We continue to use the **astype()** method to convert the digits from integers to floats so that they are scaled to range from 0 to 1 (as in Example 5.4). Also as before, we convert our integer y labels to one-hot encodings (as in Example 5.5).

The data loading and preprocessing behind us, we configure our LeNet-*ish* model architecture as in Example 9.3.

Example 9.3 CNN model inspired by LeNet-5

```
model = Sequential()

# first convolutional layer:
model.add(Conv2D(32, kernel_size=(3, 3), activation='relu',
                 input_shape=(28, 28, 1)))

# second conv layer, with pooling and dropout:
model.add(Conv2D(64, kernel_size=(3, 3), activation='relu'))
model.add(MaxPooling2D(pool_size=(2, 2)))
model.add(Dropout(0.25))
model.add(Flatten())

# dense hidden layer, with dropout:
model.add(Dense(128, activation='relu'))
model.add(Dropout(0.5))

# output layer:
model.add(Dense(n_classes, activation='softmax'))
```

All of the previous MNIST classifiers in this book have been dense networks, consisting only of **Dense** layers of neurons. Here we use convolutional layers (**Conv2D**) as our first two hidden layers.[18] The settings we select for these convolutional layers are:

- The integers 32 and 64 correspond to the number of filters we're specifying for the first and second convolutional layer, respectively.
- **kernel_size** is set to 3×3 pixels.
- We're using **relu** as our activation function.

---

18. Conv2D() is our choice here because we're convolving over two-dimensional arrays, that is, images. In Chapter 8, we'll use Conv1D() to convolve over one-dimensional data (strings of text). Conv3D() layers also exist but are outside the scope of this book: These are for carrying out the convolutional operation over all three dimensions, as one might want to for three-dimensional medical images.

- We're using the default stride length, which is 1 pixel (along both the vertical and the horizontal axes). Alternative stride lengths can be specified by providing a `strides` argument to `Conv2D`.

- We're using the default padding, which is `'valid'`. This means that we will forgo the use of padding: Per Equation 9.3, with a stride of 1, our activation map will be 2 pixels shorter and 2 pixels narrower than the input to the layer (e.g., a 28×28-pixel input image shrinks to a 26×26 activation map). The alternative would be to specify the argument `padding='same'`, which would pad the input with zeros so that the output retains the same size as the input (a 28×28-pixel input image results in a 28×28 activation map).

To our second hidden layer of neurons, we add a number of additional layers of computational operations:[19]

- `MaxPooling2D()` is used to reduce computational complexity. As in our example in Figure 9.7, with `pool_size` set to 2×2 and the `strides` argument left at its default (`None`, which sets stride length equal to pool size), we are reducing the volume of our activation map by three-quarters.

- As per Chapter 7, `Dropout()` reduces the risk of overfitting to our training data.

- Finally, `Flatten()` converts the three-dimensional activation map output by `Conv2D()` to a one-dimensional array. This enables us to feed the activations as inputs into a `Dense` layer, which can only accept one-dimensional arrays.

As already discussed in this chapter, the convolutional layers in the network learn to represent spatial features within the image data. The first convolutional layer learns to represent simple features like straight lines at a particular orientation, whereas the second convolutional layer recombines those simple features into more-abstract representations. The intuition behind having a `Dense` layer as the third hidden layer in the network is that it allows the spatial features identified by the second convolutional layer to be recombined in *any* way that's optimal for distinguishing classes of images (there is no sense of spatial orientation within a dense layer). Put differently, the two convolutional layers learn to identify and label spatial features in the images, and these spatial features are then fed into a dense layer that maps these spatial features to a particular class of images (e.g., the digit "3" as opposed to the digit "8"). In this way, the convolutional layers can be thought of as feature extractors. The dense layer of the network receives the extracted features as its input, instead of raw pixels.

We apply `Dropout()` to the dense layer (again to avoid overfitting), and the network then culminates in a softmax output layer—identical to the output layers we have used in all of our previous MNIST-classifying notebooks. Finally, a call to `model.summary()` prints out a summary of our CNN architecture, as shown in Figure 9.8.

---

19. Layer types such as pooling, dropout, and flattening layers aren't made up of artificial neurons, so they don't count as stand-alone hidden layers of a deep learning network like dense or convolutional layers do. They nevertheless perform valuable operations on the data flowing through our neural network, and we can use the Keras `add()` method to include them in our model architecture in the same way that we add layers of neurons.

Layer (type)	Output Shape	Param #
conv2d_1 (Conv2D)	(None, 26, 26, 32)	320
conv2d_2 (Conv2D)	(None, 24, 24, 64)	18496
max_pooling2d_1 (MaxPooling2	(None, 12, 12, 64)	0
dropout_1 (Dropout)	(None, 12, 12, 64)	0
flatten_1 (Flatten)	(None, 9216)	0
dense_1 (Dense)	(None, 128)	1179776
dropout_2 (Dropout)	(None, 128)	0
dense_2 (Dense)	(None, 10)	1290

Total params: 1,199,882
Trainable params: 1,199,882
Non-trainable params: 0

Figure 9.8   A summary of our LeNet-5-inspired ConvNet architecture. Note that the None dimension in each layer is a placeholder for the number of images per batch (i.e., the stochastic gradient descent mini-batch size). Because batch size is specified later (in the model.fit() method), None is used in the interim.

Let's break down the "Output Shape" column of Figure 9.8 first:

- The first convolutional layer, conv2d_1, takes in the 28×28-pixel MNIST digits. With the chosen kernel hyperparameters (filter size, stride, and padding), the layer outputs a 26×26-pixel activation map (as per Equation 9.3).[20] With 32 kernels, the resulting activation map has a depth of 32 slices.

- The second convolutional layer receives as its input the 26×26×32 activation map from the first convolutional layer. The kernel hyperparameters are unchanged, so the activation map shrinks again, now down to 24 × 24. The map is, however, twice as deep because there are 64 kernels in the layer.

- As discussed earlier, a max-pooling layer with a kernel size of 2 and a stride of 2 reduces the volume of data flowing through the network by half in each of the spatial dimensions, yielding an activation map of 12 × 12. The depth of the activation map is not affected by pooling, so it retains 64 slices.

- The flatten layer collapses the three-dimensional activation map down to a one-dimensional array with 9,216 elements.[21]

---

20. Activation map $= \frac{D-F+2P}{S} + 1 = \frac{28-3+2\times0}{1} + 1 = 26$
21. $12 \times 12 \times 64 = 9,216$

- The dense hidden layer contains 128 neurons, so its output is a one-dimensional array of 128 activation values.
- Likewise, the softmax output layer consists of 10 neurons, so it outputs 10 probabilities—one $\hat{y}$ for each possible MNIST digit.

Now let's move on to dissecting the "Param #" column of Figure 9.8:

- The first convolutional layer has 320 parameters:
  - 288 weights: 32 filters × 9 weights each (from the 3×3 filter size × 1 channel)
  - 32 biases, one for each filter
- The second convolutional layer has 18,496 parameters:
  - 18,432 weights: 64 filters × 9 weights per filter, each receiving input from the 32 filters of the preceding layer
  - 64 biases, one for each filter
- The dense hidden layer has 1,179,776 parameters:
  - 1,179,648 weights: 9,216 inputs from the preceding layer's flattened activation map × 128 neurons in the dense layer[22]
  - 128 biases, one for each neuron in the dense layer
- The output layer has 1,290 parameters:
  - 1,280 weights: 128 inputs from the preceding layer × 10 neurons in the output layer
  - 10 biases, one for each neuron in the output layer
- Cumulatively, the entire ConvNet has 1,199,882 parameters, the vast majority (98.3 percent) of which are associated with the dense hidden layer.

To compile the model, we call the `model.compile()` method as usual. Likewise, the `model.fit()` method will begin training.[23] The results of our best epoch are shown in Figure 9.9. Previously, our best result was attained by *Deep Net in Keras*—an accuracy of 97.87 percent on the validation set of MNIST digits. But here, the ConvNet inspired by LeNet-5 achieved 99.27 percent validation accuracy. This is fairly remarkable because the CNN wiped away 65.7 percent of the remaining error;[24] presumably these now correctly classified instances are some of the trickiest digits to classify because they were not identified correctly by our already solid-performing *Deep Net*.

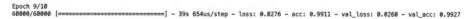

```
Epoch 9/10
60000/60000 [==============================] - 39s 654us/step - loss: 0.0276 - acc: 0.9911 - val_loss: 0.0260 - val_acc: 0.9927
```

Figure 9.9 Our LeNet-5-inspired ConvNet architecture peaked at a 99.27 percent validation accuracy following nine epochs of training, thereby outperforming the accuracy of the dense nets we trained earlier in the book.

---

22. Notice that the dense layer has two orders of magnitude more parameters than the convolutional layers!
23. These steps are identical to the previous notebooks, with the minor exception that the number of epochs is reduced (to 10), because we found that validation loss stopped decreasing after nine epochs of training.
24. 1 − (100%−99.27%)/(100%−97.87%)

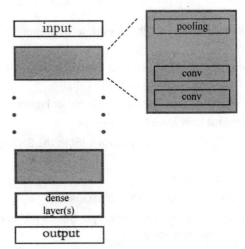

Figure 9.10   A general approach to CNN design: A block (shown in grey) of convolutional layers (often one to three of them) and a pooling layer is repeated several times. This is followed by one (up to a few) dense layers.

AlexNet and VGGNet in Keras

In our LeNet-inspired architecture (Example 9.3), we included a pair of convolutional layers followed by a max-pooling layer. This is a routine approach within convolutional neural networks. As depicted in Figure 9.10, it is common to group convolutional layers (often one to three of them) together with a pooling layer. These conv-pool blocks can then be repeated several times. As in LeNet-5, such CNN architectures regularly culminate in a dense hidden layer (up to several dense hidden layers) and then the output layer.

The AlexNet model (Figure 1.17)—which we introduced as the 2012 computer vision competition-winning harbinger of the deep learning revolution—is another architecture that features the convolutional layer block approach provided in Figure 9.10. In our *AlexNet in Keras* notebook, we use the code shown in Example 9.4 to emulate this structure.[25]

Example 9.4 CNN model inspired by AlexNet

```
model = Sequential()

# first conv-pool block:
model.add(Conv2D(96, kernel_size=(11, 11),
          strides=(4, 4), activation='relu',
          input_shape=(224, 224, 3)))
```

---

25. This AlexNet model architecture is the same one visualized by Jason Yosinski with his DeepViz tool. If you didn't view his video when we mentioned it earlier in this chapter, then we recommend checking it out at bit.ly/DeepViz now.

```
model.add(MaxPooling2D(pool_size=(3, 3), strides=(2, 2)))
model.add(BatchNormalization())

# second conv-pool block:
model.add(Conv2D(256, kernel_size=(5, 5), activation='relu'))
model.add(MaxPooling2D(pool_size=(3, 3), strides=(2, 2)))
model.add(BatchNormalization())

# third conv-pool block:
model.add(Conv2D(256, kernel_size=(3, 3), activation='relu'))
model.add(Conv2D(384, kernel_size=(3, 3), activation='relu'))
model.add(Conv2D(384, kernel_size=(3, 3), activation='relu'))
model.add(MaxPooling2D(pool_size=(3, 3), strides=(2, 2)))
model.add(BatchNormalization())

# dense layers:
model.add(Flatten())
model.add(Dense(4096, activation='tanh'))
model.add(Dropout(0.5))
model.add(Dense(4096, activation='tanh'))
model.add(Dropout(0.5))

# output layer:
model.add(Dense(17, activation='softmax'))
```

The key points about this particular model architecture are:

- For this notebook, we moved beyond the MNIST digits to a dataset of larger-sized (224×224-pixel) images that are full-color (hence the 3 channels of depth in the input_shape argument passed to the first Conv2D layer).

- AlexNet used larger filter sizes in the earliest convolutional layers relative to what is popular today—for example, kernel_size=(11, 11).

- Such use of dropout in only the dense layers near the model output (and not in the earlier convolutional layers) is common. The intuition behind this is that the early convolutional layers enable the model to represent spatial features of images that generalize well beyond the training data. However, a very specific recombination of these features, as facilitated by the dense layers, may be unique to the training dataset and thus may not generalize well to validation data.

The AlexNet and VGGNet (more about this in a moment) model architectures are very large (AlexNet, for example, has 21.9 million parameters), and you may need to increase the memory available to Docker on your machine to load it. See bit.ly/DockerMem for instructions on how to do this.

Following AlexNet being crowned the 2012 winner of the ImageNet Large Scale Visual Recognition Challenge, deep learning models suddenly began to be used widely in the competition (see Figure 1.15). Among these models, there has been a general trend toward making the neural networks deeper and deeper. For example, in 2014 the runner-up in the ILSVRC was VGGNet,[26] which follows the same repeated conv-pool-block structure as AlexNet; VGGNet simply has more of them, and with smaller (all 3×3-pixel) kernel sizes. We provide the architecture shown in Example 9.5 in our *VGGNet in Keras* notebook.

Example 9.5 CNN model inspired by VGGNet

```
model = Sequential()

model.add(Conv2D(64, 3, activation='relu',
          input_shape=(224, 224, 3)))
model.add(Conv2D(64, 3, activation='relu'))
model.add(MaxPooling2D(2, 2))
model.add(BatchNormalization())

model.add(Conv2D(128, 3, activation='relu'))
model.add(Conv2D(128, 3, activation='relu'))
model.add(MaxPooling2D(2, 2))
model.add(BatchNormalization())

model.add(Conv2D(256, 3, activation='relu'))
model.add(Conv2D(256, 3, activation='relu'))
model.add(Conv2D(256, 3, activation='relu'))
model.add(MaxPooling2D(2, 2))
model.add(BatchNormalization())

model.add(Conv2D(512, 3, activation='relu'))
model.add(Conv2D(512, 3, activation='relu'))
model.add(Conv2D(512, 3, activation='relu'))
model.add(MaxPooling2D(2, 2))
model.add(BatchNormalization())

model.add(Conv2D(512, 3, activation='relu'))
model.add(Conv2D(512, 3, activation='relu'))
model.add(Conv2D(512, 3, activation='relu'))
model.add(MaxPooling2D(2, 2))
model.add(BatchNormalization())
```

---

26. Developed by the *Visual Geometry Group* at the University of Oxford: Simonyan, K., and Zisserman, A. (2015). Very deep convolutional networks for large-scale image recognition. *arXiv: 1409.1556.*

```
model.add(Flatten())
model.add(Dense(4096, activation='relu'))
model.add(Dropout(0.5))
model.add(Dense(4096, activation='relu'))
model.add(Dropout(0.5))

model.add(Dense(17, activation='softmax'))
```

Residual Networks

As our example ConvNets from this chapter (LeNet-5, AlexNet, VGGNet) suggest, there's a trend over time toward deeper networks. In this section, we recapitulate the topic of vanishing gradients—the (often dramatic) slowing in learning that can occur as network architectures are deepened. We then describe an imaginative solution that has emerged in recent years: residual networks.

Vanishing Gradients: The Bête Noire of Deep CNNs

With more layers, models are able to learn a larger variety of relatively low-level features in the early layers, and increasingly complex abstractions are made possible in the later layers via nonlinear recombination. This approach, however, has limits: If we continue to simply make our networks deeper (e.g., by adding more and more of the conv-pool blocks from Figure 9.10), they will eventually be debilitated by the vanishing gradient problem.

We introduced vanishing gradients in Chapter 7; the basis of the issue is that parameters in early layers of the network are far away from the cost function: the source of the gradient that is propagated backward through the network. As the error is backpropagated, a larger and larger number of parameters contribute to the error, and thus each layer closer to the input gets a smaller and smaller update. The net effect is that early layers in increasingly deep networks become more difficult to train (see Figure 7.8).

Because of the vanishing gradient problem, it is commonly observed that as one increases the depth of a network, accuracy increases up to a saturation point and then later begins to degrade as networks become excessively deep. Imagine a shallow network that is performing well. Now let's copy those layers with their weights, and stack on new layers atop to make the model deeper. Intuition might say that the new, deeper model would take the existing gains from the early pretrained layers and improve. If the new layers performed simple identity mapping (wherein they faithfully reproduced the exact results of the earlier layers), then we'd see no increase in training error. It turns out, however, that plain deep networks struggle to learn identity functions.[27,28] Thus, these new layers either add new information and decrease the error, or they do not add new information (but also fail at identity mapping) and the error increases. Given that adding

---

27. Hardt, M., and Ma, T. (2018). Identity matters in deep learning. *arXiv:1611.04231*.
28. Hold tight! More clarification is coming up on the terms *identity mapping* and *identity functions* shortly.

useful information is an exceedingly rare outcome (relative to the baseline, which is essentially random noise), it transpires that beyond a certain point these extra layers will, probabilistically, contribute to an overall degradation in performance.

Residual Connections

Residual networks (or *ResNets*, for short) rely on the idea of residual connections, which exist within so-called residual modules. A residual module—as illustrated in Figure 9.11—is a collective term for a sequence of convolutions, batch-normalization operations, and ReLU activations that culminates with a residual connection. For the sake of simplicity here, we consider these various layers within a residual module to be a single, discrete unit. Following on with the most straightforward definition, a *residual connection* exists when the input to one such residual module is summed with its output to produce the final activation for that residual module. In other words, a residual module will receive some input a_{i-1},[29] which is transformed by the convolutions and activation functions within the residual module to generate its output a_i. Subsequently, this output and the original input to the residual module are summed: $y_i = a_i + a_{i-1}$.[30]

Following the structure and the basic math of the residual connection from the preceding paragraph, you'll notice that an interesting feature emerges: If the residual module has an activation $a_i = 0$—that is, it has learned nothing—the final output of the residual module will simply be the original input, since the two are summed. Following on with the equation we used most recently:

$$y_i = a_i + a_{i-1}$$
$$= 0 + a_{i-1}$$
$$= a_{i-1}$$

In this case, the residual module is effectively an *identity function*. These residual modules either learn something useful and contribute to reducing the error of the network, or they perform *identity mapping* and do nothing at all. Because of this identity-mapping behavior, residual connections are also called "skip connections," because they enable information to skip the functions located within the residual module.

In addition to this *neutral-or-better* characteristic of residual networks, we should also highlight the value of their inherent multiplicity. Consider the schematic in Figure 9.12: When several residual modules are stacked, later residual modules receive inputs that are increasingly complex combinations of the residual modules and skip connections from earlier in the network. Seen on the right in this figure, a decision tree representation shows how, at each of the three residual modules in the network, information may either pass through the residual block or bypass it via a skip connection. Thus, as is shown at the bottom of the figure, with only three residual modules there are eight possible paths the information can take. In practice, the process is not commonly as binary as it is depicted

---

29. Remember that the input to any given layer is simply the output of the preceding layer, denoted here by a_{i-1}.
30. We've opted to denote the final output of the whole residual module as y_i, but that does not mean to indicate that this is necessarily the final output of the entire model. It simply serves to avoid confusion with the activations from the current and preceding layers, indicating that the final output is a distinct entity derived from the sum of those activations.

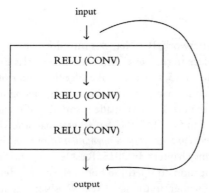

Figure 9.11 A schematic representation of a residual module. Batch normalization and dropout layers are not shown, but may be included.

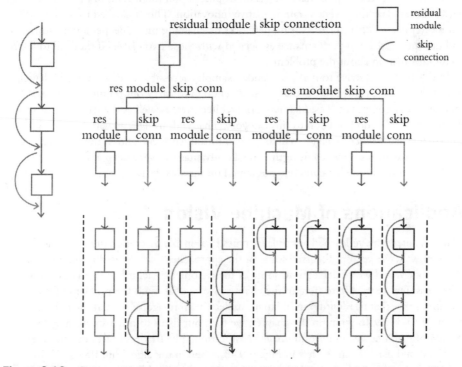

Figure 9.12 Shown at left is the conventional representation of residual blocks within a residual network. Shown at right is an unraveled view, which demonstrates how, depending on which skip connections are used, the final path of information from input to output can be varied by the network.

in this figure. That is, the value of a_i is seldom 0, and therefore the output is usually some mix of the identity function and the residual module. Given this insight, residual networks can be thought of as complex combinations or ensembles of many shallower networks that are pooled at various depths.

ResNet

The first deep residual network, ResNet, was introduced by Microsoft Research in 2015[31] and won first place in that year's ILSVRC image-classification competition. Referring back to Figure 1.15, this makes ResNet the leader of the pack of deep learning algorithms that surpassed human performance at image recognition in 2015.

Up to this point in the book, we've made it sound as if image classification is the *only* contest at ILSVRC, but in fact ILSVRC has several machine vision competition categories, such as *object detection* and *image segmentation* (more on these two machine vision tasks coming soon in this chapter). In 2015, ResNet took first place not only in the ILSVRC image-classification competition but in the object detection and image segmentation categories, too. Further, in the same year, ResNet was also recognized as champion of the detection and segmentation competitions involving an alternative image dataset called COCO, which is an alternative to the ILSVRC set.[32]

Given the broad sweep of machine vision trophies upon the invention of residual networks, it's clear they were a transformative innovation. They managed to squeeze out more juice relative to the existing networks by enabling much deeper architectures without the decrease in performance associated with those extra layers if they fail to learn useful information about the problem.

In this book, we strive to make our code examples accessible to our readers by having model architectures and datasets that are small enough to carry out training on even a modest laptop computer. Residual network architectures, as well as the datasets that make them worthwhile, do not fall into this category. That said, using a powerful, general approach called *transfer learning*—which we will introduce at the end of this chapter—we provide you with resources to nevertheless take advantage of very deep architectures like ResNet with the model's parameters pretrained on massive datasets.

Applications of Machine Vision

In this chapter, you've learned about layer types that enable machine vision models to perform well. We've also discussed some of the approaches that are used to improve these models, and we've delved into some of the canonical machine vision algorithms of the past few years. Up to here in the chapter, we've dealt with the problem of image classification—that is, identifying the main subject in an image, as seen at the left in Figure 9.13. Now, to wrap up the chapter, we turn our focus to other interesting applications of machine vision beyond image classification. The first is object detection, seen in the second panel from the left in Figure 9.13, wherein the algorithm is tasked with drawing bounding boxes around objects in an image. Next is image segmentation, shown in the third and fourth panels of Figure 9.13. *Semantic segmentation* identifies all objects of a particular class down to the pixel level, whereas *instance segmentation* discriminates between different *instances* of a particular class, also at the pixel level.

---

31. He, K., et al. (2015). Deep residual learning for image recognition. *arXiv:1512.03385.*
32. cocodataset.org

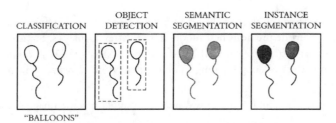

| CLASSIFICATION | OBJECT DETECTION | SEMANTIC SEGMENTATION | INSTANCE SEGMENTATION |

"BALLOONS"

Figure 9.13   These are examples of various machine vision applications. We have encountered classification previously in this chapter, but now we cover object detection, semantic segmentation, and instance segmentation.

Object Detection

Imagine a photo of a group of people sitting down to dinner. There are several people in the image. There is a roast chicken in the middle of the table, and maybe a bottle of wine. If we desired an automated system that could predict what was served for dinner or to identify the people sitting at the table, an image-classification algorithm would not provide that level of granularity—enter *object detection*.

Object detection has broad applications, such as detecting pedestrians in the field of view for autonomous driving, or for identifying anomalies in medical images. Generally speaking, object detection is divided into two tasks: detection (identifying *where* the objects in the image are) and then, subsequently, classification (identifying *what* the objects are that have been detected). Typically this pipeline has three stages:

1. A region of interest must be identified.
2. Automatic feature extraction is performed on this region.
3. The region is classified.

Seminal models—ones that have defined progress in this area—include R-CNN, Fast R-CNN, Faster R-CNN, and YOLO.

R-CNN

R-CNN was proposed in 2013 by Ross Girshick and his colleagues at UC Berkeley.[33] The algorithm was modeled on the attention mechanism of the human brain, wherein an entire scene is scanned and focus is placed on specific regions of interest. To emulate this attention, Girshick and his coworkers developed R-CNN to:

1. Perform a selective search for *regions of interest* (ROIs) within the image.
2. Extract features from these ROIs by using a CNN.
3. Combine two "traditional" (as in Figure 1.12) machine learning approaches—called *linear regression* and *support vector machines*—to, respectively, refine the locations of bounding boxes[34] and classify objects within each of those boxes.

---

33. Girshnick, R., et al. (2013). Rich feature hierarchies for accurate object detection and semantic segmentation. *arXiv: 1311.2524.*
34. See examples of bounding boxes in Figure 9.14.

R-CNNs redefined the state of the art in object detection, achieving a massive gain in performance over the previous best model in the Pattern Analysis, Statistical Modeling and Computational Learning (PASCAL) Visual Object Classes (VOC) competition.[35] This ushered in the era of deep learning in object detection. However, this model had some limitations:

- It was inflexible: The input size was fixed to a single specific image shape.
- It was slow and computionally expensive: Both training and inference are multistage processes involving CNNs, linear regression models, and support vector machines.

Fast R-CNN

To address the primary drawback of R-CNN—its speed—Girshick went on to develop Fast R-CNN.[36] The chief innovation here was the realization that during step 2 of the R-CNN algorithm, the CNN was unnecessarily being run multiple times, once for each region of interest. With Fast R-CNN, the ROI search (step 1) is run as before, but during step 2, the CNN is given a single global look at the image, and the extracted features are used for all ROIs simultaneously. A vector of features is extracted from the final layer of the CNN, which (for step 3) is then fed into a dense network along with the ROI. This dense net learns to focus on only the features that apply to each individual ROI, culminating in two outputs per ROI:

1. A softmax probability output over the classification categories (for a prediction of what class the detected object belongs to)
2. A bounding box regressor (for refinement of the ROI's location)

Following this approach, the Fast R-CNN model has to perform feature extraction using a CNN only once for a given image (thereby reducing computational complexity), and then the ROI search and dense layers work together to finish the object-detection task. As the name suggests, the reduced computational complexity of Fast R-CNN corresponds to speedier compute times. It also represents a single, unified model without the multiple independent parts of its predecessor. Nevertheless, as with R-CNN, the initial (ROI search) step of Fast R-CNN still presents a significant computational bottleneck.

Faster R-CNN

The model architectures in this section are clever works of innovation—their names, however, are not. Our third object-detection algorithm of note is Faster R-CNN, which (you guessed it!) is even swifter than Fast R-CNN.

Faster R-CNN was revealed in 2015 by Shaoqing Ren and his coworkers at Microsoft Research (Figure 9.14 shows example outputs).[37] To overcome the ROI-search bottleneck of R-CNN and Fast R-CNN, Ren and his colleagues had the cunning insight to leverage the feature activation maps from the model's CNN for this step, too. Those activation maps contain a great deal of contextual information about an image. Because

---

35. PASCAL VOC ran competitions from 2005 until 2012; the dataset remains available and is considered one of the gold standards for object-detection problems.
36. Girshnick, R. (2015). Fast R-CNN. *arXiv: 1504.08083*
37. Ren, S. et al. (2015). Faster R-CNN: Towards real-time object detection with region proposal networks. *arXiv: 1506.01497.*

Figure 9.14 These are examples of object detection (performed on four separate images by the Faster R-CNN algorithm). Within each region of interest—defined by the bounding boxes within the images—the algorithm predicts what the object within the region is.

each map has two dimensions representing location, they can be thought of as literal *maps* of the locations of features within a given image. If—as in Figure 9.6—a convolutional layer has 16 filters, the activation map it outputs has 16 maps, together representing the locations of 16 features in the input image. As such, these feature maps contain rich detail about what is in an image and *where* it is. Faster R-CNN takes advantage of this rich detail to propose ROI locations, enabling a CNN to seamlessly perform all three steps of the object-detection process, thereby providing a unified model architecture that builds on R-CNN and Fast R-CNN but is markedly quicker.

YOLO

Within each of the various object-detection models described thus far, the CNN focused on the individual proposed ROIs as opposed to the whole input image.[38] Joseph Redmon and coworkers published on You Only Look Once (YOLO) in 2015, which bucked this trend.[39] YOLO begins with a *pretrained*[40] CNN for feature extraction. Next, the image is divided into a series of cells, and, for each cell, a number of bounding boxes and

---

38. Technically, the CNN looked at the whole image at the start in both Fast R-CNN and Faster R-CNN. However, in both cases this was simply a one-shot step to extract features, and from then onward the image was treated as a set of smaller regions.
39. Redmon, J., et al. (2015). You Only Look Once: Unified, real-time object detection. *arXiv: 1506.02640.*
40. Pretrained models are used in transfer learning, which we detail at chapter's end.

object-classification probabilities are predicted. Bounding boxes with class probabilities above a threshold value are selected, and these combine to locate an object within an image.

You can think of the YOLO method as aggregating many smaller bounding boxes, but only if they have a reasonably good probability of containing any given object class. The algorithm improved on the speed of Faster R-CNN, but it struggled to accurately detect small objects in an image.

Since the original YOLO paper, Redmon and his colleagues have released their YOLO9000[41] and YOLOv3 models.[42] YOLO9000 resulted in increases in both execution speed and model accuracy, and YOLOv3 yielded some speed for even further improved accuracy—in large part due to the increased sophistication of the underlying model architectures. The details of these continuations stretch beyond the scope of this book, but at the time of writing these models represent the cutting edge of object-detection algorithms.

Image Segmentation

When the visual field of a human is exposed to a real-world scene containing many overlapping visual elements—such as the game of association football (soccer) captured in Figure 9.15—the adult brain seems to effortlessly distinguish figures from the background, defining the boundaries of these figures and relationships between them

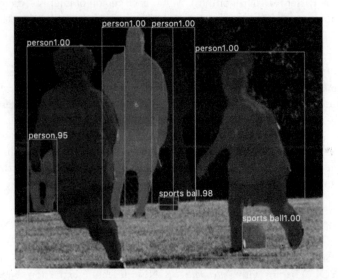

Figure 9.15   This is an example of image segmentation (as performed by the Mask R-CNN algorithm). Whereas object detection involves defining object locations with coarse bounding boxes, image segmentation predicts the location of objections to the pixel level (see page 330 for the color image).

41. Redmon, J., et al. (2016). YOLO9000: Better, faster, stronger. *arXiv: 1612.08242.*
42. Redmon, J. (2018). YOLOv3: An incremental improvement. *arXiv: 1804.02767.*

within a few hundred milliseconds. In this section, we cover *image segmentation*, another application area where deep learning has in a few short years bridged much of the gap in visual capability between humans and machines. We focus on two prominent model architectures—Mask R-CNN and U-Net—that are able to reliably classify objects in an image on a pixelwise scale.

Mask R-CNN

Mask R-CNN was developed by Facebook AI Research (FAIR) in 2017.[43] This approach involves:

1. Using the existing Faster R-CNN architecture to propose ROIs within the image that are likely to contain objects.
2. An ROI classifier predicting what kind of object exists in the bounding box while also refining the location and size of the bounding box.
3. Using the bounding box to grab the parts of the feature maps from the underlying CNN that correspond to that part of the image.
4. Feeding the feature maps for each ROI into a fully convolutional network that outputs a *mask* indicating which pixels correspond to the object in the image. An example of such a mask—consisting of bright colors to designate the pixels associated with separate objects—is provided in Figure 9.15.

Image segmentation problems require binary masks as labels for training. These consist of arrays of the same dimensions as the original image. However, instead of RGB pixel values they contain 1s and 0s indicating where in the image the object is, with the 1s representing a given object's pixel-by-pixel location (and the 0s representing everywhere else). If an image contains a dozen different objects, then it must have a dozen binary masks.

U-Net

Another popular image segmentation model is U-Net, which was developed at the University of Freiberg (and was mentioned at the end of Chapter 3 with respect to the automated photo-processing pipelines).[44] U-Net was created for the purpose of segmenting biomedical images, and at the time of writing it outperformed the best available methods in two challenges held by the International Symposium on Biomedical Images.[45]

The U-Net model consists of a fully convolutional architecture, which begins with a *contracting* path that produces successively smaller and deeper activation maps through multiple convolution and max-pooling steps. Subsequently, an *expanding* path restores these deep activation maps back to full resolution through multiple upsampling and convolution steps. These two paths—the contracting and expanding paths—are symmetrical (forming a "U" shape), and because of this symmetry the activation maps from the contracting path can be concatenated onto those of the expanding path.

43. He, K., et al. (2017). Mask R-CNN. *arXiv: 1703.06870.*
44. Ronneberger, O., et al. (2015). U-Net: Convolutional networks for biomedical image segmentation. *arXiv: 1505.04597.*
45. The two challenges were the segmentation of neuronal structures in electron microscopy stacks, and the ISBI cell-tracking challenge from 2015.

The contracting path serves to allow the model to learn high-resolution features from the image. These high-res features are handed directly to the expanding path. By the end of the expanding path, we expect the model to have localized these features within the final image dimensions. After concatenating the feature maps from the contracting path onto the expanding path, a subsequent convolutional layer allows the network to learn to assemble and localize these features precisely. The final result is a network that is highly adept both at identifying features and at locating those features within two-dimensional space.

Transfer Learning

To be effective, many of the models we describe in this chapter are trained on very large datasets of diverse images. This training requires significant compute resources, and the datasets themselves are not cheap or easy to assemble. Over the course of this training, a given CNN learns to extract general features from the images. At a low level, these are lines, edges, colors, and simple shapes; at a higher level, they are textures, combinations of shapes, parts of objects, and other complex visual elements (recall Figure 1.17). If the CNN has been trained on a suitably varied set of images and if it is sufficiently deep, these feature maps likely contain a rich library of visual elements that can be assembled and combined to form nearly any image. For example, a feature map that identifies a dimpled texture combined with another that recognizes round objects and yet another that responds to white colors could be recombined to correctly identify a golf ball. *Transfer learning* takes advantage of this library of existing visual elements contained within the feature maps of a pretrained CNN and repurposes them to become specialized in identifying new classes of objects.

Say, for example, that you'd like to build a machine vision model that performs the binary classification task we've addressed time and again since Chapter 6: distinguishing hot dogs from anything that is not a hot dog. Of course, you could design a large and complex CNN that takes in images of hot dogs and, well . . . not hot dogs, and outputs a single sigmoid class prediction. You could train this model on a large number of training images, and you'd expect the convolutional layers early in the network to learn a set of feature maps that will identify hot dog-*esque* features. Frankly, this would work pretty well. However, you'd need a lot of time and a lot of compute power to train the CNN properly, and you'd need a large number of diverse images so that the CNN could learn a suitably diverse set of feature maps. This is where transfer learning comes in: Instead of training a model from scratch, you can leverage the power of a deep model that has already been trained on a large set of images and quickly repurpose it to detecting hot dogs specifically.

Earlier in this chapter, we mentioned VGGNet as an example of a classic machine vision model architecture. In Example 9.5 and in our *VGGNet in Keras* Jupyter notebook, we showcase the VGGNet16 model, which is composed of 16 layers of artificial neurons—mostly repeating conv-pool blocks (see Figure 9.10). The closely related VGGNet19 model, which incorporates one further conv-pool block (containing three convolutional layers), is our pick for our transfer-learning starting point. In our accompanying notebook, *Transfer Learning in Keras*, we load VGGNet19 and modify it for our own hot-doggy purposes.

The chief advantage of VGG19 over VGG16 is that VGG19's additional layers afford it additional opportunities for the abstract representation of visual imagery. The chief disadvantage of VGG19 relative to VGG16 is that these additional layers mean more parameters and therefore a longer training time. Further, because of the vanishing gradient problem, backpropagation may struggle through VGG19's additional early layers.

To start, let's get the standard imports out of the way and load up the pretrained VGGNet19 model (Example 9.6).

Example 9.6 Loading the VGGNet19 model for transfer learning

```
# Load dependencies:
from keras.applications.vgg19 import VGG19
from keras.models import sequential
from keras.layers import Dense, Dropout, Flatten
from keras.preprocessing.image import ImageDataGenerator

# Load the pre-trained VGG19 model:
vgg19 = VGG19(include_top=False,
            weights='imagenet',
            input_shape=(224,224,3),
            pooling=None)

# Freeze all the layers in the base VGGNet19 model:
for layer in vgg19.layers:
    layer.trainable = False
```

Handily, Keras provides the network architecture and parameters (called *weights*, but includes biases, too) already, so loading the pretrained model is easy.[46] Arguments passed to the VGG19 function help to define some characteristics of the loaded model:

- `include_top=False` specifies that we do not want the final dense classification layers from the original VGGNet19 architecture. These layers were trained for classifying the original ImageNet data. Rather, as you'll see momentarily, we'll make our own top layers and train them ourselves using our own data.

- `weights='imagenet'` is to load model parameters trained on the 14 million-sample ImageNet dataset.[47]

- `input_shape=(224,224,3)` initializes the model with the correct input image size to handle our hot dog data.

---

46. For other pretrained Keras models, including the ResNet architecture we introduced earlier in this chapter, visit keras.io/applications.

47. The only other weights argument option at the time of writing is 'None', which would be a random initialization, but in the future, model parameters trained on other datasets could be available.

After we load the model, a quick `for` loop traverses each layer in the model and sets its `trainable` flag to `False` so that the parameters in these layers will *not* be updated during training. We are confident that the convolutional layers of VGGNet19 have been effectively trained to represent the generalized visual-imagery features of the large ImageNet dataset, so we leave the base model intact.

In Example 9.7, we add fresh dense layers on top of the base VGGNet19 model. These layers take the features extracted from the input image by the pretrained convolutional layers, and through training they will learn to use these features to classify the images as hot dogs or not hot dogs.

Example 9.7 Adding classification layers to transfer-learning model

```
# Instantiate the sequential model and add the VGG19 model:
model = Sequential()
model.add(vgg19)

# Add the custom layers atop the VGG19 model:
model.add(Flatten(name='flattened'))
model.add(Dropout(0.5, name='dropout'))
model.add(Dense(2, activation='softmax', name='predictions'))

# Compile the model for training:
model.compile(optimizer='adam', loss='categorical_crossentropy',
              metrics=['accuracy'])
```

Next, we use an instance of the **ImageDataGenerator** class to load the data (Example 9.8). This class is provided by Keras and serves to load images on the fly. It's especially helpful if you don't want to load all of your training data into memory right away, or when you might want to perform random data augmentations in real time during training.[48]

Example 9.8 Defining data generators

```
# Instantiate two image generator classes:
train_datagen = ImageDataGenerator(
    rescale=1.0/255,
    data_format='channels_last',
    rotation_range=30,
    horizontal_flip=True,
    fill_mode='reflect')
```

---

48. In Chapter 7, we mention that data augmentation is an effective way to increase the size of a training dataset, thereby helping a model generalize to previously unseen data.

```
valid_datagen = ImageDataGenerator(
    rescale=1.0/255,
    data_format='channels_last')

# Define the batch size:
batch_size=32

# Define the train and validation data generators:
train_generator = train_datagen.flow_from_directory(
    directory='./hot-dog-not-hot-dog/train',
    target_size=(224, 224),
    classes=['hot_dog','not_hot_dog'],
    class_mode='categorical',
    batch_size=batch_size,
    shuffle=True,
    seed=42)

valid_generator = valid_datagen.flow_from_directory(
    directory='./hot-dog-not-hot-dog/test',
    target_size=(224, 224),
    classes=['hot_dog','not_hot_dog'],
    class_mode='categorical',
    batch_size=batch_size,
    shuffle=True,
    seed=42)
```

The train–data generator will randomly rotate the images within a 30-degree range, randomly flip the images horizontally, rescale the data to between 0 and 1 (by multiplying by $1/255$), and load the image data into arrays in the "channels last" format.[49] The validation generator only needs to rescale and load the images; data augmentation would be of no value there. Finally, the flow_from_directory() method directs each generator to load the images from a directory we specify.[50] The remainder of the arguments to this method should be intuitive.

Now we're ready to train (Example 9.9). Instead of using the fit() method as we did in all previous cases of model-fitting in this book, here we call the fit_generator() method on the model because we'll be passing in a data generator in place of arrays of data.[51] During our run of this model, our best epoch turned out to be the sixth, in which we attained 81.2 percent accuracy.

---

49. Look back at Example 9.6, and you'll see that the model accepts inputs with dimensions of 224 × 224 × 3— that is, the channels dimension is last. The alternative is to set up the color channel as the first dimension.
50. Instructions for downloading the data are included in our Jupyter notebook.
51. As we warned earlier in this chapter, in the section on AlexNet and VGGNet, with very large models you may encounter out-of-memory errors. Please refer to bit.ly/DockerMem for information on increasing the amount of memory available to your Docker container. Alternatively, you could reduce your batch-size hyperparameter.

Example 9.9 Train transfer-learning model

```
model.fit_generator(train_generator, steps_per_epoch=15,
                    epochs=16, validation_data=valid_generator,
                    validation_steps=15)
```

This demonstrates the power of transfer learning. With a small amount of training and almost no time spent on architectural considerations or hyperparameter tuning, we have at our fingertips a model that performs reasonably well on a rather complicated image-classification task: hot dog identification. With some time invested in hyperparameter tuning, the results could be improved further.

Capsule Networks

In 2017, Sara Sabour and her colleagues on Geoff Hinton's (Figure 1.16) Google Brain team in Toronto made a splash with a novel concept called *capsule networks*.[52] Capsule networks have received considerable interest, because they are able to take positional information into consideration. CNNs, to their great detriment, do not; so a CNN would, for example, consider both of the images in Figure 9.16 to be a human face. The theory behind capsule networks is beyond the scope of this book, but machine vision practitioners are generally aware of them so we wanted to be sure you were, too. Today, they are too computationally intensive to be predominant in applications, but cheaper compute and theoretical advancements could mean that this situation will change soon.

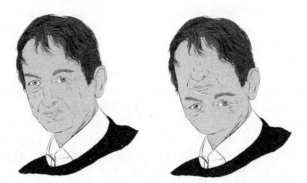

Figure 9.16   With convolutional neural networks, which are agnostic to the relative positioning of image features, the figure on the left and the one on the right are equally likely to be classified as Geoff Hinton's face. Capsule networks, in contrast, take positional information into consideration, and so would be less likely to mistake the right-hand figure for a face.

---

52. Sabour, S., et al. (2017). Dynamic routing between capsules. *arXiv: 1710.09829.*

Summary

In this chapter, you learned about convolutional layers, which are specialized to detect spatial patterns, making them particularly useful for machine vision tasks. You incorporated these layers into a CNN inspired by the classic LeNet-5 architecture, enabling you to surpass the handwritten-digit recognition accuracy of the dense networks you designed in Part II. The chapter concluded by discussing best practices for building CNNs and surveying the most noteworthy applications of machine vision algorithms. In the coming chapter, you'll discover that the spatial-pattern recognition capabilities of convolutional layers are well suited not only to machine vision but also to other tasks.

Key Concepts

Here are the essential foundational concepts thus far. New terms from the current chapter are highlighted in purple.

- parameters:
    - weight w
    - bias b
- activation a
- artificial neurons:
    - sigmoid
    - tanh
    - ReLU
    - linear
- input layer
- hidden layer
- output layer
- layer types:
    - dense (fully connected)
    - softmax
    - convolutional
    - max-pooling
    - flatten

- cost (loss) functions:
    - quadratic (mean squared error)
    - cross-entropy
- forward propagation
- backpropagation
- unstable (especially vanishing) gradients
- Glorot weight initialization
- batch normalization
- dropout
- optimizers:
    - stochastic gradient descent
    - Adam
- optimizer hyperparameters:
    - learning rate η
    - batch size

10

Deep Reinforcement Learning

In Chapter 4, we introduced the paradigm of reinforcement learning (as distinct from supervised and unsupervised learning), in which an agent (e.g., an algorithm) takes sequential actions within an environment. The environments—whether they be simulated or real world—can be extremely complex and rapidly changing, requiring sophisticated agents that can adapt appropriately in order to succeed at fulfilling their objective. Today, many of the most prolific reinforcement learning agents involve an artificial neural network, making them *deep reinforcement learning* algorithms.

In this chapter, we will

- Cover the essential theory of reinforcement learning in general and, in particular, a deep reinforcement learning model called deep Q-learning
- Use Keras to construct a deep Q-learning network that learns how to excel within simulated, video game environments
- Discuss approaches for optimizing the performance of deep reinforcement learning agents
- Introduce families of deep RL agents beyond deep Q-learning

Essential Theory of Reinforcement Learning

Recall from Chapter 4 (specifically, Figure 4.3) that *reinforcement learning* is a machine learning paradigm involving:

- An *agent* taking an *action* within an *environment* (let's say the action is taken at some timestep t).
- The environment returning two types of information to the agent:
  1. *Reward*: This is a scalar value that provides quantitative feedback on the action that the agent took at timestep t. This could, for example, be 100 points as a reward for acquiring cherries in the video game Pac-Man. The agent's objective is to maximize the rewards it accumulates, and so rewards are what *reinforce* productive behaviors that the agent discovers under particular environmental conditions.

2. *State*: This is how the environment changes in response to an agent's action. During the forthcoming timestep $(t + 1)$, these will be the conditions for the agent to choose an action in.

- Repeating the above two steps in a loop until reaching some terminal state. This terminal state could be reached by, for example, attaining the maximum possible reward, attaining some specific desired outcome (such as a self-driving car reaching its programmed destination), running out of allotted time, using up the maximum number of permitted moves in a game, or the agent dying in a game.

Reinforcement learning problems are sequential decision-making problems. In Chapter 4, we discussed a number of particular examples of these, including:

- Atari video games, such as Pac-Man, Pong, and Breakout
- Autonomous vehicles, such as self-driving cars and aerial drones
- Board games, such as Go, chess, and shogi
- Robot-arm manipulation tasks, such as removing a nail with a hammer

The Cart-Pole Game

In this chapter, we will use OpenAI Gym—a popular library of reinforcement learning environments (examples provided in Figure 4.13)—to train an agent to play Cart-Pole, a classic problem among academics working in the field of control theory. In the Cart-Pole game:

- The objective is to balance a pole on top of a cart. The pole is connected to the cart at a dot, which functions as a pin that permits the pole to rotate along the horizontal axis, as illustrated in Figure 10.1.[1]
- The cart itself can only move horizontally, either to the left or to the right. At any given moment—at any given *timestep*—the cart *must* be moved to the left or to the right; it can't remain stationary.
- Each episode of the game begins with the cart positioned at a random point near the center of the screen and with the pole at a random angle near vertical.
- As shown in Figure 10.2, an episode ends when either
  - The pole is no longer balanced on the cart—that is, when the angle of the pole moves too far away from vertical toward horizontal
  - The cart touches the boundaries—the far right or far left of the screen
- In the version of the game that you'll play in this chapter, the maximum number of timesteps in an episode is 200. So, if the episode does not end early (due to los-ing pole balance or navigating off the screen), then the game will end after 200 timesteps.
- One point of reward is provided for every timestep that the episode lasts, so the maximum possible reward is 200 points.

---

1. An actual screen capture of the Cart-Pole game is provided in Figure 4.13a.

THE CARTPOLE GAME

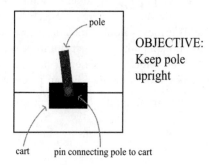

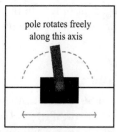

OBJECTIVE:
Keep pole
upright

Figure 10.1   The objective of the Cart-Pole game is to keep the pole balanced upright on top of the black cart for as long as possible. The player of the game (be it a human or a machine) controls the cart by moving it horizontally to the left or to the right along the black line. The pole moves freely along the axis created by the pin.

game ends early if:

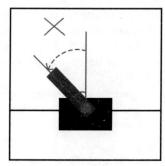

pole falls toward horizontal
(pole angle too large)

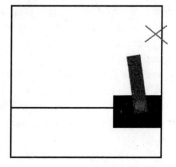

cart moves offscreen

Figure 10.2   The Cart-Pole game ends early if the pole falls toward horizontal or the cart is navigated off-screen.

The Cart-Pole game is a popular introductory reinforcement learning problem because it's so simple. With a self-driving car, there are effectively an infinite number of possible environmental states: As it moves along a road, its myriad sensors—cameras, radar, lidar,[2] accelerometers, microphones, and so on—stream in broad swaths of state information from the world around the vehicle, on the order of a gigabyte of data per second.[3] The Cart-Pole game, in stark contrast, has merely four pieces of state information:

1. The position of the cart along the one-dimensional horizontal axis
2. The cart's velocity
3. The angle of the pole
4. The pole's angular velocity

Likewise, a number of fairly nuanced actions are possible with a self-driving car, such as accelerating, braking, and steering right or left. In the Cart-Pole game, at any given timestep t, exactly one action can be taken from only two possible actions: move left or move right.

Markov Decision Processes

Reinforcement learning problems can be defined mathematically as something called a *Markov decision process*. MDPs feature the so-called *Markov property*—an assumption that the current timestep contains all of the pertinent information about the state of the environment from previous timesteps. With respect to the Cart-Pole game, this means that our agent would elect to move right or left at a given timestep t by considering only the attributes of the cart (e.g., its location) and the pole (e.g., its angle) at that particular timestep t.[4]

As summarized in Figure 10.3, the MDP is defined by five components:

1. S is the set of all possible *states*. Following set-theory convention, each individual possible state (i.e., a particular combination of cart position, cart velocity, pole angle, and angular velocity) is represented by the lowercase s. Even when we consider the relatively simple Cart-Pole game, the number of possible recombinations of its four state dimensions is enormous. To give a couple of coarse examples, the cart could be moving slowly near the far-right of the screen with the pole balanced vertically, or the cart could be moving rapidly toward the left edge of the screen with the pole at a wide angle turning clockwise with pace.
2. A is the set of all possible *actions*. In the Cart-Pole game, this set contains only two elements (*left* and *right*); other environments have many more. Each individual possible action is denoted as a.

---

2. Same principle as radar, but uses lasers instead of sound.
3. bit.ly/GBpersec
4. The Markov property is assumed in many financial-trading strategies. As an example, a trading strategy might take into account the price of all the stocks listed on a given exchange at the end of a given trading day, while it does *not* consider the price of the stocks on any previous day.

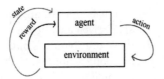

"Markov Decision Process"

S: all possible states

A: all possible actions

R: reward distribution
  given (s,a)

P: transition probability
  to s_{t+1} given (s,a)

γ: discount factor

Figure 10.3 The reinforcement learning loop (top; a rehashed version of Figure 4.3, provided again here for convenience) can be considered a Markov decision process, which is defined by the five components S, A, R, $\mathbb{P}$, and γ (bottom).

3. R is the distribution of *reward* given a *state-action pair*—some particular state paired with some particular action—denoted as (s, a). It's a distribution in the sense of being a probability distribution: The exact same state-action pair (s, a) might randomly result in different amounts of reward r on different occasions.[5] The details of the reward distribution R—its shape, including its mean and variance—are hidden from the agent but can be glimpsed by taking actions within the environment. For example, in Figure 10.1, you can see that the cart is centered within the screen and the pole is angled slightly to the left.[6] We'd expect that pairing the action of moving left with this state s would, on average, correspond to a higher expected reward r relative to pairing the action of moving right with this state: Moving left in this state s should cause the pole to stand more upright, increasing the number of timesteps that the pole is kept balanced for, thereby tending to lead to a higher reward r. On the other hand, the move right in this state s would increase the probability that the pole would fall toward horizontal, thereby tending toward an early end to the game and a smaller reward r.

---

5. Although this is true in reinforcement learning in general, the Cart-Pole game in particular is a relatively simple environment that is fully deterministic. In the Cart-Pole game, the exact same state-action pair (s, a) will in fact result in the same reward every time. For the purposes of illustrating the principles of reinforcement learning in general, we use examples in this section that imply the Cart-Pole game is less deterministic than it really is.

6. For the sake of simplicity, let's ignore cart velocity and pole angular velocity for this example, because we can't infer these state aspects from this static image.

4. $\mathbb{P}$, like $\boldsymbol{R}$, is also a probability distribution. In this case, it represents the probability of the next state (i.e., s_{t+1}) given a particular state-action pair $(\boldsymbol{s}, \boldsymbol{a})$ in the current timestep t. Like $\boldsymbol{R}$, the $\mathbb{P}$ distribution is hidden from the agent, but again aspects of it can be inferred by taking actions within the environment. For example, in the Cart-Pole game, it would be relatively straightforward for the agent to learn that the *left* action corresponds directly to the cart moving leftward.[7] More-complex relationships—for example, that the *left* action in the state s captured in Figure 10.1 tends to correspond to a more vertically oriented pole in the next state s_{t+1}—would be more difficult to learn and so would require more gameplay.

5. γ (gamma) is a hyperparameter called the *discount factor* (also known as *decay*). To explain its significance, let's move away from the Cart-Pole game for a moment and back to Pac-Man. The eponymous Pac-Man character explores a two-dimensional surface, gaining reward points for collecting fruit and dying if he gets caught by one of the ghosts that's chasing him. As illustrated by Figure 10.4, when the agent considers the value of a prospective reward, it should value a reward that can be attained immediately (say, 100 points for acquiring cherries that are only one pixel's distance away from Pac-Man) more highly than an equivalent reward that would require more timesteps to attain (100 points for cherries that are a distance of 20 pixels away). Immediate reward is more valuable than some distant reward, because we can't bank on the distant reward: A ghost or some other hazard could get in Pac-Man's way.[8,9] If we were to set $\gamma = 0.9$, then cherries one timestep away would be considered to be worth 90 points,[10] whereas cherries 20 timesteps away would be considered to be worth only 12.2 points.[11]

The Optimal Policy

The ultimate objective with an MDP is to find a function that enables an agent to take an appropriate action $\boldsymbol{a}$ (from the set of all possible actions $\boldsymbol{A}$) when it encounters any particular state $\boldsymbol{s}$ from the set of all possible environmental states $\boldsymbol{S}$. In other words, we'd

---

7. As with all of the other artificial neural networks in this book, the ANNs within deep reinforcement learning agents are initialized with random starting parameters. This means that, prior to any learning (via, say, playing episodes of the Cart-Pole game), the agent has no awareness of even the simplest relationships between some state-action pair $(\boldsymbol{s}, \boldsymbol{a})$ and the next state s_{t+1}. For example, although it may be intuitive and obvious to a human player of the Cart-Pole game that the action *left* should cause the cart to move leftward, *nothing* is "intuitive" or "obvious" to a randomly initialized neural net, and so all relationships must be learned through gameplay.

8. The γ discount factor is analogous to the *discounted cash flow* calculations that are common in accounting: Prospective income a year from now is discounted relative to income expected today.

9. Later in this chapter, we introduce concepts called value functions (V) and Q-value functions (Q). Both V and Q incorporate γ because it prevents them from becoming unbounded (and thus computationally impossible) in games with an infinite number of possible future timesteps.

10. $100 \times \gamma^t = 100 \times 0.9^1 = 90$

11. $100 \times \gamma^t = 100 \times 0.9^{20} = 12.16$

100 points
20 timesteps
away valued
at 12.2

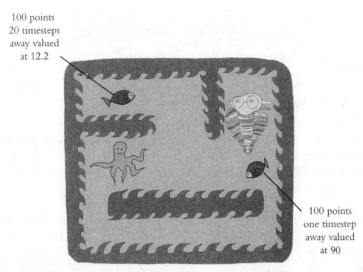

100 points
one timestep
away valued
at 90

Figure 10.4 Based on the discount factor γ, in a Markov decision process more-distant reward is discounted relative to reward that's more immediately attainable. Using the Atari game Pac-Man to illustrate this concept (a green trilobite sitting in for Mr. Pac-Man himself), with $\gamma = 0.9$, cherries (or a fish!) only one timestep away are valued at 90 points, whereas cherries (a fish) 20 timesteps away are valued at 12.2 points. Like the ghosts in the Pac-Man game, the octopus here is roaming around and hoping to kill the poor trilobite. This is why immediately attainable rewards are more valuable than distant ones: There's a higher chance of being killed before reaching the fish that's farther away.

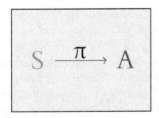

Figure 10.5 The policy function π enables an agent to map any state s (from the set of all possible states S) to an action a from the set of all possible actions A.

like our agent to learn a function that enables it to *map* $\boldsymbol{S}$ to $\boldsymbol{A}$. As shown in Figure 10.5, such a function is denoted by $\boldsymbol{\pi}$ and we call it the *policy function*.

The high-level idea of the policy function $\boldsymbol{\pi}$, using vernacular language, is this: Regardless of the particular circumstance the agent finds itself in, what is the *policy* it should follow that will enable it to maximize its reward? For a more concrete definition of this reward–maximization idea, you are welcome to pore over this:

$$J(\pi^*) = \max_{\pi} J(\pi) = \max_{\pi} \mathbb{E}\left[\sum_{t>0} \gamma^t r_t\right] \qquad (10.1)$$

In this equation:

- $J(\pi)$ is called an *objective function*. This is a function that we can apply machine learning techniques to in order to maximize reward.[12]

- π represents *any* policy function that maps S to A.

- π^* represents a particular, *optimal* policy (out of all the potential π policies) for mapping S to A. That is, π^* is a function that—fed any state s—will return an action a that will lead to the agent attaining the *max*-imum possible *discounted future reward*.

- *Expected discounted future reward* is defined by $\mathbb{E}\left[\sum_{t>0} \gamma^t r_t\right]$ where $\mathbb{E}$ stands for *expectation* and $\sum_{t>0} \gamma^t r_t$ stands for the *discounted future reward*.

- To calculate the discounted future reward $\sum_{t>0} \gamma^t r_t$, over all future timesteps (i.e., $t > 0$), we do the following.

  - Multiply the reward that can be attained in any given future timestep (r_t) by the discount factor of that timestep (γ^t).
  - Accumulate these individual discounted future rewards ($\gamma^t r_t$) by summing them all up (using $\sum$).

Essential Theory of Deep Q-Learning Networks

In the preceding section, we defined reinforcement learning as a Markov decision process. At the end of the section, we indicated that as part of an MDP, we'd like our agent—when it encounters any given state s at any given timestep t—to follow some optimal policy π^* that will enable it to select an action a that maximizes the discounted future reward it can obtain. The issue is that—even with a rather simple reinforcement learning problem like the Cart-Pole game—it is computationally intractable (or, at least, extremely computationally inefficient) to definitively calculate the maximum cumulative discounted future reward, $max(\sum_{t>0} \gamma^t r_t)$. Because of all the possible future states S and all the possible actions A that could be taken in those future states, there are *way* too many possible future outcomes to take into consideration. Thus, as a computational shortcut, we'll describe the *Q-learning* approach for *estimating* what the optimal action a in a given situation might be.

---

12. The cost functions (a.k.a. loss functions) referred to throughout this book are examples of objective functions. Whereas cost functions return some cost value C, the objective function $J(\pi)$ returns some reward value r. With cost functions, our objective is to *minimize* cost, so we apply gradient *descent* to them (as depicted by the valley-descending trilobite back in Figure 7.2). With the function $J(\pi)$, in contrast, our objective is to *maximize* reward, and so we technically apply gradient *ascent* to it (conjuring up Figure 7.2 imagery, imagine a trilobite hiking to identify the peak of a mountain) even though the mathematics are the same as with gradient descent.

Value Functions

The story of Q-learning is most easily described by beginning with an explanation of *value functions*. The value function is defined by $V^\pi(s)$. It provides us with an indication of how *valuable* a given state s is if our agent follows its policy π from that state onward.

As a simple example, consider yet again the state s captured in Figure 10.1.[13] Assuming our agent already has some reasonably sensible policy π for balancing the pole, then the cumulative discounted future reward that we'd expect it to obtain in this state is probably fairly large because the pole is near vertical. The value $V^\pi(s)$, then, of this particular state s is high.

On the other hand, if we imagine a state s_h where the pole angle is approaching horizontal, the value of it—$V^\pi(s_h)$—is lower, because our agent has already lost control of the pole and so the episode is likely to terminate within the next few timesteps.

Q-Value Functions

The *Q-value function*[14] builds on the value function by taking into account not only state: It considers the utility of a particular action when that action is paired with a given state—that is, it rehashes our old friend, the state-action pair symbolized by (s, a). Thus, where the value function is defined by $V^\pi(s)$, the Q-value function is defined by $Q^\pi(s, a)$.

Let's return once more to Figure 10.1. Pairing the action *left* (let's call this a_L) with this state s and then following a pole-balancing policy π from there should generally correspond to a high cumulative discounted future reward. Therefore, the Q-value of this state-action pair (s, a_L) is high.

In comparison, let's consider pairing the action *right* (we can call it a_R) with the state s from Figure 10.1 and then following a pole-balancing policy π from there. Although this might not turn out to be an egregious error, the cumulative discounted future reward would nevertheless probably be somewhat lower relative to taking the *left* action. In this state s, the *left* action should generally cause the pole to become more vertically oriented (enabling the pole to be better controlled and better balanced), whereas the rightward action should generally cause it to become somewhat more horizontally oriented—thus, *less* controlled, and the episode somewhat more likely to end early. All in all, we would expect the Q-value of (s, a_L) to be higher than the Q-value of (s, a_R).

Estimating an Optimal Q-Value

When our agent confronts some state s, we would then like it to be able to calculate the *optimal Q-value*, denoted as $Q^*(s, a)$. We could consider all possible actions, and the action with the highest Q-value—the highest cumulative discounted future reward—would be the best choice.

In the same way that it is computationally intractable to definitively calculate the optimal policy π^* (Equation 10.1) even with relatively simple reinforcement learning problems, so too is it typically computationally intractable to definitively calculate an

---

13. As we did earlier in this chapter, let's consider cart position and pole position only, because we can't speculate on cart velocity or pole angular velocity from this still image.
14. The "Q" in Q-value stands for *quality* but you seldom hear practitioners calling these "quality-value functions."

optimal Q-value, $Q^*(s, a)$. With the approach of deep Q-learning (as introduced in Chapter 4; see Figure 4.5), however, we can leverage an artificial neural network to *estimate* what the optimal Q-value might be. These deep Q-learning networks (DQNs for short) rely on this equation:

$$Q^*(s, a) \approx Q(s, a; \theta) \tag{10.2}$$

In this equation:

- The optimal Q-value ($Q^*(s, a)$) is being *approximated*.

- The Q-value approximation function incorporates neural network model parameters (denoted by the Greek letter theta, θ) in addition to its usual state s and action a inputs. These parameters are the usual artificial neuron weights and biases that we have become familiar with since Chapter 6.

In the context of the Cart-Pole game, a DQN agent armed with Equation 10.2 can, upon encountering a particular state s, calculate whether pairing an action a (*left* or *right*) with this state corresponds to a higher predicted cumulative discounted future reward. If, say, *left* is predicted to be associated with a higher cumulative discounted future reward, then this is the action that should be taken. In the next section, we'll code up a DQN agent that incorporates a Keras-built dense neural net to illustrate hands-on how this is done.

For a thorough introduction to the theory of reinforcement learning, including deep Q-learning networks, we recommend the recent edition of Richard Sutton (Figure 10.6) and Andrew Barto's *Reinforcement Learning: An Introduction*,[15] which is available free of charge at `bit.ly/SuttonBarto`.

Figure 10.6 The biggest star in the field of reinforcement learning, Richard Sutton has long been a computer science professor at the University of Alberta. He is more recently also a distinguished research scientist at Google DeepMind.

15. Sutton, R., & Barto, A. (2018). *Reinforcement Learning: An Introduction* (2nd ed.). Cambridge, MA: MIT Press.

Defining a DQN Agent

Our code for defining a DQN agent that learns how to act in an environment—in this particular case, it happens to be the Cart-Pole game from the OpenAI Gym library of environments—is provided within our *Cartpole DQN* Jupyter notebook.[16] Its dependencies are as follows:

```
import random
import gym
import numpy as np
from collections import deque
from keras.models import Sequential
from keras.layers import Dense
from keras.optimizers import Adam
import os
```

The most significant new addition to the list is gym, the Open AI Gym itself. As usual, we discuss each dependency in more detail as we apply it.

The hyperparameters that we set at the top of the notebook are provided in Example 10.1.

Example 10.1 Cart-Pole DQN hyperparameters

```
env = gym.make('CartPole-v0')
state_size = env.observation_space.shape[0]
action_size = env.action_space.n
batch_size = 32
n_episodes = 1000
output_dir = 'model_output/cartpole/'
if not os.path.exists(output_dir):
    os.makedirs(output_dir)
```

Let's look at this code line by line:

- We use the Open AI Gym make() method to specify the particular environment that we'd like our agent to interact with. The environment we choose is version zero (v0) of the Cart-Pole game, and we assign it to the variable env. On your own time, you're welcome to select an alternative Open AI Gym environment, such as one of those presented in Figure 4.13.
- From the environment, we extract two parameters:
    1. state_size: the number of types of state information, which for the Cart-Pole game is 4 (recall that these are cart position, cart velocity, pole angle, and pole angular velocity).
    2. action_size: the number of possible actions, which for Cart-Pole is 2 (*left* and *right*).

---

16. Our DQN agent is based directly on Keon Kim's, which is available at his GitHub repository at bit.ly/keonDQN.

- We set our mini-batch size for training our neural net to 32.

- We set the number of episodes (rounds of the game) to 1000. As you'll soon see, this is about the right number of episodes it will take for our agent to excel regularly at the Cart-Pole game. For more-complex environments, you'd likely need to increase this hyperparameter so that the agent has more rounds of gameplay to learn in.

- We define a unique directory name (`'model_output/cartpole/'`) into which we'll output our neural network's parameters at regular intervals. If the directory doesn't yet exist, we use `os.makedirs()` to make it.

The rather large chunk of code for creating a DQN agent Python class—called DQNAgent—is provided in Example 10.2.

Example 10.2 A deep Q-learning agent

```
class DQNAgent:
    def __init__(self, state_size, action_size):
        self.state_size = state_size
        self.action_size = action_size
        self.memory = deque(maxlen=2000)
        self.gamma = 0.95
        self.epsilon = 1.0
        self.epsilon_decay = 0.995
        self.epsilon_min = 0.01
        self.learning_rate = 0.001
        self.model = self._build_model()

    def _build_model(self):
        model = Sequential()
        model.add(Dense(32, activation='relu',
                        input_dim=self.state_size))
        model.add(Dense(32, activation='relu'))
        model.add(Dense(self.action_size, activation='linear'))
        model.compile(loss='mse',
                      optimizer=Adam(lr=self.learning_rate))
        return model

    def remember(self, state, action, reward, next_state, done):
        self.memory.append((state, action,
                            reward, next_state, done))

    def train(self, batch_size):
        minibatch = random.sample(self.memory, batch_size)
        for state, action, reward, next_state, done in minibatch:
            target = reward # if done
            if not done:
```

```
            target = (reward +
                    self.gamma *
                    np.amax(self.model.predict(next_state)[0]))
        target_f = self.model.predict(state)
        target_f[0][action] = target
        self.model.fit(state, target_f, epochs=1, verbose=0)
    if self.epsilon > self.epsilon_min:
        self.epsilon *= self.epsilon_decay

def act(self, state):
    if np.random.rand() <= self.epsilon:
        return random.randrange(self.action_size)
    act_values = self.model.predict(state)
    return np.argmax(act_values[0])

def save(self, name):
    self.model.save_weights(name)

def load(self, name):
    self.model.load_weights(name)
```

Initialization Parameters

We begin Example 10.2 by initializing the class with a number of parameters:

- state_size and action_size are environment-specific, but in the case of the Cart-Pole game are 4 and 2, respectively, as mentioned earlier.

- memory is for storing *memories* that can subsequently be *replayed* in order to train our DQN's neural net. The memories are stored as elements of a data structure called a *deque* (pronounced "deck"), which is the same as a list except that—because we specified maxlen=2000—it only retains the 2,000 most recent memories. That is, whenever we attempt to append a 2,001st element onto the deque, its first element is removed, always leaving us with a list that contains no more than 2,000 elements.

- gamma is the discount factor (a.k.a. decay rate) γ that we introduced earlier in this chapter (see Figure 10.4). This agent hyperparameter discounts prospective rewards in future timesteps. Effective γ values typically approach 1 (for example, 0.9, 0.95, 0.98, and 0.99). The closer to 1, the less we're discounting future reward.[17] Tuning the hyperparameters of reinforcement learning models such as γ can be a fiddly process; near the end of this chapter, we discuss a tool called SLM Lab for carrying it out effectively.

---

17. Indeed, if you were to set $\gamma = 1$ (which we don't recommend) you wouldn't be discounting future reward at all.

- **epsilon**—symbolized by the Greek letter ϵ—is another reinforcement learning hyperparameter called *exploration rate*. It represents the proportion of our agent's actions that are random (enabling it to *explore* the impact of such actions on the next state s_{t+1} and the reward r returned by the environment) relative to how often we allow its actions to *exploit* the existing "knowledge" its neural net has accumulated through gameplay. Prior to having played any episodes, agents have no gameplay experience to exploit, so it is the most common practice to start it off exploring 100 percent of the time; this is why we set **epsilon = 1.0**.

- As the agent gains gameplay experience, we very slowly *decay* its exploration rate so that it can gradually exploit the information it has learned (hopefully enabling it to attain more reward, as illustrated in Figure 10.7). That is, at the end of each

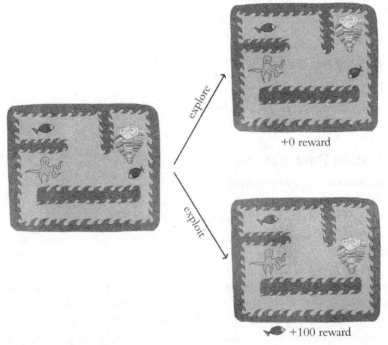

+0 reward

+100 reward

Figure 10.7   As in Figure 10.4, here we use the Pac-Man environment (with a green trilobite representing a DQN agent in place of the Mr. Pac-Man character) to illustrate a reinforcement learning concept. In this case, the concept is exploratory versus exploitative actions. The higher the hyperparameter ϵ (epsilon) in a given episode, the more likely the agent is to be in its exploratory mode, in which it takes purely random actions: By chance, an agent in this mode might navigate in the opposite direction of a fish that would have provided an immediate reward of 100 points. The alternative to the exploratory mode is the exploitative mode. Assuming the DQN agent's neural net parameters have already benefited from some previous gameplay experience, in its exploitative mode the agent's policy should be to acquire reward that is immediately available to it.

episode the agent plays, we multiply its ϵ by epsilon_decay. Common options for this hyperparameter are 0.990, 0.995, and 0.999.[18]

- epsilon_min is a floor (a minimum) on how low the exploration rate ϵ can decay to. This hyperparameter is typically set to a near-zero value such as 0.001, 0.01, or 0.02. We set it equal to 0.01, meaning that after ϵ has decayed to 0.01 (as it will in our case by the 911th episode), our agent will explore on only 1 percent of the actions it takes—exploiting its gameplay experience the other 99 percent of the time.[19]

- learning_rate is the same stochastic gradient descent hyperparameter that we covered in Chapter 7.

- Finally, _build_model()—by the inclusion of its leading underscore—is being suggested as a *private* method. This means that this method is recommended for use "internally" only—that is, solely by instances of the class DQNAgent.

Building the Agent's Neural Network Model

The _build_model() method of Example 10.2 is dedicated to constructing and compiling a Keras-specified neural network that maps an environment's state s to the agent's Q-value for each available action a. Once trained via gameplay, the agent will then be able to use the predicted Q-values to select the particular action it should take, given a particular environmental state it encounters. Within the method, there is nothing you haven't seen before in this book:

- We specify a sequential model.

- We add to the model the following layers of neurons.

  - The first hidden layer is dense, consisting of 32 ReLU neurons. Using the input_dim argument, we specify the shape of the network's input layer, which is the dimensionality of the environment's state information s. In the case of the Cart-Pole environment, this value is an array of length 4, with one element each for cart position, cart velocity, pole angle, and pole angular velocity.[20]

  - The second hidden layer is also dense, with 32 ReLU neurons. As mentioned earlier, we'll explore hyperparameter selection—including how we home in on a particular model architecture—by discussing the SLM Lab tool later on in this chapter.

---

18. Analogous to setting $\gamma = 1$, setting epsilon_decay = 1 would mean ϵ would not be decayed at all—that is, exploring at a continuous rate. This would be an unusual choice for this hyperparameter.

19. If at this stage this exploration rate concept is somewhat unclear, it should become clearer as we examine our agent's episode-by-episode results later on.

20. In environments other than Cart-Pole, the state information might be much more complex. For example, with an Atari video game environment like Pac-Man, state s would consist of pixels on a screen, which would be a two- or three-dimensional input (for monochromatic or full-color, respectively). In a case such as this, a better choice of first hidden layer would be a convolutional layer such as Conv2D (see Chapter 10).

- The output layer has dimensionality corresponding to the number of possible actions.[21] In the case of the Cart-Pole game, this is an array of length 2, with one element for *left* and the other for *right*. As with a regression model (see Example 7.11), with DQNs the z values are output directly from the neural net instead of being converted into a probability between 0 and 1. To do this, we specify the `linear` activation function instead of the sigmoid or softmax functions that have otherwise dominated this book.

- As indicated when we compiled our regression model (Example 7.12), mean squared error is an appropriate choice of cost function when we use linear activation in the output layer, so we set the `compile()` method's `loss` argument to `mse`. We return to our routine optimizer choice, `Adam`.

Remembering Gameplay

At any given timestep t—that is, during any given iteration of the reinforcement learning loop (refer back to Figure 10.3)—the DQN agent's `remember()` method is run in order to append a memory to the end of its `memory` deque. Each memory in this deque consists of five pieces of information about timestep t:

1. The `state` s_t that the agent encountered
2. The `action` a_t that the agent took
3. The `reward` r_t that the environment returned to the agent
4. The `next_state` s_{t+1} that the environment also returned to the agent
5. A Boolean flag `done` that is `true` if timestep t was the final iteration of the episode, and `false` otherwise

Training via Memory Replay

The DQN agent's neural net model is trained by *replaying memories* of gameplay, as shown within the `train()` method of Example 10.2. The process begins by randomly sampling a `minibatch` of 32 (as per the agent's `batch_size` parameter) memories from the `memory` deque (which holds up to 2,000 memories). Sampling a small subset of memories from a much larger set of the agent's experiences makes model-training more efficient: If we were instead to use, say, the 32 most recent memories to train our model, many of the states across those memories would be very similar. To illustrate this point, consider a timestep t where the cart is at some particular location and the pole is near vertical. The adjacent timesteps (e.g., $t-1, t+1, t+2$) are also likely to be at nearly the same location with the pole in a near-vertical orientation. By sampling from across a broad range of memories instead of temporally proximal ones, the model will be provided with a richer cornucopia of experiences to learn from during each round of training.

For each of the 32 sampled memories, we carry out a round of model training as follows: If `done` is `True`—that is, if the memory was of the final timestep of an episode—then we know definitively that the highest possible reward that could be attained from

21. Any previous models in this book with only two outcomes (as in Chapters 8 and 11) used a single sigmoid neuron. Here, we specify separate neurons for each of the outcomes, because we would like our code to generalize beyond the Cart-Pole game. While Cart-Pole has only two actions, many environments have more than two.

this timestep is equal to the reward r_t. Thus, we can just set our target reward equal to reward.

Otherwise (i.e., if done is False) then we try to estimate what the target reward—the maximum discounted future reward—might be. We perform this estimation by starting with the known reward r_t and adding to it the discounted[22] maximum future Q-value. Possible future Q-values are estimated by passing the next (i.e., *future*) state s_{t+1} into the model's predict() method. Doing this in the context of the Cart-Pole game returns two outputs: one output for the action *left* and the other for the action *right*. Whichever of these two outputs is higher (as determined by the NumPy amax function) is the maximum predicted future Q-value.

Whether target is known definitively (because the timestep was the final one in an episode) or it's estimated using the maximum future Q-value calculation, we continue onward within the train() method's for loop:

- We run the predict() method again, passing in the *current* state s_t. As before, in the context of the Cart-Pole game this returns two outputs: one for the *left* action and one for the *right*. We store these two outputs in the variable target_f.

- Whichever action a_t the agent actually took in this memory, we use target_f[0][action] = target to replace that target_f output with the target reward.[23]

- We train our model by calling the fit() method.

  - The model input is the current state s_t and its output is target_f, which incorporates our approximation of the maximum future discounted reward. By tuning the model's parameters (represented by θ in Equation 10.2), we thus improve its capacity to accurately predict the action that is more likely to be associated with maximizing future reward in any given state.

  - In many reinforcement learning problems, epochs can be set to 1. Instead of recycling an existing training dataset multiple times, we can cheaply engage in more episodes of the Cart-Pole game (for example) to generate as many fresh training data as we fancy.

  - We set verbose=0 because we don't need any model-fitting outputs at this stage to monitor the progress of model training. As we demonstrate shortly, we'll instead monitor agent performance on an episode-by-episode basis.

Selecting an Action to Take

To select a particular action a_t to take at a given timestep t, we use the agent's act() method. Within this method, the NumPy rand function is used to sample a random value between 0 and 1 that we'll call v. In conjunction with our agent's epsilon,

---

22. That is, multiplied by gamma, the discount factor γ.
23. We do this because we can only train the Q-value estimate based on actions that were actually taken by the agent: We estimated target based on next_state s_{t+1} and we only know what s_{t+1} was for the action a_t that was actually taken by the agent at timestep t. We don't know what next state s_{t+1} the environment might have returned had the agent taken a different action than it actually took.

epsilon_decay, and epsilon_min hyperparameters, this v value will determine for us whether the agent takes an exploratory action or an exploitative one:[24]

- If the random value v is less than or equal to the exploration rate ϵ, then a random exploratory action is selected using the randrange function. In early episodes, when ϵ is high, most of the actions will be exploratory. In later episodes, as ϵ decays further and further (according to the epsilon_decay hyperparameter), the agent will take fewer and fewer exploratory actions.

- Otherwise—that is, if the random value v is greater than ϵ—the agent selects an action that exploits the "knowledge" the model has learned via memory replay. To exploit this knowledge, the state s_t is passed in to the model's predict() method, which returns an activation output[25] for each of the possible actions the agent could theoretically take. We use the NumPy argmax function to select the action a_t associated with the largest activation output.

Saving and Loading Model Parameters

Finally, the save() and load() methods are one-liners that enable us to save and load the parameters of the model. Particularly with respect to complex environments, agent performance can be flaky: For long stretches, the agent may perform very well in a given environment, and then later appear to lose its capabilities entirely. Because of this flakiness, it's wise to save our model parameters at regular intervals. Then, if the agent's performance drops off in later episodes, the higher-performing parameters from some earlier episode can be loaded back up.

Interacting with an OpenAI Gym Environment

Having created our DQN agent class, we can initialize an instance of the class—which we name agent—with this line of code:

```
agent = DQNAgent(state_size, action_size)
```

The code in Example 10.3 enables our agent to interact with an OpenAI Gym environment, which in our particular case is the Cart-Pole game.

Example 10.3 DQN agent interacting with an OpenAI Gym environment

```
for e in range(n_episodes):
    state = env.reset()
    state = np.reshape(state, [1, state_size])
```

---

24. We introduced the exploratory and exploitative modes of action when discussing the initialization parameters for our DQNAgent class earlier, and they're illustrated playfully in Figure 10.7.

25. Recall that the activation is linear, and thus the output is *not* a probability; instead, it is the discounted future reward for that action.

```
    done = False
    time = 0
    while not done:
#         env.render()
        action = agent.act(state)
        next_state, reward, done, _ = env.step(action)
        reward = reward if not done else -10
        next_state = np.reshape(next_state, [1, state_size])
        agent.remember(state, action, reward, next_state, done)
        state = next_state
        if done:
            print("episode: {}/{}, score: {}, e: {:.2}"
                    .format(e, n_episodes-1, time, agent.epsilon))
        time += 1
    if len(agent.memory) > batch_size:
        agent.train(batch_size)
    if e % 50 == 0:
        agent.save(output_dir + "weights_"
                    + '{:04d}'.format(e) + ".hdf5")
```

Recalling that we had set the hyperparameter n_episodes to 1000, Example 10.3 consists of a big for loop that allows our agent to engage in these 1,000 rounds of game-play. Each episode of gameplay is counted by the variable e and involves:

- We use env.reset() to begin the episode with a random state s_t. For the purposes of passing state into our Keras neural network in the orientation the model is expecting, we use reshape to convert it from a column into a row.[26]

- Nested within our thousand-episode loop is a while loop that iterates over the timesteps of a given episode. Until the episode ends (i.e., until done equals True), in each timestep t (represented by the variable time), we do the following.

  - The env.render() line is commented out because if you are running this code via a Jupyter notebook within a Docker container, this line will cause an error. If, however, you happen to be running the code via some other means (e.g., in a Jupyter notebook *without* using Docker) then you can try uncommenting this line. If an error isn't thrown, then a pop-up window should appear that *renders* the environment graphically. This enables you to watch your DQN agent as it plays the Cart-Pole game in real time, episode by episode. It's fun to watch, but it's by no means essential: It certainly has no impact on how the agent learns!

  - We pass the state s_t into the agent's act() method, and this returns the agent's action a_t, which is either 0 (representing *left*) or 1 (*right*).

---

26. We previously performed this transposition for the same reason back in Example 7.14.

- The action a_t is provided to the environment's step() method, which returns the next_state s_{t+1}, the current reward r_t, and an update to the Boolean flag done.

- If the episode is done (i.e., done equals true), then we set reward to a negative value (-10). This provides a strong disincentive to the agent to end an episode early by losing control of balancing the pole or navigating off the screen. If the episode is not done (i.e., done is False), then reward is +1 for each additional timestep of gameplay.

- In the same way that we needed to reorient state to be a row at the start of the episode, we use reshape to reorient next_state to a row here.

- We use our agent's remember() method to save all the aspects of this timestep (the state s_t, the action a_t that was taken, the reward r_t, the next state s_{t+1}, and the flag done) to memory.

- We set state equal to next_state in preparation for the next iteration of the loop, which will be timestep $t + 1$.

- If the episode ends, then we print summary metrics on the episode (see Figures 10.8 and 10.9 for example outputs).

- Add 1 to our timestep counter time.

- If the length of the agent's memory deque is larger than our batch size, then we use the agent's train() method to train its neural net parameters by replaying its memories of gameplay.[27]

- Every 50 episodes, we use the agent's save() method to store the neural net model's parameters.

As shown in Figure 10.8, during our agent's first 10 episodes of the Cart-Pole game, the scores were low. It didn't manage to keep the game going for more than 42 timesteps (i.e., a score of 41). During these initial episodes, the exploration rate ϵ began at 100 percent. By the 10th episode, ϵ had decayed to 96 percent, meaning that the agent was in exploitative mode (refer back to Figure 10.7) on about 4 percent of timesteps. At this early stage of training, however, most of these exploitative actions would probably have been effectively random anyway.

As shown in Figure 10.9, by the 991st episode our agent had mastered the Cart-Pole game. It attained a perfect score of 199 in all of the final 10 episodes by keeping the game going for 200 timesteps in each one. By the 911th episode,[28] the exploration rate ϵ had reached its minimum of 1 percent so during all of these final episodes the agent is in exploitative mode in about 99 percent of timesteps. From the perfect performance in these final episodes, it's clear that these exploitative actions were guided by a neural net well trained by its gameplay experience from previous episodes.

---

27. You can optionally move this training step up so that it's inside the while loop. Each episode will take *a lot* longer because you'll be training the agent much more often, but your agent will tend to solve the Cart-Pole game in far fewer episodes.

28. Not shown here, but can be seen in our *Cartpole DQN* Jupyter notebook.

```
episode: 0/999, score: 19, e: 1.0
episode: 1/999, score: 14, e: 1.0
episode: 2/999, score: 37, e: 0.99
episode: 3/999, score: 11, e: 0.99
episode: 4/999, score: 35, e: 0.99
episode: 5/999, score: 41, e: 0.98
episode: 6/999, score: 18, e: 0.98
episode: 7/999, score: 10, e: 0.97
episode: 8/999, score: 9, e: 0.97
episode: 9/999, score: 24, e: 0.96
```

Figure 10.8   The performance of our DQN agent during its first 10 episodes playing the Cart-Pole game. Its scores are low (keeping the game going for between 10 and 42 timesteps), and its exploration rate ϵ is high (starting at 100 percent and decaying to 96 percent by the 10th episode).

```
episode: 990/999, score: 199, e: 0.01
episode: 991/999, score: 199, e: 0.01
episode: 992/999, score: 199, e: 0.01
episode: 993/999, score: 199, e: 0.01
episode: 994/999, score: 199, e: 0.01
episode: 995/999, score: 199, e: 0.01
episode: 996/999, score: 199, e: 0.01
episode: 997/999, score: 199, e: 0.01
episode: 998/999, score: 199, e: 0.01
episode: 999/999, score: 199, e: 0.01
```

Figure 10.9   The performance of our DQN agent during its final 10 episodes playing the Cart-Pole game. It scores the maximum (199 timesteps) across all 10 episodes. The exploration rate ϵ had already decayed to its minimum of 1 percent, so the agent is in exploitative mode for ~99 percent of its actions.

As mentioned earlier in this chapter, deep reinforcement learning agents often display finicky behavior. When you train your DQN agent to play the Cart-Pole game, you might find that it performs very well during some later episodes (attaining many consecutive 200-timestep episodes around, say, the 850th or 900th episode) but then it performs poorly around the final (1,000th) episode. If this ends up being the case, you can use the load() method to restore model parameters from an earlier, higher-performing phase.

Hyperparameter Optimization with SLM Lab

At a number of points in this chapter, in one breath we'd introduce a hyperparameter and then in the next breath we'd indicate that we'd later introduce a tool called SLM Lab for tuning that hyperparameter.[29] Well, that moment has arrived!

---

29. "SLM" is an abbreviation of *strange loop machine*, with the *strange loop* concept being related to ideas about the experience of human consciousness. See Hofstadter, R. (1979). *Gödel, Escher, Bach*. New York: Basic Books.

SLM Lab is a deep reinforcement learning framework developed by Wah Loon Keng and Laura Graesser, who are California-based software engineers (at the mobile-gaming firm MZ and within the Google Brain team, respectively). The framework is available at `github.com/kengz/SLM-Lab` and has a broad range of implementations and functionality related to deep reinforcement learning:

- It enables the use of many types of deep reinforcement learning agents, including DQN and others (forthcoming in this chapter).

- It provides modular agent components, allowing you to dream up your own novel categories of deep RL agents.

- You can straightforwardly drop agents into environments from a number of different environment libraries, such as OpenAI Gym and Unity (see Chapter 4).

- Agents can be trained in multiple environments simultaneously. For example, a single DQN agent can at the same time solve the OpenAI Gym Cart-Pole game and the Unity ball-balancing game Ball2D.

- You can benchmark your agent's performance in a given environment against others' efforts.

Critically, for our purposes, the SLM Lab also provides a painless way to experiment with various agent hyperparameters to assess their impact on an agent's performance in a given environment. Consider, for example, the *experiment graph* shown in Figure 10.10. In this particular experiment, a DQN agent was trained to play the Cart-Pole game during a number of distinct *trials*. Each trial is an instance of an agent with particular, distinct hyperparameters trained for many episodes. Some of the hyperparameters varied between trials were as follows.

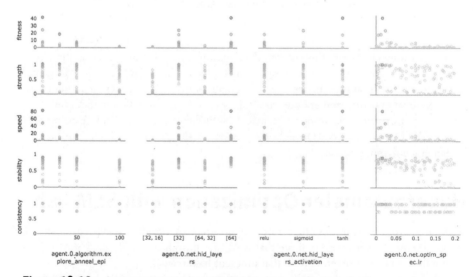

Figure 10.10 An experiment run with SLM Lab, investigating the impact of various hyperparameters (e.g., hidden-layer architecture, activation function, learning rate) on the performance of a DQN agent within the Cart-Pole environment

- Dense net model architecture
    - [32]: a single hidden layer, with 32 neurons
    - [64]: also a single hidden layer, this time with 64 neurons
    - [32, 16]: two hidden layers; the first with 32 neurons and the second with 16
    - [64, 32]: also with two hidden layers, this time with 64 neurons in the first hidden layer and 32 in the second
- Activation function across all hidden layers
    - Sigmoid
    - Tanh
    - ReLU
- Optimizer learning rate (η), which ranged from zero up to 0.2
- Exploration rate (ϵ) *annealing*, which ranged from 0 to 100[30]

SLM Lab provides a number of metrics for evaluating model performance (some of which can be seen along the vertical axis of Figure 10.10):

- *Strength*: This is a measure of the cumulative reward attained by the agent.
- *Speed*: This is how quickly (i.e., over how many episodes) the agent was able to reach its strength.
- *Stability*: After the agent solved how to perform well in the environment, this is a measure of how well it retained its solution over subsequent episodes.
- *Consistency*: This is a metric of how reproducible the performance of the agent was across trials that had identical hyperparameter settings.
- *Fitness*: An overall summary metric that takes into account the above four metrics simultaneously. Using the fitness metric in the experiment captured by Figure 10.10, it appears that the following hyperparameter settings are optimal for this DQN agent playing the Cart-Pole game:
    - A single-hidden-layer neural net architecture, with 64 neurons in that single layer outperforming the 32-neuron model.
    - The tanh activation function for the hidden layer neurons.
    - A low learning rate (η) of ~0.02.
    - Trials with an exploration rate (ϵ) that anneals over 10 episodes outperform trials that anneal over 50 or 100 episodes.

---

30. *Annealing* is an alternative to ϵ decay that serves the same purpose. With the epsilon and epsilon_min hyperparameters set to fixed values (say, 1.0 and 0.01, respectively), variations in annealing will adjust epsilon_decay such that an ϵ of 0.01 will be reached by a specified episode. If, for example, annealing is set to 25 then ϵ will decay at a rate such that it lowers uniformly from 1.0 in the first episode to 0.01 after 25 episodes. If annealing is set to 50 then ϵ will decay at a rate such that it lowers uniformly from 1.0 in the first episode to 0.01 after 50 episodes.

Details of running SLM Lab are beyond the scope of our book, but the library is well documented at `kengz.gitbooks.io/slm-lab`.[31]

Agents Beyond DQN

In the world of deep reinforcement learning, deep Q-learning networks like the one we built in this chapter are relatively simple. To their credit, not only are DQNs (comparatively) simple, but—relative to many other deep RL agents—they also make efficient use of the training samples that are available to them. That said, DQN agents do have drawbacks. Most notable are:

1. If the possible number of state-action pairs is large in a given environment, then the Q-function can become extremely complicated, and so it becomes intractable to estimate the optimal Q-value, Q^*.
2. Even in situations where finding Q^* is computationally tractable, DQNs are not great at exploring relative to some other approaches, and so a DQN may not converge on Q^* anyway.

Thus, even though DQNs are sample efficient, they aren't applicable to solving all problems.

To wrap up this deep reinforcement learning chapter, let's briefly introduce the types of agents beyond DQNs. The main categories of deep RL agents, as shown in Figure 10.11, are:

- *Value optimization*: These include DQN agents and their derivatives (e.g., *double DQN*, *dueling QN*) as well as other types of agents that solve reinforcement learning problems by optimizing value functions (including Q-value functions).

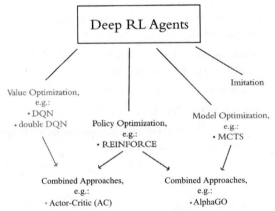

Figure 10.11   The broad categories of deep reinforcement learning agents

---

31. At the time of this writing, SLM Lab installation is straightforward only on Unix-based systems, including macOS.

- *Imitation learning*: The agents in this category (e.g., *behavioral cloning* and *conditional imitation learning* algorithms) are designed to mimic behaviors that are taught to them through demonstration, by—for example—showing them how to place dinner plates on a dish rack or how to pour water into a cup. Although imitation learning is a fascinating approach, its range of applications is relatively small and we don't discuss it further in this book.

- *Model optimization*: Agents in this category learn to predict future states based on (s, a) at a given timestep. An example of one such algorithm is Monte Carlo tree search (MCTS), which we introduced with respect to AlphaGo in Chapter 4.

- *Policy optimization*: Agents in this category learn policies *directly*, that is, they directly learn the policy function π shown in Figure 10.5. We'll cover these in further detail in the next section.

Policy Gradients and the REINFORCE Algorithm

Recall from Figure 10.5 that the purpose of a reinforcement learning agent is to learn some policy function π that maps the state space S to the action space A. With DQNs, and indeed with any other value optimization agent, π is learned indirectly by estimating a value function such as the optimal Q-value, Q^*. With policy optimization agents, π is learned *directly* instead.

Policy gradient (PG) algorithms, which can perform gradient *ascent*[32] on π directly, are exemplified by a particularly well-known reinforcement learning algorithm called REINFORCE.[33] The advantage of PG algorithms like REINFORCE is that they are likely to converge on a fairly optimal solution,[34] so they're more widely applicable than value optimization algorithms like DQN. The trade-off is that PGs have *low consistency*. That is, they have higher variance in their performance relative to value optimization approaches like DQN, and so PGs tend to require a larger number of training samples.

The Actor-Critic Algorithm

As suggested by Figure 10.11, the *actor-critic* algorithm is an RL agent that combines the value optimization and policy optimization approaches. More specifically, as depicted in Figure 10.12, the actor-critic combines the Q-learning and PG algorithms. At a high level, the resulting algorithm involves a loop that alternates between:

- *Actor*: a PG algorithm that decides on an action to take.

- *Critic*: a Q-learning algorithm that critiques the action that the actor selected, providing feedback on how to adjust. It can take advantage of efficiency tricks in Q-learning, such as memory replay.

---

32. Because PG algorithms *maximize* reward (instead of, say, minimizing cost), they perform gradient *ascent* and not gradient descent. For more on this, see Footnote 12 in this chapter.

33. Williams, R. (1992). Simple statistical gradient-following algorithms for connectionist reinforcement learning. *Machine Learning, 8,* 229–56.

34. PG agents tend to converge on at least an optimal local solution, although some particular PG methods have been demonstrated to identify the optimal *global* solution to a problem. See Fazel, K., et al. (2018). Global convergence of policy gradient methods for the linear quadratic regulator. *arXiv: 1801.05039.*

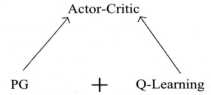

Figure 10.12   The actor-critic algorithm combines the policy gradient approach to reinforcement learning (playing the role of actor) with the Q-learning approach (playing the role of critic).

In a broad sense, the actor-critic algorithm is reminiscent of the generative adversarial networks of Chapter 11. GANs have a generator network in a loop with a discriminator network, with the former creating fake images that are evaluated by the latter. The actor-critic algorithm has an actor in a loop with a critic, with the former taking actions that are evaluated by the latter.

The advantage of the actor-critic algorithm is that it can solve a broader range of problems than DQN, while it has lower variance in performance relative to REINFORCE. That said, because of the presence of the PG algorithm within it, the actor-critic is still somewhat sample inefficient.

While implementing REINFORCE and the actor-critic algorithm are beyond the scope of this book, you can use SLM Lab to apply them yourself, as well as to examine their underlying code.

Summary

In this chapter, we covered the essential theory of reinforcement learning, including Markov decision processes. We leveraged that information to build a deep Q-learning agent that solved the Cart-Pole environment. To wrap up, we introduced deep RL algorithms beyond DQN such as REINFORCE and actor-critic. We also described SLM Lab—a deep RL framework with existing algorithm implementations as well as tools for optimizing agent hyperparameters.

This chapter brings an end to Part III of this book, which provided hands-on applications of machine vision (Chapter 9), natural language processing (Chapter 8), art-generating models (Chapter 11), and sequential decision-making agents. In Part IV, the final part of the book, we will provide you with loose guidance on adapting these applications to your own projects and inclinations.

Key Concepts

Listed here are the key concepts from across this book. The final concept—covered in the current chapter—is highlighted in purple.

- parameters:
  - weight w
  - bias b
- activation a
- artificial neurons:
  - sigmoid
  - tanh
  - ReLU
  - linear
- input layer
- hidden layer
- output layer
- layer types:
  - dense (fully connected)
  - softmax
  - convolutional
  - de-convolutional
  - max-pooling
  - upsampling
  - flatten
  - embedding
  - RNN
  - (bidirectional-)LSTM
  - concatenate

- cost (loss) functions:
  - quadratic (mean squared error)
  - cross-entropy
- forward propagation
- backpropagation
- unstable (especially vanishing) gradients
- Glorot weight initialization
- batch normalization
- dropout
- optimizers:
  - stochastic gradient descent
  - Adam
- optimizer hyperparameters:
  - learning rate η
  - batch size
- word2vec
- GAN components:
  - discriminator network
  - generator network
  - adversarial network
- deep Q-learning

IV

Appendices

Appendices

A

Formal Neural Network Notation

To keep discussion of artificial neurons as straightforward as possible, in this book we used a shorthand notation to identify them within a network. In this appendix, we lay out a more widely used formal notation, which may be of interest if you'd like to:

- Possess a more precise manner for describing neurons
- Follow closely the backpropagation technique covered in Appendix B

Taking a look back at Figure 6.12, the neural network has a total of four layers. The first is the input layer, which can be thought of as a collection of starting blocks for each data point to enter the network. In the case of the MNIST models, for example, there are 784 such starting blocks, representing each of the pixels in a 28×28–pixel handwritten MNIST digit. No computation happens within an input layer; it simply holds space for the input values to exist in so that the network knows how many values it needs to be ready to compute on in the next layer.[1]

The next two layers in the network in Figure 6.12 are hidden layers, in which the bulk of the computation within a neural network occurs. As we'll soon discuss, the input values x are mathematically transformed and combined by each neuron in the hidden layer, outputting some activation value a. Because we need a way to address specific neurons in specific layers, we'll use superscript to define a layer, starting at the first hidden layer, and subscript to define a neuron in that layer. In Figure 6.12, then, we'd have a_1^1, a_2^1, and a_3^1 in the first hidden layer. In this way, we can precisely refer to an individual neuron in a specific layer. For example, a_2^2 represents the second neuron in the second hidden layer.

Because Figure 6.12 is a dense network, the neuron a_1^1 receives inputs from all of the neurons in the preceding layer, namely the network inputs x_1 and x_2. Each neuron has its own bias, b, and we'll label that bias in exactly the same manner as the activation a: For example, b_2^1 is the bias for the second neuron in the first hidden layer.

---

1. For this reason, we usually don't need a means to address a particular input neuron; they have no weights or biases.

The green arrows in Figure 6.12 represent the mathematical transformation that takes place during forward propagation, and each green arrow has its own individual weight associated with it. In order to refer to these weights directly, we employ the following notation: $w^1_{(1,2)}$ is the weight in the *first* hidden layer (superscript) that connects neuron a^1_1 to its input x_2 in the input layer (subscript). This double-barreled subscript is necessary because the network is fully connected: Every neuron in a layer is connected to every neuron in the layer before it, and that connection carries its own weight. Let's generalize this weight notation:

- The superscript is the hidden-layer number of the input-receiving neuron.
- The first subscript is the number of the neuron receiving the input within its hidden layer.
- The second subscript is the number of the neuron providing input from the preceding layer.

As a further example, the weight for neuron a^2_2 will be denoted $w^2_{(2,i)}$ where i is a neuron in the preceding layer.

At the far right of the network, we finally have the output layer. As with the hidden layers, output-layer neurons have weights and a bias, and these are labeled in the same way.

Backpropagation

In this appendix, we use the formal neural network notation from Appendix A to dive into the partial-derivative calculus behind the backpropagation method introduced in Chapter 7.

Let's begin by defining some additional notation to help us along. Backpropagation works backwards, so the notation is based on the final layer (denoted L), and the earlier layers are annotated with respect to it ($L - 1, L - 2, \ldots L - n$). The weights, biases, and outputs from functions are subscripted appropriately with this same notation. Recall from Equations 6.5 and 6.6 that the layer activation a^L is calculated by multiplying the preceding layer's activation (a^{L-1}) by the weight w^L and bias b^L terms to produce z^L and passing this through an activation function (denoted simply as σ here). Also, we implement a simple cost function at the end; here we're using Euclidean distance. Thus, for the final layer we have:

$$z^L = w^L \cdot a^{L-1} + b^L \tag{B.1}$$

$$a^L = \sigma(z^L) \tag{B.2}$$

$$C_0 = (a^L - y)^2 \tag{B.3}$$

In every iteration, we need the gradient of the total error from the preceding layer ($\partial C / \partial a^L$); in this way, the total error of the system is propagated backwards. We'll call this value δ_L. Because backpropagation runs back-to-front, we start with the output layer. This layer is a special case given that the error *originates* here in the form of the cost function and there are no layers above it. Thus, δ_L is given as follows:

$$\delta_L = \frac{\partial C}{\partial a^L} = 2(a^L - y) \tag{B.4}$$

Again, this is a special case for the initial δ value; the remaining layers will be different (more on that shortly). Now, to update the weights in layer L we need to find the gradient of the cost *w.r.t.* (with respect to) the weights, $\partial C / \partial w^L$. According to the chain rule, this is the product of the gradient of the cost for the layer before w.r.t. its output, the gradient of the activation function w.r.t. z, and the gradient of the z w.r.t. the weights w^L:

$$\frac{\partial C}{\partial w^L} = \frac{\partial C}{\partial a^L} \cdot \frac{\partial a^L}{\partial z^L} \cdot \frac{\partial z^L}{\partial w^L} \tag{B.5}$$

Since $\partial C / \partial a^L = \delta_L$ (Equation B.4), this equation can be simplified to:

$$\frac{\partial C}{\partial w^L} = \delta_L \cdot a^{L-1}(1 - a^{L-1}) \cdot a^{L-1} \tag{B.6}$$

This value is essentially the relative amount by which the weights at layer L affect the total cost, and we use this to update the weights at this layer. Our work isn't complete, however; now we need to continue down the rest of the layers. For layer $L - 1$:

$$\delta_{L-1} = \frac{\partial C}{\partial a^{L-1}} = \frac{\partial C}{\partial a^L} \cdot \frac{\partial a^L}{\partial z^L} \cdot \frac{\partial z^L}{\partial a^{L-1}} \tag{B.7}$$

Again, $\partial C / \partial a^L = \delta_L$ (Equation B.4). In this way, the total error is being incorporated down the line, or *backpropagated*. The remaining terms have derivatives, so the equation becomes:

$$\delta_{L-1} = \frac{\partial C}{\partial a^{L-1}} = \delta_L \cdot a^L (1 - a^L) \cdot w^L \tag{B.8}$$

Now we need to find the gradient of the cost w.r.t. the weights at this layer $L - 1$ as before:

$$\frac{\partial C}{\partial w^{L-1}} = \frac{\partial C}{\partial a^{L-1}} \cdot \frac{\partial a^{L-1}}{\partial z^{L-1}} \cdot \frac{\partial z^{L-1}}{\partial w^{L-1}} \tag{B.9}$$

Once again, substituting δ_{L-1} for $\partial C / \partial a^{L-1}$ (Equation B.8) and taking the derivatives of the other terms, we get:

$$\frac{\partial C}{\partial w^{L-1}} = \delta_{L-1} \cdot a^{L-1}(1 - a^{L-1}) \cdot a^{L-2} \tag{B.10}$$

This process is repeated layer by layer all the way down to the first layer.

To recap, we first find δ_L (Equation B.4) which is the error of the cost function (Equation B.3), and we use that value in the equation for the derivative of the cost function w.r.t. the weights in layer L (Equation B.6). In the next layer, we find δ_{L-1} (Equation B.8)—the gradient of the cost w.r.t. the output of layer $L - 1$. As before, this is used in the equation to calculate the gradient of the cost function w.r.t. the weights in layer $L - 1$ (Equation B.10). And so on; backpropagation continues until we reach the model inputs.

Up to this point in this appendix, we've only dealt with networks with single inputs, single hidden neurons, and single outputs. In practice, deep learning models are never this simple. Thankfully, the math shown above scales straightforwardly given multiple neurons in a layer and multiple network inputs and outputs.

Consider the case where there are multiple output classes, such as when you're classifying MNIST digits. In this case, there are 10 output classes ($n = 10$) representing the digits 0–9. For each class, the model provides a probability that a given input image belongs to that class. To find the total cost, we find the sum of the (quadratic, in this case) cost over all the classes:

$$C_0 = \sum_{n=1}^{n} (a_n^L - y_n)^2 \tag{B.11}$$

In Equation B.11, a^L and y are vectors, each containing n elements.

Examining $\partial C / \partial w^L$ for this, the output layer, we must account for the fact that there may be many neurons in the final hidden layer, each one of them connected to each output neuron. It's helpful here to switch the notation slightly: Let the final hidden layer be i and the output layer be j. In this way, we have a matrix of weights that can be accessed with a row for each output neuron and a column for each hidden-layer neuron, and each weight can be denoted w_{ji}. So now, we find the gradient on each weight (remember, there are $i \times j$ weights: one for each connection between each neuron in the two layers):

$$\frac{\partial C}{\partial w_{ji}^L} = \frac{\partial C}{\partial a_j^L} \cdot \frac{\partial a_j^L}{\partial z_j^L} \cdot \frac{\partial z_j^L}{\partial w_{ji}^L} \tag{B.12}$$

We do this for every single weight in the layer, creating the gradient vector for the weights of size $i \times j$.

Although this is essentially the same as our single-neuron-per-layer backprop (refer to Equation B.7), the equation for the gradient of the cost w.r.t. the preceding layer's output a_{L-1} will change (i.e., the δ_{L-1} value). Because this gradient is composed of the partial derivatives of the current layer's inputs and weights, and because there are now multiple of those, we need to sum everything up. Sticking with the i and j notation:

$$\delta_{L-1} = \frac{\partial C}{\partial a_i^{L-1}} = \sum_{j=0}^{n_j-1} \frac{\partial C}{\partial a_j^L} \cdot \frac{\partial a_j^L}{\partial z_j^L} \cdot \frac{\partial z_j^L}{\partial a_i^{L-1}} \tag{B.13}$$

This is a lot of math to take in, so let's review in simple terms: Relative to the simpler network of Equations B.1 through B.10, the equations haven't changed except that instead of calculating the gradient on a single weight, we need to calculate the gradient on multiple weights (Equation B.12). In order to calculate the gradient on any given weight, we need that δ value—which itself is composed of the error over a number of connections in the preceding layer—so we calculate the sum over all these errors (Equation B.13).

PyTorch

In this appendix, we'll introduce the distinguishing elements of PyTorch, including contrasting it with its primary competition—TensorFlow.

PyTorch Features

In Chapter 12, we introduced PyTorch at a high level. In this section, we continue by examining the library's core attributes.

Autograd System

PyTorch operates using what's called an *autograd system*, which relies on the principle of reverse-mode automatic differentiation. As detailed in Chapter 6, the end product of forward propagating through a deep neural network is the result of a series of functions chained together. Reverse-mode automatic differentiation applies the chain rule to differentiate the inputs with respect to the cost at the end, working backwards (introduced in Chapter 7 and detailed in Appendix B). At each iteration, the activations of the neurons in the network are computed by forward propagation, and each function is recorded on a graph. At the end of training, this graph can be computed backwards to calculate the gradient at each neuron.

Define-by-Run Framework

What makes autograd especially interesting is the *define-by-run* nature of the framework: The calculations for backpropagation are defined with each forward pass. This is important because it means that the backpropagation step is only dependent on how your code is run, and as such the backpropagation mathematics can vary with each forward pass. This means that every round of training (see Figure 7.5) can be different. This is useful in settings such as natural language processing, where the input sequence length is typically set to the maximum length (i.e., the longest sentence in the corpus) and shorter sequences are padded with zeros (as we did in Chapter 8). PyTorch, in contrast, natively supports dynamic inputs, circumventing the need for this truncating and padding.

The define-by-run framework also means that the framework is not asynchronous. When a line is executed, the code is run, making debugging much simpler. When the code throws an error, you're able to see exactly which line caused the error. Furthermore, by running an appropriate helper function, this so-called *eager* execution can be easily replaced with a traditional graph-based model—wherein the graphs are defined in advance, which brings with it speed and optimization benefits.

PyTorch Versus TensorFlow

You might now wonder when one might select PyTorch over TensorFlow. The answer is not unambiguous, but we'll explore some of the advantages and disadvantages of each library here.

One relevant topic is adoption: TensorFlow is currently more widely used than PyTorch. PyTorch was first released to the public in January 2017, whereas TensorFlow was released a little over a year prior, in November 2015. In the rapidly developing world of deep learning, this is a significant head start. Indeed, the 1.0.0 version of PyTorch was only released on December 7, 2018. In this way, TensorFlow gained traction and a large body of tutorials and Stack Overflow posts emerged online, giving Google's library an edge.

A second consideration is that PyTorch's dynamic interface makes iteration easier and quicker relative to the static nature of TensorFlow.[1] With PyTorch you can define, change, and execute nodes as you go, as opposed to defining the entire model in advance. Debugging is significantly easier in PyTorch, largely because graphs are defined at run time. This means that errors occur when the code is executed and are more easily traceable to the offending line of code.

Visualization in TensorFlow is intuitive and easy with the built-in TensorBoard platform (see Figure 7.18). However, TensorBoard integrations with PyTorch do exist, and data are more implicitly available during PyTorch model training, so custom solutions can be built using other libraries (for example, with matplotlib).

TensorFlow is used in both development and production at Google, and for this reason the library has much more sophisticated deployment options, including mobile support and distributed training support. PyTorch has historically lagged in these departments; however, with the release of PyTorch 1.0.0, a new just in time (JIT) compiler and its new distributed library are available to address these shortcomings. Additionally, all of the major cloud providers have announced PyTorch integrations, including ones with TensorBoard and TPU support on Google Cloud![2]

When it comes to everyday use, PyTorch feels more "Pythonic" than TensorFlow: It was written specifically as a Python library, and so it will feel familiar to Python developers. While TensorFlow has an established Python implementation that's widely used, the library was originally written in C++, and so its Python implementation can feel cumbersome. Of course, Keras exists to try to solve this problem, but in the process it obscures some of TensorFlow's functionality.[3] On the topic of Keras, PyTorch has the

---

1. The Eager mode central to TensorFlow 2.0 intends to remedy this.
2. One might have expected Google to drag its feet on integrations with the library of one of its primary competitors—in this case, Facebook.
3. TensorFlow 2.0's tight coupling with Keras therein intends to correct many of these issues.

Fast.ai library,[4] which aims to provide high-level abstractions to PyTorch that are analogous to those provided by Keras to TensorFlow.

Taking all of these topics into account, if you're doing research or if your in-production execution demands are not very high, PyTorch might be the optimal choice. The speed of iteration when experimenting, coupled with simpler debugging and extensive NumPy integration, make this library well suited to research. However, if you're deploying deep learning models into a production environment, you'll find more support with TensorFlow. This is especially the case if you're using distributed training or performing inference on a mobile platform.

PyTorch in Practice

In this section, we go over the basics of PyTorch installation and use.

PyTorch Installation

Alongside TensorFlow and Keras, PyTorch is one of the libraries in the Docker container we recommended installing[5] for running the Jupyter notebooks throughout this book. So, if you followed those instructions, you're already all set. If you're working outside of our recommended Docker setup, then you can consult the installation notes that are available on the PyTorch homepage.[6]

The Fundamental Units Within PyTorch

The fundamental units within PyTorch are tensors and variables, which we describe in turn here.

Basic Operations with Tensors

As in TensorFlow, *tensor* is little more than a fancy name for a matrix or vector. Tensors are functionally the same as NumPy arrays, except that PyTorch provides specific methods to perform computation with them on GPUs. Under the hood, these tensors also keep a record of the graph (for the autograd system) and the gradients.

The default tensor is usually `FloatTensor`. PyTorch has eight *types* of tensors, which contain either integers or floats. When you define which type of tensor you'd like to use, that choice has memory and precision implications; 8-bit integers can only store 256 values (i.e., $[0 : 255]$) and occupy much less memory than 64-bit[7] integers. However, in cases where, say, integers up to 255 are all that is required, using higher-order integers would be unnecessary. This consideration is especially relevant when you're running models on GPU architectures, because memory is generally the limiting factor on GPUs, as compared to running models on the CPU, where installing more RAM is relatively cheap.

---

4. github.com/fastai/fastai
5. See the beginning of Chapter 5 for these instructions.
6. pytorch.org
7. 64-bit integers can store values as large as $2^{63} - 1$, which is 9.2 quintillion.

```
import torch
x = torch.zeros(28, 28, 1, dtype=torch.uint8)
y = torch.randn(28, 28, 1, dtype=torch.float32)
```

This code (which is available in our *PyTorch* Jupyter notebook, along with all of the other examples in this appendix) creates a $28 \times 28 \times 1$ tensor, x, that's filled with zeros, of the type uint8.[8] You could also have used torch.ones() to create a comparable tensor filled with ones. The second tensor, y, contains random numbers from the standard normal distribution.[9] By definition, these cannot be 8-bit integers, so we specified 32-bit floats here.

As mentioned initially, these tensors have a lot in common with NumPy n-dimensional arrays. For example, it's easy to generate a PyTorch tensor from a NumPy array with the torch.from_numpy() method. The PyTorch library also contains many math operations that can be efficiently performed on these tensors, many of which mirror their NumPy counterparts.

Automatic Differentiation

PyTorch tensors can natively store the computational graph for the network as well as the gradients. This is enabled by setting the requires_grad argument to True when you create the tensor. Now, each tensor has a grad attribute that stores the gradient. Initially, this is set to None until the tensor's backward() method is called. The backward() method reverses through the record of operations and calculates the gradient at each point in the graph. After the first call to backward(), the grad attribute becomes filled with gradient values.

In the following code block, we define a simple tensor, perform some mathematical operations, and call the backward() method to reverse through the graph and calculate the gradients. Subsequently, the grad attribute will store gradients.

```
import torch

x = torch.zeros(3, 3, dtype=torch.float32, requires_grad=True)

y = x - 4
z = y**3 * 6
out = z.mean()

out.backward()

print(x.grad)
```

---

8. The "u" in uint8 stands for *unsigned*, meaning that these 8-bit integers span from 0 to 255 instead of from -128 to 127.

9. The standard normal distribution has a mean of 0 and a standard deviation of 1.

Because x had its `require_grad` flag set, we can perform backpropagation on this series of computations. PyTorch has accumulated the functions that generated the final output using its autograd system, so calling `out.backward()` will calculate the gradients and store them in `x.grad`. The final line prints the following:

```
tensor([[32., 32., 32.],
        [32., 32., 32.],
        [32., 32., 32.]])
```

As this example demonstrates, PyTorch takes the hassle out of automatic differentiation. Next, we cover the basics of building a neural network in PyTorch.

Building a Deep Neural Network in PyTorch

The essential paradigm of building neural networks should be familiar: They consist of multiple layers that are stacked together (as in Figure 4.2). In the examples throughout this book, we used the Keras library as a high-level abstraction over the raw TensorFlow functions. Similarly, the PyTorch nn module contains layerlike modules that receive tensors as inputs and return tensors as outputs. In the following example, we build a two-layer network akin to the dense nets we used to classify handwritten digits in Part II:

```
import torch

# Define random tensors for the inputs and outputs
x = torch.randn(32, 784, requires_grad=True)
y = torch.randint(low=0, high=10, size=(32,))

# Define the model, using the Sequential class
model = torch.nn.Sequential(
    torch.nn.linear(784, 100),
    torch.nn.Sigmoid(),
    torch.nn.Linear(100, 10),
    torch.nn.LogSoftmax(dim=1)
)

# Define the optimizer and loss function
optimizer = torch.optim.Adam(model.parameters())
loss_fn = torch.nn.NLLLoss()

for step in range(1000):
    # Make predictions by forward propagation
    y_hat = model(x)
    # Calculate the loss
    loss = loss_fn(y_hat, y)
    # Zero-out the gradient before performing a backward pass
    optimizer.zero_grad()
```

```
# Compute the gradients w.r.t. the loss
loss.backward()
# Print the results
print('Step: :4d - loss: :0.4f'.format(step+1, loss.item()))
# Update the model parameters
optimizer.step()
```

Let's break this down step by step:

- The x and y tensors are placeholders for the input and output values of the model.
- We use the Sequential class to begin building our model as a series of layers (linear() through to LogSoftmax()), in much the same way as we did in Keras.
- We initialize an optimizer; in this case we use Adam with its default values. We also pass into the optimizer all of the tensors we'd like optimized—in this case, model.parameters().
- We also initialize the loss function, although it doesn't require any parameters. We opted for the built-in negative log-likelihood loss function, torch.nn.NLLLoss().[10]
- We manually iterate over the number of rounds of training (Figure 7.5) that we'd like to take (in this case, 1000), and during each round we
  - Calculate the model outputs using y_hat = model(x).
  - Calculate the loss using the function we defined earlier, passing in the predicted $\hat{y}$ values and the true y values.
  - Zero the gradients. This is necessary because the gradients are accumulated in buffers, and not overwritten.
  - Perform backpropagation to recalculate the gradients, given the loss.
  - Finally, take a step using the optimizer. This updates the model weights using the gradients.

This procedure diverges from the model.fit() method we employed in Keras. However, with all of the theory covered in this book and the hands-on examples we've worked through together, hopefully it's not a stretch to appreciate what's taking place in this PyTorch code. Without too much effort, you should be able to adapt the deep learning models in this book from Keras into PyTorch.[11]

---

10. Pairing a LogSoftmax() output layer with the torch.nn.NLLLoss() cost function in PyTorch is equivalent to using a softmax output layer with cross-entropy cost in Keras. PyTorch does have a cross_entropy() cost function, but it incorporates the softmax calculation so that if you were to use it, you wouldn't need to apply the softmax activation function to your model output.

11. Note that our example PyTorch neural network in this appendix isn't learning anything meaningful. The loss decreases, but the model is simply memorizing (overfitting to) the training data we randomly generated. We're feeding in random numbers as inputs and mapping them to other random numbers. If we randomly generated validation data, too, the validation loss wouldn't decrease. If you're feeling adventurous, you could initialize x and y with actual data from, say, the MNIST dataset (you can import these data with Keras, as in Example 5.2) and train a PyTorch model to map a meaningful relationship!

Index

Credits

Figure P.2: Cajal, S.-R. (1894). Les Nouvelles Idées sur la Structure du Système Nerveux chez l'Homme et chez les Vertébrés. Paris: C. Reinwald & Companie.

Figure 1.5: Hubel, D. H., & Wiesel, T. N. (1959). Receptive fields of single neurones in the cat's striate cortex. The Journal of Physiology, 148, 574–91.

Figure 1.13: Viola, P., & Jones, M. (2001). Robust real-time face detection. International Journal of Computer Vision, 57, 137-154.

Figure 1.18: Screenshot of TensorFlow Playground © Daniel Smilkov and Shan Carter.

Figure 1.19: Screenshot of TensorFlow Playground © Daniel Smilkov and Shan Carter.

Figure 2.8: Screenshot of word2viz © Julia Bazińska.

Figure 3.2: Goodfellow, I., et al. (2014). Generative adversarial networks. arXiv:1406.2661.

Figure 3.3: Radford, A., et al. (2016). Unsupervised representation learning with deep convolutional generative adversarial networks. arXiv:1511.06434v2.

Figure 3.5: Zhu, J.-Y., et al. (2017). Unpaired Image-to-Image Translation using Cycle-Consistent Adversarial Networks. arXiv:1703.10593.

Figure 3.7: Zhang, H., et al. (2017). StackGAN: Text to photo-realistic image synthesis with stacked generative adversarial networks. arXiv:1612.03242v2.

Figure 3.8: Chen, C. et al. (2018) Learning to See in the Dark. arXiv:1805.01934.

Figure 4.5: Mnih, V., et al. (2015). Human-level control through deep reinforcement learning. Nature, 518, 529–533.

Figure 4.8: Silver, D., et al. (2016). Mastering the game of Go with deep neural networks and tree search. Nature 529, 484–489.

Figure 4.9: Silver, D., et al. (2016). Mastering the game of Go without human knowledge. Nature 550, 354–359.

Figure 4.10: Silver, D., et al. (2017). Mastering Chess and Shogi by Self-Play with a General Reinforcement Learning Algorithm. arXiv:1712.01815.

Figure 4.12: Levine, S., Finn, C., et al. (2016). End-to-End Training of Deep Visuomotor Policies. Journal of Machine Learning Research, 17, 1-40.

Figure 4.13: Screenshot of OpenAI Gym © OpenAI.

Figure 4.14: Screenshot of Deep Mind lab © 2018 DeepMind Technologies Limited.

Figure 7.18: Screenshot of TensorBoard © Google Inc.

Figure 9.14: Ren, S. et al. (2015). Faster R-CNN: Towards Real-Time Object Detection with Region Proposal Networks. arXiv: 1506.01497.

Figure 10.10: Screenshot of SLM Lab © Wah Loon Keng and Laura Graesser.

Figure 10.15: He, K., et al. (2017). Mask R-CNN. arXiv: 1703.06870.

Figure 11.5: Screenshot of Jupyter © 2019 Project Jupyter.

Credits

Figure 2.7 Cajal, S. R. (1909). Les Nouvelles Idées sur la Structure du Système Nerveux chez l'Homme et chez les Vertébrés. Paris: C. Reinwald & Company.

Figure 2.9 Hubel, D. H., & Wiesel, T. N. (1959). Receptive fields of single neurones in the cat's striate cortex. The Journal of Physiology, 148, 574–591.

Figure 3.5 Viola, P., & Jones, M. (2001). Robust real-time face detection. International Journal of Computer Vision, 57, 137–154.

Figure 3.13a Screenshot of TensorFlow Playground © Daniel Smilkov and Shan Carter.

Figure 3.13b Screenshot of TensorFlow Playground © Daniel Smilkov and Shan Carter.

Figure 3.8 Screenshot of word2viz © John Brandsen.

Figure 3.22 Goodfellow, I. et al. (2014). Generative adversarial networks. arXiv:1406.2661.

Figure 3.23 Radford, A. et al. (2016). Unsupervised representation learning with deep convolutional generative adversarial networks. arXiv:1511.06434v2.

Figure 3.24 Zhu, J-Y. et al. (2017). Unpaired image-to-image Translation using Cycle-Consistent Adversarial Networks. arXiv:1703.10593.

Figure 3.25 Zhang, H. et al. (2017). StackGAN: Text to photo-realistic image synthesis with stacked generative adversarial networks. arXiv:1612.03242v2.

Figure 3.27 Chen, X. et al. (2018). Learning to see in the Dark. arXiv:1805.01934.

Figure 4.3 Mnih, V. et al. (2015). Human-level control through deep reinforcement learning. Nature, 518, 529–33.

Figure 4.5 Silver, D. et al. (2016). Mastering the game of Go with deep neural networks and tree search. Nature, 529, 484–489.

Figure 4.6 Silver, D. et al. (2016). Mastering the game of Go without human knowledge. Nature, 550, 354–359.

Figure 4.10 Silman, D. et al. (2017). Mastering Chess and Shogi by Self-Play with a General Reinforcement Learning Algorithm. arXiv:1712.01815.

Figure 4.12 Levine, S., Finn, C., et al. (2016). End-to-end Training of Deep Visuomotor Policies. Journal of Machine Learning Research, 17, 1–40.

Figure 4.13 Screenshot of OpenAI Gym © OpenAI.

Figure 4.14 Screenshot of Deep Mind lab © 2016 DeepMind Technologies Limited.

Figure 4.16 Screenshot of DishPantry © Google Inc.

Figure 5.2 Sermanet, P. et al (2014). Faster R-CNN: Towards Real-Time Object Detection with Region Proposal Networks. arXiv:1506.01497.

Figure 5.10 Screenshot of SLM Lab © Wah Loon Keng and Laura Graesser.

Figure 6.1 Dahl, R. et al (2017). Pixel Recursive R-CNN. arXiv:1702.00783.

Figure 7.8 Screenshot of OpenAI Gym © 2016 Wojciech Zaremba.

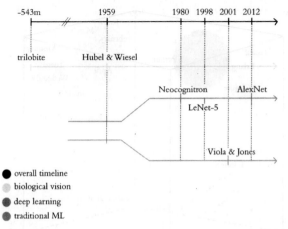

Figure 1.8 Abridged timeline of biological and machine vision, highlighting the key historical moments in the deep learning and traditional machine learning approaches to vision that are covered in this section (also see Figure 1.8 on page 9).

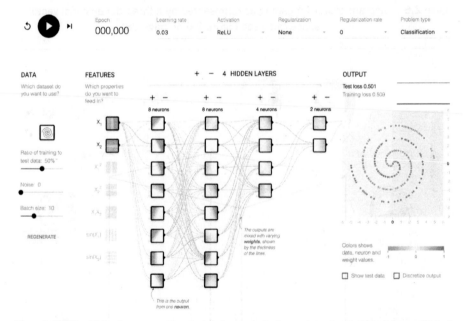

Figure 1.18 This deep neural network is ready to learn how to distinguish a spiral of orange dots (negative cases) from blue dots (positive cases) based on their position on the X_1 and X_2 axes of the grid on the right (also see Figure 1.18 on page 18).

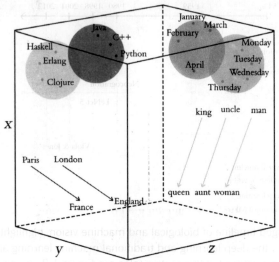

n – dimensional space

Figure 2.6 Diagram of word meaning as represented by a three-dimensional vector space (also see Figure 2.6 on page 28).

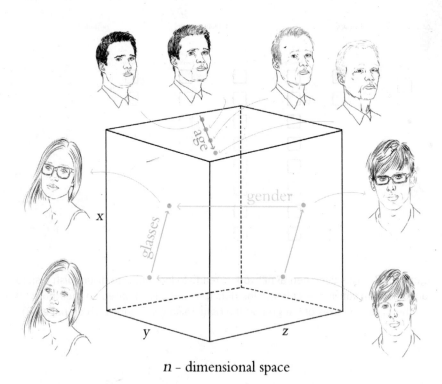

n – dimensional space

Figure 3.4 A cartoon of the latent space associated with generative adversarial networks (GANs). Moving along the purple arrow, the latent space corresponds to images of a similar-looking individual aging. The green arrow represents gender, and the orange one represents the inclusion of glasses on the face (also see Figure 3.4 on page 43).

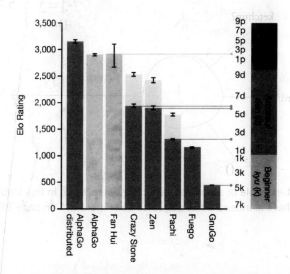

Figure 4.8   The Elo score of AlphaGo (blue) relative to Fan Hui (green) and several Go programs (red). The approximate human rank is shown on the right (also see Figure 4.8 on page 63).

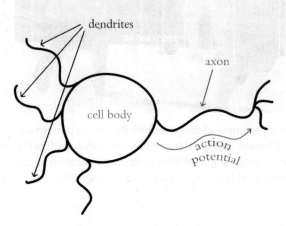

Figure 6.1   The anatomy of a biological neuron (also see Figure 6.1 on page 86).

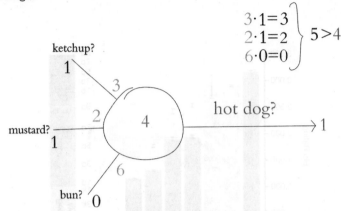

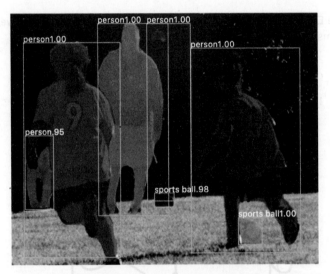

Figure 6.4   First example of a hot dog-detecting perceptron: In this instance, it predicts there is indeed a hot dog (also see Figure 6.4 on page 88).

Figure 9.15   This is an example of image segmentation (as performed by the Mask R-CNN algorithm). Whereas object detection involves defining object locations with coarse bounding boxes, image segmentation predicts the location of objections to the pixel level (also see Figure 9.15 on page 250).